Managing the Software Process

Watts S. Humphrey
SOFTWARE ENGINEERING INSTITUTE

ADDISON-WESLEY PUBLISHING COMPANY

Reading, Massachusetts ■ Menlo Park, California ■ New York
Don Mills, Ontario ■ Wokingham, England ■ Amsterdam ■ Bonn
Sydney ■ Singapore ■ Tokyo ■ Madrid ■ San Juan

 **Software Engineering Institute**

The SEI Series in Software Engineering

Library of Congress Cataloging-in-Publication Data

Humphrey, Watts S., 1927–
    Managing the software process / by Watts S. Humphrey.
      p. cm.
    Includes bibliographies and index.
    ISBN 0-201-18095-2
    1. Software engineering—Management.   I. Title.
QA76.758.H86 1989
005.1′068—dc 19   88-34453
                                                  CIP

Reprinted with corrections August, 1990.

12 13 14 15 16 17 18 19 20 AL 959493

TO MY CHILDREN

Katharine, Lisa, Sarah, Watts Jr., Peter,
Erica, and Christopher

Software Engineering Institute

The SEI Series in Software Engineering

FOREWORD

The "software crisis" is dead!

"When did it die?" you might ask. Many may not have noticed, and, indeed, we cannot pinpoint the exact moment of demise; nonetheless, it is clear that things are different today than they were a few years ago in the realm of software development.

This book is one of the best signs of that change that I have seen.

Although for two decades we have heard about, read about, and lived the "software crisis" in the popular sense of a set of terrible conditions that beset us, I am using the term "crisis" here more in its preferred dictionary sense of a decisive point or turning point. While many of those conditions (missed budgets and schedules, poor quality, unreasonable expectations) are still with us, we have changed from feeling that software is some kind of totally unmanageable beast to believing that under the right conditions we can manage it just as we have learned to manage other problematical situations in our universe.

Watts Humphrey's considerable experience as a software manager, and now as a student of the development process, has given him the insight to understand that building software is not just a monolithic process, always the same. As the central theme of this book so clearly indicates, we can classify those differences in what we actually observe in development organizations in a way that permits us to see that there is a sequence of maturity levels in the software process.

Understanding that there are different stages of maturity and understanding something of the conditions that determine where one is and where one can hope to be is often the key to growth—to turning the corner from chaotic software development to a more controlled and manageable process. That is the theme of this

highly readable, well-grounded, and pragmatic book. It will help you move beyond the turning point (or crisis) of feeling overwhelmed by the task of managing
the software process to understanding what is essential in software management
and what you can do about it.

Long live the crisis!

Peter Freeman

LAGUNA BEACH, CALIFORNIA

PREFACE

If you don't know where you're going, any road will do.
CHINESE PROVERB

If you don't know where you are, a map won't help.
WATTS S. HUMPHREY

Software engineering can be both rewarding and disappointing. The intellectual challenge of software is unsurpassed, but our business performance has all too often been abysmal. There is an urgent national need to improve this performance, and to do so we need an improvement plan and a set of priorities. Such planning calls for a vision of our goals and a clear understanding of where we are. These are the themes of this book.

While it may seem trivial to define the state of our current software process, it is not. The definition task requires an evaluation standard, a measurement framework, and much work. To intelligently attack our problems, we must know what they are. One way to measure the capability of a software organization is to observe what it does in a crisis. That is when good practices are most important, and that is when software people often have the least guidance. This book will help you deal with the following questions:

1. How good is my current software process?
2. What must I do to improve it?
3. Where do I start?

This book grew out of work at the Software Engineering Institute at Carnegie Mellon University on a U.S. Air Force project. The objective was to provide guidance to the military services in selecting capable software contractors.[1] The resulting method for evaluating their strengths and weaknesses has proved valuable for assessing other software organizations. This book describes the techni-

[1] Humphrey, W. S., and W. L. Sweet. "A method for assessing the software engineering capability of contractors," SEI Technical Report SEI-87-TR-23, September 1987.

cal and managerial topics these assessments have found most critical for improvement.

The book's individual topics are presented in relation to the basic principles of software process management. The approach is to provide a framework and some techniques for evaluating and improving the process of doing software rather than presenting a specific set of solutions. It is like the distinction between learning a story and learning to read. The software field is so new that many new tools and methods will surely be developed. The techniques outlined in these pages, however, are grounded in the durable principles that have fueled several centuries of scientific and engineering advancement. These principles provide a powerful conceptual framework for learning about and improving the software engineering process.

Individuals, Teams, and Armies

The history of software development is one of increasing scale. Initially a few individuals could hand craft small programs; the work soon grew beyond them. Teams of one or two dozen professionals were then used, but success was mixed. While many organizations have solved these small-system problems, the scale of our work continues to grow. Today large projects require the coordinated work of many teams. Complexity is outpacing our ability to solve problems intuitively as they appear. What is required is a more structured approach to software process management.

In addition to working with very large projects, however, we have found that the same methods are effective for smaller groups. In fact, in simplified form, they are even helpful for individual programmers. That, of course, is the key. If our methods do not serve the individual professionals, they will not endure.

People and the Software Process

Talented people are the most important element in any software organization. The crucial initial step is thus to get the best people available. The better and more experienced they are, the better the chance of producing first-class results.[2]

Once you have the best people you can get, however, what next? If everyone wrote in different programming languages, used special conventions, or didn't coordinate their design and code changes with their peers, the results would be chaos. Successful software organizations have learned that even the best professionals need a structured and disciplined environment in which to do cooperative work.

Software organizations that do not establish these disciplines condemn their

[2]Boehm, B. W. *Software Engineering Economics*. Englewood Cliffs, NJ: Prentice-Hall, 1981.

people to endless hours of repetitively solving technically trivial problems. There may be challenging work to do, but their time is consumed by mountains of uncontrolled detail. Unless these details are rigorously managed, the best people cannot be productive. First-class people are essential, but they need the support of an orderly process to do first-class work.

The Myth of the Super Programmers

There is a common view that a few first-class artists can do far better work than the typical software team. The implication is that they will know intuitively how to do first-class work, so no orderly process framework will be needed. If this were true, one would expect that those organizations who have the best people would not suffer from the common problems of software quality and productivity. Experience, however, shows that this is not the case. A few of the nation's leading software organizations have consistently hired the top graduates from the best computer science schools. They are thus staffed with the best available people, yet their programming groups have many of the same problems that plague everyone else. It seems that the super programmer approach requires better people than are available, even from our leading universities. While this may be a theoretical solution, it is clearly not a practical one. Attracting the best people is vital, but it is also essential to support them with an effectively managed software process.

Process and Technology

Another myth is the widespread belief that some technologically advanced tool or method will provide a magic answer to the software crisis. This is not only wrong, but it is dangerous. Technology is vital for long-term improvement, but unthinking reliance on an undefined "silver bullet" will divert attention from the need for better process management.[3]

When asked to name their key problems, few software professionals even mention technology. Their major concerns are open-ended requirements, uncontrolled change, arbitrary schedules, insufficient test time, inadequate training, and unmanaged system standards. They may mention limited machine time, poor terminal availability, or low-quality tools, but these are more management than high-technology problems.

The effective use of software technology is limited by several factors: an ill-defined process, inconsistent implementation, and poor process management.

[3]Brooks, F. P. "No silver bullet, essence and accidents of software engineering," *IEEE Computer,* April, 1987, 10–19.

Software technology cannot be fully effective until these problems have been adequately addressed.

This book focuses on software process management. The software process is that set of actions required to efficiently transform a user's need into an effective software solution. Many software organizations have trouble defining and controlling this process, which is where they have the greatest potential for improvement. This is the focus of this book.

Book Overview

The five parts of this book each cover a separate facet of software process improvement. The sequence of topics follows a prescribed model that has provided a useful improvement framework for a number of leading software organizations. The chapters in each section cover the key elements of each improvement phase. By first identifying their status in the maturity framework outlined in Chapter 1, organizations can determine where they should focus their initial improvement efforts. The organization's improvement priorities should then be focused on the topics covered in the next part of the book. Level 1 organizations, for example, should concentrate on the topics in Part II, while Level 2 organizations should focus on Part III.

As you read this book it is important to realize that most software issues are interrelated. Some aspects of every topic are thus involved in almost every phase of software activity. The key concern of process management, however, is priority: What topics should be the focus for improvement and in which order? The basic logic for the book's organization is thus management priority. For example, standards are addressed in Part III. That does not mean that standards are not important both before and after the Defined Process phase, but that this is where standards deserve priority management attention.

Each book part is introduced with a brief overview that summarizes the key topics covered and why they are important at this phase of process improvement. In brief these five parts are:

Part I, "Software Process Maturity," describes a framework for software process management, the use of this framework in process assessment, and the steps required to initiate effective software process change.

Part II, "The Repeatable Process," outlines the actions needed to establish basic control over the software process. These provide the stability needed for orderly and continuous process improvement.

Part III, "The Defined Process," describes how to specify the development process and the technical and managerial concepts needed to control it. Software development is a surprise-prone business, and a defined process permits more orderly reaction to unanticipated events.

In Part IV, "The Managed Process," the methods of quantitative software process control are introduced. At this stage data is gathered and analyzed to support quantitative quality and process management. These are the tools that can guide us to a better understanding of our work, a more precise way to control our actions, and a truly informed basis for sustained process improvement.

Part V, "The Optimizing Process," presents the final stage of software process evolution; it shifts the focus from fixing problems to preventing them. At this level software managers and professionals learn to use quantitative process methods to harness technology for continuing quality and productivity improvement.

A Suggested Approach for Reading This Book

This book is designed for direct reading from beginning to end. Some readers, however, may find it helpful to start with an overview by first reading Chapters 1, 19, and 20 and then the summaries at the ends of the other chapters. This will provide a perspective of current software issues and a vision of future process objectives. Readers should then start at the beginning of the book and work forward in step with their progress in improving their software process.

Acknowledgments

Before my early retirement from IBM in 1986, I had the good fortune to work with many stimulating people and to be given many challenging assignments. I probably owe most to Vin Learson for entrusting me with IBM's systems programming development organization through the early years of System/360. The problems of large-scale software development were new to all of us, but this talented IBM software team probably had more combined systems programming experience than any other organization in the world. While we had many problems, these people did a remarkable job. The best tribute to their skill is the growing family of 360-compatible competitors whose basic strategy is to build products that will use the systems these professionals developed. Since imitation is the sincerest form of flattery, these people clearly did a superb job. Without such dedicated and capable professionals as well as an enlightened corporate management, it would have been an impossible assignment. With this support it was both a rewarding experience and an intense personal education.

In the ensuing years I have worked for many technical leaders. George Kennard, Earl Wheeler, and Jack Kuehler all gave me invaluable support and guidance as we worked to control and improve IBM's software development process. I want to thank these executives and also to express my appreciation to the many IBM managers and professionals who have worked with and supported me during my 27 years with the company.

In writing this book, I have also come to appreciate the enormous debt we owe those professionals who publish their views and experiences. The two whose insights and ideas were uniquely pertinent to this book are Fred Brooks and Barry Boehm. While so many others have had a strong influence on this work, I want to particularly mention Joel Aron, Vic Bassili, Edsger Dijkstra, Mike Fagan, Harlan Mills, and Gerry Weinberg. Through reading their works I have gained a deeper understanding of my own experiences, and I have attempted to capture the essence of their combined perspectives in this book. For what success I have achieved, I owe them my deepest gratitude.

The conceptual framework for this book is also built in part on the pioneering work of W. E. Deming and J. M. Juran. It was their leadership in statistical quality control that lifted Japanese industry to world preeminence in the automobile, camera, steel, shipbuilding, watch, and electronics industries in the 1950s and 1960s. More recent work shows that their concepts are equally applicable to software.

I must also thank many of my professional colleagues for being so generous with their time in reviewing this manuscript and offering helpful suggestions. I particularly thank Jon Bently, Bob Goldberg, Rich Pethia, Al Pietrasanta, Bill Riddle, and Glenn Secor for their thoughtful and comprehensive reviews of all or most of the manuscript. Many others have spent countless hours reviewing one or more chapters and providing helpful comments and suggestions. For this, I thank Rodger Blair, Maribeth Carpenter, Currie Colket, Susan Dart, Betty Deimel, Jo Delgado, Ken Diamond, Larry Druffel, Bob Glass, John Goodenough, Mark Kellner, Dave Kitson, John Maher, Steve Masters, Don O'Neill, Mark Paulk, Jim Tomayko, Jay Warshowski, Jim Withey, and Janet Yodanis. I also thank the many others who have helped with suggestions, comments, and encouragement. As in programming, without the support of reviewers the quality of one's work is constrained by our individual horizons. Reviewers thus give more than their time; they offer us a share of their talents and wisdom in the hope that we can achieve excellence. I am therefore deeply grateful to all those who have been so generous, and I hope the results will justify their investment. I also want to particularly thank Peter Freeman for his helpful review comments and for agreeing to write a forward to this book.

Peter Gordon, Helen Goldstein, and Helen Wythe at Addison-Wesley have also greatly assisted me in this task. The invaluable guidance and support of Michael Bass, Ellen Silge, Randy Miyake, and Julie Anjos during manuscript editing and production have also made this job far easier than I had thought possible. Dorothy Josephson has also been enormously helpful. In addition to being a talented secretary, she has scheduled reviews, distributed manuscripts, handled correspondence, and helped with the thousands of other chores that normally consume an author's time.

Finally, I must acknowledge my wife's help and encouragement. Through long hours and closeted weekends, Barbara has stayed cheerful and good-natured. I could not have written this book without her support.

Watts S. Humphrey

PITTSBURGH, PA

CONTENTS

 **Software Engineering Institute**

PART ONE

Software Process Maturity

This book is divided into five parts, each of which corresponds roughly to a stage of software process improvement. The characteristics of these maturity stages are described in Chapter 1, and the actions normally required to advance from one maturity level to the next are listed in Appendix A at the back of the book.

Part I sets the stage for the rest of the book. It provides guidance on the questions "Where are we and where are we going?"

Chapter 1 discusses the software process maturity framework, explains why it is important, and shows how it relates to the key software problems in organizations. Chapter 1 also provides an overview of the way organizations can improve through the five maturity levels.

Chapter 2 deals with the principles of software process change and the most common problems encountered in launching an improvement program.

Chapter 3 describes how to assess software organizations and how the results are used to determine priority needs for improvement.

Chapter 4 deals with the most common software problems, why they persist, and the general approaches to resolving them. It also describes an extreme case of the initial process and the reasons some software organizations appear trapped in this initial chaotic state.

With the background provided in Part I, software organizations are ready to assess their status and determine their priority needs for improvement.

1

A Software Maturity
Framework

In launching an improvement program, we should first consider the characteristics of a truly effective software process. Fundamentally, it must be predictable. That is, cost estimates and schedule commitments must be met with reasonable consistency, and the resulting products should generally meet users' functional and quality expectations.

The software process is the set of tools, methods, and practices we use to produce a software product. The objectives of software process management are to produce products according to plan while simultaneously improving the organization's capability to produce better products. The basic principles are those of statistical process control, which have been used successfully in many fields. A process is said to be stable or under statistical control if its future performance is predictable within established statistical limits.[4]

When a process is under statistical control, repeating the work in roughly the same way will produce roughly the same result. To obtain consistently better results, it is thus necessary to improve the process. If the process is not under statistical control, sustained progress is not possible until it is.

Dr. W. E. Deming, in his work with the Japanese after World War II, applied the concepts of statistical process control to many of their industries.[4] While there are important differences, these concepts are just as applicable to software as they are to producing consumer goods like cameras, television sets, or automobiles.

The basic principle behind statistical control is measurement. As Lord Kelvin said a century ago: "When you can measure what you are speaking about, and express it in numbers, you know something about it; but when you cannot measure

3

it, when you cannot express it in numbers, your knowledge is of a meager and unsatisfactory kind; it may be the beginning of knowledge, but you have scarcely in your thoughts advanced to the stage of science.''[5]

There are several factors to consider in measuring the programming process. First, one cannot just start to use numbers to control things. The numbers must properly represent the process being controlled, and they must be sufficiently well defined and verified to provide a reliable basis for action. While process measurements are essential for orderly improvement, careful planning and preparation are required or the results are likely to be disappointing.

The second point is equally important: The mere act of measuring human processes changes them. Since people's fears and motivations are involved, the results must be viewed in a different light from data on natural phenomena. It is thus essential to limit the measurements to those with a predefined use. Measurements are both expensive and disruptive; overzealous measuring can degrade the process we are trying to improve.

1.1 Software Process Improvement

An important first step in addressing software problems is to treat the entire software task as a process that can be controlled, measured, and improved. For this purpose we define a process as that set of tasks that, when properly performed, produces the desired result. Clearly, a fully effective software process must consider the relationships of all the required tasks, the tools and methods used, and the skill, training, and motivation of the people involved.

To improve their software capabilities, organizations must take six steps:

1. Understand the current status of their development process or processes.
2. Develop a vision of the desired process.
3. Establish a list of required process improvement actions in order of priority.
4. Produce a plan to accomplish the required actions.
5. Commit the resources to execute the plan.
6. Start over at step 1.

To improve an organization, it is helpful to have a clear picture of the ultimate goal and some way to gauge progress along the way. The framework used here for this purpose roughly parallels the quality maturity structure defined by Crosby.[3] It addresses the six improvement steps by characterizing the software process into one of five maturity levels. By establishing their organization's position in this maturity structure, software professionals and their managers can more readily identify areas where improvement actions will be most fruitful.

1.2 Process Maturity Levels

The five levels of process maturity are discussed further in the balance of this chapter. They are as shown in Fig. 1.1 and have the following general characteristics:

1. *Initial*   Until the process is under statistical control, orderly progress in process improvement is not possible. While there are many degrees of statistical control, the first step is to achieve rudimentary predictability of schedules and costs.

2. *Repeatable*   The organization has achieved a stable process with a repeatable level of statistical control by initiating rigorous project management of commitments, costs, schedules, and changes.

3. *Defined*   The organization has defined the process as a basis for consistent implementation and better understanding. At this point advanced technology can usefully be introduced.

4. *Managed*   The organization has initiated comprehensive process measurements and analysis. This is when the most significant quality improvements begin.

5. *Optimizing*   The organization now has a foundation for continuing improvement and optimization of the process.

These levels have been selected because they:

  □ Reasonably represent the actual historical phases of evolutionary improvement of real software organizations
  □ Represent a measure of improvement that is reasonable to achieve from the prior level
  □ Suggest interim improvement goals and progress measures
  □ Make obvious a set of immediate improvement priorities, once an organization's status in this framework is known

While there are many other elements to these maturity level transitions, the primary objective is to achieve a controlled and measured process as the foundation for continuing improvement.

This process maturity structure is intended for use with an assessment methodology and a management system.[7, 8, 9, 12] Assessment helps an organization identify its specific maturity status, and the management system establishes a structure for implementing the priority improvement actions. Once its position in this maturity structure is defined, the organization can concentrate on those items that will help it advance to the next level.

When, for example, a software organization does not have an effective project-planning system, it may be difficult or even impossible to introduce ad-

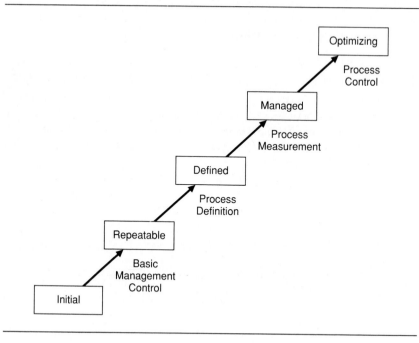

FIGURE 1.1
Process Maturity Levels

vanced methods and technology. Poor project planning generally leads to unrealistic schedules, inadequate resources, and frequent crises. In such circumstances, new methods are usually ignored and priority is given to coding and testing.

1.2.1 The Initial Process (Level 1)

The Initial Process Level could properly be called ad hoc, and it is often even chaotic. At this stage the organization typically operates without formalized procedures, cost estimates, and project plans. Tools are neither well integrated with the process nor uniformly applied. Change control is lax, and there is little senior management exposure or understanding of the problems and issues. Since many problems are deferred or even forgotten, software installation and maintenance often present serious problems.

While organizations at this level may have formal procedures for planning and tracking their work, there is no management mechanism to ensure that they are used. The best test is to observe how such an organization behaves in a crisis. If it abandons established procedures and essentially reverts to coding and testing, it is likely to be at the Initial Process Level. After all, if the techniques and methods are appropriate, then they should be used in a crisis; if they are not appropriate in a crisis, they should not be used at all.

One key reason why organizations behave in this fashion is that they have not experienced the benefits of a mature process and thus do not understand the consequences of their chaotic behavior. Because many effective software actions (such as design and code inspections or test data analysis) do not appear directly to support shipping the product, they seem expendable.

It is much like driving an automobile. Few drivers with any experience will continue driving for very long when the engine warning light comes on, regardless of their rush. Similarly, most drivers starting on a new journey will, regardless of their hurry, pause to consult a map. They have learned the difference between speed and progress.

In software, coding and testing seem like progress, but they are often only wheel spinning. While they must be done, there is always the danger of going in the wrong direction. Without a sound plan and a thoughtful analysis of the problems, there is no way to know.

Organizations at the Initial Process Level can improve their performance by instituting basic project controls. The most important are project management, management oversight, quality assurance, and change control.

The fundamental role of a *project management* system is to ensure effective control of commitments. This requires adequate preparation, clear responsibility, a public declaration, and a dedication to performance.[8]

For software, project management starts with an understanding of the job's magnitude. In any but the simplest projects, a plan must then be developed to determine the best schedule and the anticipated resources required. In the absence of such an orderly plan, no commitment can be better than an educated guess.

A suitably disciplined software development organization must have senior *management oversight*. This includes review and approval of all major development plans prior to their official commitment.

Also, a quarterly review should be conducted of facility-wide process compliance, installed quality performance, schedule tracking, cost trends, computing service, and quality and productivity goals by project. The lack of such reviews typically results in uneven and generally inadequate implementation of the process as well as frequent overcommitments and cost surprises.

A *quality assurance* group is charged with assuring management that software work is done the way it is supposed to be done. To be effective, the assurance organization must have an independent reporting line to senior management and sufficient resources to monitor performance of all key planning, implementation, and verification activities. This generally requires an organization of about 3 percent to 6 percent the size of the software organization.

Change control for software is fundamental to business and financial control as well as to technical stability. To develop quality software on a predictable schedule, requirements must be established and maintained with reasonable stability throughout the development cycle. While requirements changes are often needed, historical evidence demonstrates that many can be deferred and incorporated later. Design and code changes must be made to correct problems found in development and test, but these must be carefully introduced. If changes are not controlled, then orderly design, implementation, and test is impossible and no quality plan can be effective.

1.2.2 The Repeatable Process (Level 2)

The Repeatable Process has one important strength that the Initial Process does not: It provides control over the way the organization establishes its plans and commitments. This control provides such an improvement over the Initial Process Level that the people in the organization tend to believe they have mastered the software problem. They have achieved a degree of statistical control through learning to make and meet their estimates and plans. This strength, however, stems from their prior experience at doing similar work. Organizations at the Repeatable Process Level thus face major risks when they are presented with new challenges.

Examples of the changes that represent the highest risk at this level are the following:

□ *Unless they are introduced with great care, new tools and methods will affect the process, thus destroying the relevance of the intuitive historical base on which the organization relies.* Without a defined process framework in which to address these risks, it is even possible for a new technology to do more harm than good.

□ *When the organization must develop a new kind of product, it is entering new territory.* For example, a software group that has experience developing compilers will likely have design, scheduling, and estimating problems when assigned to write a real-time control program. Similarly, a group that has developed small self-contained programs will not understand the interface and integration issues involved in large-scale projects. These changes again destroy the relevance of the intuitive historical basis for the organization's process.

□ *Major organizational changes can also be highly disruptive.* At the Repeatable Process Level, a new manager has no orderly basis for understanding the organization's operation, and new team members must learn the ropes through word of mouth.

The key actions required to advance from the Repeatable to the next stage, the Defined Process, are to establish a process group, establish a development process architecture, and introduce a family of software engineering methods and technologies.

Establish a process group. A process group is a technical resource that focuses exclusively on improving the software process. In software organizations at early maturity levels, all the people are generally devoted to product work. Until some people are given full-time assignments to work on the process, little orderly progress can be made in improving it.

The responsibilities of process groups include defining the development process, identifying technology needs and opportunities, advising the projects, and conducting quarterly management reviews of process status and performance. While there is no published data at this point, my experience indicates that the process group should be about 1 to 3 percent the size of the software organization. Because of the need for a nucleus of skills, groups smaller than about four professionals are unlikely to be fully effective. Small organizations that lack the experience base to form a process group should address these issues by using specially formed committees of experienced professionals or by retaining consultants.

A frequent question concerns the relative responsibilities of process groups and quality assurance. While this is discussed in more detail in Chapters 8 and 14, the assurance group is focused on enforcing the current process, while the process group is directed at improving it. In a sense, they are almost opposites: assurance covers audit and compliance, and the process group deals with support and change.

Establish a software development process architecture, or development life cycle, that describes the technical and management activities required for proper execution of the development process.[11] This process must be attuned to the specific needs of the organization, and it will vary depending on the size and importance of the project as well as the technical nature of the work itself. The architecture is a structural decomposition of the development cycle into tasks, each of which has a defined set of prerequisites, functional descriptions, verification procedures, and task completion specifications. The decomposition continues until each defined task is performed by an individual or single management unit.

If they are not already in place, *introduce a family of software engineering methods and technologies*. These include design and code inspections, formal design methods, library control systems, and comprehensive testing methods. Prototyping should also be considered, together with the adoption of modern implementation languages.

1.2.3 The Defined Process (Level 3)

With the Defined Process, the organization has achieved the foundation for major and continuing progress. For example, the software teams, when faced with a crisis, will likely continue to use the process that has been defined. The foundation has now been established for examining the process and deciding how to improve it.

As powerful as the Defined Process is, it is still only qualitative: there is little data to indicate how much is accomplished or how effective the process is. There is considerable debate about the value of software process measurements and the best ones to use. This uncertainty generally stems from a lack of process definition and the consequent confusion about the specific items to be measured. With a Defined Process, we can focus the measurements on specific tasks. The process architecture is thus an essential prerequisite to effective measurement.

The key steps required to advance from the Defined Process to the next level are:

1. Establish a minimum basic set of process measurements to identify the quality and cost parameters of each process step. The objective is to quantify the relative costs and benefits of each major process activity, such as the cost and yield of error detection and correction methods.

2. Establish a process database and the resources to manage and maintain it. Cost and yield data should be maintained centrally to guard against loss, to make it available for all projects, and to facilitate process quality and productivity analysis.

3. Provide sufficient process resources to gather and maintain this process data and to advise project members on its use. Assign skilled professionals to monitor the quality of the data before entry in the database and to provide guidance on analysis methods and interpretation.

4. Assess the relative quality of each product and inform management where quality targets are not being met. An independent quality assurance group should assess the quality actions of each project and track its progress against its quality plan. When this progress is compared with the historical experience on similar projects, an informed assessment can generally be made.

1.2.4 The Managed Process (Level 4)

In advancing from the Initial Process through the Repeatable and Defined Processes to the Managed Process, software organizations should expect to make substantial quality improvements. The greatest potential problem with the Managed Process is the cost of gathering data. There are an enormous number of potentially valuable measures of the software process, but such data is expensive to gather and to maintain.

Approach data gathering with care, therefore, and precisely define each piece of data in advance. Productivity data is essentially meaningless unless explicitly defined. For example, the simple measure of lines of source code per expended development month can vary by 100 times or more, depending on the interpretation of the parameters.[6] The code count could include only new and changed code or all shipped instructions. For modified programs, this can cause variations of a factor of 10. Similarly, noncomment nonblank lines, executable instructions, or equivalent assembler instructions can be counted with variations of up to 7 times.[14] Management, test, documentation, and support personnel may or may not be counted when calculating labor months expended. Again, the variations can run at least as high as a factor of 7.[16]

When different groups gather data but do not use identical definitions, the results are not comparable, even if it makes sense to compare them. The tendency with such data is to use it to compare several groups and to criticize those with the lowest ranking. This is an unfortunate misapplication of process data. It is rare that two projects are comparable by any simple measures. The variations in task complexity caused by different product types can exceed five to one.[6] Similarly, the cost per line of code of small modifications is often two to three times that for new programs.[6] The degree of requirements change can make an enormous difference, as can the design status of the base program in the case of enhancements.

Process data must not be used to compare projects or individuals. Its purpose is to illuminate the product being developed and to provide an informed basis for improving the process. When such data is used by management to evaluate individuals or teams, the reliability of the data itself will deteriorate. The Fifth Amendment of the U.S. Constitution is based on sound principles—few people can be counted on to provide reliable data on their own performance.

The two fundamental requirements for advancing from the Managed Process to the next level are:

1. Support automatic gathering of process data. All data is subject to error and omission, some data cannot be gathered by hand, and the accuracy of manually gathered data is often poor.

2. Use process data both to analyze and to modify the process to prevent problems and improve efficiency.

1.2.5 The Optimizing Process (Level 5)

In varying degrees, process optimization goes on at all levels of process maturity. With the step from the Managed to the Optimizing Process, however, there is a paradigm shift. Up to this point software development managers have largely focused on their products and will typically gather and analyze only data that directly relates to product improvement. In the Optimizing Process, the data is available to tune the process itself. With a little experience, management will soon see that process optimization can produce major quality and productivity benefits.

For example, many types of errors can be identified and fixed far more economically by design or code inspections than by testing. Unfortunately, there is only limited published data available on the costs of finding and fixing defects.[1, 13] However, from experience, I have developed a useful rule of thumb: It takes about 1 to 4 working hours to find and fix a bug through inspections and about 15 to 20 working hours to find and fix a bug in function or system test. To the extent that organizations find that these numbers apply to their situations, they should consider placing less reliance on testing as their primary way to find and fix bugs.

However, some kinds of errors are either uneconomical to detect or almost impossible to find except by machine. Examples are errors involving spelling and syntax, interfaces, performance, human factors, and error recovery. It would be unwise to eliminate testing completely since it provides a useful check against human frailties.

The data that is available with the Optimizing Process gives us a new perspective on testing. For most projects, a little analysis shows that there are two distinct activities involved: the removal of defects and the assessment of program quality. To reduce the cost of removing defects, inspections should be emphasized, together with any other cost-effective techniques. The role of functional and system testing should then be changed to one of gathering quality data on the programs. This involves studying each bug to see if it is an isolated problem or if it indicates design problems that require more comprehensive analysis.

With the Optimizing Process, the organization has the means to identify the weakest elements of the process and to fix them. At this point in process improvement, data is available to justify the application of technology to various critical tasks, and numerical evidence is available on the effectiveness with which the process has been applied to any given product. We should then no longer need reams of paper to describe what is happening since simple yield curves and statistical plots could provide clear and concise indicators. It would then be possible to assure the process and hence have confidence in the quality of the resulting products.

1.3 People in the Optimizing Process

Clearly, any software process is dependent on the quality of the people who implement it. There are never enough good people, and even when you have them there is a limit to what they can accomplish. When they are already working 50 to 60 hours a week, it is hard to see how they could handle the vastly greater challenges of the future.

The Optimizing Process enhances the talents of quality people in several ways. It helps managers understand where help is needed and how best to provide people with the support they require. It lets the professionals communicate in concise, quantitative terms. This facilitates the transfer of knowledge and minimizes the likelihood of wasting time on problems that have already been solved. It provides a framework for the professionals to understand their work performance and to see how to improve it. This results in a highly professional environment and substantial productivity benefits, and it avoids the enormous amount of effort that is generally expended in fixing and patching other people's mistakes.

The Optimizing Process provides a disciplined environment for professional work. Process discipline must be handled with care, however, for it can easily become regimentation. The difference between a disciplined environment and a regimented one is that discipline controls the environment and methods to specific standards, while regimentation defines the actual conduct of the work.

Discipline is required in large software projects to ensure, for example, that the many people involved use the same conventions, don't damage each others' products, and properly synchronize their work. Discipline thus enables creativity by freeing the most talented software professionals from the many crises that others have created. A disciplined process, then, empowers the intellect, while regimentation supplants it.

1.4 The Need for the Optimizing Process

There are many examples of disasters caused by software problems, ranging from expensive missile aborts to enormous financial losses.[2, 10, 15] As the computerization of our society continues, the public risks due to poor-quality code will become untenable. Not only are our systems being used in increasingly sensitive applications, but they are also becoming much larger and more complex.

While questions can appropriately be raised about the size and complexity of current systems, these are human creations, and they will, alas, continue to be produced by humans beings (with all their failings and creative talents). While many of the currently promising technologies will undoubtedly help, there is an enormous backlog of needed function that will inevitably translate into vast amounts of code.

Unless we dramatically improve our error rates, this greater volume of code will mean increased risk of error. At the same time, the complexity of our systems is increasing, which will make the systems progressively more difficult to test. In combination these trends expose us to greater risks of damaging errors as we attempt to use software in increasingly critical applications. These risks will thus continue to increase as we become more efficient at producing volumes of new code.

As well as being a management issue, quality is an economic one. It is always possible to do more reviews or to run more tests, but it costs both time and money to do so. It is only with the Optimizing Process that the data is available to understand the costs and benefits of such work. The Optimizing Process provides the foundation for significant advances in software quality and simultaneous improvements in productivity.

There is little data on how long it takes for software organizations to advance through the maturity levels toward the Optimizing Process. Based on my experience, transitions from Level 1 to Level 2 or from Level 2 to Level 3 take from one to three years, even with a dedicated management commitment to process improvement. To date, I have observed only a few software teams at level 4 or 5, and no complete organizations. People could reasonably argue that this limited anecdotal evidence is hardly proof of the benefits of these process levels. They would of course be right. On the other hand, this framework has essentially fueled four centuries of scientific and engineering development. These concepts have been proven in physics, engineering, and manufacturing, and I have yet to see evidence that they won't work for software as well. While I cannot expect all readers to blindly share this conviction, I do assert that there is little alternative. Rather than continuing to struggle with their current immature processes, this framework at least offers software organizations an improvement path. I assert that it will work. If you find it doesn't precisely fit your needs, make some changes, try it out, and if it works, publish your findings so we can all learn and improve.

There is an urgent need for better and more effective software organizations. To meet this need, software managers and professionals must establish the goal of moving to the Optimizing Process.

1.5 Summary

The improvement of software development organizations follows six steps:

1. Understand the current status of the development process.
2. Develop a vision of the desired process.
3. Establish a list of required process improvement actions in order of priority.
4. Produce a plan to accomplish the required actions.
5. Commit the resources to execute the plan.
6. Start over at step 1.

A maturity structure addresses these six steps by characterizing a software process into one of five maturity levels. These levels are:

1. *Initial*   Until the process is under statistical control, no orderly progress in process improvement is possible.
2. *Repeatable*   The organization has achieved a stable process with a repeatable level of statistical control by initiating rigorous project management of commitments, costs, schedules, and changes.
3. *Defined*   The organization has defined the process. This helps ensure consistent implementation and provides a basis for a better understanding of the process.

4. *Managed*   The organization has initiated comprehensive process measurements and analyses beyond those of cost and schedule performance.

5. *Optimizing*   The organization now has a foundation for continuing improvement and optimization of the process.

The Optimizing Process helps people to be effective in several ways:

□ It helps managers understand where help is needed and how best to provide the people with the support they require.

□ It lets the professionals communicate in concise, quantitative terms.

□ It provides the framework for the professionals to understand their work performance and to see how to improve it.

References

1. Basili, V. R., and R. W. Selby. "Comparing the effectiveness of software testing strategies," *IEEE Transactions on Software Engineering*, vol. SE-13, no. 12, December 1987.

2. Borning, A. "Computer system reliability and nuclear war," *Communications of the ACM*, vol. 30, no 2, February 1987.

3. Crosby, P. B. *Quality Is Free*. New York: McGraw-Hill, 1979.

4. Deming, W. E. *Quality, Productivity, and Competitive Position*. Cambridge, MA: Massachusetts Institute of Technology Center for Advanced Engineering Study, 1982.

5. Dunham, J. R., and E. Kruesi. "The measurement task area," *IEEE Computer*, vol. 16, no. 11, November 1983.

6. Flaherty, M. J. "Programming process measurement system for System/370," *IBM System Journal*, vol. 24, no. 2, 1985.

7. Humphrey, W. S. "The IBM large-systems software development process: objectives and direction," *IBM Systems Journal*, vol. 24, no. 2, 1985.

8. Humphrey, W. S. *Managing for Innovation—Leading Technical People*. Englewood Cliffs, NJ: Prentice-Hall, 1987.

9. Humphrey, W. S., and D. H. Kitson. "Preliminary Report on Conducting SEI-Assisted Assessments of Software Engineering Capability," SEI Technical Report SEI-87-TR-16, July, 1987.

10. Myers, G. J. *Software Reliability—Principles and Practices*. New York: Wiley, 1976.

11. Radice, R. A., N. K. Roth, A. C. O'Hara, Jr., and W. A. Ciarfella. "A programming process architecture," *IBM Systems Journal*, vol. 24, no. 2, 1985.

12. Radice, R. S., J. T. Harding, P. E. Munnis, and R. W. Phillips. "A programming process study," *IBM Systems Journal*, vol. 24, no. 2, 1985.

13. Shooman, M. L., and M. I. Bolsky. "Types, distribution and test and correction times for programming errors," *Proceedings of the 1975 International Conference of Reliable Software*. New York: IEEE, 1975, pp. 347–357.

14. Shooman, M. L. *Software Engineering: Design, Reliability, and Management*. New York: McGraw-Hill, 1983.

15. *The New York Times*. "Making sure the computers keep running." February 8, 1987.

16. Wolverton, R. W. "The cost of developing large-scale software," *IEEE Transactions on Computers*, June 1974.

2

The Principles of Software Process Change

This chapter describes the principles for changing the software process and discusses some common misconceptions about software work. Software process change rests on many of the principles of organizational change, but much has been written about this subject, and it is not reproduced here. It is important, however, to have general familiarity with such issues as resistance to change, champions, sponsors, agents, unfreezing, and refreezing before launching a software process change program. These topics are therefore summarized at the end of this chapter. For those who seek deeper understanding, there is a sizable literature on these topics.[6, 8, 9, 10, 11, 13, 14, 15] W. E. Deming's *Out of the Crisis* should also be read by everyone in this field.[3]

2.1 Process in Perspective

Before discussing the principles and some of the common misconceptions about software, it is important to put the subject of process in perspective. When some approach seems to fit a need, it is often tempting to assume it will solve all the problems. While process management provides a powerful basis for assessing software problems and a consistent framework for organizational improvement, it is not a cure-all. Two other key areas that need to be considered are people and design methods.

2.1.1 The People

The extreme sensitivity of software quality to the talent of its builders presents a special challenge. Large software teams must necessarily contain a mix of talents—a few team members will be unusually talented, while many will be normally or only marginally capable. While it is possible to assign the less skilled people to the least sensitive tasks, it is not always possible to know who this is or what parts of the product have the lowest risk. Further, not all errors are made by the least skilled professionals. Everyone makes mistakes, and the most difficult errors concern the most complex parts of the design. Even when this work is done by the most talented people, they can have bad days, have mental blocks, or just overlook something.

Better people clearly do better work; we obviously want the best teams for our projects. Focusing only on talent, however, can lead into a blind alley for several reasons:

- ☐ The best people are always in short supply.
- ☐ You probably have about the best team you can get right now.
- ☐ With proper leadership and support, most people can do much better work than they are currently doing.

Talent, however, is relative. The raw programming trainee today does better work than many of our most experienced people of 10 and 20 years ago. While it is always desirable to recruit better people, it is also wise to focus on making better use of the talent we already have.[6] This always pays off.

2.1.2 Design

There is convincing evidence that superior products have superior designs. This may seem self-evident, but it is worth repeating. In studying many software products to see what separated success from failure, Curtis found that the successes were always designed by people who understood the application.[2] For example, a well-designed program to control a missile was designed by someone who understood missiles.

A program can be viewed as executable knowledge. Program designers should thus have application knowledge. When this knowledge is coupled with the ability to produce a creative design, a quality product will likely result. With such talents, an orderly process can be of great help. Without them, good product design is unlikely, regardless of the process used.

2.2 The Six Basic Principles

The basic principles of software process change are:

- □ *Major changes to the software process must start at the top.*   Senior management leadership is required to launch the change effort and to provide continuing resources and priority.
- □ *Ultimately, everyone must be involved.*   Software engineering is a team effort, and anyone who does not participate in improvement will miss the benefits and may even inhibit progress.
- □ *Effective change requires a goal and knowledge of the current process.*   To use a map, you must know where you are.
- □ *Change is continuous.*   Software process improvement is not a one-shot effort; it involves continual learning and growth.
- □ *Software process changes will not be retained without conscious effort and periodic reinforcement.*
- □ *Software process improvement requires investment.*   It takes planning, dedicated people, management time, and capital investment.

Each of these principles is expanded in the following sections.

2.2.1 Major Changes to the Software Process Must Start at the Top

Major changes require leadership. Making changes calls for a management team with the conviction that long-term improvements are both possible and essential. These managers must then set challenging goals, monitor progress, and insist on performance.

Perhaps Deming's most important contribution has been his insistence that process problems are management's responsibility.[3] Most people will generally do their best within the constraints of the system. Exhortations thus cause little improvement and often make things worse. Sustained progress, then, comes from changing the system through management action. While the managers won't actually do the work, they must set the priorities, furnish the resources, and provide continuing support. That is why changes to the software process must start at the top.

2.2.2 Ultimately, Everyone Must Be Involved

With an immature software process, the software professionals are forced to improvise solutions. While this takes considerable talent, it can also result in a good deal of interference and wasted motion. With a more mature process, these individual actions are more structured, efficient, and reinforcing. As in professional sports, all the team members need to support each other as they execute practiced plays. When they don't, they act like a mob of individual players who have lost the synergistic cohesion of a team. Such teams don't win many pennants.

In the software process, people are the most important ingredient.[5] It is essential to recognize their desire to do good work. The need is thus to focus on repairing the process and not the people. If management feels that the people are the problem, process improvement will appear threatening, the people will worry about their jobs, and this worry will likely cause resistance to change.

2.2.3 Effective Change Is Built on Knowledge

An effective change program requires a reasonable understanding of the current status. An assessment is an effective way to gain this understanding. Assessment must be done with care, however, for things are rarely done the way they are supposed to be, and the managers are often the last people to know. The assessment is a learning process, aimed at gaining a clear definition of the key problems and the professionals' views of what should be done to resolve them. Without such knowledge, priorities are hard to establish—and priorities are the most important part of an improvement program.

People often feel that their problems are unique. From assessing several dozen large software organizations, however, it is clear that they all face very similar problems.[7] What is more, these problems have all been solved before, and often *in the same organization!* Software professionals generally need most help in controlling requirements, coordinating changes, managing (and making) plans, managing interdependencies, and coping with systems design issues. Since the energy spent on these and similar problems generally consumes a large part of every software professional's time, these areas are where management can provide the most immediate help. The surprising thing is that, at least in low-maturity organizations, technical issues practically never show up at the top of these priority lists. This is not because technical issues are not important, but just that so many management problems must be handled first.

2.2.4 Change Is Continuous

One of the most difficult things for a management team to recognize is that human-intensive processes are never static. Both the problems and the people are in constant flux, and this fluidity calls for periodic adjustment of tasks and relationships. Even with a stable population, the people continually learn new skills and find different ways to solve problems. In dealing with these dynamics, three points are important:

□ Reactive changes generally make things worse.

□ Every defect is an improvement opportunity.

□ Crisis prevention is more important than crisis recovery.

The first point comes from industrial engineering. While processes *can* be improved under pressure, doing so is often a mistake. In a crisis, the focus is on quickly fixing the immediate problem, not on improving the process. While temporary process patches may be needed, it is wise to make permanent process changes in a more disciplined way. By occasionally adding new review steps or requiring additional tests, for example, the process can soon become an incoherent patchwork rather than an orderly improvement framework.

Defect prevention, discussed in detail in Chapter 17, is a powerful technique for improving the software process. The general idea is to track every problem and periodically to establish prevention action teams. Because of the problem volume in low-maturity software organizations, however, this approach is rarely practical before maturity level 3 or 4. At that point the process is sufficiently refined to permit association of problem categories with process causes.

One of the greatest conundrums of software management is maintaining sufficient priority on problem prevention. People gain greater visibility from putting out fires than from preventing them. These "heroes" are then more likely to be promoted than the quiet and effective professionals who stayed out of trouble. At the level 4 or 5 process, measurements can make this distinction clear, but at lower maturity levels management must consciously reward preventing as well as fixing.[6]

2.2.5 Software Process Changes Won't Stick by Themselves

The tendency for improvements to deteriorate is best characterized by the physics term *entropy*. It refers to the steady increase in the randomness or disorder of physical processes. In the absence of conscious effort, human processes behave much the same way. Precise and accurate work is so hard that it is rarely sustained for long without reinforcement. This means that new methods must be carefully introduced and periodically monitored, or they too will rapidly decay.

Human adoption of new process methods involves four stages:

1. *Installation*   This involves initial installation of the methods and training in their proper use.
2. *Practice*   Here the people learn to perform the methods as instructed.
3. *Proficiency*   Next comes the traditional learning curve, as people gradually improve their efficiency.
4. *Naturalness*   Finally the methods are so ingrained that they are performed without intellectual effort.

For first-class athletes, artists, or scientists, superior work is natural. A truly superior software team also behaves naturally. This "naturalness," however, is only developed through long experience and continual reinforcement.

While such ingrained behavior is highly desirable, few disciplines achieve it. The best examples are people working in the life-threatening conditions of outer space or the ocean floor, the behavior of physicists with radioactivity or near high-energy accelerators, the handling of high explosives, the operation of nuclear submarines, or the piloting of high-performance aircraft. Sloppy behavior in these fields is often instantly and painfully obvious. The fact that there are occasional accidents merely demonstrates the limited human ability to long sustain high levels of precise performance. Since periodic reinforcement is needed in these fields it is clearly essential in the less threatening environment of software engineering.

Software engineering is a tough discipline, and it is getting tougher. There are endless opportunities for error, and the need for coordination and control grows with increasing system function, team size, or process complexity. The actions of even the best-intentioned professionals must be tracked, reviewed, and checked, or process deviations will occur. If there is no system to identify deviations and to reinforce the defined process, small digressions will accumulate and degrade it beyond recognition. This lack of a tracking system is why many managers do not know what is going on—the process is not what it was when they last looked!

2.2.6 It Takes Time, Skill, and Money to Improve the Software Process

While the need for dedicating resources to improvement seems self-evident, it is surprising how often managers rely on exhorting their people to try harder. The slogans are unfurled and everyone salutes the goal of better quality. If, when the people return to their jobs, management merely continues to mouth platitudes, nothing will change. The key points are:

- □ To improve the software process, someone must work on it!
- □ Unplanned process improvement is wishful thinking.
- □ Automation of a poorly defined process will produce poorly defined results.
- □ Improvements should be made in small, tested steps.
- □ Train, train, train!

To Improve the Software Process, Someone Must Work on It!   No one questions the need to design a manufacturing process before they order the tools and go into production. They must consider raw materials handling, design the process flow, select the tools, specify the controls, and oversee ordering, installation, and operation. The software process needs the same attention. If it is not designed, it will merely be adjusted to each successive crisis. Overall performance then will be essentially unchanged: a chaotic process that is doomed to remain one. The need for resources devoted to improving the software process is discussed in more detail in Chapter 14.

Unplanned Process Improvement Is Wishful Thinking.   As F. P. Brooks has said, "There is no silver bullet."[1] Instead of looking for some magic answer to instantly solve all problems, software development must be treated like any other discipline. This requires detailed improvement plans and the resources and dedication to follow them. Plans define the resource needs and provide a framework for management tracking. *If process improvement is not rigorously planned and tracked, it will not happen!*

Automation of a Poorly Defined Process Will Produce Poorly Defined Results.   This is the normal consequence of picking a solution before understanding the problem. As with any other data processing application, when support programs are written and installed before their operational use is defined, they are generally an expensive waste of time. Investment in software process automation is essential, but it must focus on those defined tasks where the labor, time, or quality improvement potential is most promising. Until the software community can identify the highest-priority problems and define their potential for improvement, there is no business basis for investment. While such savings are hard to prove, some practical approaches are described in Chapter 18. Software process automation investments should proceed in step with software process maturity improvement. Automation should certainly be used to resolve the highest-priority problems, but little effort should be wasted until a clear definition of the process application is available. This generally means that early automation efforts should focus on planning, coordination, and change control.

Improvements Should Be Made in Small Steps.   People do not naturally perform well on highly rigorous and complex tasks. As a result, the software engineering process must be tailored to their abilities, rather than the reverse. Human memory and comprehension are limited, and it is easy to design processes that are beyond peoples' capacities. When such processes are both ill-defined and near these capability limits, they easily become unstable and erratic. Such processes must be changed with particular care. With an ill-defined process it is hard to anticipate the impact of a change on all the critical but informal activities. The results could be expensive and possibly even destructive.

The world is full of bright ideas with hidden pitfalls. In one case, for example, a management decision was made to evaluate the programmers by the number of patches they made to their code. While the number of patches dropped sharply, on closer examination it turned out that multiple changes were combined into a few large patches. The overall software change activity had not been reduced at all.

Process changes should be made in small steps, and even then they must be tested and adjusted before wide-spread implementation. Unless process improvements have the wholehearted participation and support of the people most directly involved, and unless they are carefully planned, thoroughly tested, and introduced in phased steps, they will probably be disappointing. Generally the change should be tried in a pilot project and the results evaluated before broader introduction.

Train, Train, Train!   Many organizations proudly proclaim that their people are their most important asset. While such platitudes sound good, it is instructive to compare how organizations install some of their capital equipment assets with the installation of their critical human assets. The latter is generally given little attention. While personnel briefings and facility tours can be helpful, they rarely fill the common need for training. Few software professionals are adequately prepared to use the languages and tools they are given, to understand the protocols and system services they need, to effectively use (or even know) the organization's software process, to appreciate the subtleties of the application they are implementing, or to plan and track their own work. Without such training, the necessary learning is gained through trial and error. This not only wastes time and money; it also often involves a lot of error.

Training is expensive, but not nearly as expensive as not training. A plan is required, some specialists must be hired or retained, and the required courses must be defined and offered. While the kinds of training depend on the organization's maturity level (as described in Appendix A), the key is to start by figuring out what training the people need. These needs are then reviewed with management and a training plan is developed. Finally, for the key courses, attendance must be required. If the courses are optional, few of the busy people will be able to go, and they are the ones who most need it. In sum, training must be planned, funded, scheduled, and required.

2.3 Some Common Misconceptions about the Software Process

Effective change depends on realism. Without an appreciation of the current state of the software process and a realistic view of the future, it is easy to succumb to wishful thinking or overly optimistic schemes. These then block the rational thought needed to address problems in an orderly way. Since the views in the following paragraphs are often held by people with little direct exposure to software, they may seem of little concern. Occasionally, however, such people hold key positions over a software organization. When this is the case, it is important to address these questions directly as part of the improvement process. Some of the more common software process misconceptions are:

□ *We must start with firm requirements*.   There is a widespread but fallacious view that requirements are the customers' job and that development should not start until they are explicitly defined.

□ *If it passes test, it must be OK*.   If the generally dismal record of software quality problems doesn't prove this false, nothing will.

□ *Software quality can't be measured*.   While not as well recognized, this too is false.

□ *The problems are technical*.   In spite of the many improved languages, tools, and environments, the problems of software cost, schedule, and quality remain.

□ *We need better people*.   Since the software professionals make the errors, some people erroneously feel that they should be blamed for them.

□ *Software management is different*.   While this is a new and unique field, traditional management methods can and should be used.

The remarkable thing about these misconceptions is that even though most software professionals recognize their fallacy our contracts and our management systems are largely based on them.

2.3.1 We Must Start with Firm Requirements

While we sometimes get firm requirements, a software perversity law seems to dictate that the firmer the specifications are, the more likely they are to be wrong. The fact is that the demand for firm and unchanging requirements is mostly wishful thinking and may even be an unconscious attempt to avoid blame for a poor result.

With rare exceptions, the requirements must change as the software job progresses. Just by writing a program, we change our perceptions of the task. The ripple of change starts with the requirements and continues through implementation, initial use, and even through later enhancement. Even if we could plan for all this development learning, the computer implementation of human tasks changes the applications themselves. Requirements by their very nature cannot be firm because we cannot anticipate the ways the tasks will change when they are automated.

For large-scale programs, the task of stating a complete requirement is not just difficult; it is practically impossible. Unless the job has previously been done and only modest changes are needed, it is best to assume that the requirements are wrong. Software development is a learning process, and it must generally proceed in small steps. Even with small programs, there are far too many definitions, functions, and options to possibly master in one step. Generally the most practical answer is to use an incremental development process—that is, to gradually increase the level of detail as the requirement and the implementation are mutually refined. What this means is:

- □ The customer doesn't generally know what is needed and neither does anyone else!
- □ The initial requirements are therefore often wrong and will change.
- □ You must therefore establish a link to someone who knows the application and work together until the job is completed. The larger and more complex the system, the more you will need expert domain knowledge.

Stable Requirements.   Clearly, to build anything we must have some stability, at least for long enough to get it built and tested. This means the incremental development process must start with minimal requirements that we and the user "know" are valid. These are then implemented, tested, and used in trial form. The next increment is then planned and developed. Thus, the solution is gradually evolved in a way that is more likely to meet the user's needs.

For large or integrated systems, the system design organization must also be part of this process. The crucial point is to start with expert knowledge of the users' problem and gradually augment this with a progressively refined system and software design. If the higher-level designs are selected with great insight, many of the lower-level decisions will not affect the requirements. This, however, is not guaranteed. Requirements problems can be uncovered during every development phase, and they must be properly resolved at the requirements level and not just patched in the design or the code.

Premature Requirements Freezes.   One argument against the incremental approach is that it takes too long. That is true when compared with projects with firm, accurate, and precise initial requirements, which is occasionally feasible, but not the general case. When projects are built with firm but poor requirements, the later retrofits are more expensive and time-consuming than an evolutionary process.

The requirements-based process motivates counterproductive behavior. The end users are forced to firmly state their needs before they are ready. Any changes are then frozen so a contract can be negotiated. Then the adversarial debates start on what functions are covered by the contract. Since someone must pay for every change, someone must be responsible for it. Unfortunately, without initial agreement on the job, it is impossible to reach agreement on the scope of the changes. These arguments thus often hinge on the literal interpretation of a flawed requirements document. This process results in wasted time and money, distrust, and a poor product.

With software the challenge is to balance the unknowable nature of the requirements with the business need for a firm contractual relationship. While the solution will vary with each situation, contractual deals are rarely successful if they are not based on a realistic understanding of the job. The pleasant comfort of a firm deal does not last long if it is based on vague specifications. It is far better to have the bickering up front when everyone retains their options. Whether this requires a study, a prototype, or an evolutionary development program, the resulting understanding will provide a firmer foundation for the entire project.

2.3.2 If It Passes Test, It Must Be OK

The converse is certainly true: If it doesn't pass test, it isn't OK! As we build larger and more complex programs and their operating environments become more complex and unpredictable, testing is a progressively less reliable indicator of system quality. The reason is that many design and coding errors are caused by the programmer failing to anticipate some improbable condition. As the number of possible program conditions increases, the feasibility of exhaustively testing thus declines. An example is the problem of testing a multiprogramming operating system. Here a large number of relatively independent programs interact in an almost unpredictable way. If the design of any part of the system depends in any way on the particular sequence of these programs, every such sequence must be tested. In the simple case of four parallel jobs that each have ten interruptable tasks, the total number of possible execution sequences is approximately five thousand billion billion.

One could argue that when each of these job streams is independent, all the combinations need not be tested. For truly error-free programs then, independent testing would be adequate. While this argument is entirely logical, the nature of complex systems often causes unexpected interactions, especially when heavily stressed. If the programs were supposed to be independent, the existence of errors could then mean that they had some unintentional dependencies. What this means is that if the programs don't need to be tested, the testing job is possible! For programs that contain errors, however, such highly variable environments cannot be tested with sufficient completeness to ensure a reliable system.

If we cannot completely test programs, how can we handle complex systems? The answer is that we can do some things with reasonable assurance, but not everything. While the balance of this book describes some approaches to this problem, a few simple ground rules will help:

- □ Establish as high-quality a software process as you can.
- □ Determine the most complex, essentially error-free programs you can build with this process.
- □ When highly reliable programs are needed, limit their complexity to what you know you can produce with your essentially defect-free process.
- □ Test your programs as thoroughly as you economically can.
- □ Recognize that your capability to build progressively larger defect-free programs will improve as you manage and improve your software process.

We should certainly attempt to build programs that are beyond our previous capability. We must recognize, however, that they will contain errors that might cause erratic and possibly damaging behavior. If such risks are acceptable, it makes sense to push our previous complexity limits.

2.3.3 Software Quality Can't Be Measured

There is no measure that comprehensively represents programming quality. On the other hand, such comprehensive measures don't exist for other complex products either. Quality measures are valuable, however, so we must find some and use them. Fortunately, we have found that even rudimentary measures can help to guide our work. Further, if we don't measure the quality of our products, we can only vaguely understand how good or bad they are. While a more comprehensive treatment of this topic is included in Chapters 15 and 16, discussions of software quality should use numbers, which requires measurement. Without measures, a quality program will produce little useful action.

With today's software, quality improvement is generally governed by the amount of effort we can afford to spend on quality improvement. Such decisions involve the potential social and economic damage of the errors and the cost of removing them. As the quality of our programs improves, the defect prevention and removal processes must thus become progressively more efficient. This also requires data!

The initial step must be to define the purpose for making software quality measurements. If they are to help in finding the residual errors or in setting goals and tracking against them, some useful measures are discussed later in this book. If, however, the desire is for some grand benchmark to use in evaluating all programs, such quality measurements are indeed not feasible.

2.3.4 The Problems Are Technical

There are many fascinating and important technical software problems. The issue is not whether there are such problems, but whether their solution will make much of a difference. Unfortunately, the highest-priority problems of most software organizations are not technical.[7] As pointed out in Chapter 1, most software organizations are at maturity level 1 or 2. Their highest priority is to establish an orderly process that will permit their people to operate efficiently. As long as they continue to work with a relatively confused and incoherent process, they won't have much time for sophisticated technical work.

Low-maturity software organizations spend most of their energy in controlling the high volume of changes, recovering from late-discovered defects, and reacting to unanticipated crises. While such organizations generally produce products, their costs are rarely predictable and their quality is often marginal. Their major problems are not the lack of adequate languages, reuse methods, advanced tools, or integrated environments. While these might help (but it is not likely), the critical issues are much less sophisticated. These are the topics in the first 14 chapters of this book. While the technical work cannot be ignored, it will not fix the management problems.

Perhaps the most frustrating point about our current software problems is that most of them have been solved many times before. The reason these solutions are constantly reinvented is that so many organizations have a disordered and unmanaged process. As long as all the people do their tasks each in their own way, they will continue to make and remake the same mistakes.

2.3.5 We Need Better People

I once heard a senior executive seriously propose that we find the programmers who made the errors and get rid of them. While it is true that an occasional poor performer does bad work, the true cause of errors is the process, not the people. The actual error injection is done by people, but they often have inaccurate, confusing, or incomplete information, have not been trained, have inadequate facilities, have ill-defined methods and procedures, or can't follow the procedures they have. We must certainly get the most energetic and best-qualified people we can, but this alone will not solve all the problems. Most of the problems can only be fixed through management action.

2.3.6 Software Management Is Different

Many factors make software different from other engineering fields:

- ❑ Software is generally more complex than other engineering products.
- ❑ Since software engineering is relatively new, there are not yet many managers or senior professionals with sufficient experience to appreciate the benefits of an effective process.
- ❑ The insignificant cost of reproducing software forces software solutions to many late-discovered system problems. While this is often the only practical approach, it further complicates the software job.
- ❑ In other engineering fields, release to manufacturing provides a natural discipline that is not present with software. When some independent party must sign off on production costs and schedules, the design definition is either complete or all work stops until it is.
- ❑ The software discipline is not grounded in natural science. As an artifact of human ingenuity, software does not rest on a stable foundation of physical principles.
- ❑ Software is often the system element that presents the function to the end user. It is thus the part that is most visible, most subject to complaint, and most exposed to requirements changes.

□ Software also is often the crucial ingredient that couples all the other system elements together.

□ Software is often viewed by non–software practitioners as a black art. This causes many managers to back away and not to use their management instincts to solve software problems.

The last factor is the crux of the software management problem. While there are many unique characteristics to software, they all require more management discipline, not less. Managers should thus demand detailed plans, tracking systems, and periodic technical and management reviews. Software management should be entirely traditional, only more so. Unfortunately, many managers who insist on these items for hardware let their software teams get by without them.

Above all, software managers should insist on clear answers to simple questions. They should require detailed plans and estimates with crisp checkpoints. The technical plans should be technically reviewed, and the results should be in plain English. Unless you want to dig into the technical methods, algorithms, or languages, most software process topics can be understood by experienced managers from almost any discipline. Technical background generally helps, but it is not essential. Above all, managers should not worry about looking stupid. We software people make so many mistakes that everyone feels stupid a good part of the time. Since the computer will ruthlessly expose us, we either learn a little humility, switch fields, or become managers.

2.4 A Strategy for Implementing Software Process Change

Most software organizations have plenty of room for improvement. They may, for example, need to change their management system, their procedures, their tools and methods, or even their organizational structure. The implementation of the necessary changes, however, must be handled with care. While the software people will generally welcome a concerted effort to improve their process, the changes must be handled properly or they will generate resistance.

In software, resistance to change generally takes two forms. First, the professionals see their problems as somehow immutable and incapable of solution. They don't consider them technically insoluble as much as organizationally impractical. They involve so much detail and procedure that all the existing standards, rules, facilities, and attitudes seem too much to overcome. Second, even when this inertia is overcome, management often either doesn't understand the real issues or sees them as too technically trivial to be important. They are thus prone to embrace some magic technological "silver bullet" that will painlessly solve all their problems.[1] While technology is important and is the long-term key to improving the software process, it is rarely of much help in solving problems that are not precisely understood. Since most people object to having someone else's solutions to undefined problems imposed on them, the unplanned introduction of technology generally causes resistance to change.

An effective change process has three phases: unfreezing, moving, and refreezing.[6] With the software process, unfreezing is best initiated by an effort to understand the true problems in the organization and to make people aware of the opportunities for change. One way to do this is with a software process assessment, as described in Chapter 3.

2.4.1 Champions, Sponsors, and Agents

Champions are the ones who initiate the change process. They bring management's attention to the subject, obtain the blessing of a sponsor, and establish the credibility to get the change program launched.[6, 14] The champion maintains focus on the goal, strives to overcome obstacles, and refuses to give up when the going gets rough. Many studies have shown that new ideas without champions have little chance of success.[4, 11, 12, 15] "Although champions don't always win, winners, it seems, always have champions."[6, 9]

The senior management role is equally crucial: someone in authority needs to recognize the value of the work and *sponsor* it. This is done by providing both resources and official backing. With this, the champion's job is done, and it is time to actually launch the change process.

Once it is clear that changes are needed and management sponsorship has been obtained, the essential next step is to identify the change *agents* who will lead change planning and implementation.[6, 14] They muster the resources, assign the work, and call on senior management for help when needed. In selecting such agents, the key points to consider are:[6]

"**1.** Agents should be enthusiastic about leading the change process.

2. Agents must be both technically and politically capable of understanding the problems and ensuring that effective solutions are implemented.

3. Agents need the respect of the people they are to deal with.

4. Agents must have management's confidence and support or they will not act with the assurance needed to get wide cooperation and acceptance."

Chapter 14, "The Software Engineering Process Group," describes how organizations of change agents are established to support the software change process.

2.4.2 The Elements of Change

Three key elements of effective change are planning, implementation, and communication. The planning stage should involve knowledgeable representatives from each of the affected groups. This helps to ensure that a competent plan is developed and makes its acceptance more likely. Once the plan is developed, caution is advisable when starting implementation. Some initial trial efforts can minimize the risk that an early failure will derail the entire process. Broader implementation should quickly follow these early successes.

While the proper pace must depend on the problems encountered, it is essential to maintain a continuous stream of actions and successes.[9] Such successes will not only dispel the fears of those not yet involved, but will maintain a positive image of progress. Most professionals have heard countless promises of magic results, but when the smoke clears they know they will have to deal with the resulting mess. It is thus essential to have public plans, periodic progress reports, and early demonstrations of success. These not only reassure the people; they also help to ensure continued executive support.

2.4.2 Refreezing

Refreezing can take many forms, but the basic objective is to ensure that an achieved capability is retained in general practice. Several common techniques are:[6]

- □ Retain the management team that instituted the change.
- □ Modify the organization's procedures.
- □ Establish measurements and incentives.
- □ Set up a dedicated staff to monitor and support performance.
- □ Establish an education and training program.

While all these techniques are useful in certain circumstances, some combination is generally most effective. The key needs are to ensure that the entire management team is convinced that the change is important, the people know their jobs and how to do them, the organization's procedures and systems support the new methods, and the reward system encourages their use. While the operating team that originally installed the change may not be the best one to maintain it, a transition period is generally required. In any case, skilled and knowledgeable professionals are the key ingredient to an effective software process, so education and training should be part of every software refreezing plan.

2.5 Summary

This chapter describes the principles for changing the software process and discusses some common misconceptions that can inhibit the improvement efforts. The six basic principles of software process change are:

1. Major changes to the software process must start at the top.
2. Everyone must be involved.
3. Effective change requires knowledge of the current process.
4. Change is continuous.
5. Software process changes will not be retained without conscious effort and periodic reinforcement.
6. Software process improvement requires investment.

The key topics to focus on once the decision has been made to invest in process improvement are:

- To improve the software process, someone must work on it!
- Unplanned process improvement is wishful thinking.
- Automation of a poorly defined process will produce poorly defined results.
- Improvements should be made in small, tested steps.
- Train, train, train!

Some common misconceptions about the software process are:

- We must start with firm requirements.
- If it passes test, it must be OK.
- Software quality can't be measured.
- The problems are technical.
- We need better programmers.
- Software management is different.

While the software people will generally welcome a concerted management effort to improve their process, the changes must be handled with care or they will generate resistance. Software process change must start with an unfreezing step. Once it is clear that change is needed, the essential next step is to establish resources to serve as change agents. Three key elements of making the change are planning, implementation, and communication. Refreezing can take many forms, but the basic objective is to ensure that an achieved capability is retained in general practice. Education and training should be part of every software refreezing plan.

References

1. Brooks, F. P. "No silver bullet, essence and accidents of software engineering," *IEEE Computer*, April 1987.
2. Curtis, W., H. Krasner, V. Shen, and N. Iscoe. "On building software process models under the lamppost," *IEEE Proceedings*, 9th International Conference on Software Engineering, Monterey, CA, March 30–April 2, 1987.
3. Deming, W. E. *Out of the Crisis*. Cambridge, MA: MIT Center for Advanced Engineering Study, 1982.

4. Fernilius, W. C., and W. H. Waldo. "Contribution of Basic Research to Recent Successful Industrial Innovations," Industrial Research Institute Research Corporation, St. Louis, MO. Prepared for the Division of Policy Research and Analysis, National Science Foundation (Washington, D.C.: September 1979).

5. Freeman, Peter. *Software Perspectives—The System Is the Message*. Reading, MA: Addison-Wesley, 1987.

6. Humphrey, W. S. *Managing for Innovation—Leading Technical People*. Englewood Cliffs, NJ: Prentice-Hall, 1987.

7. Humphrey, W. S., T. Kasse, and D. Kitson. "State of Software Engineering Practice," Software Engineering Institute Technical Report, CMU/SEI-89-TR-1.

8. Huse, E. F. *Organization Development and Change*. St. Paul, MN: West, 1975.

9. Irwin, Patrick H., and Frank W. Langham, Jr. "The change seekers," *Harvard Business Review*, January–February 1966.

10. Lawrence, Paul R. "How to deal with resistance to change," *Harvard Business Review*, January–February 1969.

11. Maidique, Modesto A. "Entrepreneurs, champions, and technological innovation," *Sloan Management Review*, Harvard University, Winter 1980.

12. Peters, Thomas J., and Robert H. Waterman, Jr. *In Search of Excellence: Lessons from America's Best-Run Companies*. New York: Harper & Row, 1982.

13. Pfeffer, Jeffrey. *Organizations and Organization Theory*. Marshfield, MA: Pitman, 1982.

14. Pressman, R. S. *Making Software Engineering Happen, A Guide for Instituting the Technology*. Englewood Cliffs, NJ: Prentice Hall, 1988.

15. Sherwin, Douglas S. "Strategy for winning employee commitment," *Harvard Business Review on Management*. New York: Harper & Row, 1975.

3

Software Process Assessment

Process assessment helps software organizations improve themselves by identifying their critical problems and establishing improvement priorities. The basic assessment objectives are:

- To learn how the organization works
- To identify its major problems
- To enroll its opinion leaders in the change process [3]

John Gardner described the basic reason for doing an assessment when he said that most organizations "are not suffering because they can't solve their problems but because they won't see their problems."[2]

Management is often so focused on finding solutions that it fails to define the problems. Dale Zand, a professor at NYU's School of Business, notes that when managers say, "I don't want to hear your problems, I want to hear your solutions," they are taking precisely the wrong approach.[10] On the other hand, an unconstrained search for problems without regard to solutions rarely results in much useful guidance. It is, however, important to focus first on problem definition since a complex problem must be thoroughly understood before a solution is attempted. Without preliminary problem analysis, the "solutions" are seldom effective, and they often are not even pertinent to the real problems the professionals deal with on a daily basis.

Software assessments are similar to the organizational development process used successfully for many years.[1, 6, 9] They have also been used by both IBM and the Software Engineering Institute of Carnegie Mellon University.[3, 4, 8] The essential approach is to conduct a structured series of interviews with the key people in the organization to learn their problems, concerns, and creative ideas.

Assessments differ from other common studies. Product reviews, for example, are generally used to find the status of a particular project. Such evaluations are often initiated by senior management to probe particular issues and expose the problems. While a product review is a proper exercise of management responsibility, it is often a poor way to motivate change and generally provides little guidance on how to improve the software process.

Audits are typically conducted for senior managers who suspect problems and send in some experts to uncover them. In the financial field, examples of errors and occasional wrongdoing are so common that periodic financial audits are a sign of a well-run business. With software, periodic audits are also needed to maintain consistent focus on the way the work is supposed to be done. Some responsible engineering groups even make a practice of requesting audits of their own projects. While this is not common, it can be very helpful in identifying key issues and is similar to the assessment process discussed in this chapter.

The main reason to audit software work, however, is to ensure that the professionals follow the officially approved process. Typical process deviations are not motivated by greed but by a desire to get the job done as quickly and effectively as practical. The professionals often find that some aspects of the official process are outmoded and inefficient. They properly try to get the job done in spite of these bureaucratic obstacles, and their expedient shortcuts often turn out to be very effective. Thus unless it is done extremely well, an audit can actually do more harm than good, particularly if the official process is either not defined or cannot be implemented as stated.

Software audits can be highly effective when the software process is well enough defined to provide an auditable standard. Comprehensive audits of large software organizations can be expensive, however, since they require a lot of work by teams of skilled professionals.

3.1 Assessment Overview

A software process assessment is not an audit but a review of a software organization to advise its management and professionals on how they can improve their operation. It is conducted by a team of software professionals who typically have assessment experience or training. Some or even all the members can be drawn from the organization being examined, but, as will be discussed later, it is generally desirable to have a mix of local and outside reviewers.

The purpose of an assessment is to identify the highest-priority areas for improvement and to provide guidance on how to make those improvements.

Assessments are based on the principle that the local managers and professionals want to improve their own operation and that their primary need is guidance on what to do and how to do it. While this principle generally applies, there are exceptions. Some organizations are under such extraordinary pressure, their managers are so inexperienced, or the professional skill level is so deficient that outside guidance and assistance are required.

3.2 Assessment Phases

Assessments are typically conducted in three phases: preparation, assessment, and recommendations. During preparation, senior management becomes committed to the process, agrees to participate personally, and commits to take action on the resulting recommendations or explain its reasons for not doing so. Phase one concludes with a brief one- or two-day training program for the assessment team.

Phase two is the on-site assessment period. This activity typically takes several days, although it can take two or more weeks, depending on the size of the organization and the assessment technique used. It concludes with a preliminary report of the findings to local management.

In phase three the findings and action recommendations are presented to the local managers. A local action team is then assembled to plan and implement the recommendations. The assessing organization may provide assistance during this period and may participate in a subsequent follow-up assessment.

3.3 Five Assessment Principles

As in many activities, the basic requirements for a good assessment are a competent team, sound leadership, and a cooperative organization. Because the software process is human-intensive, however, some special considerations should be kept in mind. They are:

1. The need for a process model as a basis for the assessment
2. The requirement for confidentiality
3. Senior management involvement
4. An attitude of respect for the views of the people in the organization being assessed
5. An action orientation

These points are described further in the following sections.

3.3.1 Start with a Process Model

An assessment implies a standard. The organization's process is reviewed in comparison with some vision of how such processes should be performed. This, of course, is the crux of the assessment process. As the proverb says: "If you don't know where you are going, any road will do." The maturity model described in Chapter 1 of this book provides a framework for comparison.[5]

Without such a foundation, an assessment can easily degenerate into a loosely directed intuitive exploration. If the assessment team members have extensive software experience and good intuition, such studies can be valuable. Unfortunately, the members of such groups often focus on their own particular specialties. This generally means that no topic is covered in much depth and that many areas are overlooked. If such teams split into individuals or small units to probe particular areas, there is a better chance of covering all the key topics. Unfortunately, these separate probes result in many different views of the operation and reduce the likelihood of a coherent result. Splitting the team also destroys the synergistic power of the group's diverse experience and minimizes the likelihood of agreement on anything but platitudes.

To avoid these problems, it is wise to base an assessment on a common view of the desired software process. Such a model provides a basis for orderly exploration as well as a framework for establishing problem priorities. With such a focus, the entire team can work together on the key issues and recommendations. While agreement may take some time, the discussions invariably stimulate deeper understanding, and far better conclusions are reached than would otherwise be possible. Appendix A describes a more detailed framework for the software process maturity structure.

3.3.2 Observe Strict Confidentiality

The assessment's purpose must be to support the organization's improvement program and not to report its problems to higher management. Even when initiated with this intent, it is extraordinarily difficult to maintain confidentiality, particularly when a chief executive demands to see the results. If any member of the assessment team provides such data, however, people will learn that they cannot speak in confidence. As this becomes widely known, the assessment group will find it increasingly difficult to conduct assessments that uncover the real issues.

Confidentiality permits the assessors to talk to people at all levels of the organization. If the managers suspect that the findings will be passed to higher management, they will properly insist on being present at every interview. Unfortunately, when managers are present, professionals rarely say anything that their managers don't know already or with which they might disagree. There is then no reason to have an assessment. The managers could present this official view far more efficiently in a two-hour briefing.

Confidentiality is required at all organizational levels. The professionals must know that their comments will not be attributed to them. Several projects should be reviewed at once, and the project managers should be told that the results for their projects will be given only to them. Site management is then provided a composite picture of the overall facility. This ensures that no single project or individual is identified with any specific problem.

3.3.3 Involve Senior Management

The senior manager sets the organization's priorities. This local manager typically gives final approval for software commitments and answers to corporate management when things go wrong. While some senior managers are responsible for multiple projects in several locations, it is wise to focus in a reasonably local geographic area. This focus minimizes project disruption, simplifies assessment arrangements, and generally facilitates subsequent action planning and implementation. In the following discussions, the senior manager of this total organization will be called the *site manager*.

The site manager must be personally involved in the assessment and its follow-up action plans. If not, the work will not be given sufficient priority. While some initial good-faith attempts may be made, the first crisis will soon preempt these process improvement efforts. If the assessment is to have any lasting impact, the site manager must personally participate, assign qualified people, and periodically review the progress of the resulting action plans.

Without this support the assessment will likely be a waste of time. The lower-level people can generally handle their routine problems, but lasting improvements must survive the periodic crises. That is when the process is under most stress, when management is most likely to defer nonessential work, and when serious disasters are most likely. Since software crises are common, if the site manager won't protect the process improvement efforts, they will not likely continue long enough to do much good.

3.3.4 Keep an Open Mind and a Level Head

Any assessment can easily seem arrogant. A group of remote "experts" reviews a large and complex organization and in a few days tells them what they are doing wrong and what they should do to improve. Generally the local people work hard, are dedicated to doing a good job, and are trying to improve. They are thus properly skeptical of any brief study and doubt it can have any lasting impact.

The local professionals will soon sense if an assessment team arrives thinking it has all the answers. Their natural reaction will be to show these "experts" they are not so smart after all. This leads to an unspoken wish that the assessment will fail. Under these conditions, it often will.

This distrust of outside experts is not only understandable but is quite proper. A small team of outside experts cannot hope to identify in a few days the most critical problems in any organization. Complex problems rarely have simple answers, and the subtleties of most organizations are far too intricate for any group to fathom quickly.

The fundamental assumption must be that the on-site professionals are smart, motivated, and have many good ideas. If they can be convinced to share their knowledge, the assessment can be a catalyst for self-improvement. The professionals will be willing to share, however, only when they see the assessment as a way to get help rather than as a threat of exposure.

A highly critical attitude or a lack of interest in local views by the assessment team can be deadly. When good work is found, it should be recognized and identified so other groups can take advantage of it. Surprisingly, for each software problem there is often someone in the organization who has already solved it. Making this capability visible can be one of the greatest and most immediate benefits of the assessment. Mistakes and oversights must also be identified, but they should be objectively reported without attribution, criticism, or blame. The team must recognize that its suggestions are only ideas that will have to be evaluated and adjusted to local conditions. As difficult as it is to achieve, the proper attitude is one of open-minded and supportive professionalism.

Even when the assessment team is appropriately supportive, some local people will be resentful and not cooperate. If the team members' actions clearly demonstrate their desire for active collaboration with the on-site professionals, however, this will be recognized and people generally will respond positively.

3.3.5 Focus on Action

Finally, to have lasting effect, the assessment must be directed toward improvement. An action orientation keeps the questions focused on current problems and the need to solve them. If the assessment turns into a general exploration, it will not focus on the priority issues or produce recommendations that will be implemented.

An aborted or misguided assessment will do little good and can even make the situation worse. Prior to an assessment the professionals generally are aware of their worst problems and often assume management is not. While this leads them to view management as mildly inept, they frequently assume management doesn't understand the issues and cannot be expected to solve them. After an assessment, this is no longer the case. An expert study has heard their concerns and suggestions for what should be done about them. These results are then reported to the site manager. After all this, any manager who does not take action will be seen by the people as either incompetent or unconcerned with their problems. In either case their morale will suffer. In net, management must either focus on taking action or not do an assessment.

3.4 The Assessment Process

The first step in any assessment is to identify the organization to be assessed and the team to do it. This typically requires the site manager's commitment to doing the assessment and willingness to assign sufficient skilled resources to get it done. Since professional assessment groups are rare, most organizations will have to assemble an assessment team of their own.

A small staff of assessment specialists can be extremely helpful in supporting local assessment groups. If such a group is available, through corporate or division headquarters, for example, they too must strictly observe confidentiality. The main advantage of such specialist groups is that they can maintain a relatively stable and repeatable assessment process. They can also help the local organizations track their progress and compare their performance with a composite of other similar groups.

3.4.1 Forming an Assessment Team

The assessment team leader is selected first. This is someone who has considerable software experience, has the ability to lead small groups, and is able to convincingly present the results. This leader should have assessment experience or should obtain advice and assistance from someone who has. When this is not possible, a brief study of the available assessment literature can provide useful guidance. [1, 3, 4, 6, 7, 8, 9]

The assessment team members should all be experienced software developers, and one or more should have experience in each phase of the software process. Four to six professionals typically form an adequate team, although more can be used if desired. Since larger teams cost more money and are harder to manage, an upper limit of eight to ten participants is usually wise. Table 3.1 gives some guidelines for selecting assessment team members.

The team members should be drawn from several groups within the organization being assessed, and, where possible, most should come from projects other than those selected for review. A few members can come from assurance or support groups, but the team must appreciate the pressures of line product development. No one should participate in the assessment who is otherwise personally involved in reviewing, supporting, or managing the projects being assessed. The members can be drawn from parallel projects, local test groups, or Software Quality Assurance (SQA) groups from other locations. The local SQA people, for example, should not be used. Since smaller organizations may have trouble finding enough people who meet all these criteria, they will have to make some compromises.

TABLE 3.1
GUIDELINES FOR SELECTING ASSESSMENT TEAM MEMBERS

Each assessment team member should:
Have at least eight to ten years professional software experience
Be well respected in the organization
Be able to deal with people in an informal and nonthreatening manner
Be a team player
Have attended assessment training with this team

No assessment team member should:
Be currently serving in an audit or review capacity for any of the projects being assessed
Be a line manager over any of the projects being assessed or people being interviewed
Be working directly on any of the projects being assessed or working on their direct support

With an external assessment at least one professional from the organization being assessed should participate as a full team member. This local representation facilitates the planning process, provides the rest of the team with background on the organization, and establishes a focal point for assessment logistics and follow-up action. Since this local member is critical to the success of the effort, the site manager should be personally involved in making the selection.

3.4.2 Self-Assessment Considerations

While it is possible for organizations to assess themselves, they should be aware of several potential problems.[3] First, few organizations can afford a staff of assessment experts. With a temporary team, some crisis always seems to prevent the key people from participating on the agreed date. Even when the date is finally set, a local team rarely has the clout to insist on the site manager's participation. An in-house assessment can easily become a futile staff exercise unless the site manager is personally involved.

Site managers who desire a self-assessment should thus reach agreement with their line managers on its importance and their commitment to support it. They must plan to assign people where needed, commit to attend the necessary meetings, and agree to participate in developing action plans to address the recommendations.

Before any management team members can responsibly make such commitments, they must know how much time is required from them and from their key people. Generally the time can be kept to a minimum. Except for the assessment team members, the managers and their people need only spend a few hours attending assessment meetings. Afterward, however, action planning and implementation can take much more time. This, of course, depends on the recommendations and the priorities the management team assigns to them.

3.4.3 Assessment Ground Rules

It is desirable to have a written set of assessment ground rules for the organization being assessed and for the assessment team members. For an external assessment, the site manager and the assessment team leader should sign a written agreement covering these ground rules. A copy of the standard agreement used by the Software Engineering Institute (SEI) is shown in Appendix B. Such an agreement minimizes subsequent misunderstandings and ensures agreement on the critical points. The items to be covered in such an agreement are:

□ The assessment results will be kept confidential by the assessment team members.

□ The site manager personally agrees to participate in the opening and closing assessment meetings.

□ In addition to the regular members, the site manager agrees to assign one or two local professionals to handle the assessment arrangements and to lead the follow-up action plan work. They will be full assessment team members.

□ The site manager commits to developing and implementing appropriate action plans in response to the assessment recommendations. When an action plan is not deemed appropriate, the reasons will be explained to the assessment team.

□ The site manager agrees to designate a person responsible for developing the action plans. If possible, this person should be a member of the assessment team.

While it is essential to have such an agreement for external assessments, it is perhaps even more important to document and to sign such an understanding for an in-house assessment. Without a clear statement of roles and responsibilities, the assessment team members likely will not call on management when they should. In any case, both the site manager and the team members should clearly understand how the assessment is to be conducted and what they are expected to do.

3.4.4 Assessment Team Training

As the assessment team is formed, the members must agree to participate fully during the training period, on-site review, and wrap-up meetings. Unrelated phone calls should be held, all other meetings and commitments rescheduled, and the members should be on time for every session. Assessments are intense efforts, and it is disruptive to have one or two members consistently late or preoccupied with other matters.

Typically the team leader conducts a two- or three-day training program for the entire assessment team. This program familiarizes the team members with the assessment process and helps to build a cohesive working group. Members who have previously been trained should participate in training the new team. They need to understand the organization being assessed, to contribute to assessment planning, and to be an equal member of the new team. A typical training program includes the following steps:

1. The assessment schedule and objectives are outlined.

2. The assessment principles are reviewed, together with the software process model used as the assessment framework.

3. The organization members briefly outline the organization's mission, its management structure, and its recent history.

4. The assessment guidelines are discussed and all team members are asked to sign the written agreement.

5. A team-building exercise is conducted to assist the group in developing an effective and mutually supportive mode of operation.

6. The detailed plan for the assessment period is covered, including the purpose of each session, who participates, and their roles. The plan covers:

   □ The topics for each session

   □ The discussion leader assignments

   □ Who will note the findings and how

   □ When and how team conclusions are to be reached

   □ By whom and when any reports and presentations are to be prepared and presented

7. When necessary, portions of this process are rehearsed until all members are comfortable with their roles.

8. *On-site planning*   The final training task is to work out the details of the on-site period. The organization members summarize the key active projects, and the team discusses and agrees on the most appropriate projects to assess. Several back-up projects are identified in case a desired project becomes unavailable. To provide coverage of a spectrum of the work being done, it is generally wise to review between three and six projects. While more projects require more work, five or six projects should be included if possible. Following project selection, the final details of the on-site period are settled. This involves meeting facilities, participant selection, daily schedules, and administrative support.

3.4.5 The On-Site Period

The typical SEI assessment schedule is shown in Table 3.2. The assessment starts with a presentation to the site manager and staff. The assessment ground rules are

TABLE 3.2
TYPICAL SEI-ASSISTED ASSESSMENT SCHEDULE

Day One
Assessment Overview (site manager, staff, participants)
  Purpose and conduct of the assessment
Briefing (participants)
  A detailed review of the assessment schedule
  Questions and answers
Questionnaire (project representatives)
  The questionnaire is completed for each project
Project Discussions (project representatives)
  Each project representative separately meets with the assessment team to clarify any questions and be told of any materials that the team desires to discuss on day three

Day Two
Functional Area Interviews (functional representatives)
  A series of meetings, each with four to six professionals who are experts in selected technical areas
Preliminary Findings (assessment team)
  The assessment team formulates its preliminary findings

Day Three
Project Discussions (project representatives)
  Each project representative separately meets with the assessment team to discuss the points needing clarification and to comment on the preliminary findings
Findings Formulation (assessment team)
  The assessment team formulates its findings

Day Four
Findings Dry Run (assessment team)
  The findings presentation is reviewed by the assessment team
Findings Review (project representatives)
  The findings presentation is reviewed with the project representatives
Findings Presentation (site manager, staff, participants)
  The assessment findings are presented to the site manager, staff, and all the people who participated in the assessment
Senior Management Meeting (site manager, assessment team leader)
  A discussion of any special management considerations that were not covered during the findings presentation, the next steps required, and the need to start planning for action team formation
Assessment Postmortem (assessment team)
  The assessment team reviews the assessment process and identifies any changes needed to improve it

discussed, as well as the assessment principles and the overall schedule. An overview meeting is then held with all the site participants, including the project managers and the professionals to be interviewed. When possible, these people should participate in the opening management meeting, but if not, that material is again presented together with a more detailed schedule for the assessment period.

Any questions and concerns are addressed, and copies of the ground rules and schedule are distributed.

3.5 Assessment Conduct

While most technical people enjoy discussing the products they are developing, such discussion rarely provides much insight into the organization's problems. The objective is to explore the implementation of real projects rather than the products being built or the way the work is supposed to be done. While an idealized composite of the best instances of project work might be interesting, it does not provide a useful basis for process improvement. The assessment should thus focus on what the projects actually do, how they do it, the problems encountered, and the results obtained.

A selected set of questions should be prepared in advance of the actual assessment period. This ensures an efficient use of time as well as complete coverage of the material.[3, 4, 5, 8] These questions are generally reviewed with the project managers in a small initial meeting that provides an overview of process status and suggests areas for further exploration.

Meetings are next held with small groups of selected professionals who have expertise in various facets of the software process (see Table 3.3). In free-form discussions the professionals offer their views and suggestions on the key problems. The discussions should typically end with a question such as: "If you could fix one facet of the process, what would you do and why?" With most groups this will generally elicit several creative ideas.

It is also helpful to structure these discussions in the reverse order of the development process. Often, for example, the comments of the test and release specialists will be most helpful if heard before meeting with the implementation people. This is true for the design and requirements phases as well.

3.5.1 Probing Questions

In conducting assessments it is hard to obtain really accurate information. The reasons for this are:

□ *Questions are often misunderstood.*   The English language is imprecise, and brief questions are invariably subject to several interpretations.

□ *The respondents may have a different understanding of some common terms.* For example, discussion is often required to reach common understanding on the meaning of the terms "high-level language," "review," or "reusability."

TABLE 3.3
GUIDELINES FOR SELECTING FUNCTIONAL AREA REPRESENTATIVES

Six to eight representatives are identified for each of several meetings of 90 to 120 minutes each. Potential areas of specialty for each meeting are:
    Quality Assurance and release
    Software integration and test
    Coding and unit test
    Requirements and design

Each of these representatives should be:
    A recognized opinion leader in the selected area
    Actually working on projects rather than on a staff
    A technical professional and not a manager
    Aware of the assessment process and the confidentiality arrangements

---

☐ *The respondents may not be broadly aware of the work in their own organization.* Some professionals are narrowly focused on their specialty areas. Outside this sphere, they may be uninformed or even misinformed. Managers typically have a broader view, but their hands-on experience is sometimes dated and their current knowledge is often filtered by their people.

☐ *Occasionally people are unwilling to risk the truth.* While it is rare for someone to tell an out-and-out lie, stories can generally be couched in favorable terms and the "unusual events" that "really weren't representative" can easily be overlooked.

Because of the difficulty of obtaining accurate information, probing and checking are an important part of every assessment. One way to ensure accurate information is to ask for copies of work products. When the assessment team members are sufficiently experienced, they can usually tell if the work was done as described.

It is easy to damage the trust established during an interview by showing skepticism or disbelief. The key is to assume everyone has useful knowledge to impart and to concentrate on finding it. There are invariably many creative approaches to common problems, and making them more widely used can produce early benefits. By openly searching for such examples, any probing activity is made nonthreatening and is more readily accepted.

3.5.2 Assessment Conclusions

At the assessment conclusion, the team prepares a report on its initial findings. Some suggested guidelines are shown in Table 3.4. The report should be a composite summary of site status, together with more detailed findings in key areas. Prior to reviewing this material with the site manager, the team should review it with the project managers. This should identify any overlooked problems or any misstated or overemphasized topics.

TABLE 3.4
GUIDELINES FOR FINDINGS FORMULATION

The findings should be limited to the top 10 to 12 items that are:
  Major issues for most of the projects reviewed
  Key issues for advancing to the next maturity level
  Supported by evidence from the assessment
  Addressable by an action recommendation
  Specific—avoid sweeping generalizations

The last site action is to review the composite findings with the site manager and staff. Any questions are addressed, and the schedule for follow-up work is reviewed. If possible, all the site personnel who participated in the assessment should attend this meeting. Some suggested topics to cover in this meeting are shown in Table 3.5.

3.5.3 Assessment Report

The final assessment team action is the presentation of a written final report and recommendations to the site manager and staff. The recommendations should highlight the three or four items of highest priority. Since no organization can handle more than a few priority tasks at a time, the total number of items requiring attention should be limited to around ten. These should be clearly explained, together with the assessment team's views on implementation priority. A suggested report outline is shown in Table 3.6.

The wording and format of the recommendations should be carefully considered. The recommendations should start with a brief one- or two-sentence statement of precisely what is recommended. A more complete discussion should then explain what is to be done and why, though again this should be brief. Most of these topics are complex and could easily justify pages of tutorial explanation. If this action was not justified by the assessment, however, it cannot be sold in the recommendations. If further explanation is required on how to carry out the recommendations, references should be given to separate documents or to a report appendix. It is essential to remember that the sole purpose of the recommendation is to provide the management team with items they can assign for implementation. The simplest guide is to write the recommendation report so the site manager can give it to someone with the brief note: "Do this."

A *written* assessment report should always be prepared because:

☐ Writing the actual recommendations helps the assessment team understand precisely what it is recommending. People who agree on a shorthand presentation are often surprised by the trouble they later have agreeing on a written statement of the same points.

TABLE 3.5
A TYPICAL OUTLINE OF THE FINDINGS PRESENTATION

Presentation Overview:
 Agenda
 Scope—projects assessed
 Assessment conduct—schedule
 Summary composite status—the bad news
 Strengths noted—it isn't all bad
 Findings summary
 Findings—each finding (see below)
 Next steps

Findings format:
 Finding—what the team observed
 Consequences—the implications of the finding for the organization
 Examples—specific instances of the finding (without identifying people or projects)

□ Since presentations are generally tersely worded, their interpretation is highly dependent on the listeners' background and biases. While similar problems accompany written reports, they provide a less ambiguous record of what was found, what was recommended, and why.

□ A written report provides an ideal vehicle for informing the professionals about what was found and recommended. It also provides a clear foundation for action plan preparation and implementation.

TABLE 3.6
A TYPICAL FINAL REPORT OUTLINE

Summary and Conclusions
 An executive summary of the findings and recommendations

The Assessment
 The assessment background and a description of the assessment process

Site Status
 A summary description of the site status

Key Findings
 A brief description of each finding

Recommendations
 A description of each of the recommendations in priority order

Appendices
 The assessment agreement
 Cross-reference of findings and recommendations

3.5.4 Action Plans

The action plans are next prepared by the local site organization, generally under the guidance of the team member named for this purpose. If properly chosen, this member is now fully knowledgeable on the issues and is able to start quickly.

It is wise to involve leading professionals from several projects in action plan preparation. This produces a better result and also facilitates later acceptance. It is also wise to limit the number of initial action plan efforts so they can all be fully staffed by capable professionals. A key manager should be given responsibility for tracking each one, and the site manager should periodically review staffing and progress. Since failures can discredit the entire improvement program, special pains should be taken to ensure the success of these initial efforts.

3.5.5 Reassessments

Organizations should generally conduct follow-up assessments one to two years after the initial action plans have been developed and approved. This is important for several reasons:

- □ To assess the progress that has been made
- □ To provide a visible future milestone for completion of the actions from the prior assessment
- □ To establish new priorities for continued improvement

3.6 Implementation Considerations

The greatest assessment risk is that no significant improvement actions will be taken. Without proper management focus a few superficial efforts may be made, but soon everything will revert to business as usual. A catalyst is needed to maintain the improvement priority, such as goals and management reviews. Long-term goals are first established, and then subgoals are defined for intervening two- or three-month periods. A senior management quarterly review then maintains high-level checkpoint visibility, crystallizes the plans, and creates the periodic crises required to get things accomplished.

3.6.1 Risks

Some of the other key risks and potential actions to alleviate them are schedule conflicts, inadequate support, and lack of follow-through.

Schedule Conflicts.   Despite the best intentions, crises that conflict with assessment plans often arise. The most damaging of these require the site manager to miss either the opening or the closing meeting or both. Such unfortunate schedule conflicts have happened in about one-third of the assessments I have conducted. An approach that works is to request a substitute executive who can speak for the site manager and then to arrange for a later private meeting to cover the issues with the site manager in person.

Inadequate Support.   In the few cases of inadequate management support that I have experienced, the reason was that the assessment commitment was made at too low a management level. Often only a very senior executive can take a sufficiently long-term view to avoid becoming defensive. Also, even fairly high-level managers are often only responsible for portions of the software work, so they cannot provide adequate organization-wide priority. It is very difficult if not impossible to recover from this problem.

Lack of Follow-through.   Frequently management changes or other high-priority issues reduce the focus on action plan implementation. In at least half of the organizations I have assessed, the site manager changed between the final assessment report and action plan completion. While occasionally the action priorities were lost, more frequently the improvement efforts were successfully maintained. The most important determinants of success were the presence of an aggressive manager to lead the change efforts, a capable process improvement staff, and a clearly stated improvement goal.

3.6.2 Staffing

Staffing is generally the most serious implementation problem. In addition to staffing the assessment itself, the other staffing needs will generally include:

- ☐ A small, full-time staff to focus and to guide the improvement efforts—typically a Software Engineering Process Group, as discussed in Chapter 14
- ☐ Part-time project participation in the action plan working groups
- ☐ Project review and implementation of the resulting actions

Since the best software people are always overcommitted, they will generally not be made available without the site manager's personal involvement. If this is not forthcoming, the improvement work will likely suffer and may even not be done at all.

3.7 Summary

Assessments are done:

- To learn how the organization actually works
- To identify its major problems
- To enroll its opinion leaders in the change process [3]

Assessments are typically conducted in three phases: preparation, the on-site assessment, and findings and action recommendations.

An assessment implies a standard, and it is done to support the organization's improvement program. Confidentiality permits the assessors to talk to people at all levels of the organization. The site manager is personally involved.

The assessment team leader should be someone with considerable software experience, the ability to lead small groups, and the ability to convincingly present the results. The assessment team members should all be experienced software developers. Four to six professionals typically form an adequate team, although more can be used if desired.

Senior management must assign sufficient priority to the assessment and improvement effort, or adequate resources will not be assigned and no significant actions will likely result.

References

1. Conference Report No. 605, "Organizational Development: A Reconnaissance." New York: 1973.

2. Gardner, J. "Renewal of Organizations." 20th Annual Meeting of the Board of Trustees, Midwest Research Institute, Kansas City, MO, May 3, 1965.

3. Humphrey, W. S. *Managing for Innovation—Leading Technical People*. Englewood Cliffs, NJ: Prentice-Hall, 1987.

4. Humphrey, W. S., and D. H. Kitson. "Preliminary Report on Conducting SEI-Assisted Assessments of Software Engineering Capability." Software Engineering Institute, Carnegie Mellon University Technical Report SEI-87-TR-16, July 1987.

5. Humphrey, W. S., and W. L. Sweet. "A Method for Assessing the Software Engineering Capability of Contractors," Technical Report CMU/SEI-87-TR-23. Software Engineering Institute, Carnegie Mellon University, September 1987.

6. Huse, E. H. *Organization Development and Change*. St. Paul, MN: West, 1975.

7. Pressman, R. S. *Making Software Engineering Happen, A Guide for Instituting Technology*. Englewood Cliffs, NJ: Prentice-Hall, 1988.

8. Radice, R. A., J. T. Harding, P. E. Munnis, and R. W. Phillips. "A programming process study," *IBM Systems Journal,* vol. 24, no. 2, 1985.

9. Rodgers, David. *Can Business Management Save the Cities.* New York: MacMillan, Free Press, 1978.

10. Zand, Dale. Peter Drucker Management Conference, New York City, April 22, 1982.

4

The Initial Process

Most software organizations operate in the Initial Process Level at least some of the time; many organizations never leave it. Though it is so common, this chaotic state is as hard to describe as darkness; it is easier to point out what it lacks. The Initial Process is the lack of a managed, defined, planned, and disciplined process for developing software. Since there can be many degrees to this lack, there are obviously many gradations to the Initial Process. Table 4.1 summarizes the basic characteristics of each process level and the actions required to improve to the next higher maturity level.

To emphasize the characteristics of the often chaotic Initial Process, this chapter starts with an extreme example. While few organizations have all these problems, many will find the symptoms familiar. Next some external characteristics are summarized, as well as the impact such environments have on the professionals working in them. Finally the reasons organizations fall into this chaotic trap are discussed, as are (briefly) the methods for escaping. There is, of course, a way out—but that is the subject of the entire book.

4.1 The Nature of the Initial Process

In the Initial Process, the professionals are driven from crisis to crisis by unplanned priorities and unmanaged change. From the outside, such groups are often hard to identify, at least in the short term. Over time, however, they are easy to recognize because they generally do not meet commitments. While their managers often

TABLE 4.1
THE LEVELS OF SOFTWARE PROCESS MATURITY

Level 1—Initial
Characteristics: Chaotic—unpredictable cost, schedule, and quality performance
Needed Actions: Planning (size and cost estimates and schedules), performance tracking, change control, commitment management, Quality Assurance

Level 2—Repeatable
Characteristics: Intuitive—cost and quality highly variable, reasonable control of schedules, informal and ad hoc process methods and procedures
Needed Actions: Develop process standards and definitions, assign process resources, establish methods (requirements, design, inspection, and test)

Level 3—Defined
Characteristics: Qualitative—reliable costs and schedules, improving but unpredictable quality performance
Needed Actions: Establish process measurements and quantitative quality goals, plans, measurements, and tracking

Level 4—Managed
Characteristics: Quantitative—reasonable statistical control over product quality
Needed Actions: Quantitative productivity plans and tracking, instrumented process environment, economically justified technology investments

Level 5—Optimizing
Characteristics: Quantitative basis for continued capital investment in process automation and improvement
Needed Actions: Continued emphasis on process measurement and process methods for error prevention

present a convincing and impressive story and they may even meet their interim checkpoints, there is often some last-minute crisis that blows the plan out the window. Such groups occasionally even deliver on schedule, but these accidents are the exception and are generally due to herculean individual efforts rather than the strength of the organization.

These groups are often staffed with well-intentioned and competent people. They are anxious to do an effective job and are both busy and overcommitted. The lack of effective management and planning, however, means fluid schedules, inadequate resources, poor coordination, and vague status reports. This results in frequent disasters and almost constant surprises. Unfortunately, the surprises are rarely pleasant.

From their customers' perspective, such organizations are tolerated only as long as there is no alternative. Senior management is equally unhappy. These managers must make operating plans, and when one group does not meet commitments, the total organization misses its plan. Management frustration increases as new plans are successively missed, and soon they no longer believe anything the software people say. Software managers are frequently replaced, but when the new managers learn the problems, they sound like their predecessors and they too are discredited. In its frantic search for a magician to clear up the problems, senior management often makes things worse.

As far as the professionals and their immediate managers are concerned, the Initial Process is extraordinarily frustrating. Senior management makes unreasonable demands while cutting resources. Schedules are the only priority, but when they do deliver, nobody likes the result. Many first-class professionals leave as soon as they can. Most of the rest either have strong local ties or have given up hope for improvement and just put in time to collect their pay.

For creative professionals, the most frustrating part of this environment is that the same problems constantly recur. Plans are ad hoc, schedules are arbitrary, design control is nonexistent, and resources are always inadequate. Few people learn from past mistakes, and those who do are so discredited they have little influence. The remaining senior people become cynics whose "I told you so's" are often maddeningly accurate.

The "old salts" know what will happen because they have seen it all before. When the time comes to ship a new program, nobody will remember what test cases were run, or some module update will inadvertently be left out of the new version. Regression is common, and old problems that were fixed continually recur. Even after shipment, the "official" copy is sometimes lost and somebody has to scurry around to reconstruct a new master.

4.2 A Case Study of a Chaotic Project

I once participated in the review of a large military software development contract. The project was seriously late, and the review was to see if the current schedule would be met. After extended discussion we concluded the basic system should be completed within a few months of the current schedule. We also learned that a small amount of additional function was required but that it would not present a problem. We did not, however, see a plan. We reported that the project was in good technical shape but that there was modest further schedule exposure. While we were concerned about the lack of documented planning, the technical work looked good, and we really did expect the project to finish nearly on schedule.

After this report I periodically checked to see if the project had been completed. Every time, I was told it was almost done. Some months later I heard that the "small amount" of added code turned out to be 250,000 lines! It had seemed so simple that no one bothered to make a plan. Without a plan, they had no idea how big the job really was, no basis to know where they stood, and no way to justify added resources when they got into trouble. Even though the technical work was sound, the customer was convinced the project would be a disaster. The project was ultimately completed and was reasonably successful, but the customer lost so much confidence in the software people that he refused to pay for much of this work. As is often the case with the Initial Process, inadequate project management nearly destroyed years of good technical work.

4.3 Why Software Organizations Are Chaotic

The simplest explanation for the chaotic behavior of Level 1 organizations is human nature: People don't like to admit they don't know. Unfortunately, in software development there are an enormous number of unknowns. Without some work we generally have no idea how much code a given function will require or how much effort it will take. What is worse, in many cases the software team doesn't even know how to go about finding out.

When political pressures mount for a commitment, it takes guts to say you don't know. This is known as betting your job. If you insist on taking the time to make a good plan, you may be replaced by someone who promises to be more responsive. On the other hand, if you cave in to the pressure, you have to come up with a number. With nothing to guide you, you play it safe and put in the largest number the traffic will bear.

The software graveyard is strewn with the carcasses of partially completed projects that were three to five times larger than anyone dreamed. No responsible builder would contract for a house without reviewing the plans and specs. Some software managers have learned this painful lesson, but those who have not will continue to suffer the chaos of the Initial Process. Few escape until they learn to dig in their heels and refuse to commit until they have done their homework.

While lack of a commitment discipline is the most common reason for chaotic behavior, there are other forces. These are discussed in more detail in the following sections, but the logic is roughly as follows:

1. Under extreme pressure, software managers often make a guess rather than a plan. When the guess is drastically low, as it usually is, chaos ensues. Intuitive commitments occasionally are accurate, but generally only when the project scale and function are similar to the guesser's prior experience.

2. When the going gets rough, there is a strong temptation to believe in magic. Some "savior" may appear, or a new technology may be the answer. Since this hope is often an excuse for not planning, it merely postpones the problem.

3. The scale of software projects follows an escalating cycle:

   □ Programs generally take far more code than expected.

   □ As the programs become larger, new technical and management issues come up.

   □ Since these are unlike previous experience, they are a surprise.

□ As the scale increases, the surprises continue, but at dramatically increased cost.

4. Even after a higher maturity level is reached by an organization, new management, increased competition, or new technical challenges put pressure on the process. With the maturity of our field and the general lack of training for our people, this often means that organizations under pressure revert to the Initial Process.

4.3.1 Chaotic Forces—Unplanned Commitments

The most insidious and probably most difficult software management problem is the unplanned commitment. One software development group I studied was responsible for providing programs to support a large payroll application. In one typical case, a change in the tax laws affected the withholding calculations. Since the new law went into effect on the first of the year, the programmers were faced with a firm schedule. This schedule, however, represented what was needed and had nothing to do with an achievable plan to do the work. The programmers struggled valiantly to meet this arbitrary need, and they did manage to make the date. Unfortunately, there had not been enough time to do adequate testing, so the program had many bugs. It was so bad, in fact, that it was almost unusable. During the months it took to clean it up, the tax calculations for the entire payroll had to be done by hand.

When people are directed by top management to run a mile in two minutes, what should they do? Experienced hardware engineers have learned to first test the directive. If it is truly firm, the best ones develop a comprehensive comparison of this job with their prior experience to show management why this schedule is unrealistic. They also dig in their heels and insist that management either change the schedule to one that makes sense or relieve them of responsibility for meeting the dates. When the better engineers all do this, the managers have little choice, unless they want to do the design themselves. Unfortunately, all too many programmers start looking for their running shoes.

There are many reasons why commitments are made before a work plan can be developed, and they have considerable justification. While software developers are not responsible for all these problems and clearly cannot fix them, they suffer the consequences of chaos just the same. Until they learn to resist these pressures, however, such problems will continue. As we shall see, there are other steps that software professionals can take to mitigate these problems, but they all start with the professionals refusing to commit to a date without a plan to meet it.

Minor Commitments Can Also Cause Problems.   When a new requirement seems simple, the manager is tempted to merely commit to do it. Since software is a matter of detail, however, simple-looking functions often have hidden traps.

When these are not found until after the commitment, the manager is in an impossible situation. The normal result is an inadequately staffed crash effort to meet the date, regardless of job size. If the function really had been simple, the planning would have been equally simple and a well-thought-out commitment could have been made in the first place.

The Unplanned Commitment Trap.   The unplanned commitment is a trap because of the forces it generates. First, lack of an orderly plan generally means there are insufficient time and resources to do the job. This results in confusion, no time to think through the problems, and an unwillingness to use any but the lowest-risk, brute-force methods. Under these conditions, things generally get worse.

As managers struggle to recover from a first disaster, they feel increased pressure to be responsive. Like gamblers playing double or nothing, they soon lose their money, the house, and the farm. The users and senior managers become increasingly impatient and less willing to listen to problems and explanations. These managers are progressively driven into making more aggressive commitments, and the senior managers are progressively less inclined to be reasonable. Soon, the only way out is to find replacements. The new managers, however, are soon in exactly the same boat. Unless they have enough experience to stand up to these pressures, the spiral will continue.

4.3.2 Chaotic Forces—Gurus

The technical wizard can be a powerful asset. Unfortunately, gurus sometimes believe they can do no wrong. After they have led a small team to produce a superbly crafted program, they sometimes believe they can develop anything. While this overstates the case for many astute and highly competent professionals, some will accept almost any challenge with supreme confidence. When pressed for a plan, they refuse to be pinned down and point to their prior success to support their infallibility. As long as they continue to be successful, they will be given progressively larger and more demanding assignments until they hit one that is beyond them.

Unfortunately, when the crisis hits, there is almost no way to recover. Gurus typically run projects out of their heads. With nothing written down, everyone must come to them for guidance. At the breaking point, the limits of this intuitive approach have been reached and there is no simple recovery. A project within weeks of delivery is suddenly delayed by many months, and no one but the discredited guru understands what happened. While disaster frequently educates some bright gurus, it often results in drastic management action. Since the managers can't find anyone to trust, they are reluctant to invest any more time and money and often cancel the entire project.

4.3.3 Chaotic Forces—Magic

Human beings are inherently repelled by complexity. Scientists and engineers have historically searched for elegantly simple solutions to complex problems, and system developers are no different. Somehow there must be some grand solution to all this detail and confusion. Maybe we are using the wrong technology or the people have taken a wrong tack. This, however, is rarely the case. As Dr. F. P. Brooks says, "There is no silver bullet."[2]

While there are many cases in which improved technology can help, there are many more that need effective management. It is both understandable and desirable to search for better methods and people, but when the hope is for magical results, such quests take on a Holy Grail quality that blocks rational thought. Belief in magic makes all the details seem so unnecessary that the hard work is deferred while Rome burns.

4.3.4 Chaotic Forces—Problems of Scale

One of the fundamental reasons for problems of scale is the large size of many programs. Software size is insidious because of its impact on the development process. Having learned to build a small program, we are not fully prepared to build a large one, though we often think we are. The problems of scale can be summarized as follows:

□ As software products become larger, they are much more difficult to understand. These progressive levels of scale are roughly as follows:

1. One person knows the details of the program.

2. One person understands it but can't remember it so the design must be documented.

3. One person understands the overall design of a program, but the details of its component modules are each understood by separate experts.

4. A large software product is defined and understood at the product management level, but a separate team understands the characteristics and design of each of its component programs.

5. With software systems, the high-level design may be well defined and understood by the system management team, but each of its component products is only understood by the respective product management organizations.

6. When the system is very large and has evolved through many versions, there may be no one who understands it.

□ As software knowledge is more widely distributed:

1. Common notations are needed for precise communication.

   2. These standards must be documented, interpreted, and updated.

   3. Conflicts in standards must be identified and resolved.

   4. Standards changes must be controlled and distributed.

- With larger-scale software, similar control is needed for requirements, design, code, and test.

- As software size increases, prototypes or multiple releases are needed because:

   1. The total function cannot be implemented in time.

   2. Some needs cannot be understood without operational experience on a partial system.

   3. Some design issues cannot be resolved until a preliminary system has been built and run.

   4. A release discipline helps sort out user priorities.

   5. No one successfully builds large software systems in one shot anyway.

- With multiple releases, new complications arise:

   1. The requirements must be phased to meet end user needs.

   2. Each software component design must synchronize with these needs.

   3. Product interdependencies are orchestrated to meet release functional prerequisites.

   4. The build and integration plans are scheduled around these interdependencies.

   5. Early system drivers are scheduled to meet component test needs.

   6. The tight schedule requires subsequent release development to start before the prior releases are finished.

Experience in building a 10,000-line product will certainly help, but the 100,000 line product that follows will bring many new lessons. This is equally true at 1 million and 10 million lines. While a few groups have experience with 10- to 30-million line programs, no one has gone much beyond. There undoubtedly will be new surprises when we reach this next level, as we ultimately must. The software development process hasn't scaled up so far, and we cannot expect that it will start to do so now.

4.3.5 The Implications of Software Scale

The problems of software scale affect the individual, the management system, and the technical methods and tools that we use. Most people begin their software careers by writing small programs. They find it so stimulating and rewarding to produce a program that runs that they think they have the software problem licked. They "know" how to write programs and wonder what all the fuss is about.

Nuclear experience is of considerable value, but only for small-scale work. Unfortunately, when managers and professionals start at this level and when their educational experience reinforces it, the larger-scale system problems come as a shocking surprise. They have little trouble completing their own modules, but they become increasingly frustrated at having to coordinate with so many others. Everything they do seems to have an impact on someone else, and they spend most of their time reacting to remote requests for a seemingly endless string of changes.

The problem, of course, is scale. It is much like taking a beachhead. If the air strikes, the naval guns, and the landing craft are not precisely in sync, they will likely end up shooting at each other. When a large-scale process veers out of control, seemingly proper nuclear actions can have potentially serious large-scale consequences.

4.4 Software Process Entropy

There are many forces on the software process that push us toward disorganization (or increased entropy). Even when we have established a sound project management system, three classes of forces tend to disrupt it: dynamic requirements, increasing system size, and human nature.

As we build new systems we learn what we should have built. In fact, we often do not really understand what we want or how to build it until we have finished. This is a good reason for building prototypes, and it is what led Dr. Brooks to suggest we throw away our first system and concentrate on the second.[1]

The evolutionary process is driven by requirements dynamics. Each new development uncovers new issues that lead to changes. In addition to being unplanned, changes are highly error-prone and thus especially disruptive. A natural law of software development seems to require that all changes increase the total amount of code. Change disruption is thus compounded by increasing project scale.

Human nature, of course, is the ultimate limitation on our development process. In addition to intellectual constraints, people have emotions and ambitions. They want to get ahead, to belong, or to feel they have done something important. These feelings often motivate conformity and responsiveness to management's wishes. This response is a positive force because it helps make the management system work. The negative, however, is the hierarchy of response that flows from the top of the organization. Since schedule and cost are generally most visible to senior management, junior managers will give them highest priority, naturally reducing the attention they can give to other issues. Since all management levels are similarly responsive, these priorities dominate the entire operation. This domination results in a management system focused on responding to the current crisis.

Without planning, the problems of scale are not understood or adequately anticipated. In large software systems, the most severe problems are not obvious until testing gets into trouble. Without a plan, the response-driven management system treats testing as the problem. Such irrational priorities produce increasingly chaotic behavior.

4.5 The Way Out

If the chaos of the Initial Process Level were a simple problem, it would have been solved and this would be a history book. By examining many organizations that have worked their way out of the chaos trap, however, the outlines of a general solution are clear:

1. Apply systematic project management—the work must be estimated, planned, and managed.

2. Adhere to careful change management—changes must be controlled, including requirements, design, implementation, and test.

3. Utilize independent software assurance—an independent technical means is required to assure that all essential project activities are properly performed.

These basic steps involve much detail, but, as Robert Frost once said, "The best way out is always through."* Every successful construction superintendent, factory manager, battalion commander, and programming manager has learned this, often the hard way. The management of any large, complex activity requires mountains of detail. Unfortunately, few people enjoy detail work or do it naturally, but where details make the crucial difference, they are only overlooked at the manager's peril.

The solution to the chaos trap depends, of course, on the discipline of the software professionals themselves. When faced with an ill-defined or impossible job, they must act responsibly. That is the only way their managers can understand the risks they face. The managers have a similar obligation. When pressured into an unplanned or unreasonable commitment, they too must act responsibly. It is

---

*Copyright 1930 by Holt, Reinhart and Winston and renewed 1958 by Robert Frost. Reprinted from *The Poetry of Robert Frost* edited by Edward Connery Lathem. By permission of Henry Holt and Company, Inc.

usually effective to say: "I understand your requirement and we will do our utmost to meet it, but until I make a plan, I can't responsibly commit to a date." Most executives will accept this, and, if they really have a firm need, they will know what risks they face. Any organization that will not deal responsibly with such professional behavior is a risky place to work.

Many essential actions are described in the balance of this book and their use will materially assist organizations in working their way out of the chaos trap. Because large software systems are so complex and each organization has unique problems, no single action plan can possibly solve all problems. An appreciation of some principles should thus help to see where new or different approaches are needed. To summarize, the basic principles for controlling the chaos in software organizations are:

1. Plan the work.
2. Track and maintain the plan.
3. Divide the work into independent parts.
4. Precisely define the requirements for each part.
5. Rigorously control the relationships among the parts.
6. Treat software development as a learning process.
7. Recognize what you don't know.
8. When the gap between your knowledge and the task is severe, fix it before proceeding.
9. Manage, audit, and review the work to ensure it is done as planned.
10. Commit to your work and work to meet your commitments.
11. Refine the plan as your knowledge of the job improves.

Point 3 is so important that it deserves further comment. The basic approach to any large job is to break it into smaller parts that can each be implemented independently. This general approach turns out to be the driving force behind many of the technical directions in software engineering, such as subroutines and modularization. As systems grow larger, it is progressively more important to partition them cleanly. With clean partitioning methods, we shall be able to treat large systems as collections of smaller ones. When we can do that, we shall have learned how to scale up our software process.

4.6 Summary

The Initial Process is a largely chaotic state in which the professionals are driven from crisis to crisis by unplanned priorities and unmanaged change.

For creative professionals, the most frustrating part of this environment is that the same problems keep repeating. Plans are ad hoc, schedules are arbitrary, design control is nonexistent, and resources are always inadequate.

Human beings are inherently repelled by complexity. Somehow, there must be some grand solution to all this detail and confusion. This belief often causes a search for a technical wizard or a magic technology that will solve all these problems.

Even with a sound project management system, there are disruptive forces: dynamic requirements, increasing system size, and human nature. These often cause organizations to fall back into the chaos trap.

The outlines of a general solution to this problem are described in the balance of this book.

References

1. Brooks, F. P. *The Mythical Man-Month,* New York: Addison-Wesley, 1975.

2. Brooks, F. P. "No silver bullet, essence and accidents of software engineering," *IEEE Computer,* April 1987.

Software Engineering Institute

PART TWO

The Repeatable Process

Once an organization has conducted an assessment, as outlined in Chapter 3, it is then in a position to address its key improvement priorities. Assuming it is at Level 1, the Initial Process, its highest-priority needs will most likely be those described in Chapters 5 through 8 in Part II.

It is important to realize, however, that the software process is complex and involves a host of different activities. The reason the four topics of Part II are addressed at this point is not that they cover all important issues but that they likely represent the highest-priority areas for organizational improvement at this point. While many other areas probably need attention, it is essential to establish priorities. Otherwise, resources will be dissipated on many small efforts and little will be accomplished.

Some examples of topics that must continue to be handled according to the organization's traditional methods are standards, inspections, and testing, which are required in every software organization, regardless of maturity level. These are not addressed in Part II, however, because they are of lower priority until the items in Chapters 5 through 8 are under reasonable control. At that point the topics for Level 3 can be addressed, as described in Part III. Appendix A provides a more complete summary of many of the lower-priority topics that require continuing attention as organizations work to improve the maturity of their software process.

The main issues described in the chapters in Part II are commitments, planning, configuration management, and Quality Assurance.

Chapter 5 deals with the way software commitments are made and managed. It outlines the principles of the commitment process, how commitments relate to the management system, and how an effective commitment system can be implemented and managed.

Chapter 6 reviews software planning principles and goals, the Work Breakdown Structure, size estimating, resource estimating, and project tracking.

Chapter 7 explains why configuration management is important and describes the capabilities with highest initial priority. The principles and basic functions of configuration management are covered, with prime focus on managing source code, object code, and code change. While many important configuration management topics remain, these are deferred for attention in Chapter 12 in Part III.

Chapter 8 describes the benefits and goals of Software Quality Assurance (SQA), how it is organized, and some of the key considerations in establishing and managing an SQA organization.

The reason these topics are selected for attention at this point is that they establish a sound basis for project planning and process management. Until the organization effectively handles commitments, planning, configuration management, and Quality Assurance, the process will be too erratic to permit orderly improvement.

5

Managing Software Organizations

The role of the management system is to ensure that projects are successfully completed. This implies some organization-wide agreement on the meaning of the terms "success" and "completion." It also requires a continuing management focus on the progress of each project. Project management starts with a definition of the job to be done and the plan to do it. Since the specifics of such plans are discussed in the next chapter, the focus here is on the organizational and management framework for making and managing such plans. This involves managing commitments, project oversight, and contention. The basic principles of project management are:

□ Each project has a plan that is based on a hierarchy of commitments.

□ A management system resolves the natural conflicts between the projects and between the line and staff organizations.

□ An oversight and review system audits and tracks progress against the plans.

5.1 Commitment Discipline

The foundation for software project management is the commitment discipline. This is supported by plans, estimates, reviews, and tracking systems, which focus on ensuring that the organization meets its commitments. Commitments are not met by reviews, procedures, or tools, however; they are met by committed people.

The next few paragraphs cover commitment principles, how commitments are managed, and how to establish a commitment discipline.

5.1.1 Making a Commitment

In simplest terms a commitment is an agreement by one person to do something for another. Typically this involves a planned completion date and some consideration or payment. Salancik describes commitments as "a way to sustain action in the face of difficulties."[4] Commitment is thus the essential foundation for large-scale work. When the coordinated efforts of many professionals are involved, mutual commitments are essential.

When, for example, two programmers cooperate on a single project, they must divide up the work. This division starts with agreement on the distribution of functions, common interfaces, standard formats, and naming conventions. As work progresses, test plans are needed, and each may require design data from the other, as well as preliminary program versions, or test cases. For either programmer to perform effectively, each must know what the other is doing and be able to rely on its being done as agreed. This reliance is achieved through a commitment process.

Most modern, large software projects involve the cooperative efforts of many individuals. As such projects grow larger, more people are involved and more detailed coordination is necessary. The commitment discipline thus becomes progressively more important. Commitment is not just a matter of honor, for it forms the foundation on which everyone bases their daily work.

The elements of an effective commitment are:[3]

1. The person making the commitment does so willingly.
2. The commitment is not made lightly; that is, the work involved, the resources, and the schedule are carefully considered.
3. There is agreement between the parties on what is to be done, by whom, and when.
4. The commitment is openly and publicly stated.
5. The person responsible tries to meet the commitment, even if help is needed.
6. Prior to the committed date, if it is clear that it cannot be met, advance notice is given and a new commitment is negotiated.

5.1.2 The Commitment Hierarchy

While commitments are met by committed individuals, the work is not done in a vacuum. As long as the professionals feel they are part of an organization that treats its commitments seriously, they will strive to do their part. This calls for a management team that takes care in making commitments and then insists on extraordinary efforts to meet them.

A commitment attitude is highly visible. One action that always impresses the software professionals is strong management support in negotiating requirements changes with the customer. With this backing, they are better able to develop and meet their plans and estimates. Other examples of management's commitment attitude are support on obtaining needed facilities and services and a general practice of holding meetings on schedule.

Commitment is a way of life. Committed organizations meet their large and their small commitments. When organizations are sloppy about their minor commitments, the people sense the lack of concern and the big ones are treated with less care as well. As Brooks has said, schedules are missed a day at a time.[1]

5.1.3 The Software Commitment Process

To be effective, the software commitment process must reach to the top of the organization. This requires that:

1. All commitments for future software delivery are personally made by the organization's senior executive.
2. These commitments are made only after successful completion of a formal review and concurrence process.
3. An enforcement mechanism ensures that these reviews and concurrences are properly conducted.

The senior executive's personal involvement is what motivates the entire commitment process. The people know they must justify their recommendations in a visible process and that poor work will likely be exposed.

To do this, the senior manager should require evidence that the following work was done prior to approving a commitment:

1. The work has been defined and agreed to between the developers and their customer.
2. A documented project plan has been produced, including a resource estimate, a schedule, and a cost estimate.
3. All directly involved parties have agreed to this plan in writing.
4. Adequate business and technical preparation has been done to ensure that the commitment represents a reasonable risk.
5. An independent review has been conducted to ensure that this planning work was done according to the organization's standards and procedures.
6. The groups participating in the work have or can acquire the resources required.

5.1.4 Establishing a Commitment Process

A commitment process can be established very quickly. The basic requirement is a senior executive who is willing to insist that the required planning be done before any commitment is made. In addition, since the people must know how to make schedules and estimates, training courses are required, as are specific estimating, review, and approval procedures. Once the senior manager decides to implement a commitment process, however, these items can be readily accomplished.

5.2 The Management System

An organization can be viewed as a complex machine with gears and levers, lubrication, and motive power. Management's goals and objectives are the fuel that drive this engine, while the commitment process is the lubrication. The management system is the gear train that distributes the power, sets the pace, and points the organization's direction.[2]

While every organization will have unique objectives, there are generally four components:

- □ To have a technical and business strategy that aims at such long-term goals as growth rate or market position
- □ To provide quality products that meet customers' needs in a timely and effective way
- □ To perform the assigned mission competitively and economically
- □ To improve continually the organization's ability to handle more challenging work

These general objectives, applicable to most organizations, demonstrate the inherent conflicts common to most software groups. Since resources are generally limited it is not possible to do everything that should be done. Priorities and trade-offs are needed between long-term performance and short-term response. An example is the balance required between improving productive capability and delivering products.

One cause of these conflicts is senior management's period focus. Management generally operates against annual revenue, profit, and productivity measures. Corporations produce quarterly and annual reports, work from annual operating plans, and establish annual objectives for their people. This period focus is further reinforced when senior management compensation is based on quarterly or annual profits. At the very top, the board of directors represents the stockholders. A quarterly earnings surprise can affect the stock market, cause investor concern, disturb the board members, and require management response.

On the other hand, development projects are typically measured by schedule performance, customer satisfaction, and profitability. In short-range terms, when projects succeed, organization performance will likely improve. When the projects have mixed success, however, conflicts between period and product measures are inevitable.

The conflict between period and product measures is roughly the same as that between line and staff. On one side, line management focuses on getting the product out the door, while the staff is building the organization's competence. The staff is also generally responsible for monitoring product management's performance and reporting shortcomings.

5.2.1 Product and Period Plans

To resolve the inherent conflict and to establish a framework for operations, most organizations produce annual operating plans. These specify the tasks to be performed and assign the responsibilities and resources to accomplish them. Since skilled resources are the single most important need of every project and staff, their allocation is the essential first step in producing these plans.

The operating plan deals with technical and business issues in annual and organizational terms. Thus expenses, capital requirements, and product delivery commitments are established for each period by each organizational entity. Similarly, annual productivity and profitability objectives may be stated, together with strategies for achieving them.

Product plans, on the other hand, focus on the activities and objectives of each project. Here the issues are function, cost, schedule, and quality, together with related resources and checkpoints. While each project has its own management and some dedicated resources, all projects rely on common resources for some of their work. They also report to senior management on a periodic oversight basis. Typically they are monitored by common staffs and audit groups who inform management of the problems and risks of meeting the period and product goals.

This distinction between period and product is often the source of considerable confusion. Project personnel view their work as the fundamental business of the organization and have little appreciation of the need for period information. The project is not set up on an annual basis and often has considerable difficulty in producing annual data on such items as cost, quality, or productivity. Organizations, however, are generally measured and managed on a period basis, and the project data must be translated into period terms for inclusion in annual budgets, plans, or stockholder reports.

While it is clear that project success is essential for long-term organizational success, it is rarely sufficient. The reason is that project work is driven by external customer desires with little regard for the organization's mission or continuing needs. While this concern for the customer is natural, any organization that manages by reacting to project priorities can have no coherent direction of its own. It thus lacks a strategic framework for selecting which project opportunities to pursue or how to allocate scarce resources.

The organization's direction is set in its strategy. The strategy is a period instrument that deals with the problems and issues five or more years ahead. It typically includes a statement of management's long-term objectives, the anticipated technical, resource, and marketplace issues, and the key programs to address them. The strategic plan thus provides the framework for continual organizational improvement.

5.2.2 Management Oversight

An effective management system typically uses reviews and a contention system to resolve product and period conflicts and establish the balance between line and staff. Each line and staff organization prepares its annual plan and reviews it with all involved parties. The issues are then resolved, the separate plans are consolidated into a total organization plan, and this total plan is incorporated in the plan for the next higher organizational level. Similarly, each project area establishes its own plan prior to project initiation and periodically reviews and updates it.

To couple these disparate planning systems, the senior manager should conduct quarterly oversight reviews. These reviews compare project performance with the plans and strategies and include staff reports on project monitoring and support. The quarterly review provides the forum for resolving conflicts and balancing line and staff resources. It also sets the priorities for long-term organizational improvement. The quarterly review process is covered in more detail later in this chapter.

5.2.3 The Contention Process

An effective review system requires a parallel contention system to encourage the open expression of differences and their rational resolution. The principle behind the contention system is that the best decisions are based on a full understanding of the relevant issues. There are many ways to solve most problems and there is rarely agreement on the best approach. Most successful organizations have found that the contention system helps them arrive at better decisions. "This is why Alfred P. Sloan, the founder of General Motors, used to say that no important decision should be made unless there is some contention."[3]

The principles of the contention system are:[3]

1. All major decisions are reviewed with the involved parties in advance, and the parties are requested to agree. Where possible, any issues are resolved before proceeding.

2. When the time comes for the decision, all dissenting parties are present and asked to state their views.

3. When there is no disagreement, the senior manager determines if there is knowledgeable agreement, if any disagreeing parties are absent, or if more preparation is needed. In the latter two cases, the decision is deferred until the necessary homework has been done.

The contention system does not generate disagreement because that already exists. Delegation in every organization assigns responsibility for subsets of the overall mission, and many of these assignments conflict. The contention system makes these inherent disagreements visible in a way that encourages an objective search for the best answers. While the disagreeing parties will rarely find a solution that meets all objections, the resulting discussions invariably produce better understanding and an improved result.

Except at specified checkpoints or for certain key decisions, it is wise to let the responsible managers proceed unless the dissenting parties can convince senior management to stop them. As long as there is an environment in which dissenting views are encouraged and issues are resolved in an objective manner, progress will be made even when there is serious disagreement.

The basic principles of the contention system can be used effectively in even the smallest organizations. As organization size grows, however, it is important to make the process more explicit. Without a stated way to handle contention, many people in large organizations are reluctant to voice their concerns, so issues often fester without resolution. Since the early seeds of most disasters are sensed by the professionals, an effective contention system can provide valuable advance warning.

5.2.4 The Quarterly Review

The quarterly review provides a forum for resolving conflicts and monitoring progress against period and product objectives. The topics should typically include an assessment of project performance against plan and the organization's performance against its goals. A typical agenda is shown in Table 5.1.

The quarterly review agenda of Table 5.1 assumes a typical organization such as the very simple one shown in Fig. 5.1. In this example, the site manager is the senior executive over an operation that has three main functions: projects, technical support, and finance. The technical support organization includes the central computing services for the laboratory, the Software Configuration Management (SCM) group, the Software Quality Assurance (SQA) organization, and the Software Engineering Process Group (SEPG). These last three activities are discussed in Chapters 7, 8, and 14, respectively. The other parts of the organization include the normal functions their titles imply.

The project portion of the quarterly review examines the status of each major project against its plan and objectives. Each project should thus have an approved plan against which progress is reported. Since project plans are discussed in the

TABLE 5.1
EXAMPLE OF A QUARTERLY REVIEW AGENDA

Opening Comments	**Site Manager**
Project A Review	
Milestone Status	Project A Manager
Financial Status	Finance Manager
Issues	Project A Manager
Staff Comments	Finance and SQA
Project B Review	
Milestone Status	Project B Manager
Financial Status	Finance Manager
Issues	Project B Manager
Staff Comments	Finance and SQA
Project C Review	
Milestone Status	Project C Manager
Financial Status	Finance Manager
Issues	Project C Manager
Staff Comments	Finance and SQA
Remaining Project Overviews	
Milestone Status	Development Manager
Financial Status	Finance Manager
Issues	Development Manager
Staff Comments	Finance and SQA
Computing Support	
Performance Measures	Computing Manager
Issues	Computing Manager
Project Comments	Development Manager
Process Status	
Assessment Update	SEPG Manager
Action Plan Status	SEPG Manager
Technology Plan Status	SEPG Manager
Organization Performance	
Productivity	Finance/SEPG
Quality	SQA/SEPG
Action Item Summary	Site Manager

next chapter, the details of such reviews will not be described here. The key is for each project manager to summarize each quarter what was accomplished in the previous quarter and what is planned for the next. If the work is proceeding as planned, these reports are generally crisp and brief. A lot of discussion is often the best indication that the project is in trouble.

A summary status report such as that shown in Table 5.2 can be useful in identifying project status against specific checkpoints. The ones shown here imply

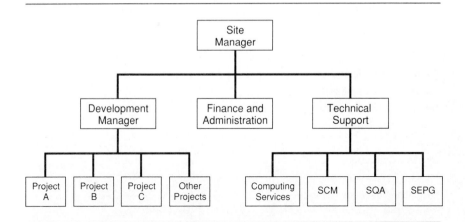

FIGURE 5.1
Typical Software Laboratory Organization

a simple sequential process, but others could be picked depending on the process used. A later discussion of phase reviews further describes these items. The milestones selected should be unambiguous; otherwise, coding will be 90 percent complete for most of the project.[1]

Other measures of progress can also be tracked, such as resources used, software size versus plan, or quality status. These topics are discussed in Chapters 6 and 16, and appropriate review measures are given there.

In addition to monitoring product progress, the quarterly reviews maintain focus on *organizational improvement*. This concerns the management control system, the development and introduction of a standardized software process, the introduction of improved methods and technologies, and tracking of overall organizational quality and productivity. These topics are discussed further in Chapters 6, 13, 16, 17, and 18.

A reasonably frequent management review process emphasizes those areas in which senior management wishes to make changes. In any organization the people quickly learn which subjects are most important by watching where the senior managers spend their time. Since most professionals have much more to do than they can handle, the items senior management is most interested in are done first. The others are deferred and often never done at all.

Organizational improvement is a matter of priorities. For any improvements to be implemented, they must be given sufficient priority to get on the immediate action lists of some key people. By being included in the quarterly reviews, the items will get the priority attention required to produce results. For example, in many software organizations the professionals hear management's periodic exhor-

TABLE 5.2
SIMPLE PROJECT SCHEDULE CHECKPOINTS

Project: _____ Manager: _____ Date: _____

Item	Planned	Projected	Actual	Difference
Functional Rqts. Approval	____	____	____	____
Phase 1 Review Approval	____	____	____	____
Design Reviews Complete	____	____	____	____
Phase 2 Review Approval	____	____	____	____
Code Reviews Complete	____	____	____	____
Unit Test Complete	____	____	____	____
Phase 3 Review Approval	____	____	____	____
Integration Test Entry Complete	____	____	____	____
System Test Complete	____	____	____	____
Phase 4 Review Approval	____	____	____	____
Customer Shipment	____	____	____	____

tations about quality and productivity, but they don't see any time or money spent on them. While they do not question management's conviction on these topics, when they have no quality or productivity tasks to report on, their work is not affected.

When the management team decides to make improvements, it must assign people to do the work. If, for example, a software estimating and scheduling system is to be implemented, someone must work out the details. Since capable professionals are always in short supply, the best people will be fully occupied. If senior management does not intervene, no one will be assigned and nothing will be done. Staffing of organizational improvement tasks should thus be reviewed monthly, at least at the outset.

The organization's Software Engineering Process Group and Software Quality Assurance staffs should conduct the quarterly management reviews. The SQA staff assesses project and subcontractor status, and the SEPG staff covers management controls, process status, technology status, and quality and productivity tracking. When such staffs are not available, finance should run the quarterly review until they are set up. The primary focus of these reviews should be on financial and resource status and on establishing the technical staffs required to conduct more comprehensive reviews.

5.2.5 Project Phase Reviews

In addition to the quarterly review process, management must assess project progress periodically. This is typically accomplished through a sequence of reviews at key points in each project. For government contractors, such reviews are contractually specified in such Department of Defense (DoD) standards as 2167. Regardless of the customer, however, all reasonably sized projects should be reviewed periodically. The review is done by dividing the program into appropriate phases, depending on project size and anticipated risk. These reviews ensure coordination of the technical and business tasks, make all participating groups aware of project status, and either resolve or escalate the key issues.

The final step in each phase review is approval to proceed to the next phase. The project manager obtains this agreement either at the phase review or at a subsequent escalation meeting.

The definition of each phase and the phase review meeting contents must be tailored to the specific needs of the organization. The basic topics are resources and schedules, but further items are included as the software process is further defined. Regardless of the specific meeting contents, however, the principles of the phase review process are:

1. Before initiation and at predetermined points during the project, detailed technical and management reviews are conducted.

2. The particular review points are selected based on the following criteria:

   ▫ Whenever major resource commitments are required

   ▫ At key technical milestones such as project initiation, high-level design complete, prototype completion, unit test complete, and so forth

   ▫ At reasonable calendar intervals, with special milestones established for unusually short or long projects

3. The review is conducted by the project manager.

4. All involved line and staff organizations participate.

5. The meeting is not to resolve issues but to identify them and assign resolution responsibility.

6. The project manager, with finance and Software Quality Assurance concurrence, decides whether:

   ▫ The phase was successfully completed.

   ▫ After issue resolution, the phase is to be considered complete.

   ▫ Another review is required.

   ▫ Escalation should be made to senior management.

7. The review is concluded, and the project manager notifies senior management of the final conclusion. A review report is also distributed summarizing the key issues and the responsibilities and dates for their resolution.

The involved business and technical groups are represented at the phase review, and their concurrence indicates their agreement with the status and plan and their ability to commit the required resources to do the work. Concurrence by Software Quality Assurance is based on their independent review of the technical and planning work to date. They assure management that the work has been done according to organization practices and that the conclusions presented properly represent the work accomplished.

At each subsequent phase, estimates, schedules, and plans are updated consistent with technical progress. In each case, the involved business and technical groups participate in the review and Software Quality Assurance verifies that the work has been properly done according to the organization's standards and procedures and that the results are accurately represented.

Management thus has a solid basis for deciding to continue with the project or make changes.

5.3 Establishing a Project Management System

The most important management review system is that conducted by the project management team itself. If project management is not aware of and actively involved in project issues, no other management system can be fully effective. With effective and involved project managers, however, a management system is still needed to resolve conflicts between the projects and between the line and the staff organizations.

Even with capable project managers, the effectiveness of the management system depends on the quality of the project schedules and resource estimates and the capability of Software Quality Assurance to monitor project performance. When the organization reaches the Defined maturity level (Level 3), reports on progress against quality plans should be initiated. These topics are discussed in Chapters 6, 8, and 16, respectively.

While the actions required to set up a project management system are relatively straightforward, they are not trivial. The first step is to get agreement from the senior management team that such a system is needed. The responsibility and resources for doing the work are then designated. The next steps are:

1. The commitment system is defined:

   □ What commitments require senior management approval?

   □ When are these approvals needed?

   □ What preparation and concurrences are required prior to requesting this approval?

   □ What are the mechanisms for stopping or delaying projects that have not been approved?

2. The quarterly review system is established:

□ What is to be covered and who will do it?

□ Who manages the agenda and schedule?

□ Who attends?

□ Who prepares the minutes and tracks the action items?

3. The phase review system is established:

   □ What projects are to be covered?

   □ At what project checkpoints will phase reviews be conducted?

   □ What special criteria will be used for very large and very small projects?

   □ Who is responsible for scheduling and conducting the reviews?

   □ Who is responsible for reporting the results and tracking the action items?

   □ Who attends?

   □ What are the procedures for handling issues and escalation?

   □ What mechanisms ensure that projects do not proceed without successfully completing the phase review or receiving management exception approval?

Since the quarterly review system provides the oversight assurance that all these steps are taken, such a senior management review system should be instituted as soon as possible, even before all the procedures and definitions have been established. The phase reviews should also be launched as quickly as they can be defined, even before an estimating and scheduling system is fully in place. While a formal planning system will facilitate the review process, the phase reviews will significantly improve issue identification and resolution.

5.4 Summary

Software project management starts with a definition of the job to be done and the plan to do it. Its foundation is the way commitments are made and the various plans, estimates, reviews, and tracking systems that support them.

Organizations have line and staff groups with conflicting goals. Line management focuses on getting the product out the door, while the staff is concerned with the organization's long-term capability.

An effective management system uses reviews and a contention system to resolve product and period conflicts and establish the balance between line and staff.

Each line and staff organization prepares its annual plan and reviews it with all involved parties. Similarly, each project area establishes its own plans, which are reviewed prior to project initiation and then periodically updated and re-reviewed.

These disparate planning systems are coupled through senior management quarterly oversight reviews that provide the forum for resolving conflicts and balancing resources between the line and staff organizations.

An effective review system requires a parallel contention system to encourage the open expression of differences and their rational resolution.

In addition to the quarterly review process, management needs to periodically assess project progress. This is accomplished through a sequence of phase reviews held at key points in the project schedule.

In establishing a project management system, the first essential action is to obtain agreement from the senior management team that such a system is needed. Then:

1. The commitment system is defined.

2. The quarterly review system is established.

3. The phase review system is initiated.

References

1. Brooks, F. P., Jr. *The Mythical Man-Month.* New York: Addison-Wesley, 1975.

2. Freeman, P. *Software Perspectives.* Reading, MA: Addison-Wesley, 1987.

3. Humphrey, W. S. *Managing for Innovation—Leading Technical People.* Englewood Cliffs, NJ: Prentice-Hall, 1987.

4. Salancik. In M. Tushman and W. Moore ed., *Readings in the Management of Innovation,* p. 208. Boston: Pitman, 1982.

6

The Project Plan

The project plan defines the work and how it will be done. It provides a definition of each major task, an estimate of the time and resources required, and a framework for management review and control. The project plan is also a powerful learning vehicle. When properly documented, it is a benchmark to compare with actual performance. This comparison permits the planners to see their estimating errors and to improve their estimating accuracy.

This chapter starts with a brief overview of project planning principles and the project plan. This overview is followed by an extended discussion of software estimation that includes size measures, estimating methods, and productivity factors. The chapter then concludes with discussions of scheduling, tracking, plan reviews, and planning models. The reason for the heavy emphasis on size and resource estimating is that poor resource plans invariably lead to inadequate resources, schedule delays, and cost overruns. Since resource estimates are directly derived from software size estimates, poor size estimating is thus the root cause of many software problems.

6.1 Project Planning Principles

The project plan is developed at the beginning of the job and is successively refined as the work progresses. Initially, since the requirements are often vague and incomplete the focus is on determining where more knowledge is needed and how to get it. Without this guidance, programmers often start enthusiastically building what they understand best, leaving the unknowns until later. Since the unknowns generally have the highest risk, this progression frequently leads to trouble. The logic for software project planning is:

1. While requirements are initially vague and incomplete, a quality program can only be built from an accurate and precise understanding of the users' needs. The project plan thus starts by mapping the route from vague and incorrect requirements to accurate and precise ones.

2. A conceptual design is then developed as a basis for planning. This initial structure must be produced with care since it generally defines the breakdown of the product into units, the allocation of functions to these units, and the relationships among them. Since this provides the organizational framework for planning and implementing the work, it is almost impossible to recover from a poor conceptual design.

3. At each subsequent requirements refinement, resource projections, size estimates, and schedules are also refined.

4. When the requirements are sufficiently clear, a detailed design and implementation strategy is developed and incorporated in the plan.

5. As various parts of the project become sufficiently well understood, implementation details are established and documented in further plan refinements.

6. Throughout this cycle, the plan provides the framework for negotiating the time and resources to do the job.

6.1.1 Planning Considerations

With rare exceptions, initial resource estimates and schedules are unacceptable. This is not because the programmers are unresponsive but because the users generally want more than they can afford. When someone wants to build a house and the first estimate is beyond their means, it is pointless to blame the builder. Software planning should be viewed in much the same way. If the job doesn't fit the available schedule and resources, it must either be pared down or the time and resources increased.

Similarly, most new product functions are usually needed before they can possibly be ready. After some experience users will generally recognize that building software takes time. Few users, however, have this background, and even those who do often have trouble anticipating their needs two or three years in advance. As a result, the function *is* needed immediately and the software engineers really *can't* produce it on time.

This natural conflict has existed since the first days of computer programming, and those programmers who cut their estimates under pressure have invariably been wrong. History demonstrates that even initial "inflated" estimates are generally optimistic.

This does not mean that software managers should dig in their heels and refuse to discuss changes to their resource estimates and schedules. It is best to reach early agreement on the essential functions and to defer the rest until later. A good rule of thumb is that the schedule and estimate will be too high if the first release includes any functions that are not absolutely essential. If early agreement is not reached on this point, the users and software engineers will likely have continuing disagreements for the duration of the project. Quality products are an artistic blend of needs and solutions, requiring harmonious teamwork between the users and the software engineers.

The planning negotiations are the critical test of a software management team. The team must treat the initial plan as a starting point and when schedule or cost must be reduced, job scope must be cut as well. While these negotiations proceed, it is crucial to remember that the most important single factor in determining the delivery date is the date when work begins. Until agreement is reached and work can start, final delivery slips day by day.

6.1.2 The Planning Cycle

The following iterative plan negotiation process is shown graphically in Fig. 6.1:

1. The cycle starts with the initial requirements (top left in Fig. 6.1).

2. The response to every demand for a commitment must be: "I understand your requirement and will produce a plan with that objective, but without a plan, I cannot make a commitment."

3. The plan is produced by first breaking the work into key elements, called a Work Breakdown Structure (WBS). This implies that a conceptual design has been developed.

4. The size of each product element is estimated.

5. The resource needs are projected.

6. The schedule is produced.

The resulting schedule and estimate are then compared with the initial need, and, if they fit, the commitment can be made and work can proceed. If, as is more usual, the cost is too high or the schedule is too long, requirements negotiation and replanning are needed.

Figure 6.1 also shows that as the plan is produced, the process database provides estimating factors and stores historical records. This database provides the organization with the ability to make progressively better plans. This planning process is further described in the balance of this chapter.

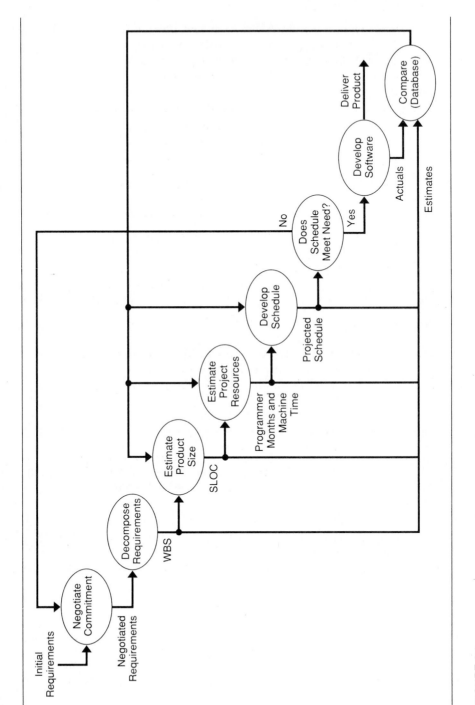

FIGURE 6.1
The Software Development Planning Cycle

6.2 Project Plan Contents

The elements of a software plan are:

- □ *Goals and objectives*   These describe what is to be done, for whom, and by when, as well as the criteria for determining project success.
- □ *Work Breakdown Structure (WBS)*   The WBS subdivides the project into tasks that are each defined, estimated, and tracked.[21]
- □ *Product size estimates*   These are quantitative assessments of the code required for each product element (subsystem, component, or module). Contingencies are applied to these estimates based on prior project experience.
- □ *Resource estimates*   Based on prior experience, known productivity factors are applied to yield reasonable estimates of the resources required for each WBS element.
- □ *Project schedule*   Based on the available project staffing and resource estimates, a schedule for the key tasks and deliverable items is produced.

In addition to defining the work, this plan provides management the basis for periodically reviewing and tracking progress against the plan.[8] As the work definition is progressively refined, the plan is periodically updated, the estimates are revised, and the schedules are reviewed. These reviews and updates are managed through the quarterly and phase review processes described in Chapter 5.

6.2.1 Goals and Objectives

The project's goals and objectives are established during the requirements phase. This is also a negotiation period between the software engineers and the users on what is to be done, how success will be measured, and how much time and resources are needed. Since the users' needs generally change when they look closely at their problems, requirements invariably change as the work progresses. A design and implementation effort, however, must start from a reasonably stable requirements definition. Requirements change is thus a continuing problem for software engineering. To have any chance of managing this problem, the software team must follow a few simple rules:

1. Implement the product in small incremental steps.
2. Select each increment to support succeeding increments and/or improve requirements knowledge.
3. Freeze the requirements for each incremental step before starting design.
4. When the requirements change during implementation, defer the change to a subsequent increment.

5. If the changes cannot be deferred, stop work, modify the requirements, revise the plan, and start again on the design.

These incremental steps, or *builds,* are aimed at producing running code as soon as possible. The process starts with minimal function and gradually expands until a functionally useful level is reached. Then testing is done to validate the requirements before development proceeds.

These rules are best understood by analogy with an airline. Requirements changes are analogous to aircraft modifications in that they must be made when the plane is on the ground. Once it starts down the runway, all change activity must stop until the flight is over. With software development, once design starts, you are "in the air" until the code is written and tested. Changes made in the middle of this cycle are generally destructive. When changes are made in flight, their design is generally incoherent and the code is error-prone. Requirements and objectives must be set at the beginning and not changed during a build. When they must change, as occasionally happens, the current build must stop and a new cycle starts over.

The key considerations of the requirements phase are:

- □ *Functional requirements*   The product functions are listed, together with any performance or other constraints. Where possible, a draft user's manual is produced or a prototype is built to test any questionable items.

- □ *System needs*   Target system configurations are specified, together with any standards, compatibility, or environmental constraints.

- □ *Customer identification*   The users are identified, as well as their support needs, including: delivery mechanics, product packaging, installation support, documentation requirements, and training. The extent of user involvement during the software life cycle is also defined.

- □ *Measures of success*   Cost, schedule, performance, quality, size, and other measures of success are quantified in advance. Such measures are often initially stated in general terms and refined at each program phase.

- □ *Validation and acceptance*   The means for determining success are established, including responsibility for acceptance testing, the criteria to be used, and any warranties or other consequences of failure.

- □ *Support*   Continuing support requirements are stated, including defect reporting and correction and subsequent enhancement plans.

While production of running code is often considered the most critical part of software engineering, the items listed above often have a greater impact. A superbly crafted program has little value if it cannot be operated by the intended users in the required environment. Even the best projects have errors, changes, and enhancements, and lack of early agreement on these other needs will cause later problems. They should thus be resolved before substantial resources are expended and while both the software engineers and the users have the flexibility to stop work. Such early terminations are rare, but negotiations at a later date are complicated by the money already spent and the severe schedule and resource consequences of late changes.

6.2.2 The Work Breakdown Structure (WBS)

Project planning starts with an estimate of the size of the product to be produced. This estimation begins with a detailed and documented breakdown of the product into work elements.[3, 21] The breakdown generally has two parts: the product structure and the software process. The WBS then provides the framework for relating them. The product design typically has a hierarchical structure, as shown in Fig. 6.2. For larger jobs, the subsystems hierarchy might consist of systems, subsystems, products, components, and modules. A five-level structure is usually adequate to support a system of several million lines of code. This product structure must reflect the overall design concept for the project, which is then reflected in allocations of functions to each of the components and modules. This is where advanced design concepts and prototyping methods can be most effectively used (see Chapter 13).

As this product structure is refined, the process tasks required to produce each product element are defined. Next, these tasks are allocated to the various organizational groups. The objective is to structure the WBS into small enough increments so each can be developed by an individual or a small team in a relatively short amount of time. In general the more detailed the WBS is, the more accurate the product estimates, the better the project plan, and the more precisely it can be tracked.[21]

A size estimate is then made of each product element. The prime considerations in making such estimates are:

1. Start with as detailed a product structure as is technically possible.
2. Precisely define the standard of measurement.
3. Estimate the size of each product element.
4. Sum these elements to produce a total estimate.
5. Apply appropriate contingencies.

6.3 Size Measures

The measure used in program size estimation should be reasonably easy to use early in the project and readily measurable once the work is completed. Subsequent comparisons of the early estimates to the actual measured product size then provide feedback to the estimators on how to make more accurate estimates.

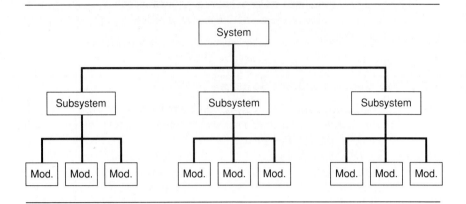

FIGURE 6.2
Typical WBS Structure

While debates continue on the best measures of software size, there is no answer that meets all objectives. At one extreme, a simple count of the number of lines of source code is easy to define, is widely applicable, and facilitates automated counting. Unfortunately, it is often hard to relate lines of code to early functional requirement descriptions. To solve this problem, Albrecht devised an estimating method called function points.[1] In simplest terms, function points start from the user's perspective and estimate the size of the application. Lines of code, however, are a product measure and relate more closely to what the software engineer intends to build. They both have advantages and disadvantages, however, so before proceeding to describe the estimating process, these two methods are briefly described.

6.3.1 Line-of-Code Size Estimates

Line-of-code (LOC) estimates typically count all source instructions and exclude comments and blanks.[12] Automated tools, for example, are often designed to count semicolons. Even though it is difficult to estimate lines of code from high-level requirements statements, this measure does facilitate a learning process that leads to improved estimating. As software groups gain development experience, they accumulate a wealth of functional examples that form a comparison basis for new estimates. The finer the product structural detail, the more likely relevant examples are available, and the more accurate the subsequent estimates. The simplicity of the LOC metric also facilitates storing and retrieving the size data needed to improve estimating accuracy. Perhaps the most important advantage of the LOC is that it directly relates to the product to be built. It can thus be measured after the fact and compared to the initial plans.

6.3.2 Function Points

With function points, initial application requirements statements are examined to determine the number and complexity of the various inputs, outputs, calculations, and databases required. By using values that Albrecht has established, points are assigned to each of these counts.[1, 2] These points are then summed to produce an overall function point rating for the product. Based on prior experience, this final function point figure can be converted into a reasonably good estimate of the development resources required. The general approach is as follows:[1, 2]

1. Count the number of inputs, outputs, inquiries, master files, and interfaces required.
2. Multiply these counts by the following factors:

   □ Inputs   4
   □ Outputs   5
   □ Inquiries   4
   □ Master files   10
   □ Interfaces   10

3. Adjust the total of these products by +25 percent, 0, or −25 percent, depending on the estimators' judgment of the program's complexity.

While function points help in making early size estimates of application programs, they have drawbacks.[20] The most important are that the complexity factors are judgmental and it is not possible to automatically measure the function point content of programs. Albrecht thus advised that function points be used to make initial estimates and then, based on experience, these function point values are converted to LOC. Planning then proceeds using the LOC measure.

The function point metric is most helpful when:

□ A new program development is being estimated.
□ The applications involve considerable input-output or file activity.
□ An experienced function point expert is available.
□ Sufficient data is on hand to permit reasonably accurate conversion from function points to LOC.

6.4 Estimating

Once a size measure has been established, an estimating procedure is needed. Probably the most accurate one is the Wideband Delphi Technique originated by the Rand Corporation:[3]

1. A group of experts is each given the program's specifications and an estimation form.
2. They meet to discuss the product and any estimation issues.
3. They then each anonymously complete the estimation forms.
4. The estimates are given to the estimate coordinator, who tabulates the results and returns them to the experts, as illustrated in Fig. 6.3.
5. Only each expert's personal estimate is identified; all others are anonymous.
6. The experts meet to discuss the results, revising their estimates as they feel appropriate.
7. The cycle continues until the estimates converge to an acceptable range.

This group procedure typically makes far better estimates than any individual estimator. The accuracy is further improved if the estimates are done for the smallest practical product elements. Generally this involves use of a composite estimating form, as shown in Fig. 6.4.

6.4.1 Estimating Inaccuracies

Regardless of the method used, software estimates will be inaccurate. The inaccuracies must be compensated for, however, because a poor size estimate results in an inappropriate resource plan and a generally understaffed project. To date, at least, software size estimates have almost invariably erred in being too low. These low estimates typically result in a last-minute crisis, late delivery, and poor quality.

There are two types of estimating inaccuracies, and they can both be compensated for, at least to some degree. Normal statistical variations can be handled by using multiple estimators, as in the Wideband Delphi Technique or by using some other independent means to check the results. The other source of error is the estimating bias caused by the project stage at which the estimate is made. The earlier the estimate, the less is known about the product and the greater the estimating inaccuracy. Again, with software, the resulting estimates have generally been on the low side.

Project:

Estimator: Date:

Here is the range of estimates from the _____ round:

	X X*		X!	X	X
0	20	40	60	80	100

X —estimates
X*—your estimate
X!—median estimate

Please enter your estimate for the next round: _____ SLOC
Please explain any rationale for your estimate.

FIGURE 6.3
Sample Estimation Form

6.4.2 Estimating Contingencies

When programmers estimate the code required to implement a function, their estimates are invariably low. While there are many potential explanations, the important point is that their optimism is a relatively predictable function of project status. While there is no good published data to support these figures, the author's rules of thumb are shown in Table 6.1. These amounts should be added as an estimating contingency at the end of the indicated project phase. Depending on the experience of the programmers, the data available from prior projects, and the level of knowledge about the new product, the contingency number should be selected within these ranges. Such contingencies may seem excessive, but code growth is the most important single factor in cost and schedule overruns. Every software size estimate should include a contingency, and the only debate should be over the amount to use.

Because contingencies inflate the resource estimates, add to the schedule, and increase costs, they are energetically resisted by almost everyone on the project. The programmers argue that they understand the product and won't make the same mistakes again. Marketing argues that the costs and schedules are excessive, and management wants the contract. Experience shows, however, that until enough is known to partition the product into modules of a few hundred LOC each, substantial contingencies are required.

FIGURE 6.4
Sample Composite Estimation Form

Project:

Estimator: Date:

Here is the range of estimates from the _____ round:

    Range: Next:

Module A:

0	20	40	60	80	100

_____ SLOC

Module B:

0	20	40	60	80	100

_____ SLOC

Module C:

0	20	40	60	80	100

_____ SLOC

Module D:

0	20	40	60	80	100

_____ SLOC

Module E:

0	20	40	60	80	100

_____ SLOC

Module F:

0	20	40	60	80	100

_____ SLOC

Module G:

0	20	40	60	80	100

_____ SLOC

FIGURE 6.4 (continued)

X —estimates
X* —your estimates
X! —median estimates

Please enter your estimates for the next round: Total SLOC
Please explain any rationale for your estimates.

Even after the program is implemented and in test, code expansion of 10 percent to 25 percent is likely. This is not a theoretical safety factor; late changes will be required that will add significant amounts of code. Such contingencies will be hard to support, however, until each organization accumulates its own historical data and develops its own contingency factors based on this data.

6.4.3 A Size Estimating Example

An example of a program size estimate is shown in Table 6.2. This is a hypothetical satellite ground station control program estimated during the requirements phase. The lack of detailed knowledge about the program is indicated by the size of the units being estimated. For such gross estimates, large contingencies are generally warranted. Because significant knowledge and experience were assumed for components A, B, and C, their contingencies were selected as 100 percent. Since components D and E were areas in which the group had no prior experience, 200 percent contingencies were used.

While this example is only for the delivered product code, estimates are also often needed for test cases, development aids, installation tools, and diagnostic programs. Nonoperational code can be four or more times larger than that required for the basic functions.[3] Software projects also generally need documentation, training, system and acceptance testing, human factor considerations, packaging, shipment, and support. Each involved group should estimate its work products in much the same way already described for the delivered code. Similarly, each group, based on its own experience, should apply appropriate contingency factors.

6.5 Productivity Factors

Once we have an estimate of the amount of code to be implemented, the amount can be converted into the number of programmer months and time required. While some programmers can intuitively estimate their work, most of us need a more

TABLE 6.1
CODE GROWTH BY PROJECT PHASE

Completed Project Phase	Code Growth Range (%)
Requirements	100–200
High-level design	75–150
Detailed design	50–100
Implementation	25–50
Function test	10–25
System test	0–10

orderly procedure, particularly when the projects are large and many people are involved. This involves productivity factors, or standard factors for the number of lines of code that, on average, can be produced per programmer month.[12]

There are many kinds of potentially useful software productivity factors, and each organization should select those most relevant to their situation. Since few organizations have such data at hand, however, several examples are provided in the next few paragraphs. Organizations can gather their own data and compare it with some of these factors. They will then better be able to intelligently establish reasonable numbers to use for their own work.

A set of relative productivity factors has been developed from data on over 500 of IBM's System/370 programming development projects, as shown in Table 6.3 and Table 6.4.[9] These figures represent a composite of several years of development experience on a total of nearly ten million lines of source code. What they show is that productivity varies significantly depending on product type, program size, and the percent of the program being changed.

TABLE 6.2
EXAMPLE PROGRAM SIZE ESTIMATE—SATELLITE GROUND STATION
CONTROL PROGRAM

Date: 5/25/87	Estimator: WSH			Program: Satellite
	Base	Contingency		Total
Component	KLOC*	%	KLOC*	KLOC*
A Executive	9	100	9	18
B Function Calculation	15	100	15	30
C Control/Display	12	100	12	24
D Network Control	12	200	24	36
E Time Base Calculation	18	200	36	54
Total	66	145	96	162

*KLOC = thousands of lines of source code

Examination of these data show some interesting comparisons. For example, productivity on large language compiler programs was 4 times that of small data communications programs. Similarly, the productivity for new or largely modified language programs was 4.7 times larger (6.6/1.4) than that for small percentage modifications to communications programs. One possible reason for this is that the IBM database contains a mix of new and modified programs of all sizes and types. Even with some 500 programs, there was not enough data to permit construction of Table 6.3 for new programs only. It is likely that the degree of modification is different for different program size classes. For instance, many of the small programs could consist of small modifications to large programs rather than new small programs. If this were the case, it could account for much of the productivity variation between the large and small programs. Exactly the same explanation could be true for the modification data as well. Unfortunately, data on this point is not available.

Even with data on more than 500 programs and over ten million lines of code, however, statistically significant factors could not be obtained for the combination of Tables 6.3 and 6.4. That is, it was not possible to show the productivity variation on large language programs depending on the percent of their modification. D. N. Card has, however, obtained some more direct data that shows that productivity varies significantly with the degree of program modification.[4] For product enhancements, productivity was only 70 percent as high as for new development and maintenance was only 25 percent as high. Since the repair of defects found in test is quite similar to maintenance work, the advantages of early defect prevention and detection are clear.

DeMarco and Lister have identified a set of environmental factors that make a significant difference in team productivity, as shown in Table 6.5.[6] These numbers show the characteristics of the work environment for the top 25 percent of the programmers, the bottom 25 percent, and the average. The critical point is that the performance of the programmers in the top 25 percent of their study population was 2.6 times greater than those in the bottom 25 percent. The nature of the development environment appeared to have a significant effect on this productivity difference.

TABLE 6.3
RELATIVE PRODUCTIVITY VERSUS PROGRAM
SIZE AND PRODUCT CLASS [9]

	Size in KCSI*		
Product Class	<10	10–50	>50
Language	1.8	3.9	4.0
Control	1.6	1.8	2.4
Communications	1.0	1.6	2.0

*KCSI = thousands of new or changed source instructions

6.5.1 Organization Productivity Data

In productivity calculations, it is important to use factors that relate to the specific organization doing the work and not to use more factors than the available data warrants. Since all productivity factors are at best averaged data from several projects done by different people with various levels of ability, it is not wise to try to account for more than a few of the most significant variables. Because so many factors affect productivity and because there is no way to adjust standardized productivity numbers to account for all these variations, each organization should gather its own data to use as a baseline for productivity calculations. Adjustments can then be made to account for those variations that are considered most significant.

Another reason to calibrate all calculations to the organization is that the productivity factors described in the literature generally do not include precise unit definitions. As Flaherty points out, variations in the definition of lines of code or programmer months can change productivity numbers by factors of more than 50.[9]

Organizations can develop their own productivity factors by examining a number of recently produced programs, counting their lines of code in a consistent and defined manner, and calculating the programmer months (PM) required to do the job. In doing this, the definitions for LOC and PM should be thoughtfully established and documented. It is even desirable to obtain or develop a program to count the new and changed source LOC in each program produced.

6.5.2 Developing Productivity Data

Since software organizations generally have some records of the work they have produced, the first step in developing productivity data is to see what is available. With this information, the following approach should produce the needed data:

TABLE 6.4
RELATIVE PRODUCTIVITY VERSUS PERCENT
OF PROGRAM NEW OR CHANGED AND
PRODUCT CLASS [9]

Product Class	% New or Changed		
	<20%	20–40%	>40%
Language	3.0	6.0	6.6
Control	1.5	2.3	2.3
Communications	1.4	1.8	1.9

TABLE 6.5
EFFECTS OF ENVIRONMENT ON PERFORMANCE [6]

Environmental Factor	Top 25%	Bottom 25%	All
Dedicated floor space?			
Square feet:	78	46	63
Workspace % yes:			
Quiet workspace?	57%	29%	42%
Private workspace?	62%	19%	39%
Silence phone?	52%	10%	29%
Divert calls?	76%	19%	57%
Needless interruptions?	38%	76%	62%
Their workspace makes them feel appreciated?	57%	29%	45%

1. Identify a number of recently completed programs that are as similar to the new program as possible in size, language used, application type, team experience, and so forth.
2. Get data on the size, in LOC, of each project. Try to use the same counting scheme for each program.
3. For modified programs, note the percent of code modified and count only the number of new or changed LOC in the productivity calculations. Special management emphasis on the advantages of reuse is needed to counteract the bias toward new code that this measure might cause.
4. Obtain a count of the programmer months expended for each project, but be sure to include or exclude the same labor categories for each program. Generally the categories to include are direct design and implementation programmers, test, and documentation. To minimize the number of variables, it is often wise to exclude SQA, managers, clerical, requirements, and computing operations. The requirements effort in particular should often be excluded because it is highly dependent on customer relationships and application knowledge.

Often not all the desired data will be available. If there is not enough to produce a meaningful basis for estimating, it may be necessary to use approximate information. This can be done by having some of the more experienced professionals estimate the size of some previously produced products. The financial people will often have records of labor expenditures, but, if not, they may have some cost data. With a little searching, they can usually separate out the machine costs and calculate the labor months expended for each project.

Approximations based on labor expenditure are a crude way to gather productivity data and should only be used as an interim stopgap until more accurate data can be generated. These crude approximations, however, directly represent the anticipated development environment and provide an important base for judging the appropriateness of data from other organizations.

6.5.3 Using Productivity Data

With the basic data in hand, it is now possible to derive base productivity numbers. Since the data gathered will be for various sizes and classes of programs, will involve different degrees of modification or new development, and may have used a variety of different languages or environments, some adjustments may be needed. With some local data, it is thus reasonable to examine some of the published productivity figures to see which ones might apply to your organization.[2, 9, 11, 15, 19] In using this productivity data, you should keep the following points in mind:

- ☐ Even with a large experience base, your productivity estimates will only be crude approximations.
- ☐ Real productivity data generally has large standard deviations.
- ☐ With enough data, the extreme cases should be discarded.
- ☐ Most of the factors that affect productivity cannot be determined or compensated for.
- ☐ If a mix of program types is involved and some selections appear warranted, the selections should be made based on program characteristics only. If this is not done, people have a tendency to exclude the low productivity cases, resulting in an optimistic estimating bias.

This same approach can be used with different program classes or to adjust for degree of program modification. Until there is statistical validation for any adjustment factors, however, only one set of adjustments should be made.

If not used with care, productivity figures can be misleading. For example, the data in Table 6.4 implies that the productivity in developing new language or application programs is 3.5 times (6.6/1.9) that for new real-time programs. The problem is that these are productivity figures for people experienced at that work. A team that has built several real-time programs but no application programs could not conceivably be 3.5 times as productive with their first application project. They would have to learn the application, the product technology, and all the undocumented tricks and techniques that come with experience.

6.5.4 A Resource Estimating Example

The actual process of making a resource estimate is quite simple once the size estimates and productivity factors are available. To show how this is done, the

TABLE 6.6
PROGRAM RESOURCE CALCULATION EXAMPLE

Program Name	Program Class	Size KLOC	Productivity Base	Productivity Adjust.	LOC/PM	PM
A Executive	Control	18	400	1.8/3.9	185	97
B Function Calculation	Language	30	400	3.9/3.9	400	75
C Control and Distribution	Control	24	400	1.8/3.9	185	130
D Network Control	Communication	36	400	1.6/3.9	164	220
E Time Calculation	Language	54	400	4.0/3.9	410	132
Total		162			248	654

example from Table 6.2 is used again in Table 6.6. Assuming that the organization has determined that its typical productivity for moderate-sized language and application programs is 400 LOC/PM, this figure is used as the base for the productivity calculations. These are next adjusted to reflect the lower productivity generally achieved with communications and control programs. If suitable factors are not otherwise available, the figures from Table 6.3 can be used. Since this example organization's productivity for language programs in the 10 to 50 KLOC range is 400 LOC/PM the productivity figure for moderate-sized control programs is 400 × 1.8/3.9 = 185 LOC/PM. Using these figures the total programmer months required can be calculated.

This simple estimating procedure can be used for any other factors that are pertinent for the organization and products involved. For example, if a particular project includes a mix of new and modified code, it might be wise to adjust for the degree of modification involved.

6.6 Scheduling

Once the total resource needs have been calculated, the project schedule can be developed by spreading these resources over the planned product development phases. This is best done by using data on the organization's historical experience with similar projects. When such data is not available, publicly available factors such as those shown in Table 6.7 can be used for guidance.[3] These numbers are based on TRW's experience, so they are not necessarily correct for all organizations. For example, Griffin has derived the breakdown in Table 6.8 from Martin Marietta's experience.[10] The large differences between these resource profiles are undoubtedly due to at least some of the following factors:

- □ Different definitions of project phases
- □ Different resource categories included
- □ Differences in software methods used
- □ Differences in the product types being developed
- □ Different programmer skill levels
- □ Differing degrees of urgency on the project

Since all these conditions generally vary among organizations and projects, it is essential for each organization to gather its own resource distribution data. Once the project resource distribution is known, an overall project schedule can be produced as follows:

1. Based on the overall project schedule objective, a staffing plan is developed.

2. A preliminary schedule for each phase is next established by comparing the cumulative resource needs with those expected to be available. An initial schedule is then made.

3. This preliminary plan is then reviewed to ensure that reasonable staffing assignments can be made consistent with this schedule and resource profile. Adjustments are generally required.

The detail used in the schedule depends on the detail available from the Work Breakdown Structure, which in turn depends on the current project phase and previous experience with similar products. As the project progresses, successively more detailed schedules are made to permit more accurate planning and status assessments.

TABLE 6.7
PHASE DISTRIBUTION—RESOURCE AND TIME [3]

	Product Size			
Phase	Small 2 KLOC	Intermediate 8 KLOC	Medium 32 KLOC	Large 128 KLOC
Resource:				
Product Design	16%	16%	16%	16%
Programming:				
Detailed Design	26%	25%	24%	23%
Code & Unit Test	42%	40%	38%	36%
Integration & Test	16%	19%	22%	25%
Schedule:				
Product Design	19%	19%	19%	19%
Programming	63%	59%	55%	51%
Integration & Test	18%	22%	26%	30%

Barry W. Boehm, *Software Engineering Economics,* © 1981, p. 65. Reprinted by permission of Prentice-Hall, Inc., Englewood Cliffs, NJ.

TABLE 6.8
DEVELOPMENT EFFORT PER PROGRAM
PHASE [10]

Program Phase	% Effort
Design	3.49%
Detailed Design	11.05%
Code and Unit Test	23.17%
Unit and Integration Test	27.82%
Qualification Test	34.47%

6.7 Project Tracking

One requirement for sound project management is the ability to determine project status. The planning process should thus produce a schedule and enough check-points to permit periodic tracking. One way to do this is with earned-value project scheduling.[18] This is done as in the following example:

1. Several checkpoints are determined for each project phase. These must each represent completion of precisely defined tasks, such as:

   □ Module specifications complete and approved

   □ Module design complete, inspected, and corrections made

   □ Module unit test plan complete, reviewed, and approved

   □ Module coding complete, and first clean compilation

   □ Module code inspection complete and corrections made

   □ Module through unit test and delivered to SCM for integration in the baseline

2. The resources required to complete each checkpoint are determined as a percent of the total project. For the above example, the dates might be as shown in Table 6.9.

3. This plan is plotted as shown in Fig. 6.5.

4. As the project progresses, actual performance against the plan is tracked, as shown by the dotted line in Fig. 6.5.

In this example it is clear that module implementation is four weeks behind schedule at this point and is exposed to further slippage.

   When this scheduling method is applied to an entire project, a reasonably clear picture of overall status emerges. For large projects, however, several points must be kept in mind:

TABLE 6.9
SCHEDULE TRACKING EXAMPLE

Module Implementation—Total Resources 17 Programmer Weeks

Checkpoint	Scheduled		Cumulative Resources	Resources %
	Date	Week		
Specifications Complete	2/12	2.0	2.0	11%
Design Complete	3/18	7.0	7.0	41%
Unit Test Plan Complete	3/25	8.0	8.0	47%
First Clean Compile	4/22	12.0	12.0	71%
Code Complete	5/6	14.0	14.0	82%
U. T. Complete	5/27	17.0	17.0	100%

□ Every checkpoint must be specific and measurable.

□ As more is known about the project, more detailed plans can be made. This permits such checkpoints as:

1. 50 percent of module designs complete, design reviews conducted, and corrections made

2. 25 percent of compiler test cases compile without error

3. 15 percent of compiled test programs execute without error

4. First draft of user's manual complete and ready for technical review

□ The official project plan numbers are used as the basis for determining percent complete. If they are no longer appropriate, a new plan must be developed, or all status measures will be inaccurate.

□ Partial credit is not permitted. For example, a 50 percent module design complete checkpoint means that design is 100 percent complete for 50 percent of the modules, not that the average level of completion of the individual modules is 50 percent.

6.8 The Development Plan

After completing the estimates and schedule, the full development plan is assembled in a complete package and submitted to management for review and approval. The summary sheet for such a plan is shown in Table 6.10.

In addition to the estimate and schedule, many items can be usefully included in such plans.[8] Figure 6.6 shows some of the elements that should be considered for inclusion, depending on the particular needs of the project and the organization's practices.[7]

After preparation, the plan is circulated to all involved groups for review and sign-off. Every group must agree that the plan represents their commitment to do

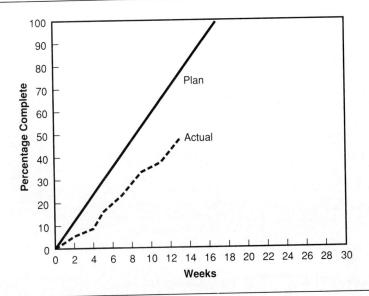

FIGURE 6.5
Module Checkpoint Plan

the work in the time and with the resources specified. This calls for a review and management signature by such groups as:

- Software engineering
- Documentation
- Test and test development
- Packaging and release
- Tools and facilities support
- Training
- Installation support
- Maintenance
- Acceptance test
- Administration
- Software Quality Assurance

At each phase review the development plan is updated. The schedules show task status and current projections compared to the plan. The development plan sum-

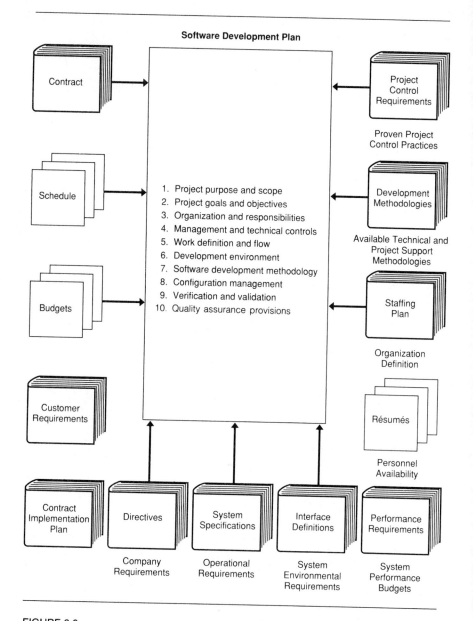

FIGURE 6.6
Example Development Plan Contents [7]
Source: Evans, M. W., P. H. Piazza, and J. B. Dolkas, *Principles of Productive Software Management.* New York: Wiley, 1983.

TABLE 6.10
DEVELOPMENT PLAN SUMMARY—EXAMPLE

Date: _____ Estimator: _____ Project: _____

Product Manager Approval: _____ Date: _____

Estimate Summary:
  Size:
    KLOC
    Contingency
    Total

  Programmer Months:
    High-Level Design
    Detailed Design
    Code and Unit Test
    Integration and Test
    Total Development

Phase Review Dates:
Phase 0
Phase 1
Phase 2
Phase 3
Phase 4

Plan Contents
  Plan Summary
  Program
  Documentation
  DP Support
  Integration
  Test and Release
  Support
  Training
  Approvals
  Estimating and Contingency Factors

mary is updated to reflect changes in program size estimates, resources used to date, and projected phase review dates, as shown in Table 6.11. The actual dates, resources expended, or LOC completed are shown in the column at the right. The regular use of such summaries will quickly inform senior management of any significant changes in the program. The phase review report should then inform them of the resolution of any schedule, resource, or staffing issues.

Some of the items to be considered in phase reviews are:

  □ *The base project schedule is retained and updated unless a major project change is introduced and a full replanning cycle is completed and approved.* The updated schedule shows the original start and end dates for each item, the

TABLE 6.11
DEVELOPMENT PLAN UPDATE SUMMARY—EXAMPLE

Date: _____ Estimator: _____ Project: _____

Product Manager Approval: _____ Date: _____

Estimate Summary:		Plan					Actual
Phase:	1	2	3	4	5		
Size:							
KLOC							
Contingency							
Total							
Programmer Months:							
High-Level Design							
Detailed Design							
Code and Unit Test							
Integration and Test							
Total Development							
Phase Review Dates:							
Phase 0							
Phase 1							
Phase 2							
Phase 3							
Phase 4							

actual dates for each item, and any new item completion projections. If this is not done, scheduling will be informal and every project will always appear to be on schedule at each review.

☐ *The final product delivery date is shown on the overall schedule, and all subsidiary schedules are posted against this master.*   This ensures the impact of schedule slippages is apparent well before final test and delivery.

☐ *The development teams participate in planning their own work.*   They then understand the overall project and are more committed to the final result.

☐ *When a development schedule or estimate is outside the user's acceptable range, it is rarely wise to arbitrarily make reductions.*   Most estimates, no matter how unacceptable, are generally too optimistic. This is why contingencies are needed. Management must question the initial plans but, unless this plan has obvious errors or is out of line with prior experience, they should concentrate on ways to reduce the work, provide added resources, or remove other constraints.

6.9 Planning Models

Software cost models can be helpful in making product plans, but they should be used with care. Experience has shown that models, if not calibrated to the specific organization's experience, can be in error by 500 percent or more.[11, 13] Models should thus be used to augment the estimating process and not to replace it. No model can fully reflect the product's characteristics, the development environment, and the many relevant personnel considerations.

In order to improve their accuracy, some software cost models have been enhanced to the point at which misuse is a real danger. Organizational estimating capability improves because the professionals have gained experience by thinking through the product and task details. As they compare subsequent experience with earlier estimates, their intuition steadily improves. A good intuition, supported by documented experience, is generally far more accurate than any cost model.

When models are used to produce software cost estimates, their results are often blindly accepted and the project plan is not properly developed. The people then do not fully understand the project, appreciate their roles, or feel committed to the plan. They also do not learn how to make better estimates.

Once the size and resource estimates have been made, it is necessary to spread these resources over the planned schedule. If the organization does not have a good historical basis, a number of modeling techniques can be of help.[3, 14, 16, 17] Models such as COCOMO and SLIM, for example, can be used effectively to check the estimates for errors or oversights and to help in assessing risks. Under no circumstances, however, should such models be relied on to produce the final estimates.

6.10 Final Considerations

The most important single prerequisite to good software cost estimating is the establishment of an estimating group. The group ensures that the cost estimate and actual performance data are retained in a database, that the available data is analyzed to establish the productivity factors and contingencies, and that the development groups are competently assisted in preparing and documenting their plans. When development teams are so supported, they are in the best position to capitalize on their planning experience and to progressively improve their estimating accuracy.

When IBM's Federal Systems Division (FSD) introduced software cost estimating methods in the late 1960s and early 1970s, their subsequent experience showed rapid and continuous improvement in estimating accuracy.[5] Table 6.12

shows the progressive improvement in software development cost accuracy for ten projects that were completed in IBM FSD in 1977, 1978, and 1979. As can be seen, estimating accuracy progressively improved as the organization gained experience. While experience is the key, experienced software groups rarely improve their estimating accuracy to this degree without the support of an orderly planning process.

6.11 Summary

The project plan provides a definition of each major task, an estimate of the time and resources required, and a framework for management review and control. It is developed at the beginning of the job and is successively refined as the work progresses.

With rare exceptions, initial resource estimates and schedules are unacceptable. This is not because the programmers are unresponsive, but because the users generally want more than they can afford. If the job doesn't fit the available schedule and resources, it must either be pared down or the time and resources increased.

The elements of a software plan are: goals and objectives, a sound conceptual design, Work Breakdown Structure (WBS), product size estimates, resource estimates, and the project schedule. In addition to defining the work, this plan provides management the basis for periodically reviewing and tracking progress against the plan.

TABLE 6.12
COMPLETED PROJECT ACTUAL VERSUS BUDGET PERFORMANCE [5]

Project Completion Year	Project	% Variance	Average
1977	A	56.2	
	B	99.4	77.8
1978	C	19.4	
	D	31.4	
	E	14.3	
	F	33.6	
	G	15.2	22.8
1979	H	23.7	
	I	2.2	
	J	9.6	11.8

The measure used in program size estimation should be reasonably easy to use early in the project and readily measurable once the work is completed. Subsequent comparison of the early estimates to the actual measured product size then provides feedback to the estimators on how to make more accurate estimates. Once an estimate of the amount of code to be developed is obtained, this can be converted into the number of programmer months and time required. From the total resource needs, the project schedule can be developed by spreading these resources over the planned software engineering phases.

After the estimates and schedule are completed, the full development plan is assembled in a complete package and circulated to all involved groups for review and sign-off. At each phase review, the development plan is updated. The schedules show task status and current projections compared to the plan. The most important single prerequisite to good software cost estimating is the establishment of an estimating group.

References

1. Albrecht, A. J. "Measuring application development productivity," *Proceedings of the Joint SHARE/GUIDE/IBM Application Development Symposium,* October 1979, pp. 83–92.

2. Albrecht, A. J., and J. E. Gaffney, Jr. "Software function, source lines of code, and development effort prediction: a software science validation," *IEEE Transactions of Software Engineering,* vol. SE-9, no. 6, November 1983.

3. Boehm, Barry W. *Software Engineering Economics.* Englewood Cliffs, NJ: Prentice-Hall, 1981.

4. Card, D. N., D. V. Cotnoir, and C. E. Goorevich. "Managing software maintenance, cost and quality," *IEEE Proceedings, Conference on Software Maintenance*—1987, Austin, Texas, September 21–24, 1987, pp. 145–152.

5. Cruickshank, R. D., and M. Lesser. "An approach to estimating and controlling software development costs," in Goldberg and Loren, eds., *Economics of Information Processing,* vol. I & II. New York: Wiley, 1981.

6. DeMarco, Tom, and Tim Lister. "Programmer performance and the effects of the workplace," *Proceedings of the 8th International Conference on Software Engineering,* August 28–30, 1985, IEEE Catalog No. 85CH2139-4.

7. Evans, M. W., P. H. Piazza, and J. B. Dolkas. *Principles of Productive Software Management.* New York: Wiley, 1983.

8. Fairley, R. E. "A Guide for Preparing Software Project Management Plans." Technical Report TR-86-14, Wang Institute of Graduate Studies, November 3, 1986.

9. Flaherty, M. J. "Programming productivity measurement system of System/370," *IBM Systems Journal,* vol. 24, no. 2, 1985.

10. Griffin, E. L. "Real-time estimating," *Datamation,* June 1980, pp. 188–197.

11. Jeffery, D. R. "Time-sensitive cost models in the commercial MIS environment," *IEEE Transactions on Software Engineering,* vol. SE-13, no. 7, July 1987.

12. Jones, T. C. "Measuring programming quality and productivity," *IBM Systems Journal,* vol. 17, no. 1, 1978.

13. Kemerer, C. F. "An empirical validation of software cost estimation models," *Communications of the ACM,* May 1987, vol. 70, no. 5.

14. Londeix, B. *Cost Estimation for Software Development.* Reading, MA: Addison-Wesley, 1987.

15. McGarry, F. E. "What have we learned in the last 6 years—measuring software development technology," *Proceedings of the Seventh Annual Software Engineering Workshop,* Goddard Space Flight Center, December 1982.

16. Putnam, L. H. "A general empirical solution to the macro software sizing and estimating problem," *IEEE Transactions on Software Engineering,* vol. SE-4, no. 4, July 1978, pp. 345–361.

17. Putnam, L. H. "Measurement data to support sizing, estimating and control of the software life cycle," *IEEE Proceedings COMPCON,* 1978, pp. 352–352F.

18. Snyder, T. R. "Rate charting," *Datamation,* November 1976.

19. Stephenson, W. E. "An analysis of the resources used in the Safeguard System software development," *IEEE Proceedings of the 2nd International Conference of Software Engineering,* 1976.

20. Symons, C. R. "Function point analysis: difficulties and improvements," *IEEE Transactions on Software Engineering,* vol. 14, no. 1, January 1988, p. 2.

21. Tausworthe, R. C. "The Work Breakdown Structure in software project management," *Journal of Systems and Software,* vol. 1, 1980, pp. 181–186.

7

Software Configuration Management—Part I

Change management is one of the fundamental activities of software engineering. Changes to the requirements drive the design, and design changes affect the code. Testing then uncovers problems that result in further changes, sometimes even to the original requirements. The change process is simple in concept but complex in detail. For even modest-sized projects, the number of people involved and the change volume generally require a formal change management system. That is the reason for software configuration management.

Since a key objective of the software process is to have change activity converge until the final product is stable enough to ship, the management of all changes is important. This chapter focuses on code control because that is generally the most practical area for initial attention. Control of requirements and design changes is also critically important, but these functions can often be handled as enhancements to a code management system. Their discussion is thus deferred to Chapter 12.

7.1 The Need for Configuration Management

The most frustrating software problems are often caused by poor configuration management. The problems are frustrating because they take time to fix, they often happen at the worst time, and they are totally unnecessary. For example, a difficult bug that was fixed at great expense suddenly reappears; a developed and tested feature is mysteriously missing; or a fully tested program suddenly doesn't work. Configuration management helps to reduce these problems by coordinating the work products of the many different people who work on a common project.[2] Without such control, their work will often conflict, resulting in such problems as:[1]

☐ *Simultaneous update*   When two or more programmers work separately on the same program, the last one to make changes can easily destroy the others' work.

☐ *Shared code*   Often, when a bug is fixed in code shared by several programmers, some of them are not notified.

☐ *Common code*   In large systems, when common program functions are modified, all the users need to know. Without effective code management, there is no way to be sure of finding and alerting every user.

☐ *Versions*   Most large programs are developed in evolutionary releases. With one release in customer use, another in test, and a third in development, bug fixes must be propagated between them. If found by the customer, for example, a bug should be fixed in all the later versions. Similarly, if a bug is found in a development release, it should be fixed in those prior versions that contained it. In larger systems with several simultaneous active releases and many programmers working on bug fixes and enhancements, conflicts and confusion are likely.

These problems stem from confusion and lack of control, and they can waste an enormous amount of time. The key is to have a control system that answers the following questions:[2]

☐ What is my current software configuration?

☐ What is its status?

☐ How do I control changes to my configuration?

☐ How do I inform everyone else of my changes?

☐ What changes have been made to my software?

☐ Do anyone else's changes affect my software?

The key role of Software Configuration Management (SCM) is to control change activity so these questions can be answered. If, however, SCM is viewed merely as a management tool or a contractual obligation, it can easily become a bureaucratic roadblock that impedes the work. While such systems may be contractually required, the real need is to assist the programmers in controlling and tracking their work, while ensuring that nothing is lost or destroyed.[5]

7.2 Software Product Nomenclature

Since the role of configuration management is to control the development of the system elements as they are built and then combined into a full system, it is

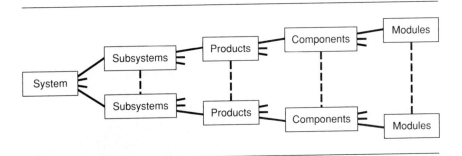

FIGURE 7.1
Software Product Nomenclature

important to use common system terminology. The design process starts by successively partitioning the system until a satisfactory level of detail is reached. At this point, implementation begins with these smallest pieces, which are progressively assembled and tested until the total system is completed. Since there is no standardized nomenclature for these levels, the terms shown in Fig. 7.1 will be used:

- □ *System* The package of all the software that meets the user's requirements.

- □ *Subsystem* Large systems can have many subsystems, such as communications, display, and processing.

- □ *Product* Subsystems typically contain many products. For example, an operating system might contain a control program, compilers, utilities, and so forth.

- □ *Components* At the next level, a control program could be made up of such components as the supervisor, scheduler, and I/O control system.

- □ *Module* At the lowest level, components consist of a number of modules. Modules typically implement individual functions that are relatively small and self-contained, such as queue management, interrupt dispatcher, and command interpreter.

During the implementation process two things are happening at the same time. First, the modules are being developed, enhanced, tested, and repaired from detailed design and implementation through system test. Second, the modules are being assembled into components, products, subsystems, and systems. During this building process, the modules are constantly being changed to add functions or repair problems. This process is supported by a hierarchy of tests:

- □ *Unit test*   This is a separate test of each individual module.
- □ *Integration test*   As the modules are integrated into components, products, subsystems, and systems, their interfaces and interdependencies are tested to ensure they are properly designed and implemented.
- □ *Function test*   When integration results in a functionally operable build, it is tested successively in component test, product test, subsystem test, and finally in system test.
- □ *Regression test*   At each integration step (which is here called a *spin*), a new build is produced. This is first tested to ensure that it hasn't regressed, or lost functions that were present in the previous build.

While different organizations call these activities by different names, they all follow essentially the same process. These various test phases are treated in more detail in Chapter 11.

7.3 Basic Configuration Management Functions

Figure 7.2 gives an overview of SCM code management. Once an initial product level has stabilized, a first baseline is established. With each successive set of enhancements, a new baseline is established in step with development. Each baseline is retained in a permanent database, together with all the changes that produced it. The baseline is thus the official repository for the product, and it contains the most current version. Only tested code and approved changes are put in the baseline, which is fully protected. It is the official source that all the progammers use to ensure their work is consistent with that of everyone else.

The key SCM tasks are:[1]

- □ Configuration control
- □ Change management
- □ Revisions
- □ Versions
- □ Deltas
- □ Conditional code

7.3.1 Configuration Control

The task of configuration control revolves around one official copy of the code. The simplest way to protect every system revision is to keep a separate official copy of each revision level. While this can take a lot of storage, the most serious

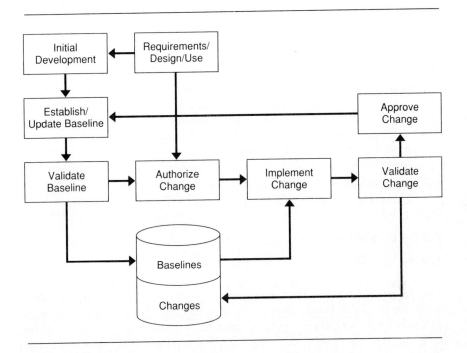

FIGURE 7.2
Configuration Management Overview

issue concerns code divergence. When two or more groups work on separate copies of the same or similar versions of common code, they often make different changes to correct the same problems. The ultimate cost of this can be understood by considering system drivers. For example, one programmer may need a copy of the system control program for unit test. Even though the control program may not be completed, the functions this programmer needs may be usable. It is therefore desirable to provide a control program copy with this function rather than waste the developer's time writing test scaffolding to simulate it. If, during this test, the programmer finds a problem in the control program driver, fix X may be made to permit continued testing. At the same time, other drivers and the control program itself are being tested by other programmers, and fix Y may be added to solve the same problem.

Since several such changes could involve the same code, coordination can be a problem. Unless all the drivers are periodically regenerated from the same baseline, each test may be invalidated by other changes. A good rule of thumb is that no two separate copies of a program can be kept identical. If separate copies exist, they must be assumed to differ since, even if they originally were the same, they will soon diverge.

The practical answer to this problem is to keep only one official copy of any code that is commonly used by several groups. Working copies may occasionally be used, but a common library must be the official source for all this common code, and only officially approved changes can be permitted to this library. Drivers then can be constructed from a driver contents table that identifies all the code to be included.

With such a library facility, programmers can be sure that their control program drivers include the latest revision levels. Further, if they encounter problems in test, these problems can be passed to control program development for repair in the official library. While temporary driver patches may be needed to complete test, the official program copy is only stored once and only fixed in one place.

7.3.2 Revisions

Keeping track of revisions is an important task of configuration management. In large systems, some programs, such as the control program, provide essential function for all the others. Once a component's modules have been integrated into a testable unit, it is then tested with the latest control program level. When new problems are found, previous tests can be rerun to trace the problem source. If an early driver is now reproduced using the latest versions of the control program modules, some of these modules will likely be different, so the prior tests will not be exactly reproduced. The answer is to keep track of every change to every module and test case. There is one latest official version and every prior version is identified and retained. These obsolete copies can then be used to assist in tracing problems.

Development is thus a repetitive cycle of revision, integration, and test. To track the revision level of every item, a numbering system must separately identify each test, module, component, product, and system. For example, module MEM might have multiple revisions as MEM8901 for the first revision in 1989 and MEM8902 for the next. Each revision of each module can then be uniquely identified and retrieved when needed. Further, the testers can check successive driver builds starting with MEM8901 and working up to the most current level to see where the problem first occurred. When the changes made in MEM at that point are identified and compared to the expected functions, problem identification is facilitated.

7.3.3 Derivations

The ability to determine what has changed is one of the most powerful software testing aids. For example, when a program worked one day and not the next, the first step is to find out what changed. As illustrated in Fig. 7.3, a derivation record would show that Test A was run on control program level 116 and the rerun was attempted on level 117. Changes X and Y could then be identified readily. Some of the information that might be maintained in such derivation records is:

1. The revision level of each module
2. The revision levels of the tools used to assemble, compile, link, load, and execute the programs and tests
3. The test cases used and their revision levels
4. The test data employed
5. The files used
6. The software and hardware system configuration, including peripherals, features, options, allocations, assignments, and hardware change levels
7. The operational procedures
8. If not a stand-alone test, a record of the job streams being executed

While this is an enormous amount of information, any change in any area could prevent problem reproduction. The first five areas are the responsibility of configuration management, while items 6, 7, and 8 should be recorded in a log maintained by the personnel operating the test system.

The key is to establish a foolproof way to identify every change in test conditions. Then when a problem occurs after introduction of multiple changes, it is possible to reproduce the prior conditions, verify correct operation, and individually reintroduce the changes until the problem recurs. While this level of detail is rarely needed, it is not difficult to retain in an automated SCM system. When the occasional tough problem arises, the derivation record provides the most informed basis for rapidly identifying the problem's precise cause.

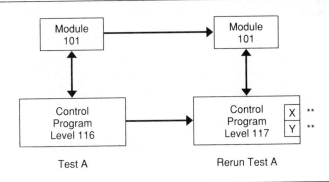

FIGURE 7.3
Derivations

7.3.4 Versions

There are other potential issues with module changes. Often, several different functions can be implemented by the same module with only modest coding differences. For example, different memory management code may be needed to handle expansion beyond the normal 512K addressing range of a computer. As shown in Fig. 7.4, a standard memory management module would be used below 512K, and one using a mode switch would handle the larger memory sizes. Since these are different programs they would have different designations, such as MEMS and MEML for the standard and large memory management modules, respectively. Each would, of course, have its own sequence of revisions and revision numbering schemes.

7.3.5 Deltas

Another task of configuration management is the implementation of deltas. The use of versions solves the problem of different functional needs for the same module but introduces multiple copies of the same code. The reason is that most of the code in the two memory management modules would be identical. One, however, would have an additional routine to handle memory limits testing and mode switching. Since they are stored as separate modules, however, there is no way to ensure that all the changes made to one are incorporated in the other.

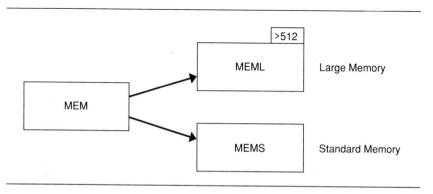

FIGURE 7.4
Versions

One way to handle this is to use deltas, as shown in Fig. 7.5. This involves storing the base module, say MEM, together with the changes required to make it into MEML. When maintenance is required on MEM, those changes can be made directly, with the single caveat that they not interfere with the delta code. Changes to MEML alone are then made to the delta, and the MEM code is left undisturbed.

The delta system is very useful in some situations but has some disadvantages. First, it is possible for versions to be made of versions, and so on indefinitely, enormously complicating the problems of working on the base code. Further, if for some reason one element was lost or corrupted in this chain of base plus delta changes, it might be difficult to reconstruct the entire chain. Finally, since some of these modules will likely last a long time, the deltas could have long lives as well, and each could grow into a large block of code.

The most practical answer is to use the delta approach for temporary variations. This, for example, is the approach typically used with a development library. When a programmer starts work on a module enhancement, a development version is released from the baseline. The programmer then implements and unit tests the desired changes in delta form. While this is being done, the baseline module will likely be changed by other programmers, so it could not merely be replaced with the new one. With deltas, however, the changes can be separately incorporated. To ensure that the changes don't conflict, they must all be regression tested.

Permanent module variations that leave the bulk of the code undisturbed can be handled by splitting the module into two or more parts. The common element would be retained as an identical module for all uses, and a separate module would be added for each variation. For the memory management case, there would

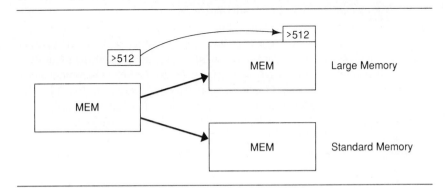

FIGURE 7.5
Deltas

then be a memory management base module MEB, a large variation MEL, and a small one MES. Here, changes need only consider one module at a time, and each can have its own separate stream of revisions.

7.3.6 Conditional Code

Another way to handle slight variations between modules is to use some form of conditional program construction. For example, the billing program shown in Fig. 7.6 might include different functions depending on the need for a state sales tax. The source program would contain various sales tax versions, but none would be included in the final system unless called for at system installation. This need for conditional code is often met by using system generation options. These might include conditionally selecting one of several optional modules depending on the particular state where the program was used. In any case, all modules would be in the source library, but only one would be used at any time.

The use of conditions simplifies code control because there is only one official copy of each module. The number of version combinations is also minimized. For example, if a system had 2 module variations for memory size, 3 for printer type, 6 for communications mode, 4 for terminal type, and 2 for I/O channel configuration, a total of 288 configurations would be possible. By using variations, all these combinations could be generated with 17 module types and 5 system generation parameters. With larger systems, the number of possibilities is so great that some form of conditional code is essential.

The use of conditional code has the advantage of providing one complete copy of the entire program. All the code is present, and the users each select the particular combinations needed for their installations. The use of conditional code does, however, have disadvantages. The most important is that the end users must specify all the parameters and then perform a special and possibly complex installation process. Since they are the only ones who understand their detailed needs, however, there may be no alternative. Another disadvantage is that the system generation process becomes progressively more complex with system growth. When it has been used on the same program for a long time, the multiple interdependencies can make the process hard to use, understand, and maintain.

It is therefore wise to restrict conditional code to an absolute minimum and to periodically review each condition to see if it can be standardized. Finally, since conditional code requires that all the program options and features be shipped to the end users, it is more difficult to control unauthorized distribution and use.

7.4 Baselines

The baseline is the foundation for configuration management.[1,4] It provides the official standard on which subsequent work is based and to which only authorized

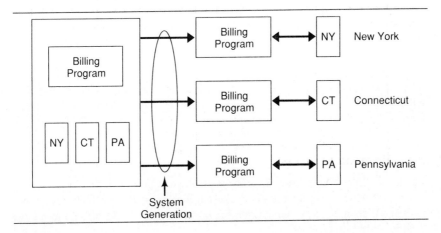

FIGURE 7.6
Conditional Code

changes are made. After an initial baseline is established and frozen, every subsequent change is recorded as a delta until the next baseline is set.

It is desirable to establish a baseline at an early point in every project. Establishing a baseline too early, however, will impose unnecessary procedures and slow the programmers' work. While there are no hard and fast rules, the trade-offs are relatively clear. As long as the programmers can work on individual modules with little interaction, a code baseline is not needed. As soon as integration begins, however, formal control is essential.

7.4.1 Baseline Scope

For code control, the baseline contains all the project code. The items to be included for the implementation phase are:

- ☐ The current level of each module, including source and object code
- ☐ The current level of each test case, including source and object code
- ☐ The current level of each assembler, compiler, editor, or other tool used
- ☐ The current level of any special test or operational data
- ☐ The current level of all macros, libraries, and files
- ☐ The current level of any installation or operating procedures
- ☐ If the project involves operating system or control program changes, it may also be necessary to retain data on the computing system configuration and its change level

Each level is uniquely named so it can be distinguished from all others. If the levels are not differentiated and if copies and change records are not retained for each modification, it may not be possible to recreate a test environment precisely. While it may not seem that critical to save every single change, some such minor omission always seems to cause the most devastating problems in final system or acceptance test. With large, complex systems, the only way to handle this is to anticipate it by retaining every change that could possibly be significant. The rule is, *unless you know it isn't important, it is!*

7.4.2 Baseline Control

SCM must ensure appropriate baseline control while providing flexible service to the programmers. On the one hand, the baseline must be protected against un-authorized change; at the same time, the programmers should be able to readily modify and test their code.

This controlled flexibility is accomplished by providing the programmers with private working copies of any part of the baseline. They can thus try out new changes, conduct tests, or make trial fixes without disturbing anyone else. When they are ready to incorporate their work into a new baseline, however, care must be taken to ensure that the new changes are compatible and that no new code causes regressions.

Every proposed change must then be tested against a trial version of the new baseline to make sure that it does not invalidate any of the other changes. Since such tests take time and since changes are being made all the time, a locking mechanism is needed to ensure that none of these updated modules are changed during this final regression test. One approach is to break this problem into two parts: locking and regression testing. The locking capability is handled through a charge-out, charge-in procedure. In building a new baseline, each module must be updated and tested with all the others. Since the module changes may conflict, it is important to do the final baseline regression test with all the new code.

As will be discussed in Chapter 11, changes should not all be integrated and tested in one big bang. Typically the integration plan specifies the order in which one or a few modules are added to the trial baseline. As each module is charged out for this trial update, it is locked to prevent anyone else from changing it. When that trial update is completed and verified, it is charged back in. This removes the lock, and the module is available for the next trial update.

To protect against module changes causing broader problems, a comprehen-sive regression testing procedure is required. This is generally handled by running periodic regression tests on the trial baseline to ensure that all the changes made to that point have not caused problems. A large set of previously operable test cases is used, and any bug indicates that a new change has caused problems. The new changes are then backed out and the programmers responsible are instructed to find and fix the problems. Regression testing is then repeated.

7.4.3 Configuration Management Records

To maintain control over all code changes, several procedures are used. First, every change proposal is documented and authorized before being made. The documentation includes the reason for the change, the potential cost in time and LOC, the person responsible for the change, and any products affected. The basic information included in a change request is shown in Table 7.1.[4] While this data may not all be needed for every change, it is wise to err on the side of completeness since such information is often impossible to reconstruct later.

As the change is made, a record is kept of what was done. This change log includes the information shown in Table 7.2.[1, 2, 4] This change log data should permit the change to be later backed out of the system if necessary. All tests must also be completely identified so the identical tests can later be repeated if needed. The change log should either include the detail on the tests or specify where it is retained (usually in the test report or test log).

The results of each test should be documented as shown in Table 7.3. Each test is a major investment, and data should be kept for later reference. It is surprising how often some test must be rerun because no one can find a record of the results. Since the need could arise months or even years later, the critical information should be retained: the source and object code, the test data and test cases, the system hardware and software configuration, any special test tools or scaffolding, any special operational considerations such as timing or error conditions, and, of course, the test results.

Detailed test records are particularly crucial when hardware and software changes are made simultaneously. Programmers often feel that if their code runs, they don't need to worry about machine problems. In one case, for example, everyone thought that the final software tests were run on the final hardware level. Some machines, however, were not up to the final change level. Some problems were thus missed, and they were expensive to fix after customer installation.

Perhaps the single most important project control document is the problem report. This records every problem and the precise conditions that caused it. While most such reports originate in test, they can be submitted by anyone working with the program, including other developers, the testers, computer operations, documentation, Quality Assurance, or even the customer during field test. The information required in the problem report is shown in Table 7.4.[5] The problem is defined in sufficient detail here so it can be reproduced later. The problem report need not include a description of the proposed fix unless a temporary fix or bypass was applied. Such information, when available, is very useful in defining the problem and its solution.

Another important report is the expect list. This is a detailed listing of every function and feature planned for every component in each new baseline. All developers who work on program changes for a new baseline should maintain a current list of all the functions, features, fixes, and interfaces to be provided by

TABLE 7.1
SAMPLE CHANGE REQUEST CONTENTS

Status:
  Change number
  Authorization level
  Date opened
  Date closed: (planned, actual)

Change Information:
  Change description
  Change approach (if available)
  Change source:
    Organization
    Activity and phase
  Change priority:
    Problem severity
    Requirements priority
    Other

Originator:
  Name, address, phone, organization

Implementation Responsibility:
  Name, address, phone, organization

Implementation Information:
  Change type:
    Problem (number)
    Planned (WBS identification)
    Unplanned (authorization)
  Size (planned and actual):
    LOC: new, changed, deleted
    Documentation: new, changed, deleted pages
  Programmer hours (planned and actual)
  Schedule checkpoints:
    Design
    Implementation
    Inspection
    Test
    Integration
    Regression test
  Products affected (name, level)
  Related changes (numbers)

their program when delivered to integration. This information is made available to all development groups, so they know of any changes affecting them. On large projects, there are many interdependencies, and when one programmer makes a functional change, every involved activity must be informed promptly. Even if no other program depends on this function, the change will likely affect test, documentation, and integration.

TABLE 7.2
SAMPLE CHANGE LOG CONTENTS

Change Identification:
  Change number
  Date changed

Implementation Responsibility:
  Name, address, phone, organization

Implementation:
  Source and object code
  Documentation (document numbers, pages, changes)
  Reason(s) for change (change request number)
  Change dependencies
  Tests run and results

7.5 Configuration Management Responsibilities

To implement the necessary controls and procedures, a number of responsibilities need to be established. Depending on the size of the system and the number of people involved, they may be handled by a single individual, several people, or an entire organization. The basic responsibilities are: the configuration manager, module ownership, and the Change Control Board (CCB).

TABLE 7.3
SAMPLE TEST REPORT CONTENTS

Responsibilities:
  Developer
  Development manager
  Tester

Test Identification:
  Test date
  Product name (revision number)
  Test cases used (identification or bucket numbers)
  Test data used (identification numbers)
  Test configuration (hardware and software)

Test Results:
  Problem reports (numbers)
  Test result summary (by test case)

TABLE 7.4
SAMPLE PROBLEM REPORT CONTENTS

Problem Identification:
  Problem number
  Date discovered
  Date reported
  Product(s) involved
  System(s) involved

Originator Identification:
  Name, address, phone, organization, function

Problem Description:
  Severity:
    Critical (system down)
    Severe (user/application down)
    Normal (functional/operational problem)
    Inconvenience (feature, documentation error)
    Suggestion
  Status:
    Waiting
    Bypass
    Temporary fix
  Symptom description
  Probable cause (if known)
  Conditions (to recreate):
    Test cases/job streams (identification numbers)
    Hardware/software configuration (identification)
    Operational circumstances

Problem Fix/Bypass Description (if available):
  Source and object changes
  Other actions

The configuration manager is the central control point for system change and has the following responsibilities:[1]

☐ Develop, document, and distribute the SCM procedures.

☐ Establish the system baseline, including backup provisions.

☐ Ensure that no unauthorized changes are made to the baseline.

☐ Ensure that all baseline changes are recorded in sufficient detail so they can be reproduced or backed out.

☐ Ensure that all baseline changes are regression tested.

☐ Provide the focal point for exception resolution.

The configuration manager ensures that answers are always available for such questions as: what code is this, what changed, what tests were run, what were the test results, and where is this code. This crucial responsibility must be vested in someone, even for two-person projects. For projects involving hundreds or thousands of people, entire SCM departments may be needed. Developed and tested code is expensive, and it must be retained and protected. That is the configuration manager's basic responsibility.

7.5.1 Module Ownership

Even with a well-established and effective SCM function, provisions are also needed to ensure the design integrity of each module. This task is not just historical but involves understanding the design as well as future enhancement plans. For example, when bugs are fixed, there are often alternative design approaches. If enhancements are also being considered, the bug repair should be consistent with future plans.

Maintaining design integrity is a common problem in large systems with periodic enhancements. One simple but effective approach is to designate a programmer as owner of each module. Since there are often many more modules than programmers, one person generally owns several modules at one time. The module owner's responsibilities are:

- □ Know and understand the module design.
- □ Provide advice to everyone who works on or interfaces with the module.
- □ Serve as technical control point for all module modifications, including both enhancement and repair.
- □ Ensure module integrity by reviewing all changes and conducting periodic regression tests.

Module ownership ensures design continuity by providing a single focus for all module changes. It is also useful on both small and large software projects. Its disadvantages are that it depends on the skill and availability of individuals and it only provides design control at the detailed level. These disadvantages can be countered by establishing a back-up "buddy system" between module owners and maintaining an overall design responsibility to monitor and control the software structure, interfaces, macros, and conventions.

7.5.2 The Change Control Board

On moderate to very large projects, a central control mechanism is needed to ensure that every change is properly considered and coordinated. This is the role of the Change Control Board (CCB), sometimes called the Configuration Control Board.[4, 5] It should at least include members from development, documentation, test, assurance, maintenance, and release. Its purpose is to ensure that every baseline change is properly considered by all concerned parties and that every change is authorized before implementation. The CCB, for example, is the body that reviews each change request and approves it, disapproves it, or defers it for more information.

Depending on project size, several CCBs may be needed, each with expertise and authority over a particular area. Some examples are: overall design and module interfaces, the control program, the application components, user interfaces, and development tools. Each board must have a chairman with authority to resolve disputes. With multiple CCBs, a system-level CCB is needed as a resolution point for disputes between these lower-level boards.

A CCB typically needs the following information on each proposed change:[5]

- *Size* How many new and/or changed lines of code will likely be required?
- *Alternatives* What, if any, are the alternatives to making the change and, if there is more than one way to do it, why was the proposed one selected?
- *Complexity* Is the change within a single component or does it involve others?
- *Schedule* What are the required and planned dates?
- *Impact* What are the future product consequences of this change?
- *Cost* What are the potential costs and savings from making the change?
- *Severity* How critical is the change?
- *Relationship to other changes* Will another change supersede or invalidate this one, or does it depend on other changes?
- *Test* Are there any special test requirements?
- *Resources* Are the needed people available to do the work?
- *System impact* What are the memory, performance, or other system consequences of the change?
- *Benefits* Are there special advantages to be derived from the change?
- *Politics* Are there special considerations such as who is requesting the change or whom it will affect?
- *Change maturity* How long has the change been under consideration?

If the change is to fix a customer-reported problem, other information may also be required:[4]

- A definition of the problem the change is intended to fix
- The conditions under which the problem was observed
- A copy of the trouble report
- A technical description of the problem
- The names of any other programs affected

Additional information should also be available prior to release:[4]

- □ Final source and/or object code for the change
- □ Final documentation changes
- □ Evidence of successful inspection and test of the code and documentation

The CCB not only determines whether the change should be made but also the conditions under which it can be released. For example, the change may be so critical that the CCB will want to review the final inspection and test results before approving release. Special conditions such as an interface test, a performance analysis, a user review, or a field test may also be deemed appropriate.

This amount of information can become a burden to the development people, particularly during final test. When many changes arise from a single test phase, for example, it is often desirable to group them together in one CCB review. Each problem and its fix should be uniquely identified, but much of the justification material could be common.

7.5.3 CCB Problems

Since the CCB must consider every change, its workload can become excessive, particularly during the final test and release phases of a large project. This is one reason why multiple CCB's are established for specific components or test phases. It is not wise, however, to waive CCB review just because change activity has become a bottleneck. It is precisely at times of heaviest change and testing activity that loss of system control is most likely and CCB review is most needed.

It is important to select the CCB members with care. They have the power to block any part of the project so these assignments should not be treated lightly. Generally, in fact, the project's software development manager should personally chair the highest-level CCB.

7.5.4 The SCM Organization

A further question concerns the dividing line between configuration management and computer operations. While no criteria can fit every case, several ground rules are appropriate. First, these two organizations must coordinate, control, and track every change so that between them they can reproduce every program or test environment. Next, project-unique changes generally should be handled by configuration management and system-wide changes by computer operations. There will, of course, be gray areas, so a complete set of mutually agreed-upon procedures should be developed and documented.

7.6 The Need for Automated Tools

The final development stages of even modest-sized projects involve a lot of detail. Regardless of the care taken in product design, quality can be destroyed by sloppy last-minute changes. For example, to avoid recompilation, such changes may be made as object patches with the intent of later updating the source. These can cause serious problems if precisely equivalent source changes are not later made and tested for every case. In final test, precious time can be lost in a frantic search to correct some inexplicable last-minute regression. The most disastrous mistakes are often made when the project is under the greatest schedule pressure. These are often caused by a loss of change control that started with a quick object patch. While the harried programmers invariably intended to document their changes when there was time, it is later extremely difficult to remember precisely what was done and why.

If any one change is overlooked or its consequences are not properly considered, unpleasant problems are likely in system test, acceptance test, or customer use. Automated systems are thus generally needed to handle the large amount of detail.

7.6.1 The Change Management System

The change management system tracks the change requests, problem reports, CCB actions, and activity log entries. Data is recorded on what was done, by whom, when, what remains to be done, any special conditions, and current status. The system should maintain a record of the changes not closed, the changes to a particular component, and the oldest outstanding changes. This system tracks the mean time to change closure and maintains statistics on the change backlog.

Change activity is also a powerful indicator of project status. With change data like that shown in Fig. 7.7 for each module, management can pinpoint problems early and take timely action in those areas where the problems are most severe. In one case, a development manager tracked the change rate for every module. In most cases this rate steadily declined from unit test through function and integration test. A couple of modules, however, had erratic change patterns. On closer examination, these programmers were found to have design problems they didn't understand. By tracking their change activity, the manager was able to provide them with timely help.

7.6.2 The System Library

The system library stores the development work products, including the source and object code for every baseline and change, the test cases, and the development

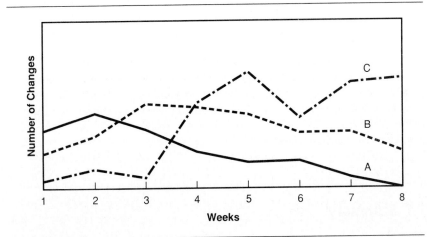

FIGURE 7.7
Module Change Tracking

tools.[3, 4] It provides locks to prevent unauthorized changes, and it has the capability to build the various system configurations, test drivers, and test scenarios or buckets required by development. Its primary functions are:

- Retrieving objects by name, date of creation, author, component, or development status
- Identifying object relationships, such as shared interfaces, the required order of change application, or where-used directories for shared code
- Executing a make function, such as building a product release, building a private system copy, reconstructing a previous version, constructing a driver system, or making up a test bucket
- Performing such service functions as checking status, verifying the presence of all build items, performing compiles, integrating changes into a new baseline, producing listings, or verifying that the source and object files contain identical change levels
- Providing the required levels of control and protection
- Gathering and reporting any desired statistical and accounting information such as change activity by category, test case usage, and size measures

There are many ways to use a system library, and there is wide variability in the functions available. Software organizations should thus make a careful investigation to ensure that the system they select meets their needs. Unless it is absolutely essential, they should use an unmodified commercial library and avoid making special adaptations or improvements.

One indication of how expensive these systems can become is IBM's experience with the library system for OS/360 and OS/370 software development. This system was initially developed in the late 1960s, and a team of 10 to 20 programmers has worked on maintaining and enhancing it ever since. Even after all this work, there still remains a large backlog of desired enhancements.

Development libraries are so powerful that their use will generate many ideas on how they could be even more effective. When these are implemented, even more ideas will be generated, and so on for 20 or more years. Unless an organization is willing to make such a never-ending investment, it should stick with commercially available libraries.

7.7 Summary

Change management is one of the fundamental activities of software engineering. Configuration management helps control changes and coordinate the work products of the many different people who work on a common software project.

The baseline is the official source for code and the repository for all completed work. It is the official standard on which subsequent work is based and to which only authorized changes or additions are made. The baseline contains all the project code, and each level is uniquely named so it can be distinguished from all others. Procedures are established to maintain control over all code changes.

To implement these controls and procedures, responsibility assignments are made for the configuration manager, module ownership, and the Change Control Board (CCB). The change management system tracks the change requests, problem reports, CCB actions, and activity log entries. Data is recorded on what was done, by whom, when, what remains to be done, any special conditions, and current status.

The system library stores the development work products. This includes the source and object code for every baseline and change, the test cases, and the development tools. It has locks to prevent unauthorized changes and the capability to build the various system configurations, test drivers, and test scenarios or buckets required by development.

References

1. Babich, W. A. *Software Configuration Management, Coordination for Team Productivity,* Reading, MA: Addison-Wesley, 1986.

2. Beresoff, E. H., V. D. Henderson, and S. G. Siegel. "Software configuration management: a tutorial," *IEEE Tutorial: Software Configuration Management,* IEEE cat. no. EHO 169-3, October 27, 1980, pp. 24–32.

3. Cristofor, E., T. A. Wendt, and B. C. Wonsiewicz. "Source control + tools = stable systems," *Proceedings COMPSAC 80,* October 27–31, 1980, Chicago.

4. "Software requirements, baselining, and control" (*Proceedings, Twelfth Annual Configuration and Date Management Workshop,* EIA, October 1978, pp. 67–77), *IEEE Tutorial: Software Configuration Management,* IEEE cat. no. EHO 169-3, October 27, 1980, pp. 156–166.

5. Tomayko, J. E. "Support Materials for Software Configuration Management," SEI-SM-4-1.0, September 1986, Carnegie Mellon University, Software Engineering Institute, Pittsburg, PA.

8

Software Quality Assurance

One of the critical challenges for any quality program is to devise a way for ordinary people to review the work of experts. Management properly wants the best designers to design the products, so Software Quality Assurance (SQA) can't have them. The need is to focus on those SQA methods that permit the development work to be reviewed by people who are not primarily developers. The SQA role is to monitor the methods and standards the software experts use and to verify that they have properly applied their expertise. SQA is a valid discipline in its own right, and people can be SQA experts without being software design experts. This SQA expertise is what is required to establish a strong quality program. It includes knowledge of statistical methods, quality control principles, the software process, and an ability to deal effectively with people in contentious situations.

8.1 Quality Management

A key management axiom says that: "What is not tracked is not done." In software there are so many things that need to be done that the manager can't possibly track them all. Since effective management of software requires that thousands of things be done precisely right, some organization is needed to do the tracking. This is the role of SQA.

Before establishing an SQA organization, it is essential to first decide how important software quality is to the organization. Is it, for example, more important than meeting a critical delivery schedule? Just how much quality is important? Should the product be delayed to fix 1 more bug, or 10 more, or 100 more, or. . . ?

As long as software quality is treated as a matter of faith, no painful actions are required. Incantations about the need to believe in quality will change nothing. If management's commitment to software quality does not come down to day-to-day actions, no consistent improvement is likely.

Similarly, if management views the mere act of setting up an SQA organization as satisfying its quality responsibilities, it will have wasted a lot of money, established another bureaucratic bottleneck, and probably damaged product quality. SQA is a management tool that must be properly used to be effective.

The prime benefit of an SQA program is the assurance it provides management that the officially established process is actually being implemented. More specifically, it ensures that:[8]

- □ An appropriate development methodology is in place.
- □ The projects use standards and procedures in their work.
- □ Independent reviews and audits are conducted.
- □ Documentation is produced to support maintenance and enhancement.
- □ The documentation is produced during and not after development.
- □ Mechanisms are in place and used to control changes.
- □ Testing emphasizes all the high-risk product areas.
- □ Each software task is satisfactorily completed before the succeeding one is begun.
- □ Deviations from standards and procedures are exposed as soon as possible.
- □ The project is auditable by external professionals.
- □ The quality control work is itself performed against established standards.
- □ The SQA plan and the software development plan are compatible.

8.1.1 The Benefits of SQA

The reasons for concern about software quality are compelling. Everyone who flies in an airplane agrees on the importance of quality software for air traffic control. Similarly, the Internal Revenue System software should not have errors, nor should the software that controls air defenses, flies aircraft, steers ships, runs banking systems, forecasts weather, directs police, and so on. Software has an enormous impact on almost everything we do, and this impact will only increase in the future.

Beyond logical arguments on the need for SQA, experience also provides a useful guide. Thayer, for example, has studied software managers' views of the reasons for project success or failure.[10] While the value of SQA was not explicitly addressed, it was found that when the project managers' standards were enforced, 76 percent of the projects were successful, as opposed to only 60 percent when no standards were followed. Obviously, this leaves open the question of what the standards were and how well they were enforced.

The experiences with IBM System/360 and 370 software development also demonstrate the value of SQA in enforcing development standards.[6] IBM reported software quality improvements of three to five times over an eight-year period. While this was due to many factors, SQA was an important part of their quality program. In describing TRW's experiences, Boehm has said that "We are finding it increasingly advantageous, from both product quality and cost-effectiveness standpoints, to have an explicit quality assurance activity on our software projects."[1] Similarly, Walker reports that Digital Equipment Corporation found that SQA "significantly increased ability . . . to predictably engineer reliable systems."[11]

8.1.2 The Need for SQA

It is hard for anyone to be objective about auditors. We generally do our own jobs pretty carefully and resent any contrary implication. The need for "outside" review, however, is a matter of perspective. Suppose you had just packed a parachute and were about to take a jump. The odds are you would be happy to have a qualified inspector monitor your every step to make sure you did it just right. When quality is vital, some independent checks are necessary, not because people are untrustworthy but because they are human. The issues with software are not whether checks are needed, but who does them and how.

In very small organizations it is often possible for the software managers to monitor the work so closely that no SQA activity is needed. As the size of the staff grows, the managers become involved with other duties, and they quickly lose touch with the day-to-day technical work. This is when they need to do one of the following:

- Find some way to handle their other workload so they can monitor more closely their people's work.

- Hire someone to do the audit work.

- Motivate the people to monitor each other.

From a technical, economic, and morale viewpoint, the last alternative is generally the most desirable. Unfortunately, as software organizations grow beyond a few dozen people, these "buddy systems" have historically broken down. This is when management must resort to the SQA solution.

8.1.3 The Goals of SQA

Broadly stated, the goals of SQA are:

- ❑ To improve software quality by appropriately monitoring both the software and the development process that produces it
- ❑ To ensure full compliance with the established standards and procedures for the software and the software process
- ❑ To ensure that any inadequacies in the product, the process, or the standards are brought to management's attention so these inadequacies can be fixed

The SQA organization is not responsible for producing quality products or for making quality plans; these are development jobs. SQA is responsible for auditing the quality actions of the line organization and for alerting management to any deviations.

To be effective, SQA needs to work closely with development. They need to understand the plans, verify their execution, and monitor the performance of the individual tasks. If the development people view SQA as the enemy, it will be hard for them to be effective. The key is an SQA attitude of cooperation and support. If they are arbitrary, antagonistic, or nit-picking, no amount of management support can make them effective.[2]

8.2 The Role of SQA

The people responsible for the software projects are the only ones who can be responsible for quality. The role of SQA is to monitor the way these groups perform their responsibilities. In doing this, there are several potential pitfalls:[2]

- ❑ It is a mistake to assume that the SQA people themselves can do anything about quality.
- ❑ The existence of an SQA function does not ensure that the standards and procedures are followed.
- ❑ Unless management periodically demonstrates its support for SQA by following their recommendations, SQA will be ineffective.
- ❑ Unless line management requires that SQA try to resolve their issues with project management before escalation, SQA and development will not work together effectively.

All SQA can do is alert management to deviations from established standards and practices (see, for example, "The Contention Process," page 74). Management must then insist that the quality problems be fixed before the product is shipped; otherwise SQA becomes an expensive bureaucratic exercise.

8.2.1 SQA Responsibilities

SQA can be effective when they report through an independent management chain, when they are properly staffed with competent professionals, and when they see their role as supporting the development and maintenance personnel in improving product quality. When all these conditions are met, SQA can help remove the major inhibitors to producing quality software. This requires that they be given the following responsibilities:

- Review all development and quality plans for completeness (see Chapter 16).
- Participate as inspection moderators in design and code inspections (see Chapter 10).
- Review all test plans for adherence to standards (see Chapter 11).
- Review a significant sample of all test results to determine adherence to plans (see Chapter 11).
- Periodically audit SCM performance to determine adherence to standards (see Chapters 7 and 12).
- Participate in all project quarterly and phase reviews and register nonconcurrence if the appropriate standards and procedures have not been reasonably met (see Chapter 5).

If SQA fulfills its responsibilities and if senior management refuses to allow line management to commit or to ship products until the SQA issues have been addressed, then SQA can help management improve product quality. Specific examples of the kinds of audits and reviews that SQA might perform are shown in Table 8.1. Since the potential workload is enormous, some of these reviews are generally done on statistically selected samples of the work.

8.2.2 SQA Functions

In establishing an SQA function, the basic organizational framework should include the following:[5]

- *Quality Assurance practices*   Adequate development tools, techniques, methods, and standards are defined and available for use as standards for Quality Assurance review.
- *Software project planning evaluation*   If adequate quality practices are not planned at the outset, they will not be implemented.
- *Requirements evaluation*   Since high-quality products are rarely developed from low-quality requirements, the initial requirements must be reviewed for conformance to quality standards.
- *Evaluation of the design process*   Means are required to ensure that the design follows the planned methodologies, that it implements the requirements, and that the quality of the design itself is independently reviewed.

TABLE 8.1
EXAMPLE ITEMS FOR SQA REVIEW

1—SQA ensures that a requirements traceability matrix or similar tool is used to show that the product specifications cover the requirements.

2—SQA verifies that an implementation traceability matrix or similar tool is used to show that the product specifications are implemented in the design.

3—SQA reviews documentation samples to verify that they are produced and maintained according to standards.

4—SQA checks appropriate samples of development records to ensure they are properly maintained and adequately represent the software design.

5—SQA periodically verifies that SCM is maintaining proper baseline control as well as full change records for requirements, design, code, test, and documentation.

6—SQA certifies that all subcontractors' SQA functions are adequately monitoring the performance of their organizations.

7—SQA reviews all plans to ensure they include the required content.

8—SQA selectively monitors the performance of the development, documentation, and test activities to ensure consistency with the approved plans and standards.

9—SQA verifies that all specified tests and peer reviews are properly conducted, that the required results and data are recorded, and that suitable follow-up actions are performed.

10—SQA audits the Change Control Board procedures to verify that they are effectively implemented as planned.

11—SQA selectively reviews the resulting design, code, and documentation to ensure that they adhere to standards.

- □ *Evaluation of coding practices*   Appropriate coding practices must be established and used.
- □ *Evaluating the software integration and test process*   A quality testing program has been established, testing is performed by an independent group that is both motivated and capable of finding problems (i.e., not development), test planning begins early, and the quality of the testing itself is reviewed.
- □ *In-process evaluation of the management and project control process*   By making sure that the management processes are working, SQA helps ensure that the entire organization is focused on producing a quality result.
- □ *Tailoring of Quality Assurance procedures*   The Software Quality Assurance plan should be tailored to the unique needs of each project.

A sample set of SQA tasks for the various project phases is shown in Table 8.2.

8.2.3 SQA Reporting

It is easy for an SQA organization to become ineffective. Without some motivating force they will often degenerate to counting defects and arguing over unimportant details. One SQA organization played it safe by non-concurring with every product shipment. In the escalation meetings, they justified their story by presenting a long list of defects. These were always a surprise, so days were wasted before development could show that the defects were largely punctuation or spelling issues that would not affect operational quality. These details were fixed, of course, and the product was quickly shipped.

The one simple rule on SQA reporting is that it not be under the software development manager. Project schedules are always tight, so these line managers are not likely to listen sympathetically to reports of inadequate test plans, human factors problems, or documentation errors. SQA should report to a high-enough management level to have some chance of influencing priorities and obtaining the resources and time to fix the key problems.

Reporting level, however, is a trade-off. With lower-level reporting, working relationships with development are generally better, while the ability to influence priorities is reduced. Since there is no simple solution that meets all needs, a specific reporting level decision should be made for each organization. There are, however, a few general guidelines:

- SQA should not report to the project manager.
- SQA should report somewhere within the local laboratory or plant organization.
- There should typically be no more than one management position between SQA and the senior location manager.
- SQA should always have a "dotted-line" relationship to a senior corporate quality executive.
- Whenever possible, SQA should report to someone who has a vested interest in software quality, like the staff head responsible for field service.

It is easy for SQA to become discouraged and revert to bureaucratic defect counting. Since it is hard to fight indefinitely for an abstract principle, it helps to have SQA report to someone who is actually affected by poor software quality. What better organization to have the parachute packing QA group report to than to the paratroopers' commander?

8.3 Launching the SQA Program

The essential first step in establishing an SQA function is to secure top management agreement on its goals. Since the senior managers must resolve all major SQA issues, they must agree in advance on the basis for doing so. If they do not, they will not back SQA in disputes with line management, and without such backing SQA cannot be effective.

TABLE 8.2
SAMPLE SQA TASKS BY PROGRAM PHASE

	Software Development Phases		
	Concept Exploration	Requirements Analysis	Preliminary Design
Configuration management	Assist on policy development	Review SCM plan and develop audit procedures	Audit for SCM plan compliance
Reviews and audits	Participate in requirements review	Participate in software design reviews	Participate in preliminary design inspections
Software specification design and production	Review software specifications for compliance with customer specs	Review preliminary interface specs	Review preliminary design and final interface specs Review preliminary operator manual Audit initial development records
Tools, techniques, and methodology	Review what is available	Review for applicability	Review validation of tools
Software testing			Review requirements for testability
Corrective action	Define corrective action procedure for software and documentation		Monitor design deficiency correction procedure
Subcontractor	Review subcontractor QA system and policy Write SQA requirements for subcontractor	Review subcontractor specs for requirements traceability Approve subcontractor SQA plan	Audit subcontractor SQA program with respect to design standards Monitor subcontractor SQA plan implementation
Plan implementation	Define SQA responsibilities, personnel requirements, and tools	Implement SQA plan	Review SQA plan and monitor for compliance
Management monitoring	Review software development plan and audit procedures	Participate in status meetings Review status reports	Audit development plan for work assignments Participate in status meetings Review reports
Delivered item inspections		Inspect preliminary interface specs	Inspect preliminary design and final interface specs, and preliminary operator manuals

TABLE 8.2 (continued)

Software Development Phases

Detailed Design	Coding	Integration/Test	Operation/ Maintenance
Audit for SCM plan compliance	Audit for SCM plan compliance to standards Audit development records for maintenance	Audit Library Audit SCM compliance Audit baselines Review development records	Audit Library Participate in CCB Audit SCM compliance
Participate in design inspections	Participate in code inspections		
Review final design specs and final operator manual Audit development progress Verify requirements traceability matrix	Audit code for compliance to standards Audit development records for maintenance	Review product specs Final development audit Verify test verification and design implementation matrices	Review updated documents Audit development record updates
Review use of tools in design	Monitor use and maintenance of tools	Monitor use and maintenance of tools	Review validation of operational tools
Review preliminary test plans, procedures, and tools	Review final test plans and procedures Witness development tests	Witness integration tests and acceptance tests Certify test reports	
Audit all deficiencies for correction Audit problem/change request system Analyze design problems for trends	Audit code deficiencies for correction Audit problem/change request system Analyze code problems for trends	Audit for correction of test deficiencies Audit problem/change system Analyze problems for trends	Audit for correction of customer problems Audit problem/change system Analyze problems for trends
Audit subcontractor compliance with design standards Monitor subcontractor SQA plan implementation	Audit subcontractor compliance with coding standards Monitor subcontractor SQA plan implementation	Monitor subcontractor test Witness final tests and acceptance Monitor subcontractor SQA implementation	Review/approve subcontractor changes
Review/update SQA plan Monitor SQA plan compliance	Review/update SQA plan Monitor SQA plan compliance	Review/update SQA plan Monitor SQA plan compliance	Update SQA plan
Audit development records for work initiation, management review of status, resources, schedules	Participate in status meetings Review status reports Audit development records	Participate in status meetings Review status reports Audit development records after final test	
Inspect final design specs, operator manuals, and preliminary test plans/procedures	Inspect final test plans/procedures	Inspect product specs Inspect test report and deliverables	Inspect updated documents

The eight steps for launching an SQA program are:[8]

1. *Initiate the SQA program*   The key SQA roles are defined and management publicly commits to them. This results in documented goals and responsibilities and an identified leader.

2. *Identify SQA issues*   The SQA leader and initial staff work with project management to identify the key issues for SQA attention.

3. *Write the SQA plan*   The SQA plan defines SQA's audit and control activities and identifies the required standards and procedures. The SQA plan is integrated with the SCM and project plans.

4. *Establish standards*   The standards and procedures that guide SQA are developed and approved. Any special project provisions are also reviewed and approved.

5. *Establish the SQA function*   The SQA function is staffed to perform the established plan.

6. *Conduct training and promote the SQA program*   SQA personnel are briefed on the SQA plan and given needed training on the project and SQA methods. Appropriate meetings and reviews are held to acquaint project personnel with the purpose and roles of SQA.

7. *Implement the SQA plan*   Each key SQA activity is assigned to specific SQA personnel, a schedule is developed, management monitoring is established, and an issue resolution system is implemented.

8. *Evaluate the SQA program*   The SQA function is periodically audited to determine its effectiveness in performing its mission. Needed corrective actions are identified and implemented.

While these basic actions are reasonably self-evident, a reading of some of the available SQA literature provides helpful background on the expected issues and the most practical approaches.[3, 5, 7, 8, 9]

Points 3 and 8, however, deserve further elaboration. In producing the SQA plan, a statistically sound sampling approach is essential. It is generally not practical for SQA to review every development action or product item, so the plan should identify the sampling system that will most effectively use the available SQA resources. Examples of possible sampling methods are:

- □ Ensure that all required design and code inspections are performed, and participate (possibly as monitor) in a selected set (see Chapter 10).
- □ Review all inspection reports and analyze those outside of established control limits (see Chapters 10 and 15).
- □ Ensure that all required tests are performed and test reports produced (see Chapter 11).
- □ Examine a selected set of test reports for accuracy and completeness (see Chapter 11).

▢ Review all module test results and further study the data on those modules with test histories that are outside of established control limits (see Chapters 11, 15, and 16).

With an immature software process it is difficult for SQA to do an effective statistical sampling job, but as maturity improves, the assurance function itself will become more effective.

Regarding point 8, SQA evaluation, it is important to establish means to evaluate SQA effectiveness. One way is to gather data on post-shipment product quality and relate it to the prior SQA evaluations. While this may appear to hold SQA responsible for product quality, it does provide an objective measure. Every product that has serious end user quality problems should be studied to see what was wrong with the software process that produced it. If the established process was not used, both SQA and development management should be faulted for not doing their jobs properly. If, however, the process had been properly implemented, then the process itself needs attention. This is not an SQA problem (see Chapters 13 and 14).

Another way to evaluate SQA performance is to periodically establish review teams consisting of members from other SQA organizations, if available, as well as some experienced software professionals who are not currently involved in product development work. Such peer reviews can help to identify the strengths and weaknesses of the SQA operation.

8.4 The SQA Plan

Each development and maintenance project should have a Software Quality Assurance plan (SQAP) that specifies its goals, the SQA tasks to be performed, the standards against which the development work is to be measured, and the procedures and organizational structure.

The IEEE standard for SQAP preparation contains the following outline:[7]

1. Purpose
2. Reference Documents
3. Management
4. Documentation
5. Standards, Practices, and Conventions
6. Reviews and Audits
7. Software Configuration Management
8. Problem Reporting and Corrective Action
9. Tools, Techniques, and Methodologies

10. Code Control

11. Media Control

12. Supplier Control

13. Records Collection, Maintenance, and Retention

Many of these topics are relatively clear from their headings, but a few warrant further comment.

The documentation section should describe the documentation to be produced and how it is to be reviewed. An example of a minimum set of items is shown in Table 8.3.

The section on standards, practices, and conventions specifies a minimum content of:

□ Documentation standards

□ Logic structure standards

□ Coding standards

□ Commentary standards

As will be seen in the next chapter, many more standards are required to properly define the operation of a software organization.

The SQAP section on reviews and audits should describe both the technical and the managerial reviews and audits to be conducted. The IEEE standard includes the items shown in Table 8.4. A more detailed discussion of reviews and inspections is included in Chapter 10.

8.5 SQA Considerations

Many Software Quality Assurance organizations fail to have much impact on software quality. While there are many potential reasons, the most common ones are:

□ *SQA organizations are rarely staffed with sufficiently experienced or knowledgeable people.* Recruiting for SQA is difficult because software professionals typically prefer development assignments and management understandably wants to assign the best designers to design work.

□ *The SQA management team is often not capable of negotiating with development.* This depends on the caliber of the SQA management team, which in turn is governed by the caliber of the SQA professional staff.

□ *Senior management often backs development over SQA on a large percentage of issues.* Development then ignores the SQA issues, and SQA degenerates into a series of useless low-level debates.

TABLE 8.3
SUGGESTED SQAP DOCUMENTATION [7]

The Software Requirements Specification   Each required software function, performance parameter, interface, or other attribute should be specified with sufficient precision to permit its verification. The SQAP identifies the verification methods to be used.

The Software Design Description   A description of the major components, databases, and internal interfaces.

The Software Verification and Validation Plan   A description of the methods used to verify that the requirements are implemented in the design, that the design is implemented in the code, and that the code meets the requirements.

The Software Verification and Validation Report   The means used to report on the SQA verification and validation activities.

User Documentation   The documentation required for proper installation, operation, and maintenance of the software, together with the planned review methods.

Other   Other documentation as called for in the Software Development Plan, the Software Configuration Management Plan, and the Standards and Procedures Manual, together with the planned review methods.

□ *Many SQA organizations operate without suitably documented and approved development standards and procedures.*   Without such standards, they do not have a sound basis for judging development work, and every issue becomes a matter of opinion. Development invariably wins such generalized debates, particularly when schedules are tight.

□ *Software development groups rarely produce verifiable quality plans.*   SQA is then trapped into arguments over specific defects rather than overall quality indicators. In such cases, they win the individual battles but invariably lose the war.

The final point, the lack of verifiable quality plans, is worth elaboration. It is typical for SQA to non-concur with a system shipment because too many errors were found in test. Development then proposes to fix the most critical bugs before shipment. The debate then revolves around which bugs should be fixed before shipment and how the balance should be handled.

While this resolution may seem reasonable, it misses the key point. SQA properly sensed that the product was deficient but was trapped into arguing about details. If product quality really was poor, however, the repair of these few bugs would not fix it. SQA should thus concentrate on whether all steps of the development process were properly followed. Those steps that were either incompletely performed or entirely omitted should be identified and corrective actions taken. If comprehensive inspections were not conducted, for example, then quality is likely poor, regardless of the test results. Similarly, if data was not gathered on all test phases, no trends are available to estimate product quality. These issues are discussed in more detail in Chapter 16.

TABLE 8.4
EXAMPLES OF SQAP REVIEWS AND AUDITS [7]

Software Requirements Review   To ensure the adequacy of the requirements

Preliminary Design Review   To evaluate the adequacy of the preliminary design

Critical Design Review   To determine if the Software Design Description satisfies the Software Requirements Specification

Software Verification and Validation Review   To evaluate the adequacy and completeness of the Software Verification and Validation Plan

Functional Audit   An audit prior to software delivery to verify that the requirements were met

Physical Audit   An audit prior to software delivery to determine that the software and documentation are consistent with the design and ready for delivery

In-Process Audits   A statistical sample of the development process is audited to verify the consistency of the code versus the design and interface specifications, the design versus the requirements, and the test plans versus the requirements

Managerial Reviews   Independent reviews are conducted of the execution of the Quality Assurance plan

The most effective SQA arguments are based on established quality standards and plans that spell out the required steps for proper development work. When these standards are not followed, SQA should promptly non-concur rather than wait until the last minute. After system test, management is faced with the choice of shipping a poor product or missing an external commitment. Not surprisingly, they generally side with the developers when they propose to fix the known bugs before shipment. Since no one knows how many more bugs are in the product, any other approach is guesswork. In guessing games, software quality generally suffers. The best answer is a quantified and verifiable quality plan with appropriate standards and procedures to support it (see Chapter 16).

8.6 SQA People

Getting good people into SQA is one of the most difficult problems software managers face. The practice of starting new hires in SQA is a partial solution that can be effective only if there are enough experienced people there already. Rotation schemes can also be effective, but unfortunately software development is generally adept at transferring their poorer performers to SQA and not taking them back.

One effective solution is to require that all new development managers be promoted from SQA. This would mean that potential managers would spend six months to a year in SQA before being promoted into management back in their home departments. While this is an extreme measure, it can be effective.

Any reasonable system can work if it has the full backing of senior management, but no staffing method will work if it does not. For SQA to be effective, they must have good people and full management backing.

8.7 Independent Verification and Validation

In DoD contracts, it is often common to have a separate Independent Verification and Validation (IV&V) organization involved. Its role is to provide an independent monitor of the development or maintenance organization's performance. While there can easily be confusion regarding the relative roles of IV&V and SQA, the distinction should be clear. Development management uses SQA to monitor its own organization and to ensure that established standards and procedures are followed. IV&V does essentially the same thing for the customer.

Another important difference between IV&V and SQA is that IV&V can and should capitalize on the existence of SQA. If SQA is working effectively, IV&V need not duplicate its work, and if it is not, IV&V must not try to replace it. Their role is to highlight this shortcoming and to get it fixed.

Another important IV&V role is to ensure that the customer's needs are adequately reflected in the work. While a structured set of standards, procedures, and requirements can greatly improve the chances of producing a good result, no bureaucratic approach can possibly produce truly great products. This is done through the interaction of creative designers and thoughtful application experts in a supportive development environment.

The crucial role of IV&V is to ensure that the right skills and attitudes are in place. While they should also review the standards and procedures, they must look beyond them to see if a first-class software engineering job is being done and if the key risks and feasibility issues are being addressed. Even when no formal IV&V function is used, either the customer or senior development management should have some independent consulting or advisory group perform this role.

As shown in Table 8.5, DeMillo has studied the performance of several DoD contractors on the respective roles of SQA and IV&V.[4] While there is considerable variation, and two contractors did not report any IV&V activity, it is clear that SQA is more involved in the internal workings of the contracting organization, while IV&V tends to look more at application-related issues.

Since IV&V groups are often expensive, they should focus on the way the contractor's work is done rather than try to duplicate it. They should also, of course, focus on the broader issues just outlined.

TABLE 8.5
SQA AND IV&V Activities [4]

Summary	Contractor					
SQA Activities	1	2	3	4	5	6
Review requirement and design specs	X	X			X	X
Review test plans and procedures	X	X		X		
Review all deliverables		X	X			
Attend design reviews	X		X		X	X
Attend code reviews	X		X		X	
Witness acceptance tests	X	X	X	X	X	X
Perform final configuration audit		X	X		X	X
IV&V Activities						
Independent requirements and design analysis		X		X		X
Algorithm studies		X		X		X
Participation in code inspections		X				
Independent code analysis		X		X		
Witness acceptance tests		X				
Approve test plans and procedures						X
Independent testing			X			

R. A. DeMillo, W. M. McCracken, R. J. Martin, and J. F. Passafiume, *Software Testing and Evaluation,* © 1987, p. 219. Reprinted by permission of The Benjamin/Cummings Publishing Company, Menlo Park, CA.

8.8 Summary

The role of SQA is to assure management that the software development work is performed the way it is supposed to be. Its prime benefit to management is the assurance it provides them that their directions are actually implemented. The

SQA organization is not responsible for producing quality products or for making quality plans; these are development jobs. SQA is responsible for auditing the quality actions of the line organization and alerting management to any deviations.

SQA can be effective when they report through an independent chain of command, when they are properly staffed with competent professionals, and when they see their role as supporting the development and maintenance personnel in improving product quality. If SQA fulfills its role, and if senior management refuses to allow line management to commit or to ship products until the SQA issues have been addressed, then SQA can help management improve product quality.

Each development and maintenance project should have a software quality assurance plan that specifies its goals, the SQA tasks to be performed, the standards against which the development work is to be measured, and the procedures and organizational structure to be used.

There are five common reasons why many Software Quality Assurance organizations fail to be effective in improving software quality: they are rarely staffed with sufficiently experienced or knowledgeable people; their management team is not capable of negotiating with development; senior management backs development over SQA on a large percentage of the issues; SQA operates without suitably documented and approved development standards and procedures; and most software development groups do not have verifiable quality plans.

Getting good people into SQA is one of the most difficult problems software managers face. Any reasonable staffing system can work, however, if it has the full backing of senior management—but no staffing method will work if it does not.

References

1. Boehm, B. W., J. R. Brown, and M. Lipow. "Quantitative evaluation of software quality," *Proceedings of the 2nd International Conference on Software Engineering,* IEEE, San Francisco, October 13–15, 1976, pp. 592–605.

2. Buckley, F. J. "The search for software quality, or one more trip down the yellow brick road," *ACM SIGSOFT,* vol. 11, no. 1, January 1986, pp. 16–18.

3. Chow, T. S. "Tutorial, Software Quality Assurance," IEEE cat. no. EH0223-8, 1984.

4. DeMillo, R. A., W. M. McCracken, R. J. Martin, and J. F. Passafiume. *Software Testing and Evaluation,* Menlo Park, CA: Benjamin/Cummings, 1987.

5. Evans, M. W., and J. J. Marciniak. *Software Quality Assurance and Management,* New York: Wiley, 1987.

6. Humphrey, W. S. "The IBM large-systems software development process: objectives and direction," *IBM Systems Journal,* vol. 24, no. 2, 1985.

7. "IEEE Standard for Software Quality Assurance Plans," IEEE Std. 730-1984, New York.

8. Kalmback, H. "Software Quality Assurance in a changing development environment," *AFIPS National Computer Conference Proceedings,* vol. 55, June 16–19, 1986, Las Vegas, NV.

9. Schulmeyer, G. G., and J. I. McManus. *Handbook of Software Quality Assurance,* New York: Van Nostrand Reinhold, 1987.

10. Thayer, R. H., A. Pyster, and R. C. Wood. "Validating solutions to major problems in software engineering project management," *IEEE Computer,* vol. 15, no. 8, August 1982, pp. 65–77.

11. Walker, M. G. "Auditing software development projects: a control mechanism for the Digital Systems development methodology," *Proceedings,* IEEE COMPCON, Spring 1979, pp. 310–314.

 **Software Engineering Institute**

PART THREE

The Defined Process

Once organizations have mastered the basic capabilities described in Part II, the performance of their projects will have sufficiently stabilized to permit orderly process improvement. The priority needs are then to improve from Level 2 to Level 3. This improvement will establish a more consistent and uniform process across the organization and provide a coherent framework for organized learning. Part III describes the key topics that Level 2 organizations must address to advance to Level 3. A more detailed listing of the total set of improvement actions is included in Appendix A. The subjects requiring priority management attention at this point are standards, software inspections, testing, advanced configuration management topics, process models and architecture, and the Software Engineering Process Group.

Chapter 9 describes the benefits of standards, gives examples of their use, and discusses the establishment of a standards program.

Chapter 10 answers the questions: What are software inspections, how are they conducted, and what are their benefits? This chapter also describes how an inspection program is initiated. More detailed inspection guidelines are included in Appendix C.

Chapter 11 covers the principles of testing, some basic testing methods, test planning, and test management.

Chapter 12 builds on the basic configuration management topics of Chapter 7. It covers the management of requirements and design changes as well as configuration accounting and auditing.

A defined software process provides a framework for orderly planning, management, and process improvement. Chapter 13 covers process models and process architectures, and how these can be used to support and improve the software process.

Chapter 14 describes the Software Engineering Process Group (SEPG), why it is important, and what it does. It also outlines the considerations involved in establishing an SEPG.

Once the topics in Part III have been mastered, the organization's process will be sufficiently well defined and standardized to permit measurement and statistical control. These are the topics of Part IV.

9

Software Standards

A standard is a rule or basis for comparison that is used to assess the size, content, value, or quality of an object or activity. In software, two kinds of standards are used to define the way the software is developed and maintained. One class describes the nature of the object to be produced, while the other defines the way the work is to be performed. Typical examples of software standards are shown in Table 9.1.[9] There are also standards for languages, coding conventions, commenting, change flagging, error reporting, and so forth.

Procedures are closely related to standards. For example, Tables 9.1 and 9.2 show several instances of a standard and a procedure for essentially the same topic. There are standards for software reviews and audits as well as procedures for conducting them. The distinction is that a review standard specifies review contents, preparatory materials, participants, responsibilities, and the resulting data and reports. The procedure for conducting the review describes how the work is actually to be done, by whom, when, and what is done with the results. These standards and procedures are what Deming refers to as operational definitions: something everyone can communicate about and work toward.[5]

There are many different ways to establish standards for an organization. Figure 9.1 shows the overall framework that TRW established for its development policies, procedures, and standards.[7] TRW has also published a guidebook of DoD regulations, specifications, and standards. Although it is somewhat out of date, the guidebook does provide a helpful overview of a number of military software standards.[2]

TABLE 9.1
REPRESENTATIVE SOFTWARE STANDARDS

Software quality assurance plans
Software development notebooks
Software development plans
Software reviews and audits
Software requirements
Software design documentation
Software test plans
Software Quality Assurance reviews
Software Configuration Management
Problem reporting/corrective action
Software documentation

9.1 Definitions

Before discussing standards and procedures, it is necessary to establish some definitions. A number of software terms are commonly used almost interchangeably, so it is easy to be confused. These terms can be usefully grouped into categories, with the meanings understood in this book, as follows:

1. Authoritative direction on what is to be done

   □ *Policy* A governing principle, typically used as the basis for regulations, procedures, or standards and generally stated by the highest authority in the organization.

   □ *Regulation* A rule, law, or instruction, typically established by some legislative or regulatory body with penalties for noncompliance.

   □ *Specification* The precise and verifiable description of the characteristics of a product. A process specification would similarly define a method, procedure, or process to be used in performing a task. Specifications are often produced by technical experts as part of a contractual agreement.

2. The characterization of how a task is to be performed or the required characteristics of the result

   □ *Guideline* A suggested practice, method, or procedure, typically issued by some authority.

   □ *Procedure* A defined way to do something, generally embodied in a procedures manual. Alternatively, as in programs, a named portion of a computer program that performs a specific task.[8]

   □ *Standard* A rule or basis for comparison that is used to assess size, content, or value, typically established by common practice or by a designated standards body.

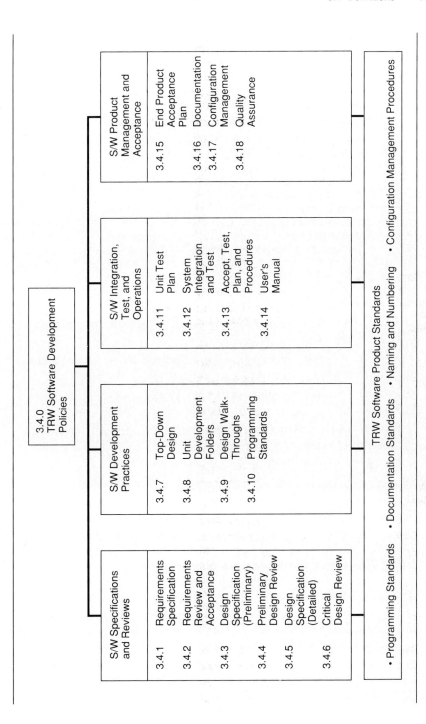

FIGURE 9.1
TRW software development policies, procedures, and standards.[7]
E. A. Goldberg, "Applying corporate development policies," *Software Development: Management.* The 71st Infotech State of the Art Conference, Maidenhead, England: Infotech, Ltd., 1980.

TABLE 9.2
REPRESENTATIVE SOFTWARE PROCEDURES

Auditing software development notebooks
Reviewing a software development plan
Conducting software reviews
Conducting software audits
Reviewing software requirements
Reviewing software design documents
Reviewing software test plans
Auditing the software testing process
Conducting SQA reviews
Performing Software Configuration Management
Auditing Software Configuration Management systems
Handling problem reporting/corrective action
Auditing problem reporting/correction action systems
Reviewing software documentation

3. The ways in which tasks are accomplished

☐ *Convention*   A general agreement on practices, methods, or procedures, typically arrived at by explicit agreement.

☐ *Method*   A regular, orderly procedure or process for performing a task, typically defined by an expert.

☐ *Practice*   A usual procedure or process, typically a matter of habit or tacit agreement.

☐ *Process*   A defined way to perform some activity, generally involving a sequence of methods or procedures designed to accomplish a specified result, and typically established by technical specialists.

The focus in this chapter is on the second group, guidelines, procedures, and standards.

9.2 The Reasons for Software Standards

Standards are needed when many people, products, or tools must coexist. They are essential for establishing common support environments, performing integration, or conducting system test. Aron points out that "large software organizations are finding that the value of one set of uniform procedures for the whole shop justifies a significant investment in training and procedure development."[1] The fact that everyone knows and understands a common way of doing the same tasks makes it easier for the professionals to move between projects, reduces the need for training, and permits a uniform method for reviewing the work and its status.

Standards also promote the consistent use of better tools and methods. When everyone uses common coding conventions and commenting guidelines, for example, it is practical for programmers to review each others' work and easier for them to understand it. This both facilitates design and code inspections and improves the maintainability of the finished product. It would be hard to conceive of an efficient programming shop in which everyone used different languages and conventions.

While the standardization of programming languages is generally recognized as necessary, the need for standards on documentation, error reporting, test plans, and estimating, for example, is just as great. With modern, large-scale programs we have passed the point where the lone genius can personally support an undocumented creation. Too many people are involved and most programs last far too long to make such private arrangements advisable.

Finally, as discussed in Chapter 8, the SQA people need approved standards and procedures to do their work. Without them most quality debates reduce to generalized disagreements. Since these disagreements usually arise when schedules are tight, management is anxious to find a quick fix. The lack of an approved standard leaves the organization with no framework for such decisions.

9.3 Benefits of Standards

While there is little quantitative evidence that supports the use of standards, most experienced software managers can cite at least one standard that was key to a program's success. In the case of IBM's OS/360, a standard assembler language permitted cooperative development by 13 laboratories in 6 countries. The later use of a standard higher-level language (PLS) also saved a great deal of money in development and support.

Thayer has surveyed software managers to determine their views on the key software problems and their most effective solutions.[14] Of all the solutions listed, the use and enforcement of standards and procedures ranked first. Not surprisingly, Thayer also found that standards were most effective when the project manager personally implemented them on a project basis. While standards alone will not make the difference between project success and failure, they clearly help.

9.4 Examples of Some Major Standards

IBM's Federal Systems Division (FSD) has established a family of standards for software development, as shown in Table 9.3.[11] These were developed by a

TABLE 9.3
IBM FSD SOFTWARE DESIGN PRACTICES [11]

Systematic programming practices

Logical expression	Prescribes mathematics-based techniques for precise expression and reasoning that apply to all phases of software development
Program expression	Defines control, data, and program structures for recording program designs
Program design	Specifies a process of stepwise refinement for recording structured program designs
Program design verification	Prescribes function-theoretic techniques for proving the correctness of structured programs

Systematic design practices

Data design	Specifies the use of abstract data objects and operations in a high-level design framework
Modular design	Defines techniques for designing synchronous software systems, based on state machines and design modules

Advanced design practices

Software system specification	Defines a process based on state machines for creating a specification as the cornerstone documentation of a software system
Real-time design	Defines a stagewise process for designing asynchronous software to achieve correct concurrent operation, with optimization to meet real-time processing requirements

Copyright 1980 International Business Machines Corporation. Reprinted with permission from the *IBM Systems Journal*, vol. 19, no. 4.

central group, an education program was established, and the management team was trained before the professionals took the courses. Under the leadership of Dr. H. D. Mills, a mathematical approach to programming was coupled with a management-first introduction plan.[10] The standards have been an important contributor to the high quality and productivity of IBM's FSD programming groups.

Dyer has also described a set of code management standards that are used by IBM FSD.[6] These cover programming languages, coding standards and conventions, computer product support software, the hierarchical program control library, and the software development environment. The language standard specifies the use of high-order programming languages (HOLs), with the limited exceptions shown in Table 9.4. For example, HOLs are to be used entirely for the top category of programs listed in this table.

Some of the other items covered by these IBM standards and conventions were coding standards, interfaces with operating system software, procedures for using a program support library, and the packaging of code into controllable

TABLE 9.4
IBM FSD LANGUAGE RECOMMENDATIONS FOR CLASSES OF
SOFTWARE PRODUCTS [6]

Language Recommendation	Class of Software
High-order language (HOL)	Program development and generation Compiler/assembler Link editor/loader Utilities Library support Data reduction Applications
HOL with assembly assist	Program development and generation Hardware simulation System simulation Diagnostics
Assembly with HOL elements	Executive
Assembly	Data recording/measurement Microcode

objects. The conventions included rules for naming programs, for designating variables, and for writing comments. To permit consistent and efficient use of a library system, naming practices were provided for version numbering, revision levels, and statement identification. Provisions were also made for standard operating system interfaces, library conventions for identification and status reporting, and packaging standards. Examples of other practices and procedures for use in software development and maintenance are provided by R. C. Tausworthe in his book on software standards.[13]

9.5 Establishing Software Standards

Before establishing an aggressive standards development program, it is wise to formulate an overall plan that considers the available standards, the priority needs of the organization, the status of the projects, the available staff skills, and the means for standards enforcement. While it is important to establish standards, it is also important to concentrate on those standards that can be implemented in a reasonable period and that will provide the most immediate benefit to the organization.

The establishment of standards starts with an examination of the organization's standards and procedures needs. These should be considered in three categories, and an effort should be made to maintain a balance of emphasis among them. Suggested categories and examples are:

1. Management and planning standards and procedures
   □ Configuration management
   □ Estimating and costing
   □ Software Quality Assurance
   □ Status reporting

2. Development process standards and methods
   □ Requirements specification
   □ Design
   □ Documentation
   □ Coding
   □ Integration and test
   □ Reviews, walkthroughs, and inspections

3. Tool and process standards
   □ Product naming
   □ Size and cost measures
   □ Defect counting and recording
   □ Code entry and editing tools
   □ Documentation systems
   □ Languages
   □ Library system

There are many potentially valuable standards that can be produced in each category. Unfortunately, when a standards group has unique skills or convictions, it often focuses in one area to the exclusion of the others. This is invariably a mistake, for each area has critical needs and it is important to maintain a balanced focus on all key topics.

9.5.1 The Standards Development Process

Standards development involves the following steps:

1. Establish a standards strategy that defines priorities and recognizes prior work.
2. Distribute, review, and maintain this strategy.
3. Select individuals or small working groups to develop the top-priority standards.

4. This development effort should build on prior work where available, define the areas of applicability, specify the introduction strategy, and propose an enforcement plan.

5. The draft standards should be widely distributed and reviewed.

6. The standards should be revised to incorporate the review comments and then re-reviewed if the changes are extensive.

7. The standards should initially be implemented in a limited test environment.

8. Based on this test experience, the standards should again be reviewed and revised.

9. Implement and enforce the standards across the defined areas of applicability.

10. Evaluate the effectiveness of the standards in actual practice.

The work of establishing a standard should be done by individuals or small working groups of technical experts. While it is important to use people who have detailed technical knowledge of the subject, it is also essential to involve representatives of the groups who will implement and enforce the standards. Once competent professionals from these key groups have been selected, however, further additions should be restricted. If too many people are involved in this creative process, much time will be wasted and the result is more likely to lack technical coherence.

In establishing a new standard, it is rarely wise to adopt one from another organization without carefully examining its fit to the unique needs of the local users. While it is always helpful to build on prior work, those who will use and enforce the standard must agree that it fits their situation.

Since standards reviews serve both a management and a technical purpose, they should involve all facets of the organization. This involves wide distribution for comment and a fairly formal review process (see Chapter 10). Reviewers should consider the introduction plan, the implementation approach, and the enforcement provisions.

Following the review period, the standard or procedure should be introduced on a trial basis with one or more projects. While it may seem pointless to test something as simple as a standard, there are always implementation problems, and a broadside implementation will invariably raise enough questions to erode management support for the overall standards program. While the degree and extent of testing should be based on individual circumstances, some testing is always advisable.

9.5.2 Maintaining Standards

Standards must be kept current. They should be modified and adjusted based on the experiences in using and enforcing them, on the changes in available technology, and on the varying needs of the projects. If the standards are not maintained, they will gradually become less pertinent to working conditions and enforcement will become progressively less practical. If not corrected, the standard will ultimately become a bureaucratic procedure that takes time without adding value.

The responsibility for maintaining each standard should be assigned to an individual or group. This could be the Software Engineering Process Group described further in Chapter 14, or some other group that has the technical capability and the management charter to handle such technical functions. Generally it is not advisable to assign such responsibilities to the development projects or to the SQA group, who since they are both involved in standards enforcement cannot be objective standards owners. Their people, of course, should participate in any working committees or review groups to the extent they are qualified to do so.

The key responsibilities of standards maintenance are:

▫ Stay aware of standards implementation problems.

▫ Be a source of guidance and advice on using the standard.

▫ Maintain the standards baseline and control changes.

▫ Periodically review the standards to ensure their effectiveness and pertinence.

Standards maintenance should not involve a great deal of work. If a standard needs frequent changes, it probably covers a subject that is not ready for standardization. Until the technology and methods for an area are well known and reasonably stable, standardization should not be attempted. When standards are established too early, they can limit the creative process and impede technology.

The standards and procedures should also be reviewed at least once every three to five years to ensure they are current and needed. If not, they should either be updated or dropped.

9.5.3 Enforcing Standards

As described in Chapter 8, standards enforcement is the basic role of the SQA organization. They do this with a mix of reviews and tests. Exhaustive reviews are most appropriate when automated tools can be used to support the monitoring process or when the standard is so critical that no single deviation is acceptable. Otherwise, statistical samples are sufficient unless major problems are encountered.

Automated tools can be most helpful for policing such items as coding conventions, documentation rules, and naming conventions. Exhaustive reviews are advisable for product plans, delivery commitments, test plans, acceptance tests, configuration management plans, change control procedures, maintenance plans, and requirements walkthroughs. The standards and procedures to be exhaustively reviewed should be selected with care since they are the single most important determinant of SQA resources.

Statistical reviews are used for all other standards and procedures. While the level of sampling should be determined for each case, it is often possible for SQA to provide useful help to development as part of the review. If SQA has a staff of trained inspection moderators, for example, they could act as design and code inspection moderators while simultaneously making sure that the inspections were properly conducted (see Chapter 10).

The effective use of statistical reviews requires that SQA have control over which cases to review and management's support in follow-up actions when the review finds problems. Assuming the samples were properly selected, problems found with the sample must be assumed to exist in the entire population. This is the critical point of any review system, for when deviations are found, the identified problems must be fixed and the full process reexamined to see if there are broader compliance problems. Since much extra work will be required for all the involved parties, management support is essential.

9.6 Standards Versus Guidelines

A standard is appropriate when no further judgment is needed. Standardization makes sense when items are arbitrary and must be done uniformly or when there is one clearly best alternative. The definition of coding or naming conventions, the selection of a programming language, and the use of common design methods are good examples. There are many possible selections, and there may be no clear right or wrong choice, but they must all be done the same way by everyone. These are appropriate subjects for standardization.

Similarly, some standards are essential to the maintenance of business or technical control. Examples are standard cost categories, reporting forms, change approval procedures, and schedule checkpoints. Again, the particular choices are somewhat arbitrary, but standard methods are needed because the support of several different approaches would be expensive and confusing.

There are also many cases in which standards are totally inappropriate. Typically these are cases involving technical judgment. One of the best examples is the specification of limits on module size. Here the evidence is overwhelming that arbitrarily large modules are likely to be complex and hard to maintain. A firm rule that no module can exceed some limit like 200 source statements, however, is not wise. There is conflicting evidence on the effect of module size on the quality or cost of programs, while there is clear evidence that too many small modules cause performance problems.[3, 4] It is unquestionably wise to construct modular programs, but this is too complex a question for arbitrary rules. One approach that has been used successfully is to require that all modules over some limit, say 200 LOC, require special approval. Another approach is to use a complexity metric, such as

McCabe, and require that all modules with complexity over 10 be specially authorized.[12]

Clearly it is not wise to establish a standard unless there is convincing evidence that it is always the right thing to do. In questionable cases, a guideline should be used or the standard should have some well-known and practical escape provisions. While such approaches have much the same effect as standards, they recognize that exceptions occasionally make sense.

9.7 Summary

A standard is a rule or basis for comparison that is used to assess the size, content, value, or quality of something. While there are many aspects to this topic, the focus in this chapter is on guidelines, procedures, and standards.

Standards promote the consistent use of better tools and methods, and they support the SQA people in doing their work. Before establishing an aggressive standards development program, it is wise to formulate an overall plan that considers the available standards, the priority needs of the organization, the status of the projects, the available staff skills, and the means for standards enforcement. The actual work of establishing a standard should be done by individuals or small working groups of technical experts.

Standards must be kept current, but standards maintenance should not involve a great deal of work. If a standard needs frequent changes, it probably covers a subject that is not ready for standardization. The standards and procedures should also be reviewed at least once every three to five years to ensure they are current and needed. Standards enforcement is the basic role of the SQA organization. Automated tools can be most helpful for policing some items, exhaustive reviews are advisable for others, and statistical reviews are used for the balance.

A standard is appropriate when no further judgment is needed. There are also many cases in which standards are totally inappropriate. Typically these are cases involving technical judgment. Clearly it is not wise to establish a standard unless there is convincing evidence that it is always the right thing to do.

References

1. Aron, J. D. *The Program Development Process, Part II*. Reading, MA: Addison-Wesley, 1983.

2. "ASD TR-78-6, Airborne Systems Software Acquisition Engineering Guidebook for Regulations, Specifications, and Standards," Redondo Beach, CA: TRW Defense and Space Systems Group, November 1977.

3. Bowen, J. B. "Module size: a standard or heuristic," *The Journal of Systems and Software*, 4, 327–332, 1984.

4. Camp, J. W., and E. P. Jensen. "Cost of modularity," *Proceedings of Symposium in Computer Software Engineering,* Polytechnic Institute of New York, 1976, pp. 215–224.

5. Deming, W. E. *Out of the Crisis.* Cambridge, MA: MIT Center for Advanced Engineering Study, 1982.

6. Dyer, M. "The management of software engineering, part IV: software development practices," *IBM Systems Journal,* vol. 19, no. 4, 1980.

7. Goldberg, E. A., "Applying corporate development policies," *Software Development Management,* The 71st Infotech State of the Art Conference, Maidenhead, England: Infotech, Ltd., 1980 (in J. D. Aron, part II, p. 533).

8. "IEEE Standard Glossary of Software Engineering Terminology," ANSI/IEEE Std. 729-1983.

9. Kalmbach, H. "Software Quality Assurance in a changing development environment," *AFIPS Conference Proceedings,* vol. 55, pp. 51–59, National Computer Conference, June 16–19, 1986, Las Vegas, NV.

10. Linger, R. C., H. D. Mills, and B. I. Witt. *Structured Programming, Theory and Practice.* Reading, MA: Addison-Wesley, 1979.

11. Linger, R. C., "The management of software engineering, part III: software design practices," *IBM Systems Journal,* vol 19, no. 4, 1980.

12. McCabe, T. J. "A complexity measure," *IEEE Trans. on Software Engineering,* vol. SE-2, no. 4, December 1976.

13. Tausworthe, R. C. "Standardized Development of Computer Software, part II, Standards." Pasadena, CA: Jet Propulsion Laboratory, California Institute of Technology, 1978.

14. Thayer, R. H., A. Physter, and R. C. Wood. "Validating solutions to major problems in software engineering project management," *IEEE Computer,* vol. 15, no. 8, August 1982, p. 65–77.

10

Software Inspections

Software inspections provide a powerful way to improve the quality and productivity of the software process. This chapter describes inspections and provides an overview of how they are conducted. Additional details on specific inspection methods and techniques are included in Appendix C. The software inspection is a peer review of a programmer's work to find problems and to improve quality. It is based on Weinberg's concept of egoless programming.[13] Weinberg refers to *cognitive dissonance* as the human tendency to self-justify actions. Since we tend not to see evidence that conflicts with our strongly held beliefs, our ability to find errors in our own work is impaired. Because of this tendency many programming organizations have established independent test groups that specialize in finding problems. Similar principles have led to software inspections.

The fundamental objective of inspections is to improve the quality of programs by assisting programmers to recognize and fix their own errors early in the software engineering process. With large-scale, complex programs, a brief inspection by competent co-workers invariably turns up mistakes the programmers could not have found by themselves. Self-hypnosis carries over into testing also. An error often starts with an early misconception that is repeated in the design, the code, the documentation, and even the testing. This is why many logic bugs are not found until final program use—unless, that is, they are spotted by someone in an inspection.

Inspections help to motivate better work. When programmers know their work will be critically examined by their peers in an inspection, they are encouraged to work more carefully either to avoid being embarrassed by sloppy mistakes or through the pride of exhibiting a quality work product. By enlisting others in identifying their errors, programmers actually end up doing better work themselves.

While inspections will not solve all problems, they are enormously effective. As shown in more detail at the end of this chapter, inspections have been demonstrated to improve both quality and productivity by impressive factors. Inspections are not magic and they should not be considered a replacement for testing, but all software organizations should use inspections or similar technical review methods in all major aspects of their work. This includes requirements, design, implementation, test, maintenance, and documentation.

10.1 Types of Reviews

There are many different kinds of reviews and many different names for them, so it is important to draw some distinctions. A detailed characterization of the most common types of software reviews is shown in Table 10.1.[11] Management and technical reviews are generally conducted for management and typically provide information for management action. Inspections and walkthroughs, on the other hand, are peer examinations aimed at assisting the producers in improving their work.

Inspections are the focus of this chapter. Their intent is to examine work technically and provide the producers with an independent assessment of those product areas where improvements are needed. As can be seen in Table 10.1, walkthroughs are generally less formal and are often conducted in an educational format. Inspections, on the other hand, generally have a formal format, attendance is specified, and data is reported on the results.

There are as many types of inspections as there are types of work products. It is helpful to inspect requirements before the high-level design starts, the high-level design before detailed design starts, the detailed design before implementation begins, and implementation before the start of test. This does not mean that all high-level design must be inspected before any detailed design starts but just that the specific design to be done must be based on work that has been inspected. It is also helpful to inspect the test cases and documentation.

While there is almost no limit on what can be inspected, there is a question of cost. Since inspections are expensive, they should be limited to those items where the benefit is likely to be worth the cost. As is shown at the end of this chapter, inspections are invariably cost-effective for design and code and often for requirements, test cases, and documentation. Where the cost of inspections does not seem warranted, a less formal walkthrough process is generally adequate. Technical reviews can also be used for such items as development and test plans.

As is discussed further in Chapters 15 and 17, it is difficult to make informed decisions on the software process without data. This, of course, is the logic behind the process maturity framework: to define and measure the process so data can be obtained to improve it. While inspections are labor-intensive, they are often more effective than testing for removing defects. This trade-off changes, however, as the maturity of the process improves. Modern tools and methods can reduce error-injection rates, and better environmental support can detect problems more economically than by hand. Without data, however, it is difficult to make informed decisions on the most appropriate methods or support tools to use.

10.2 Inspection Objectives

The basic objectives of inspections are:

- □ To find errors at the earliest possible point in the development cycle
- □ To ensure that the appropriate parties technically agree on the work
- □ To verify that the work meets predefined criteria
- □ To formally complete a technical task
- □ To provide data on the product and the inspection process

Inspections also provide a host of secondary benefits:

- □ They ensure that associated workers are technically aware of the product.
- □ They help to build an effective technical team.
- □ They help to utilize the best talents in the organization.
- □ They provide people with a sense of achievement and participation.
- □ They help the participants develop their skills as reviewers.

These results can all generally be achieved by inspections of the type discussed in the following sections.

10.3 Basic Inspection Principles

The inspection process follows certain basic principles:

1. The inspection is a formal, structured process with a system of checklists and defined roles for the participants. It provides an orderly means to implement a standard of software engineering excellence throughout an organization.
2. Generic checklists and standards are developed for each inspection type and, where appropriate, they are tailored to specific project needs. These checklists cover inspection planning, preparation, conduct, and exit and reporting

TABLE 10.1
TYPES OF REVIEWS [11]

Category/Attribute	Management Review	Technical Review	Software Inspection	Walkthrough
Objective	Ensure progress. Recommend corrective action. Ensure proper allocation of resources.	Evaluate conformance to specifications and plans. Ensure change integrity.	Detect and identify defects. Verify resolution.	Detect defects. Examine alternatives. Forum for learning.
Delegated Controls Decision making	Management team charts course of action. Decisions are made at the meeting or as a result of recommendations.	Review team petitions management of technical leadership to act on recommendations.	Team chooses predefined product dispositions. Defects must be removed.	All decisions made by producer. Change is the prerogative of the producer.
Change verification	Change verification left to other project controls.	Leader verifies as part of review report.	Moderator verifies rework.	Change verification left to other project controls.
Group Dynamics Recommended Size	2 or more people	3 or more people	3–6 people	2–7 people
Attendance	Management, technical leadership, and peer mix.	Technical leadership and peer mix.	College of peers meet with documented attendance.	Technical leadership and peer mix.
Leadership	Usually the responsible manager.	Usually the lead engineer.	Trained moderator.	Usually producer.

TABLE 10.1 (continued)

Procedures			
Material volume	Moderate to high, depending on the specific "statement of objectives" for the meeting.	Moderate to high, depending on the specific "statement of objectives" for the meeting.	Relatively low.	Relatively low.
Presenter	Project representative.	Software element representative.	Presentation by "reader" other than producer.	Usually the producer
Data collection	As required by applicable policies, standards, or plans.	Not a formal project requirement. May be done locally.	Formally required.	Not a formal project requirement. May be done locally.
Outputs				
Reports	Management review report.	Technical review report.	Defect list. Defect summary. Inspection report.	Walkthrough report.
Database entries	Any schedule changes must be entered into the project tracking database.	No formal database required.	Defect counts, characteristics, severity, and meeting attributes are kept.	No formal database required.

IEEE STD 1028-1988 © 1988 IEEE

criteria. Examples of the types of checklists and standards used to evaluate the work are style guides and criteria for completeness and correctness (see Appendix C).

3. The reviewers are prepared in advance and have identified their concerns and questions before the inspection starts.

4. The focus of the inspection is on identifying problems, not resolving them. This focus, together with the preparation mentioned in point 3, ensures that the inspection can be conducted with a minimum of wasted time.

5. An inspection is conducted by technical people for technical people. Managers do not attend, but they are informed of the findings and the dates on which the identified problems will be resolved.

6. As described in Chapter 16, the inspection data is entered in the process database and used both to monitor inspection effectiveness and to track and manage product quality.

10.4 The Conduct of Inspections

Inspections should be conducted at every point in the development or maintenance process at which intermediate products are produced. Because they are time-consuming, involve people from several groups, and use scarce resources, they must be planned well in advance. To guarantee that they are done, inspections must be an explicit part of every project plan. A suggested basic set of inspections is shown in Table 10.2.

In addition to these basic reviews, reinspections are needed when the inspection and test results indicate unusual problems. There are several ways to determine inspection effectiveness, and when parts of a product have not been adequately inspected, reinspections should be held. The various ways to ascertain inspection effectiveness are pointed out in Chapter 15, and suggested reinspection criteria are discussed later in this chapter.

10.4.1 Inspection Participants

The inspection participants include the following people:[6]

- □ *The moderator* (or inspection leader)   The person responsible for leading the inspection expeditiously and efficiently to a successful conclusion
- □ *The producers*   The person or persons responsible for doing the work being inspected
- □ *The reviewers* (or inspectors)   Generally people who are directly concerned and aware of the work being inspected

TABLE 10.2
BASIC SET OF INSPECTIONS

Phase	Inspections	Walkthroughs	Technical Reviews
Requirements		Detailed requirements	Initial requirements
Plans			Development plans
Development		System design High-level design	
	Detailed design Code		
Publications		Draft publication Final publications	
Test		Test implementation	

□ *The recorder* (or scribe)   Someone who records the significant inspection results

While many more people may be interested in the inspection results, the purpose of the inspection is to assist the producers in improving their work. This can best be done by limiting attendance to five or six reviewers.

The key point of this attendance list is that only technical peers attend. The moderator is not the manager of the work being reviewed, and neither are any of the other participants. The inclusion of managers changes the inspection process and distorts the participants' objectivity. Regardless of the manager's behavior, the participants will feel that it is they who are being reviewed rather than the product.[14]

Managers are properly interested in the results of every inspection. For example, they should ensure that the identified action items are completed, examine the data on inspection effectiveness, require that all product results are inspected, and respect the reviewers' judgments on troublesome product areas.

The managers' use of inspection data can be a source of concern. Some programmers feel that by reporting data on an inspection, they are exposing themselves to personal evaluation. While managers can use such data in this way, they must be careful not to do so. Inspection data is gathered to see how well the project is progressing, not to evaluate the people. Since reviewers are human, however, they are subject to error, and managers need to study the inspection data to see where improvements are needed. Specific criteria and techniques for making such studies are discussed in Chapters 15 and 17.

10.4.2 Preparing for the Inspection

The full inspection process consists of a preparation phase, the inspection itself, and some post-inspection activity. As a first step the producers and their manager decide that the product is ready for inspection and agree on the inspection objectives. Next the inspection participants are identified, the inspection entry criteria are prepared, and the supporting materials are produced for the opening meeting with the entire inspection group. The moderator opens this meeting with a brief statement of the subject to be inspected, the inspection objectives, and, if needed, an overview of the inspection process. The moderator then provides a copy of the inspection package to each of the participants.

Following this introductory meeting the reviewers individually prepare for the inspection. During preparation the reviewers record their time and the errors identified on the error log form. They then submit the log and the completed entry preparation form to the inspection moderator before or at the opening of the inspection meeting. Experience has shown that about three-quarters of the errors found in well-run inspections are found during preparation. Good preparation is thus essential.

10.4.3 The Inspection and Post-Inspection Actions

In conducting the inspection meeting, the moderator first checks to see if all participants are prepared and obtains copies of any preparation reports not already submitted. The producer(s) then review each major error either to clarify why it is not an error, to understand what the reviewer(s) meant, or to accept it. Pertinent data on each error is recorded. After discussing all major errors, the product is briefly reviewed to identify any other areas of confusion or concern. Based on the inspection results, and after asking the reviewers for their views, the moderator decides whether a reinspection is required. Sample reinspection criteria are shown in Table 10.3.

Following the inspection, the producer(s) fixes the identified problems and either reviews the corrections with the moderator or in a reinspection. Even if the previous decision had been not to hold a reinspection, the moderator may decide that these changes warrant one. As the final inspection action, the moderator makes sure that the inspection results and data are inserted in the process database and that management is informed that the inspection has been successfully completed.

10.5 Inspection Training

Moderator training courses are absolutely essential. The moderators need a complete grounding in the principles and methods of inspection before they can do a

TABLE 10.3
SAMPLE REINSPECTION CRITERIA

Inspection rates unusual:
    Inspection time per LOC too short
    Inspection time per LOC too long
    Too many errors per programmer hour
    Too few errors per programmer hour

Error data out of line:
    Too many minor errors, and too few major errors (preoccupied with details)
    Too many major errors
    Unusual error distribution
    Too low a percent of errors found during preparation

Other:
    Any module with more than N errors (N set in project plan)
    Any module with persistently high error rates
    The reviewers suggest a reinspection
    The moderator suggests a reinspection
    The testers suggest a reinspection
    The module contains uninspected changes

competent job. This gives them the basic skills and helps to provide the self-confidence needed to lead such a potentially contentious activity.

As for the participants, training is also highly desirable. If a competent moderator is available, however, the software professionals can often learn how to be inspectors by participating in well-run inspections. Courses should teach inspection principles and provide practice sessions with the checklists and methods involved. It is not a good idea, however, to delay the introduction of inspections until a full set of such courses is available. A brief overview by the moderator at the opening of the inspection is often sufficient to cover the purposes and principles of inspections. After the initial moderator training needs have been met, it is then desirable to broaden the training program to include all potential inspection participants.

10.6 Reports and Tracking

There are several reasons for gathering data and making reports on the inspection process. First, it is essential to track inspection completions to ensure they are done as required. Second, much can be learned about inspection effectiveness from a brief study of the data gathered. Inspection metrics and data gathering are discussed in more detail in Chapter 15.

Sample inspection report and summary forms are shown in Tables 10.4 and 10.5.[9] These forms include the basic information needed to determine if the

TABLE 10.4
INSPECTION REPORT [9]

PROJECT: _____   DATE: _____

SYSTEM NAME: _____   UNIT: _____

MODERATOR: _____ ROOM: _____   PHONE: _____

MEETING TYPE:

OVERVIEW: _____   REINSPECTION _____

REQUIREMENTS: _____   DESIGN: _____   CODE: _____

NUMBER OF INSPECTIONS: _____   INSPECTION DURATION: _____

TOTAL NUMBER OF REVIEWERS: _____   INSPECTION PREP TIME: _____

TOTAL LINES INSPECTED: _____   PAGES OF DIAGRAMS: _____

DISPOSITION: ACCEPT: _____   CONDITIONAL: _____   REINSPECT: _____

ESTIMATED REWORK EFFORT: _____ (HOURS)

REWORK TO BE COMPLETED BY: _____

REINSPECTION SCHEDULED FOR: _____

REVIEWERS:

_____   _____

_____   _____

_____   _____

PRODUCER(S):

_____   _____

RECORDER:

_____

MODERATOR CERTIFICATION: _____   DATE: _____

ADDITIONAL COMMENTS: _____

_____

_____

Distribution: Project Manager
               Quality Assurance
               Process Group
               Producer(s)
               Inspection Coordinator

TABLE 10.5
INSPECTION SUMMARY [9]

PROJECT: _____   DATE: _____

SYSTEM NAME: _____   UNIT: _____

MODERATOR: _____ ROOM: _____   PHONE: _____

MEETING TYPE:

OVERVIEW: _____   REINSPECTION _____

REQUIREMENTS: _____   DESIGN: _____   CODE: _____

| | MAJOR ERRORS* | | | | MINOR ERRORS** | | | |
	M	W	E	TOTAL	M	W	E	TOTAL
FUNCTION								
INTERFACE								
DATA								
LOGIC								
I/O								
PERFORMANCE								
MAINTENANCE								
STANDARDS								
DOCUMENTATION								
HUMAN FACTORS								
SYNTAX								
OTHER								
TOTALS								

Distribution: Project Manager
            Quality Assurance
            Process Group
            Producer(s)
            Review Coordinator

*Major—a defect that would likely cause a problem in program operation
**Minor—all other defects

M = Missing—required code is not present
W = Wrong—the code includes some errors
E = Extra—unneeded code is included

inspection was performed as planned, the types of errors found, and the costs of the inspection process. With this data, management can decide which inspections have been done properly, where the product is likely to have design weaknesses, and how to improve product quality. These topics are also covered in more detail in Chapter 15.

A final summary is made for all the inspections held on a particular project. This summary provides the overview information required for the analyses mentioned above.

10.7 Other Considerations

Since well-run inspections require intense concentration from all participants, they can be very tiring. As a result, inspection sessions should generally not exceed about two hours.[6] Inspections involving the same people should not be scheduled back-to-back since the participants will often be too tired to be fully productive. One inspection session a day is generally all that is advisable for any one individual. The moderator should check on this at the time the inspection is scheduled.

Some projects have found it helpful to use special "hot-shot" inspection teams to conduct detailed inspections of problem modules. While this is often a desirable approach, the participants can easily suffer from inspection fatigue if they are used too frequently. After a while they will lose their ability to concentrate and to think critically. They will think they have seen the code before or they will confuse one design with another.

It is also helpful to assign some inspectors to specific product areas for the project duration. If the assignment is done early in the design phase and maintained for the entire project, the inspectors' growing product knowledge will greatly facilitate inspection productivity and quality. This can also help to build a team attitude and a sense of product ownership. Since one principal value of inspections is the fresh perspective it brings to the material, however, it is wise to include some new reviewers in each inspection. When the same reviewers have seen identical or similar material several times, they may lose their ability to see the problems, and the process will lose effectiveness. It is thus generally unwise to establish a special group of inspection specialists, except to handle short-term emergencies.

Groups commonly try to cover too much material in a single review. Even if the code is relatively small, it is rarely desirable to cover two different designs at the same time. The work should be split into two inspections, even if each will take less than one hour. Putting two programs in the same inspection generally results in one being slighted. Often some of the reviewers will concentrate on one and some on the other, so that both programs suffer from partial attention. Probably the most important single inspection guideline is the upper limit on the size of the product to be inspected. While this should be set by each organization based on its unique situation and experience, an upper limit for code inspections should probably not exceed about 500 LOC.

It is also wise to focus on the quality of the result being produced rather than on the number of errors being found. Errors are a fact of life that must be expected. The need is to improve the methods and tools the software professionals use so the most prevalent error causes can be reduced or eliminated. This requires knowledge of the error classes. But while the categories are important, it is not essential to classify every error precisely or to accurately determine what caused it. As is pointed out in Chapters 16 and 17, these are important questions, but every error is a special case and often there is no exactly correct classification. The best rule is for the recorder to note quickly the basic facts and views of the group and then to move on.

Finally, some types of errors cannot be found very efficiently by inspections. If, for example, a large number of minor errors were found during preparation, it is wise to discontinue the inspection and have the producers desk check their work more carefully before starting again. It is often helpful to ask one or more of the more experienced reviewers to assist the producers while they recheck. When reviewers become embroiled in minor details, they often overlook more important problems.

10.8 Initiating an Inspection Program

Inspections have been installed successfully in many organizations with very positive results.[1, 3, 5, 6, 7, 9] The way the inspection program is introduced, however, can have an important impact on its effectiveness. The AT&T Bell Laboratories introduced inspections in conjunction with an extensive program of education and consultation. This required a central group of experts who worked with selected development groups to establish introduction plans, train the people, and provide consultation. This program had the following basic elements:[1, 9]

1. Select a location and a key project for the initial effort. This is done with local management concurrence.

2. Introduce the concept of inspections to the managers and key professionals in a three- to five-hour overview session.

3. Form a working team with one or two project members to determine training requirements, develop the needed forms and procedures, and establish the introduction plan.

4. If trained moderators are not available, conduct a two- to three-day moderator training class.

5. A two-day developer workshop is held to introduce the methods and obtain the support of the professional personnel who will use them.

6. After a couple of months' experience in conducting inspections, a management seminar is held to outline the results and emphasize the need for continuing management support. At this time the considerations involved in successful inspection programs are reemphasized, and any concerns the participants have voiced during the introduction program are discussed.

7. Periodically, the inspection program is assessed and any indicated changes made.

After the initial projects have obtained some early successes, inspections are introduced throughout the organization. It is important, however, to get some early successes with one or two projects before broadening the effort. When too much is attempted too quickly, mistakes will be made and it will be extremely difficult for a limited support team to straighten out every project simultaneously. Such mistakes often result in seriously delaying the entire inspection program.

The final implementation step is to incorporate the use of inspections into the organization's official development process and establish an SQA monitoring program to advise management whenever the established procedures are not followed. It is also desirable to establish a technical group to provide inspection training and consultation.

10.8.1 Inspection Costs

The effectiveness of inspections depends on the time and effort spent in preparing for and conducting them. IBM has found, for example, that when certain recommended inspection rates are exceeded, inspection efficiency drops by a factor of 2.[4] Optimum inspection rates depend on the type of product involved and the skill and experience of the people doing them. For design and code inspections, some available data on inspection rates is shown in Table 10.6. Here the rates are 6 to 8 times higher for COBOL application programs than for system programs and some 15 times higher than for performance-sensitive microcode. Since this data is from a limited number of cases, however, these figures should be used with considerable caution. The best course is for each organization to gather its own data and to develop the most appropriate factors to use with its own projects.

Organizations become progressively more efficient at doing inspections as they gain experience. Table 10.7 shows some data on the learning rate of one organization during three successive releases of a large system program. On release 1 (R1), an inspection program had just been initiated and inspection efficiency was a relatively low 15 percent. This means that for release 1, for example, of every 100 errors found in development, 15 were found by inspections and the balance in test. The quality index of 100 percent means that the end users then also found 100 errors. By release 3, of every 100 errors found in development, 61 were found by inspections and 39 by test. Overall product quality was improved sufficiently so the customers now found only 25 errors.

TABLE 10.6
SAMPLE RATES FOR SOFTWARE INSPECTIONS*

Example	Detailed Design		Code		Reference
	Prep.	*Review*	*Prep.*	*Review*	
IBM COBOL	898	652	709	539	[6]
IBM System	100	130	125	150	[6]
IBM System			125	90	[4]
Bell Labs System				100	[1]
Bell Labs, microcode				40	[1]

*Lines of source code (noncomment, nonblank) per programmer hour

By improving inspection efficiency, the organization depicted in Table 10.7 was able to find a far larger percentage of the errors before customer product shipment. The relative amount of time taken for inspections also changed dramatically. The average hours required to inspect 1000 lines of source code increased by 1.68 times for I0 (high-level design inspection) and by 7.0 times for I1 (detailed design inspection). By taking this additional time for design inspections early in the program, however, only 76 percent as much time was required per KCSI for I2 (code inspections). More significantly, however, the number of defects found per hour of code inspection increased by three times. While some of this improvement was undoubtedly due to the groups' improving knowledge of the product, it also appears that the ability to do good inspections is a learned skill that can significantly improve with experience. Although test time was presumably reduced significantly, such data is not available.

TABLE 10.7
RELATIVE INSPECTION RATES WITH EXPERIENCE

Release	Relative* Hours/KCSI			Relative* Hours/Defect			Inspection Efficiency*	Quality Index*
	I0	*I1*	*I2*	*I0*	*I1*	*I2*		
R1	1.00	1.00	1.00	1.00	1.00	1.00	.15	100%
R2	1.27	8.16	.99	2.79	1.00	.46	.41	55%
R3	1.68	7.00	.76	.18	.53	.33	.61	25%

*Definitions:
  KCSI = thousands of changed source instructions
  I0 = High-level design inspection
  I1 = Detailed design inspection
  I2 = Code inspection

Inspection Efficiency:

$$\frac{\text{defects found by inspections}}{\text{total defects found by inspection and test}}$$

Quality Index:

$$\frac{\text{defects found in field use}}{\text{total defects found during development}}$$

10.8.2 Inspection Benefits

There are many examples of inspection quality and productivity benefits, and there are no documented cases of poor experience. This, of course, is partly due to people's natural reluctance to write about project failures. It is becoming clear, however, that inspections can be highly effective and that they should be widely used in software development and maintenance.

To the author's knowledge, the cases in which inspections have not been effective have generally had errors in the way they were conducted. Either the preparation was not adequate, too many people were involved, the wrong people attended, or too much material was covered at one time. The biggest single problem is generally the combination of management inattention and schedule pressure. This combination causes inspections to become a pro forma exercise in which the inspection effort is expended but the desired results are not obtained.

On the positive side, there is an impressive and growing list of evidence that well-handled inspections pay enormous dividends in both quality and productivity:

- □ Yourdon reports that he and three experienced programmers inspected a 200 line PL/1 program in 45 minutes and found 25 bugs, 5 of which could not have been caught in testing.[14] While the program appears to have been of poor quality to start with, Yourdon judged the inspection to have been more effective than a test.

- □ In software maintenance, Freedman and Weinberg report that 55 percent of one-line maintenance changes were in error before the introduction of inspections and, immediately after, the error rate dropped to 2 percent.[8]

- □ In another case the introduction of inspections in software maintenance reduced the number of production crashes by 77 percent.[8]

- □ The dramatic improvement that can be expected at the initial use of inspections is shown in Table 10.8. This data is on 11 COBOL programs that were consecutively developed by the same people. After completion of the first 5 programs, inspections were instituted, and the error rates on the next 6 programs showed an average improvement of over five times. The numbers shown in the right-hand column refer to the number of errors found in the first 16 weeks of production use of the programs.[8]

- □ In one AT&T Bell Laboratory case a project of approximately 200 professionals instituted several changes, including inspections. Productivity improved by 14 percent and quality by a factor of ten. While several changes were involved and only early data was available, the results are still impressive.[9]

- □ In another AT&T Bell Laboratories example with a large electronic switching system, the cost of finding errors was reduced by ten times through the use of inspections.[9]

TABLE 10.8
COBOL PROGRAM QUALITY BEFORE AND AFTER CODE INSPECTIONS [8]

Weeks Before Inspections Started	Size (LOC)	Errors	Errors/100 LOC
−9	463	19	4.1
−7	198	17	3.54
−7	146	4	2.73
−4	880	41	4.66
−3	712	37	5.19
Total	2825	127	4.50
Weeks after Inspections Started			
2	117	2	1.13
3	134	1	0.75
6	664	7	1.05
6	484	4	0.82
7	379	3	0.79
8	580	3	0.52
Total	2418	20	0.82

Daniel P. Freedman, and Gerald M. Weinberg, *Handbook of Walkthroughs, Inspections, and Technical Reviews,* © 1982, 1979. Reprinted by permission of Scott Foreman and Company.

□ In a AT&T Bell Laboratories dial-up central switching system application, inspections were reported to be 20 times more effective than testing in finding errors.[9]

□ The Aetna Insurance Company reported that inspections found 82 percent of their errors in a COBOL program, while coding productivity was increased by 25 percent.[6]

□ In another COBOL example, 80 percent of the development errors were found by inspections, productivity was increased by 30 percent, and no errors were found in the first two months of program use.[10]

□ TRW did a study of one large program and found that a total of 2019 user-found problems resulted in code changes. These errors were analyzed to see what techniques could have been used to prevent or detect them prior to program shipment. The percent that could have been found by code inspections was 62.7 percent, and design inspections would have caught 57.7 percent. The figures for all the techniques considered are shown in Table 10.9.[12]

Clearly, inspections are an important way to find errors. Not only are they more effective than testing for finding many types of problems, but they also find them earlier in the program when the cost of making the corrections is far less.

Inspections should be a required part of every well-run software process, and they should be used for every software design, every program implementation, and every change made either during original development, in test, or in maintenance.

TABLE 10.9
ERROR PREVENTION OR DETECTION
PROBABILITIES [12]

Prevention Techniques	
Design standards	28.7%
Coding standards	26.3
Design inspections*	57.7
Code inspections*	62.7
Detection Techniques	
Unit test	72.9
Algorithm test	8.3
Integration test	46.1
Requirements test	45.7

*While inspections are listed in the reference as error
prevention techniques, they are also an important means
of error detection.

10.9 Future Directions

While inspections are highly cost-effective with the quality of the programs generally produced today, they are also labor-intensive. Each inspection requires the
concentrated involvement of a number of talented software professionals who
together review each element of the product's design and implementation. As
Britcher points out, with improved product quality, we will need to find more cost-
effective methods [2]. While newer, more productive techniques will likely be
found, some form of inspections will undoubtedly be needed as long as software
engineering remains a human-intensive process. Improved knowledge of our process and more rigorous technical and management practices, however, should help
us to use them efficiently. As described in Chapters 17 and 18, defect prevention
and improved technology will likely provide the best long-term solutions to our
productivity and quality needs.

10.10 Summary

The fundamental purpose of inspections is to improve the quality of programs by
assisting the software engineers to recognize and correct their errors. While inspections will not solve all problems, they are enormously effective, and all software
organizations should use inspections, walkthroughs, or technical reviews in all

major aspects of their work. This includes requirements, design, implementation, test, maintenance, and documentation.

The basic objectives of inspections are to find errors at the earliest possible point in the development cycle, to ensure that the appropriate parties technically agree on the work, to verify that the work meets predefined criteria, to complete formally a technical task, and to provide data on the product and the inspection process. (An overview of the inspection process is described in this chapter, and more details on inspection methods, participant qualifications, checklists, and responsibilities are given in Appendix C.)

Inspections have been installed successfully in many organizations with very positive results. Since the effectiveness of inspections depends on the time and effort spent in preparing for and conducting them, however, the way the inspection program is introduced can have an important impact on its effectiveness.

Inspections are an important way to find errors. Not only are they more effective than testing in finding many types of problems, but they also find them early in the project when the cost of making the corrections is far less.

Inspections should be a required part of every well-run software process, and they should be used for every software design, every program implementation, and every change made either during original development, in test, or in maintenance.

References

1. Ackerman, A. F., and P. J. Fowler. "Software inspections and the industrial production of software," in Hans-Ludwig Hausen, ed., *Software Validation*. Amsterdam: North-Holland, 1984.

2. Britcher, R. N. "Using inspections to investigate program correctness," *IEEE Computer*, November 1988.

3. Bruggere, T. H. "Software engineering: management, personnel, and methodology," *Proceedings*, Fourth International Conference on Software Engineering, 1979, pp. 361–368.

4. Buck, F. O. "Indicators of Quality Inspections," IBM Technical Report TR21.802, Systems Communications Division, Kingston, NY, 1981.

5. Card, D. N., F. E. McGarry, and G. T. Page. "Evaluating software engineering technologies," *IEEE Transactions on Software Engineering*, vol. SE-13, no. 7, July 1987.

6. Fagan, M. E. "Design and code inspections to reduce errors in program development," *IBM Systems Journal*, vol. 15, no. 3, 1976.

7. Fagan, M. E. "Advances in software inspections," *IEEE Transactions on Software Engineering*, vol. SE-12, no. 7, July 1986.

8. Freedman, D. P., and G. M. Weinberg. *Handbook of Walkthroughs, Inspections, and Technical Reviews, Evaluating Programs, Projects, and Products*, 3rd edition. Boston: Little, Brown, 1982.

9. Fowler, P. J. "In-Process inspections of work products at AT&T," *AT&T Technical Journal*, March-April, 1986.

10. Gilb, T. *Software Metrics,* Bromley, England: Winthrop Publishers, 1977.

11. "IEEE Draft Standard for Software Reviews and Audits" (IEEE STD 1028-1988), IEEE Computer Society, January 22, 1988.

12. Thayer, T. A., M. Lipow, and E. C. Nelson. "Software Reliability, A Study of Large Project Reality, Volume 2," TRW Series of Software Technology, Amsterdam: North-Holland, 1978.

13. Weinberg, Gerald M. *The Psychology of Computer Programming.* New York: Van Nostrand Reinhold, 1971.

14. Yourdon, E. *Structured Walkthroughs,* 2nd edition. Englewood Cliffs, NJ: Prentice-Hall, 1979.

11

Software Testing

Software testing is defined as the execution of a program to find its faults. While more time typically is spent on testing than in any other phase of software development, there is considerable confusion about its purpose. Many software professionals, for example, believe that tests are run to show that the program works rather than to learn about its faults.

As long ago as 1969, Dijkstra said that "program testing can be used to show the presence of bugs, but never their absence!"[9] In fact, testing is an inefficient way to find and remove many types of bugs. Software organizations can often improve product quality while at the same time reducing the amount of time they spend on testing (see, for example, Chapter 10 on software inspections). In spite of its limitations, however, testing is a critical part of the software process.

Today there is no question that if a software product has not been tested, it will not work. It is equally true, however, that once the program has been tested, the odds that it will work correctly under all conditions are only moderately improved. We should think of testing like weeding a garden: Individual bugs can be found with tests but more powerful methods are needed for the thickets. Unfortunately, with programs it is hard to know if we are dealing with a garden or a jungle. The first job of the tester is thus to determine the state of the product: Is it a jungle with a few beaten paths or a garden with an occasional weed?

The straightforward approach to testing is to find problems and fix them. This approach is appropriate as long as we really understand the problems. To do this, one must closely examine the product to decide if it is worthwhile to work on the weeds a few at a time. With a jungle, however, the real problem is likely caused by a jumble of code that cannot be fixed with patches. It is then often better to clear the field and start over. There are an almost limitless number of potential paths through any jungle. While repeated testing and patching will hack out a few more paths, some new testing combination will generally expose new problems. Even with relatively small programs, this can go on almost indefinitely.

Programers generally do a remarkably good job at building large and complex software products. Just to get them into test, the code must be very high quality.[7] Based on my experience with the maintenance of large programs, over half the modules are often error-free. In fact, the percentage is frequently as high as 80 percent. While there are many unappreciated gardens, the few remaining thickets get all the users' attention.

11.1 Definitions

Myers has provided some useful testing definitions:[18]

□ *Testing*   The process of executing a program (or part of a program) with the intention of finding errors

□ *Verification*   An attempt to find errors by executing a program in a test or simulated environment (it is now preferable to view verification as the process of proving the program's correctness)

□ *Validation*   An attempt to find errors by executing a program in a real environment

□ *Debugging*   Diagnosing the precise nature of a known error and then correcting it (debugging is a correction and not a testing activity)

11.1.1 The Seven Types of Software Tests

The seven basic types of software tests are:[18]

1. *Unit or module tests* verify single programs or modules. These are typically conducted in isolated or special test environments.

2. *Integration tests* verify the interfaces between system parts (modules, components, and subsystems).

3. *External function tests* verify the external system functions, as stated in the external specifications.

4. *Regression tests* run a subset of previously executed integration and function tests to ensure that program changes have not degraded the system.

5. *System tests* verify and/or validate the system to its initial objectives.

6. *Acceptance tests* validate the system or program to the user's requirements.

7. *Installation tests* validate the installability and operability of the user's system.

These tests are discussed in more detail later in this chapter.

11.1.2 Testing Methods

There are two basic ways of constructing tests: "white box" and "black box." White box tests examine the internal design of the program and require that the tester has detailed knowledge of its structure. Black box tests, however, are designed without knowledge of the program's internals and are generally based on the functional requirements.

Integration is the process of assembling the parts of a system into a working whole. It is the inverse of the disintegration (or decomposition) design process used to parcel out work to the development teams. Integration is thus a natural consequence of large-scale development and is required whenever development teams cooperatively work on parts of a common system.

Integration testing thus forms a bridge between functional (black box) and unit (white box) testing. Integration testing is the process of assembling enough of the program components so that functional testing can be performed. With most large systems the individual program modules are generally so small and special-purpose that no particularly useful external function can be performed. In most cases these modules cannot even be run except with special support that provides needed system functions.

11.2 Software Testing Principles

Software testing presents a problem in economics. With large systems it is almost always true that more tests will find more bugs. The question is not whether all the bugs have been found but whether the program is sufficiently good to stop testing. This trade-off should consider the probability of finding more bugs in test, the marginal cost of doing so, the probability of the users encountering the remaining bugs, and the resulting impact of these bugs on the users.

Unfortunately, the general lack of data on the software process prevents us from making this trade-off intelligently. Usually testing is stopped when testing time is used up, even with ample evidence that one or more tangled thicket remains. When we ship such code we generally spend more time and money fixing the problems in the customers' office than it would have taken to do the job properly.

A common view of testing is that all untested code has a roughly equal probability of containing defects. DeMarco asserts, however, that the incidence of defects in untested code varies widely and that no amount of testing can remove more than 50 percent of them.[6] While DeMarco is right in principle, there is data that shows that properly run unit tests are potentially capable of detecting as many as 70 percent of the defects in a program.[25] The objective should therefore be to remove as many defects as possible before test since the quality improvement potential of testing is limited.

11.2.1 The Axioms of Testing

A test is an experiment and should be approached as such.[4] A properly disciplined experiment starts with a hypothesis the experiment is designed to verify or disprove. Good practice is to design the experiment so the minimum number of conditions are changed at one time. These experimental conditions are recorded, and data is gathered so the experiment can be repeated if necessary. Finally, the test data is analyzed to see if the hypothesis is proven.

Test hypotheses concern the types and quantity of defects in the program. The test experiment is then designed to verify or to adjust these numbers. This view of testing is reflected in the testing axioms that Myers stated in 1976:[18]

- A good test case is one that has a high probability of detecting a previously undiscovered defect, not one that shows that the program works correctly.
- One of the most difficult problems in testing is knowing when to stop.
- It is impossible to test your own program.
- A necessary part of every test case is a description of the expected output.
- Avoid nonreproducible or on-the-fly testing.
- Write test cases for invalid as well as valid input conditions.
- Thoroughly inspect the results of each test.
- As the number of detected defects in a piece of software increases, the probability of the existence of more undetected defects also increases.
- Assign your best programmers to testing.
- Ensure that testability is a key objective in your software design.
- The design of a system should be such that each module is integrated into the system only once.
- Never alter the program to make testing easier (unless it is a permanent change).
- Testing, like almost every other activity, must start with objectives.

11.2.2 The Proper Role of Testing

An examination of even relatively simple programs demonstrates that exhaustive testing is generally impossible. If a program were to analyze a string of only ten alphabetic characters, there would be 26^{10} possible combinations. Testing one condition every microsecond would take four and a half million years. While most of these tests would be redundant, even this brute-force approach would omit many other conditions such as longer strings and illegal characters.

Test design thus reduces to the judicious selection of a small subset of conditions that will reveal the characteristics of the program. Since, as Myers points out, the programs that have the most bugs in test are the most likely source of future problems, testing must be viewed as a search for symptoms rather than bugs. While the bugs found must be fixed, the real value is the data obtained. A little analysis quickly shows which program sections are gardens and which are jungles.

11.3 Types of Software Tests

The following paragraphs discuss each of the key types of tests: unit, integration, function, regression, system, acceptance, and installation. The methods for planning, preparing, conducting, and analyzing the tests are then discussed in subsequent sections.

11.3.1 Unit Testing (White Box)

When unit tests are done on a white box basis, they are essentially path tests. The idea is to focus on a relatively small segment of code and aim to exercise a high percentage of the internal paths. A path is an instruction sequence that threads through the program from initial entry to final exit. The simplest approach is to ensure that every statement is exercised at least once. A more stringent criterion is to require coverage of every path within a program. For this purpose each traverse of a loop is considered another path so, for even relatively small programs, there are a very large number of possible paths. This procedure is thus not generally practical. Further, even testing all paths would not guarantee that all problems were detected. A more practical criterion is to exercise each condition for each decision statement at least once and ensure that all variables and parameters are exercised at and below minimums, at and above maximums, and at intermediate values. Some of the considerations involved in designing such tests are discussed further in Section 11.5 (page 207).

One disadvantage of white box testing is that the tester may be biased by previous experience. The tests are often designed by the programmers who produced the code since they may be the only ones who understand it. Unfortunately, those who created the programs' faults are least likely to recognize them. Another limitation is coverage. Even if each instruction is tested and every branch traversed in all directions, many other possible combinations may still be overlooked. Has every loop been executed in all possible combinations, has every parameter been set to all possible values, has every error condition been tested, and have all variables been evaluated over all allowed and unallowed but possible values? Myers has a nice discussion of this subject in his book *The Art of Software Testing*.[19]

While its disadvantages are significant, white box testing generally has the highest error yield of all testing techniques. In fact, in a retrospective study, Thayer and Lipow state that comprehensive path and parameter testing could potentially have caught 72.9 percent of all the problems encountered by the users of one large program.[25]

11.3.2 Integration Testing

The proper approach to integration depends on both the kind of system being built and the nature of the development project. With a new system, for example, there is no foundation on which to assemble and to run newly developed program fragments. The initial problem is thus to establish a test framework on which to run these various elements.

With a new control program, for example, basic system services are required for such functions as interrupt handling, memory allocation, and I/O management. Since it is generally impractical for each of these functions to be scaffolded by every development group, a common system driver is usually constructed. Building drivers, however, is generally a complex process, so it is typically handled by a combined team of the developers and the integration test group.

Many system driver functions are internal to the system and may not be testable with traditional functional tests. These initial integration tests are thus generally some combination of black and white box tests to ensure that the relevant system functions and interfaces are properly implemented.

Once a basic system driver is available, functional elements can be added one at a time. Their integration may involve an intricate sequencing of functional dependencies to minimize the amount of special scaffolding code needed. Therefore the functions of each component are precisely defined and a driver plan is established to provide them in a logical and economical order.

Integration Testing Approaches.   On very large systems it is often wise to do integration testing in several steps.[14] Such systems generally have several relatively large components that can be built and integrated separately before combination into a full system. Since components, such as compilers and database managers, are often functionally viable entities, separate integration and functional testing will find many problems earlier than would a single integration cycle. It also simplifies the overall system integration process to handle most of the problems in a simpler component environment.

Myers's summary of top-down and bottom-up integration testing approaches is shown in Table 11.1.[18] In bottom-up testing the modules are individually tested, using specially developed drivers that provide the needed system functions. As more modules are integrated, these drivers are replaced by the modules that perform those functions. The disadvantages of bottom-up testing are the need for drivers and the amount of testing required before functional testing is possible.

Top-down testing is essentially a prototyping philosophy. The initial tests establish a basic system skeleton from the top and each new module adds capability. The problem is that the functions of the lower-level modules that are not initially present must be simulated by program stubs. While producing such stubs may at first seem easy, as with a simple subroutine return, this is rarely the case. It is also difficult to test thoroughly each module as it is integrated, since this often requires very sophisticated stubs. Finally, with top-down testing it may be difficult or impossible to test certain logical conditions such as error handling or special checking until most of the system has been integrated.

"Big bang" testing is perhaps the most common and least effective way to integrate. Here each module is individually tested and then they are all assembled and run. If the system executes, the requirement for stubs is eliminated. The need for very high-quality modules, however, means that very sophisticated special drivers are needed. Less effort is spent on module testing, of course, and less preparatory work is required, but when each module is only given a cursory test, the likelihood of a total system integration disaster is great.

For very small programs with a few high-quality modules, big bang testing may make sense. The larger the program, however, the more likely the big bang test will complicate the problems of getting a running system. Since the entire system is turned on together at one time, there will likely be a large number of problems, and debugging will be horrendously complex. Such tests are often a desperate last resort to get a project back on schedule. The resulting disaster can thus be a serious setback.

Myers describes some compromises between bottom-up and top-down testing that involve varying the degree of top-down testing while providing more thorough testing of the modules to be integrated later in the cycle.[18] With all these variations, however, control can be a problem, due to the need to satisfy the large number of module dependencies that are necessary both for the individual module tests and as each module is integrated. In planning such tests, it is essential to consider the schedule dependency on individual modules. When a critical module hits unexpected problems, the entire integration effort may be delayed. One programmer may need to resolve a knotty problem while everyone else waits. When provisions are not made to wring out each module thoroughly before integration, such crises are frequent.

TABLE 11.1
TOP-DOWN AND BOTTOM-UP INTEGRATION [18]

Bottom-up	
Major Features:	Allows early testing aimed at proving feasibility and practicality of particular modules
	Modules can be integrated in various clusters as desired
	Major emphasis is on module functionality and performance
Advantages:	No test stubs are needed
	It is easier to adjust manpower needs
	Errors in critical modules are found early
Disadvantages:	Test drivers are needed
	Many modules must be integrated before a working program is available
	Interface errors are discovered late
Comments:	At any given point, more code has been written and tested than with top-down testing
	Some people feel that bottom-up is a more intuitive test philosophy
Top-down	
Major Features:	The control program is tested first
	Modules are integrated one at a time
	Major emphasis is on interface testing
Advantages:	No test drivers are needed
	The control program plus a few modules forms a basic early prototype
	Interface errors are discovered early
	Modular features aid debugging
Disadvantages:	Test stubs are needed
	The extended early phases dictate a slow manpower buildup
	Errors in critical modules at low levels are found late
Comments:	An early working program raises morale and helps convince management progress is being made
	It is hard to maintain a pure top-down strategy in practice

Source: Myers, G. J., *Software Reliability, Principles and Practices.* New York: Wiley, 1976.

System Build.   Since integration is a process of incrementally building a system, there is often a need to have special groups do this work. In building large software systems, build experts often integrate the components in system builds (spins), maintain configuration management control, and distribute the builds back to development for module and component test. These experts work with development to establish an integration plan and then build the drivers and integrate the system.

The key considerations in system build are detailed planning and tight control. The build plan specifies the number of spins and their schedules. At one extreme, with only one spin, is big bang integration. The opposite extreme, called continuous integration, has turned out to be the most successful approach for large systems such as IBM's OS/360.[18]

The build plan specifies the content of each spin, the cut-off date for submitting components, and the regression and functional testing requirements. Spin contents are defined in something called an "expect list" that identifies each module, its update level, the external functions it provides, and all the error fixes that it contains.

The build control process establishes criteria for including components in a spin. Generally this requires source and object code, accompanied by the final verified version of the component expect list, the component test history, the bugs found and fixed since the previous spin, any special instructions required for component build and test, and an updated set of component regression tests. When some function is left out of a module at the last minute, it can force other components to either discard or redo part or all of their integration and test plan. This need for tight schedule control and rigid integration criteria requires that the development work be synchronized. As systems grow larger, synchronization becomes less and less practical. One solution is to break the system into subsystems that are separately integrated and released. If the subsystem interdependencies can be minimized, this approach can be reasonably effective.

11.3.3 Function Testing (Black Box)

Functional or black box tests are designed to exercise the program to its external specifications. The testers are typically not biased by knowledge of the program's design and thus will likely provide tests that resemble the user's environment. The two most typical problems with black box testing are the need for explicitly stated requirements and the ability of such tests to cover only a small portion of the possible test conditions. If sufficiently detailed requirements are not available to design the functional tests, it is also likely that the requirements were inadequate for program design as well.

Since exhaustive black box testing is generally impossible, these test should be viewed as statistical sampling; when errors are found, a closer examination is required. By examining the test data it should then be possible to identify the jungles that should be returned for rework. The gardens can then be examined for any pathological cases that might have been overlooked.

Functional testing starts by examining the functions the program is to perform and devising a sequence of inputs to test them. Myers suggests that test cases be developed for all valid input conditions and options at nominal values, at their limits, and beyond these limits.[18] Test cases should also examine the program's behavior at the various volume or environmental extremes and with invalid or unexpected inputs.

11.3.4 Regression Testing

As Aron points out, testing is both progressive and regressive.[2] The progressive phase introduces and tests new functions, uncovering problems in the newly added or modified modules and in their interfaces with the previously integrated modules. The regressive phase concerns the effects of the newly introduced changes on all the previously integrated code. Problems arise when errors made in incorporating new functions affect previously tested functions. In large software systems these regression problems are common.

Regression testing is particularly important in software maintenance, where it is not uncommon for bug fixes to disrupt seemingly unrelated functions. Since these regressed functions have often been available and may be essential to users' system operations, errors that slip through the maintenance test process can be very disruptive.

The basic regression testing approach is to incorporate selected test cases into a regression test bucket that is run periodically in an attempt to detect regression problems. The decision on what to include in this bucket involves a trade-off between a comprehensive bucket that is run infrequently and a subset that is run more often. In many software organizations regression testing consists of rerunning all the functional tests every few months. This delays the discovery of regression problems and generally results in significant rework after every regression run.

The strategy that has proved most effective for many large systems is to accumulate a comprehensive regression bucket but also to define a subset. The full bucket is run only occasionally, but the subset is run against every spin. The spin subset should include all the test cases for any recently integrated functions and a selected sample from the full regression bucket.

The next problem is to decide how much of a subset to use and which tests to select. While such decisions must consider the complexity and criticality of the program, they also should be based on the success history of the test cases themselves. Generally some will be effective in finding regression problems, while others will be better at uncovering new function problems. The problems in newly integrated functions are usually associated with the beaten paths in the jungle, while regression problems generally concern the rare pathological cases that are often overlooked in functional testing.

Regression testing is more art than science, but a little data on test case run time and effectiveness can help to optimize the process. It is best to select tests that have been demonstrably effective at finding regression and that take minimal run or set-up time. Since few, if any, cases will ideally fit these conditions, trade-offs are required. During system integration, however, some regression tests should be run against every spin.

11.3.5 System Test

Myers has said, "If you do not have written objectives for your product, or if your objectives are unmeasurable, then you cannot perform a system test."[18]

The program objectives should specify what is to be done for the end users. When these objectives are not specific, neither the testing nor the system design and implementation can be accurately planned. When systems are built without good objectives, they must often be rebuilt before they can be used. Finally, even if the objectives are clear, they may not accurately reflect the end users' needs. System tests can only identify this problem if there is some connection between the ultimate users and the people designing the system tests. This is why system test planning should be done by a special test organization with a reasonably direct link to the end users, possibly through a users group or by close contact with selected key users. With such knowledge, system test planning will often uncover problems that have been undiscovered throughout the entire development process. As is often said at the time, "If only someone had talked to the users."

As shown in Table 11.2, Myers has defined several categories of system tests.[18] Their purpose is to find those cases in which the system does not work as intended, regardless of the specifications. If the system fails these tests, the debate about whether or not it meets the specifications is really an argument over who is at fault and who should pay for repair. Concern about these issues often causes management to insist that system testing be limited to the requirements and specifications. While this defers such problems, it makes them more damaging and expensive when later found by the users. Regardless of what the contract says, if the system does not meet the users' real needs, everyone loses.

Some areas that need special system test attention are operational errors and intentional misuse. People do strange things to systems, particularly when they are disgruntled or tired. With the increasingly pervasive use of sophisticated computing systems in modern society, we must also be more concerned about the problems of intentional misuse by vandals, criminals, and even terrorists. System tests should thus examine as many of these pathological situations as practical to ensure that the system does not behave pathologically as well.

While Myers's 11 types of system tests may seem impractically expensive, they each play a role in determining system effectiveness. Some tests may not be needed, and others may be abbreviated, but most are generally required before any reasonably sophisticated system can be installed in a sensitive operational environment.

As applications become more critical, behavior under stressful or anomalous conditions becomes more important. It is at the point of highest system stress when system behavior is generally most critical and when there will be the least tolerance for error. These high-stress periods are precisely when failures are most likely, when system behavior is least predictable, and when the operators are least able to handle the problems. The most critical systems should thus be stressed most thoroughly during tests that include performance, recovery, and human factors issues.

TABLE 11.2
SYSTEM TEST CATEGORIES [18]*

Load/Stress

Objective: To identify the peak load conditions at which the system fails.

Conditions: The system is subjected to peak rates for the key operational parameters, including transaction volume, operator/user load, file activity, error rates, and key combinations.

Considerations: While essential for all critical applications, such tests are rarely run because they require large configurations, need extensive preparation and support, and the stress conditions are considered unlikely. It is, however, precisely these unlikely conditions that are the most dangerous.

Volume

Objectives: This test is to determine the level of continuous heavy load at which the system will fail.

Conditions: The system is subjected to continuous heavy load conditions, as opposed to the short peak loads used for stress testing.

Considerations: The test should determine the limits of system behavior by pushing the volume beyond normal limits to see where it fails and in what way.

Configuration

Objectives: This test is intended to find those planned legal hardware and/or software configurations on which the system will not operate correctly.

Conditions: All legal hardware and software types should be tested at the maximum and minimum configurations.

Considerations: Because of the large costs or installation facilities required, such tests are often limited to the largest end user facilities that can be obtained for the test period. Such limited tests are generally inadequate and should be repeated whenever larger facilities can be obtained.

Compatibility

Objectives: This test is intended to expose those areas where the system has improper incompatibilities.

Conditions: All the compatibility objectives should be tested, including those concerning hardware and software interfaces, data and language classes, and system conversion.

Considerations: This can be an expensive and time-consuming test, but it is particularly crucial when system conversions are planned.

Security

Objectives: This test is to find ways to break the security provisions of the system.

Conditions: Because most security breaches are due to inadequate physical protection, this test should include facilities, procedures, hardware, system service, communications, and software.

Considerations: While some of this testing can be done by the systems test people, expert advice is generally advisable.

TABLE 11.2 (continued)

Performance
  Objectives: This test is intended to determine the actual performance of the sys-
                   tem against the performance objectives under peak and normal
                   conditions.

  Conditions: Typical transaction rates and response times are measured.

  Considerations: Performance measurement requires performance specifications, which
                   are difficult to produce. When practical, actual predecessor system
                   performance should be measured to determine the types of parame-
                   ters, job streams, scenarios, or other measures that would indicate
                   suitable performance.

Installability
  Objectives: This test is to identify the ways in which the system installation pro-
                   cedures lead to incorrect results.

  Conditions: Here the need is to test the installation instructions and facilities to see
                   how they work in real or simulated environments.

  Considerations: Generally the program developers know too much about the system
                   to produce understandable instructions. It is thus wise to try the
                   installation procedures on typical users to see where they
                   have trouble understanding or following the instructions pre-
                   cisely.

Reliability / Availability
  Objectives: This test measures reliability and availability while the system is oper-
                   ating with a typical workload.

  Conditions: This generally involves operating the system for long periods and mea-
                   suring both its reliability and availability.

  Considerations: While these system characteristics are of great importance, they are
                   typically not directly testable. They are thus often estimated by mea-
                   suring mean time to failure and availability during the other system
                   tests. When time and facilities are available, long-term burn-in tests
                   with simulated or actual application loads provide the best basis for
                   determining these characteristics.

Recovery
  Objectives: This test determines the behavior of the system after the occurrence of
                   an error or other abnormal condition.

  Conditions: Again, this test is often best conducted during the other system tests
                   or with special burn-in tests.

  Considerations: Recovery performance is often not specified but is generally critical
                   both to the using environment and for timely problem identification
                   and repair. If sufficient information cannot be obtained from the other
                   tests, then special tests should be run with artificially induced anom-
                   alies.

TABLE 11.2 (continued)

Serviceability

Objectives: The serviceability test objective is to identify conditions in which suffi-
                cient serviceability information and facilities will not be available to
                service personnel following erroneous system operation.

Conditions: This test involves inducing the most likely system errors and assessing
                the information provided and the system's behavior.

Considerations: This is one of the more difficult system tests because it requires hard-
                ware, software, and application knowledge as well as special facilities
                to simulate the important anomalous hardware and system conditions.

Human Factors

Objectives: This test is to identify those operations that will be difficult or inconve-
                nient for the users or operators.

Conditions: Human factors tests must include the publications, software facilities,
                and the planned operating procedures. Where possible, end user
                personnel should use the actual documentation in circumstances
                that closely approximate the expected operating environment.

Considerations: Regardless of code quality, poor documentation generally results in
                poor human factors and poor operational system performance. Such
                tests are thus mandatory.

---

*This is an edited version of Myers's original text, but it retains the basic material.

Source: Myers, G. J. *Software Reliability, Principles and Practices.* New York: Wiley, 1976.

11.3.6 Acceptance and Installation Tests

After all development testing is completed, it is often advisable to try the system in
a real user's environment. Even though such field tests generally require special
support, the results are invariably worth far more than the added costs. Often when
software is developed under contract, some form of acceptance testing is required
in a real or simulated user environment. When this is not the case, the developers
can often arrange with selected users to act as special "beta test" sites in return for
special installation support and early program availability.

If end user testing is not practical, it may be possible to try the system in an
internal application environment. Large corporations, for example, often can use
such programs in their regular internal computer operations. These tests are not as
useful as user testing, but they are better than not obtaining any early installation or
operational experience at all.

11.4 Test Planning

Metzger reports asking many integration testers from many projects what they
would do differently on their next project. They invariably say they would do a

better job of test planning. As he says, "It's too late to begin test planning when testing actually begins. All that you can do then is fumble and pray that baseline designing and unit testing have been done so well that things fall into place easily."[14] Unfortunately, disaster generally strikes when organizations most desperately need things to fall into place. Planning is the only reliable way to mitigate such problems. In fact, Beizer claims that test planning can uncover at least as many problems as the actual tests themselves.[4]

Test planning starts with an overall development plan that defines the functions, roles, and methods for all test phases.[16] An appropriate planning checklist is given in Table 11.3.[4] To be fully effective, test planning must start during the requirements phase. Some items needed for a good test plan must come from this phase, and they must be tracked throughout development. It is thus wise to conduct an early requirements inspection or walkthrough and to hold a re-review after every major change. To ensure that the requirements provide a reasonable basis for testing, the test group should participate in these reviews.

Myers describes test planning in considerable detail, but the major test plan elements are:[18]

- □ Establish objectives for each test phase.
- □ Establish schedules and responsibilities for each test activity.
- □ Determine the availability of the tools, facilities, and test libraries.
- □ Establish the procedures and standards to be used for planning and conducting the tests and reporting the test results.
- □ Set the criteria for test completion as well as for the success of each test.

11.4.1 The Test Files

It is helpful to establish a development file system to retain this information both for the test plan in general and for each test and test case.[3] These files should be defined and provisions made to retain them as part of the configuration management plan. Such files provide a useful way to relate all the material on each test and help to establish a test database. This file should also contain the specifications, design, documentation, review history, test history, test instructions, anticipated results, and success criteria for each test case. As discussed later, retention of the test results is also critically important.

11.4.2 Test Success Criteria

Establishing the test success criteria is probably the most difficult part of test planning, due to both the developers' attitudes and to their general lack of quantitative experience. The developers' viewpoint is that a successful test is one that

TABLE 11.3
TEST PLAN REVIEW CHECKLIST [4]

Testing Structure

Are the testing levels (including informal tests) defined? Are the scope and objectives for each testing level stated?

Are the test support software and hardware needed for testing identified?

Are the organizations responsible for each testing level identified? Are their responsibilities clearly defined? Are the testers independent from the software developers?

Are independent internal reviews planned? Are the organizations responsible for these reviews identified? Will these reviews include:
   software design
   test plans
   test procedures
   test results

Are standards given for these reviews? Are correction procedures stated?

Is a schedule shown for the testing activities?

Are formal reviews and audits identified? Is a schedule shown for each? Is the documentation to be available for each review and audit listed?

Is an independent Quality Assurance organization identified? Do you know what QA's role in software testing will be? Do you know what its relationship to CM is?

Testing Control

Is an organization identified to control software products and documents?

Are the products and documents that will be controlled identified?

Does the configuration management plan state when these items will be baselined?

Does the development plan state how items will be controlled prior to formal baselining?

Is a mechanism given to implement this control stating:
   how changes to controlled items are proposed
   how requests for changes are reviewed and resolved
   how controlled items are changed
   who has the responsibility for each of the above activities

Testing Standards

Are standards listed for the testing activities?

Is an organization identified with the responsibility to enforce the standards? Does this organization "sign off" on the completed test procedures and report?

Is a mechanism identified to map requirements and specifications to test cases?

Testing Objectives and Priorities

Is the testing philosophy defined? Is it shown how this leads to the final acceptance tests?

Is the importance of testability relative to other software characteristics discussed?

Documentation

Is the documentation approach discussed?

Is each contractually deliverable testing document identified?

Is the organization responsible for each contractually deliverable document shown?

---

executes completely without encountering a problem. The testers measure success, however, by bugs found. Each test should be planned against yield criterion (bugs per test run) that is determined from prior experience. The testers' goal should then be to increase test case yield, while the developers' is to produce code that will reduce test yield.

When the testers acknowledge that they cannot meet their yield objectives, their work should be technically reviewed to see if it is adequate. If the tests were competently prepared and run, the programs should be passed to the next phase and subsequent experience tracked. The testers should determine why they did not catch any bug that is later found and how to improve their tests so they would catch similar problems in the future.

11.5 Test Development

After developing the test plan, the next job is to produce the test cases. The decision on what test cases to develop is complicated by two factors. First, as already pointed out, full test coverage is generally impossible. Second, there is no proven comprehensive method for selecting the highest yielding test conditions.

Myers used to have his programming classes design the tests needed to prove that a simple program was absolutely correct.[18] The program read three integers representing the sides of a triangle and printed out whether the triangle was scalene, isosceles, or equilateral.

This almost trivial program must meet a total of 14 conditions to function correctly under all input combinations. Even with very experienced programmers, Myers found that the likelihood of their producing tests that covered a reasonably complete set of these combinations was quite small. On average, experienced programmers only tested about 8 of the 14 conditions, and a surprising six out of ten students failed to state the expected results for each of their tests.[22] The percentages of programmers who checked for specific bugs are shown in Table 11.4.[18]

Judging by the performance of experienced programmers on such a simple test design problem, it is clear that test case design is not simple. This is why system testing is essential and why trial system operation in a real environment is equally important. Because even experienced software professionals make errors and overlook conditions, it is essential to hold walkthroughs of the test plans and inspections of the test cases. Table 11.5 gives a checklist for a unit test review.

11.5.1 Test Coverage Techniques

One approach to the test coverage problem is to view the program as a graph with nodes and to ensure that these nodes and the paths between them are adequately

TABLE 11.4
TEST RESULTS FOR TRIANGLE PROGRAM [18]

Hypothetical Bug	Percent of Students That Would Have Detected the Bug
Program doesn't check to see if input forms a triangle	56
Program checks for triangle, but only $A < B + C$	28
Program doesn't check for scalene	84
Program doesn't check for isosceles	95
Program checks for isosceles but only for $A = B \neq C$	46
Program doesn't check for equilateral	100

Source: Myers, G. J., *Software Reliability, Principles and Practices*. New York: Wiley, 1976.

covered by the tests. With white box testing, the structure of the program itself is reduced to a graph on which, in general, the branch instructions define the nodes and the remaining instructions make up the paths. Means are devised to get as good coverage of this graph as practical.

The adequacy of test coverage can be roughly assessed by comparing the number of test paths executed with the complexity of the program graph. A metric such as that suggested by Card and Agresti can help with this analysis.[5] The idea is to measure module complexity in terms of the numbers of parameter values the module produces in response to inputs and the number it receives from other modules. The more complex the modules the more testing they should receive.

11.5.2 Path Selection in Unit Test

While there are no simple rules for selecting testing paths to achieve adequate test coverage, some general guidelines can help:[4]

1. Pick defined (in the requirements) functional paths that simply connect from entrance to exit.
2. Pick additional paths as small variations, favoring short paths over long ones, simple paths over complicated ones, and logically reasonable paths over illogical ones.
3. Next, to provide coverage, pick additional paths that have no obvious functional meaning.

Even a plan for full path coverage does not guarantee that all the paths will be covered or that all the errors will be found. Path testing may be blocked by bugs

TABLE 11.5
UNIT TEST REVIEW CHECKLIST

Is the design clear? Does it do what is intended?

Is the coding clear? Did you have trouble understanding it?

Are the comments helpful in understanding the routine?

Would you have trouble modifying it?

Would you be proud of this work if it were yours?

Does the code meet the established coding standards?

Do the tests meet the established unit test standards?

Does input data vary, including maximum, minimum, and nominal values? (All alike data, especially all zeros, is usually a poor choice.)

Is erroneous input data used? (All error conditions should be checked.) Can you think of erroneous data conditions that were not used?

Do the tests show that the routine has the functional capabilities allocated to it?

Do the tests demonstrate that the code completely satisfies each requirement allocated to it?

Does the actual output match the expected output?

---

and may not detect wrong or missing functions, interface errors, database errors, or initialization errors.[4] There are a number of alternate strategies for conducting structural or white box tests and Ntafos provides a useful comparison of them.[20]

11.5.3 Path Coverage in Functional Testing

For functional or black box testing, one technique for selecting tests is based on functional paths. Here the program functions are considered as a set of transaction flows that form functional paths through the program. These transaction flows can be reduced to graphs of nodes and paths much as in white box testing, and the tests are again designed to achieve coverage of these nodes and paths. These then form the paths to be covered by the functional tests in much the way as with unit tests.[4]

For this testing to be effective, all the functional paths should be defined in the requirements and they should explicitly state what the program is supposed to do. When these paths have not been well defined, it is unlikely that the program could have been designed properly. This is not inherently a testing problem, although it is often uncovered by testing.

Path Selection.   With a defined set of functional paths it is necessary to decide which paths to cover. While there are no guidelines for functional path selection, it is generally a good idea to start by considering the data handled by the program. Howden has suggested some data selection steps that have proven effective for scientific routines, as given in Table 11.6.[12] His general principles for test data selection should also be considered for functional tests of other types of programs.

TABLE 11.6
FUNCTIONAL TESTING DATA SELECTION GUIDELINES [12]

Input Numeric Variables

For small domains of discrete values of input variables, test all values.

For large domains or ranges of input variables, test at the range extremes and at selected intermediate values.

Each variable should be tested for all valid types and value classes; i.e., zero, blank, negative, etc.

Each input variable should be tested for invalid conditions; i.e., alpha in numeric field, negative in positive field, fractional in integer field, etc.

Where two or more variables are related (i.e., $x > y$), tests should be selected both for legal and illegal values.

Output Numeric Variables

For small domains or discrete output variable values, select input combinations that test all values.

For large domains or ranges of output variables, select input combinations that test at all extreme values and selected intermediate values.

Each variable should be tested for all valid types and value classes; i.e., zero, blank, negative, etc.

Attempts should be made to find input variable combinations that will drive each output variable to illegal values.

When two or more variables are related (i.e., degrees of freedom in a Chi-square distribution), both identical values should be tested, as well as distinct values over all pertinent domains defined above.

Where two or more variables are related (i.e., $x > y$), tests should be selected both for legal and illegal values.

Arrays and Vectors

The individual elements of arrays and vectors should be tested as with numeric values above.

The set of allowable values for the dimensions of the arrays should be tested at the limits, within allowable ranges, and outside.

The structure as a whole should be tested under special conditions; i.e., all 0 values, all identical values, all but one 0, diagonal, etc.

Where any substructure such as a row or column has a special identity, its variables should be tested as above.

Selecting test data for a telecommunications message handling routine, for example, would involve examining program behavior for a subset of normal values for each element of a message, as well as for all the special cases. Such testing would identify program behavior for all correct and incorrect values of the control characters, as well as for pathological conditions such as zero-length messages, blank messages, unusually long messages, and so forth.

While there is no magic way to select a sufficient set of practical tests, the objective is to test reasonably completely all valid classes for normal operation and to exhaustively test behavior under unusual and illegal conditions.

One way to look at the adequacy of a test is to determine the degree to which all the requisite conditions have been covered. Goodenough and Gerhart have suggested a systematic approach for defining the essential conditions of a program as a means for determining the required minimum set of test predicates.[11] They use decision tables to identify systematically the classes of conditions to be tested. Every class is then tested to ensure reasonable coverage of the normal and pathological cases.

A Suggested Path Selection Technique.   Prather and Myers also have suggested techniques for handling path selection.[19, 21] Their general approach is to establish equivalence classes based on the various parameters and conditions for the program. For each parameter or condition, an equivalence class would cover all valid values. An equivalence class would also be established for each invalid class, such as above range or below range. This would also include the use of incorrect names and pathological cases (such as zero-length messages). The tests are then designed to cover every equivalence class at least once. The invalid classes should, however, be treated singly because one invalid condition can cause the program to behave abnormally so that other invalid conditions may not be encountered during the test.

While this brief description only indicates the general approach, Myers's text *The Art of Software Testing* provides a more detailed explanation.[19]

11.5.4 Test Case Design Guidelines

Even though there are no simple rules for test case design, some general guidelines can be helpful:[4]

- ☐ Do it wrong.
- ☐ Use wrong combinations.
- ☐ Don't do enough.
- ☐ Do nothing.
- ☐ Do too much.

In addition, some more general overall considerations are:[4]

- ☐ *Don't forget the normal cases!*
- ☐ Don't go overboard with cases.
- ☐ Don't ignore structure.
- ☐ Remember that there is more than one kind of test.

Since the objective of test case design is to catch errors rather than to prove the program works, it is wise to consider the common types of errors. Goodenough and Gerhart have classified the major errors into three types:[11]

1. *Missing control flow paths*   Where the program fails to test particular conditions or to include unique sequences of conditions

2. *Inappropriate path selection*   Where a condition is expressed incorrectly so that an action is not performed when it should be or is performed when it should not be

3. *Inappropriate or missing action*   Where, for example, an algorithm is either omitted or is implemented but results in an incorrect value

In designing tests one should assume that such errors are distributed throughout the program and devise ways to find all of them.

11.6 Test Execution and Reporting

Every test should be treated like an experiment to be carefully controlled and recorded so that it can be reproduced. This experimental view requires that all anomalous behavior be noted and investigated. As many researchers have learned, dogged curiosity about strange and unexpected events often produces the most important results.

Testing is just this type of dogged exploration. A program is examined to determine its behavior. Though the standard functions may perform as predicted, there are often subtle clues that, if investigated, can lead to further discoveries. For example, when a program is incorrectly initiated, it may behave in a strange way. While it is appropriate to restart the test correctly, such anomalies should be noted and later explored.

The experimental approach also requires meticulous care in defining and recording the test environment, the procedures, and the test cases. Many organizations have found it valuable to keep a special test library with all copies of such material, together with the test reports, incident forms, test analyses, and test plans. Since just about everything goes through test at some time or other, such files often become gold mines of information, particularly when historical data is needed or when something has been lost and can't be found anywhere else.

11.6.1 Test Reports

At the conclusion of each test, a test report should be produced. The amount of detail included depends on the purpose of the test and the audience for the report. In the case of acceptance tests, a considerable amount of detail is generally required, including the qualifications of the test observers, detailed data on test results, and the plans to resolve the troubles reported.

A typical test report would include the following information:

1. The names of the project and programs being tested (with their IDs), the purpose of the test, and the relevant test plan

2. The responsible project and test people involved together with the run ID

3. The specific test cases (with their IDs), procedures, and data, including identifying numbers, report references, versions, and dates

4. Any special tools, drivers, stubs, or scaffolding used (see page 196).

5. The hardware and software system configurations used, including types, features, models, engineering change levels, configuration connections, layouts, and memory and file maps

6. Test results, including all incidents by type and incident report number, all bugs found with bug report numbers and the test cases that generated them, and any statistics on test operation including test time, number of runs, and personnel required

7. Identification of those items retained in the test library and those that are not and where they can be found

8. Signatures of those responsible for monitoring and conducting the tests, and certification that the appropriate procedures have been followed and the data recorded

While this is a substantial amount of data, it is relatively easy to obtain if a test log is maintained and care is taken to record every event as it occurs. Even with such care, after-the-fact generation of such reports is very difficult if not impossible. Typical test incident and software trouble report forms are shown in Table 11.7 and Table 11.8. These forms are based on ones used in a large military software system.

11.6.2 Bug Classification

As part of the test reporting process, it is desirable to have standard definitions for bug severity. This allows the follow-up actions to be prioritized and the critical items to be tracked. An example of bug severity classification is shown in Table 11.9. This classification is also taken from a military software system designed for use under field conditions. Clearly, severity classifications must consider the operational circumstances of the resulting system.

A somewhat different classification system has been proposed by Beizer, as shown in Table 11.10.[4] While this ten-level priority system is more detailed than is generally appropriate for defect reporting, it provides a valuable framework for considering what can happen to systems and how to judge bug severity. It is,

TABLE 11.7
SAMPLE TEST INCIDENT FORM

TEST INCIDENT FORM

DATE: _____ FORM #: _____ TEST ID: _____

EQUIPMENT/SYSTEM: _____

_____

_____

PROBLEM DESCRIPTION: _____

_____

_____

_____

_____

_____

_____

_____

_____

_____

_____

ACTION TAKEN:

   STEP REPEATED: _____   TEST CONTINUED: _____

   TEST RESTART: _____   TEST STOP: _____

   OTHER (EXPLAIN): _____

DISPOSITION:

   BR* GENERATED (#): _____   OPERATOR ERROR: _____

   TEST ERROR: _____   H/W TROUBLE: _____

   DOCUMENTATION: _____   CP* GENERATED (#): _____

   OTHER (EXPLAIN): _____

TESTER: _____ DATE: _____

TEST MANAGER: _____ DATE: _____

QUALITY ASSURANCE MANAGER: _____ DATE: _____

---

*BR = bug report
 CP = change proposal

TABLE 11.8
SAMPLE BUG REPORT FORM

BUG REPORT FORM

DATE: _____ BR #: _____ PROJECT: _____

DESCRIPTIVE NAME: _____

CORRECTION NEEDED BY/PRIORITY: _____

IDENTIFIERS AND VERSION NUMBERS: _____

_____

_____

PROBLEM DESCRIPTION (test details, system, data): _____

_____

_____

_____

_____

_____

_____

_____

ORIGINATOR: _____ DATE: _____

CHANGE #: _____ DATE: _____

ASSIGNED TO: _____ DATE: _____

PRIORITY: _____

CHANGE CONTROL BOARD COMMENTS: _____

_____

_____

_____

CHANGE CONTROL BOARD APPROVAL: _____ DATE: _____

FIX #: _____ DATA: _____

TABLE 11.8 (continued)

COMPLETE WHEN FIX COMPLETED AND LOGGED:

IDENTIFICATION OF ALL ITEMS CHANGED: _____

_____

_____

_____

_____

_____

_____

_____

RESOLVED BY: _____ DATE: _____

ORIGINATOR COMMENTS: _____

_____

_____

ORIGINATOR ACCEPT: _____ DATE: _____

SOFTWARE QUALITY ASSURANCE COMMENTS: _____

_____

_____

SOFTWARE QUALITY ASSURANCE VERIFY: _____ DATE: _____

SOFTWARE CONFIGURATION MANAGEMENT LOGGED: _____ DATE: _____

SOFTWARE CONFIGURATION MANAGEMENT COMMENTS: _____

_____

_____

SOFTWARE CONFIGURATION MANAGEMENT CLOSE: _____ DATE: _____

however, more common to have the most severe problems labeled "Severity 1" and to have decreasing severity indicated by larger numbers. It is also wise to limit the number of categories to four or five.

11.6.3 Test Analysis

Since tests are intended to gather data on programs, the resulting information should be analyzed and used to make decisions. The principle behind test analysis was stated by Myers when he said that "as the number of detected errors in a piece of software increases, the probability of the existence of more undetected errors also increases."[18] This increasing probability indicates a likely jungle.

In general the evidence for junglelike conditions can be found by examining the test results and the characteristics of the problems found. Some of the indicators are:

▢ The occurrence of problems does not decline monotonically with testing.
▢ Occasionally, when new test environments or test cases are tried, a new crop of problems shows up.
▢ The errors generally have their roots in design problems.
▢ The code has undergone several changes by several different programmers.

An effective way to determine the quality of a program's code is to hold inspections of those segments with the worst error histories. When possible, the review team should include the original designers and some programmers with independent experience with similar programs. If the reviewers conclude that there are serious design problems, the offending segment should be completely overhauled.

Another important area for analysis concerns the types of problems found. If, for example, several interface problems are found in one module, it would be wise to check the other modules for problems with these interfaces and this module for problems with other interfaces. Similarly, the distribution of defect types is often fairly stable within a project or development group. If this is the case and if some programs deviate widely from this norm, the test and inspection processes should be checked to see if they are sufficiently thorough.

Finally, data should be gathered on test case yield. This metric will show the effectiveness of the test cases at finding bugs as a function of size or run time. Those tests with the highest yield during regression testing should be identified for continued inclusion in the regression test buckets. Test effectiveness should be checked periodically and the regression buckets updated.

It is also desirable to tune the regression buckets to place particular emphasis on those system areas that have been changed most recently. When some test cases are demonstrably effective at finding errors caused by changes in the I/O routines, for example, they should be used to test any builds that include such changes.

TABLE 11.9
BUG SEVERITY CLASSIFICATION—MILITARY SYSTEM

Severity 1   An error that prevents the accomplishment of an operational or mission-essential function, prevents the operator/user from performing a mission-essential function, or jeopardizes personnel safety

Severity 2   An error that adversely affects the accomplishment of an operational or mission-essential function and for which no acceptable alternative workarounds are available

Severity 3   An error that adversely affects the accomplishment of an operational or mission-essential function for which acceptable alternative workarounds are available

Severity 4   An error that is an operator/user inconvenience and affects operational or mission-essential functions

Severity 5   All other errors

11.7 Test Tools and Methods

A discussion of the wide variety of tools and methods available to assist with the test process is beyond the scope of this book. There is, however, an extensive literature on this subject.[1, 3, 4, 8, 10, 12, 16, 17, 18, 19] A document TRW prepared for the Air Force on "Software Testing and Evaluation" also gives a listing of some available testing tools.[3] It is reproduced in Table 11.11.

TABLE 11.10
BUG SEVERITY CLASSIFICATIONS [4]

1—mild—an aesthetic problem such as a misspelling or output formatting problem

2—moderate—misleading or redundant outputs with small but measurable impact on system performance

3—annoying—the system behavior is dehumanizing: truncated names, nonsense outputs, etc.

4—disturbing—the system refuses to handle legitimate transactions

5—serious—loses track of transactions

6—very serious—the system executes the wrong transactions

7—extreme—the above problems frequently and arbitrarily occur

8—intolerable—long-term, unrecoverable corruption of the database occurs and is not readily apparent

9—catastrophic—the system fails

10—infectious—the system, when malfunctioning, corrupts other systems: a system that kills

This list probably does not include automatic test case generators because they are not generally cost-effective. As Munoz points out, where such generators can be used to produce large numbers of essentially random test cases, they can be very effective.[17] The first of their three main problems is that randomly generated tests rarely have high bug yield. Second, while such tools can usually produce large numbers of random input conditions, they are rarely able to generate the anticipated outputs. Analysis of the test results is thus time-consuming. Finally, the programmer who develops the random generator will also likely fail to consider some key conditions and may thus overlook an entire functional area. Though certain well-structured problems can be effectively tested this way, test case generators are not generally effective in finding pathological cases and subtle error conditions.

Another and possibly more promising technique was originally proposed by Mills.[15] The idea of *error seeding* is to purposefully inject known defects into a program and then note the percent of them that are found during testing. The implication is that the percents of these injected defects found in test provides a reasonable indication of the efficiency of the tests at finding the other defects as well. While there have been doubts about the validity of this approach, Knight and Amman have reported experimental results that support the concept.[13] The method should thus be considered, at least for experimental use.

11.8 Real-Time Testing

Real-time testing can be particularly difficult because the development work is done on a host system and then compiled for execution on a target system. Typically a reasonable set of test and debug facilities is available for the host environment but the target system is generally much more sparsely equipped. Some of these problems are discussed by Taylor.[24] Tausworthe also provides some rules for testing real time programs that resulted from the extensive experience of the Jet Propulsion Laboratory with the U.S. space program.[23] In summary, these rules are:

- Devise ways to exercise each system state either in real time or in simulated parametric time.
- Design ways to simulate any modules missing in the current test phase so the real-time tests can operate.
- Evaluate possible deadlocks, thrashing, or sensitivity to special timing conditions.
- Use tests that simulate hardware faults or special system conditions.
- Use hardware simulation to stress the software design.

TABLE 11.11
TEST TOOLS [3]

Purpose	Tool	Description
Enforcement of software standards	Code auditor	Checks that appropriate structure and coding constraints were observed
	Test auditor	Determines number of branches exercised and not exercised during a series of test runs
Requirements verification	Test requirements Verification Matrix	Lists each requirement and the test(s) that demonstrates the software satisfies the requirements
Product management	Checksum or comparator	Compares two sets of code or data to determine that they are identical
	Software patch manager	Creates files of software patches for use by test teams
	Software library manager	Aids in creating and maintaining files of baselined software products for users
Error detection and performance analysis	Editor or static analyzer	Analyzes source code for coding errors and obtains information used to check relationships between sections of code, determines data usage (elements, input, output), checks error-prone constructions, determines inaccessible instructions
	Flow chart generator	Creates a flow chart from the code (it may show where data elements are set and used)
	Instrumenters	Inserts instructions into code to record the value of data elements during execution
	Dump and/or data logging	Records the value of data elements under specific conditions (the data may be formatted and may be selected by the tester)
	Pathfinders	Records the history of routines called prior to the occurrence of a specified condition (usually an error condition)
	Simulator (or simulator interface)	Simulates external devices or environments (or provides an interface between an existing simulator and the software) to provide a more realistic environment for testing
	Data reduction programs	Provides a language that allows easier access to output data
	Summaries, plots, graphics, statistical charts	Summarizes software performance for analysis, presentation, and generation of reports

TABLE 11.11 (continued)

Purpose	Tool	Description
	Dynamic analyzer	Collects statistics on software characteristics, such as paths executed, frequency of execution of sections of code, percentage of total execution time used by sections of code, queue lengths, and waiting times
	Timing analyzer	Monitors and reports execution time of program elements
	Driver	Simulates calling routines to allow called routines to be executed
	Stubs	Simulates called routines not yet developed to allow developed routines to be tested
	Computer simulator or interpretive computer simulator	Simulates the execution characteristics of a target computer (for which the software is written)—the program is executed on another computer (a host computer)
	Emulator	Computer firmware tailored to operate exactly like the computer it replaces
	Data analyzer	A program that checks the definition and use of data items for consistency, proper specification, and use
	Hardware monitor	A hardware device that obtains signals from probes inserted in a host computer's circuitry
	Interface checker	A computer program that checks the ranges of variables to ensure compliance with interface design specifications
Production of test scripts	Test data generators	Creates test data, usually in a form directly accessible to the software being tested
	Job control language (JCL) data	Sequences of JCL allowing a tester to execute one or more tests and obtain output easily (especially useful for retesting, when the same tests are executed repeatedly)

11.9 The Test Organization

Beizer talks about something he calls "bug guilt."[4] This refers to the way programmers often feel about the errors they make in programming. Even though they know that code is rarely produced without errors, they somehow feel they shouldn't make any and the fact that they do reflects on them personally.

The fact is that programmers who produce code usually also produce bugs. It is not that they necessarily want to, but that many programs are so complex as to stretch the limits of human comprehension. Even if we could truly visualize all the possible combinations and interactions of data and control flow in a program, we would immediately challenge ourselves with another and greater level of complexity. The true limit on the size and complexity of programs is the human intellect. The issue is not that programs are inherently complicated but that people are so ingenious. Programs solve problems that people define, and as soon as we learn how to define and meet a more complex need, the knowledge gained opens up new ideas and opportunities that lead to further complexity. We will thus always be faced with finding bugs in programs, and we will likely always be faced with programmers who feel guilty about producing them. These are natural consequences of our humanity.

The implication for programming organizations is that programmers are inherently incapable of effectively testing their own programs. Not only do they feel guilty about the existence of bugs, but they are biased by the creative work they have done. This inherently blinds them to their errors, not because they won't see them but because they can't.

One remedy is to separate testing from program design and implementation. Such special test groups often assume test responsibility after unit testing. This generally makes sense because white box unit tests generally require an intimate knowledge of the program's internal structure. While the programmers may not be as fiendish in their search for bugs as they should be, this lack of zeal is often counterbalanced by their understanding of the program structure and their ability to quickly devise intricate ways to exercise all its elements. Unit test standards and walkthroughs of unit test plans can also help the programmers do a reasonably effective job of unit testing their own code.

Following unit test it is generally advisable to transfer test responsibility to a dedicated test group. This group's role is to find as many bugs as possible. As they gain experience, such groups can become extraordinarily effective at finding those odd pathological cases that will only come up once in a billion executions. As unlikely as such cases may seem, with modern hardware technologies, a billion executions can happen pretty quickly.

11.10 Summary

Software testing is the execution of a program to find its faults. We should think of testing like weeding a garden: Individual bugs can be found with tests, but more powerful methods are needed for cleaning up the jungle thickets.

A test is an experiment and should be approached as such. A properly disciplined experiment starts with a hypothesis that the experiment is designed to verify or to disprove. Testing hypotheses should concern the types and quantity of defects in the program.

White box tests examine the basic design of the program and require that the tester have detailed knowledge of the program's internal structure. Black box tests examine the program to see if it meets the functional specifications. Integration is the process of assembling the parts of a system into a working whole, and it forms a bridge between black box and white box testing. Regression testing concerns the effects of newly introduced changes on all the previously integrated code. The prime objective of system testing is to find those cases in which the system does not work as intended, regardless of the specifications.

Effective test planning starts with an overall development plan that defines the functions, roles, and methods for all test phases. The conduct of every test is carefully controlled and recorded so it can be reproduced. The test results are then detailed in a test report and retained in a configuration management database along with other key test data.

Bug guilt refers to the way programmers often feel about the errors they make in programming. The fact is that programmers who produce code usually also produce bugs. We will always be faced with finding bugs in programs, and we will likely always be faced with programmers who feel guilty about producing them. The implication for programming organizations is that programmers are inherently incapable of effectively testing their own programs. One remedy is to separate testing from program design and implementation. Following unit test, it is generally advisable to transfer test responsibility to a dedicated test group whose role is to find as many bugs as possible.

References

1. Adrion, W. R., M. A. Bransted, and J. C. Cherniavsky. "Validation, verification, and testing of computer software," *Computing Surveys,* vol. 14, no. 2, June 1982.

2. Aron, J. D. *The Program Development Process, Part II, The Programming Team.* Reading, MA: Addison-Wesley, 1983.

3. Barry, M. "Airborne Systems Software Acquisition Engineering Guidebook for Software Testing and Evaluation," Redondo Beach, CA: TRW Defense and Space Systems Group, March 1980.

4. Beizer, B. *Software Testing Techniques,* New York: Van Nostrand Reinhold, 1983.

5. Card, D. N., and W. W. Agresti. "Measuring software design complexity," *Journal of Systems and Software,* vol. 8, no. 3, June 1988.

6. DeMarco, T. *Controlling Software Projects, Management, Measurement and Evaluation.* New York: Yourdon Press, 1982.

7. DeMillo, R. A. "Hints on test data selection: help for the practicing programmer," *IEEE Computer,* April 1978.

8. DeMillo, R. A., W. M. McCracken, R. J. Martin, and J. F. Passafiume. *Software Testing and Evaluation,* Menlo Park, CA: Benjamin/Cummings, 1987.

9. Dijkstra, E. W. "Structured programming," in J. N. Buxton and B. Randell, eds., *Software Engineering Techniques.* Brussels, Belgium: NATO Science Committee, 1970.

10. Fairley, R. E. *Software Engineering Concepts,* New York: McGraw-Hill, 1985.

11. Goodenough, J. B., and Susan L. Gerhart. "Toward a theory of test data selection," *IEEE Transactions on Software Engineering,* vol. SE-1, no. 2, June 1975.

12. Howden, W. E. "Functional program testing," *IEEE Proceedings COMPSAC 78,* 1978.

13. Knight, J. C., and P. E. Amman. "An experimental evaluation of error seeding as a program evaluation technique," *Proceedings of the Tenth Annual Software Engineering Workshop,* Software Engineering Laboratory, Goddard Space Flight Center, December 1985.

14. Metzger, P. W. *Managing a Programming Project,* Englewood Cliffs, NJ: Prentice-Hall, 1973.

15. Mills, H. D. "On the statistical validation of computer programs," in H. D. Mills, ed., *Software Productivity.* New York: Dorset House, 1988.

16. Mullin, F. J. "Considerations for a Successful Software Test Program," TRW-SS-77-01, TRW Software Series, Redondo Beach CA: TRW Systems Engineering and Integration Division, January 1977.

17. Munoz, C. U. "An approach to software product testing," *IEEE Transactions on Software Engineering,* vol. 14, no. 11, November 1988.

18. Myers, G. J. *Software Reliability, Principles and Practices,* New York: Wiley, 1976.

19. Myers, G.J. *The Art of Software Testing,* New York: Wiley, 1979.

20. Ntafos, S. S. "A comparison of some structural testing strategies," *IEEE Transactions of Software Engineering,* vol. 14, no. 6, June 1988, pp. 868–874.

21. Prather, R. E., and J. P. Myers, Jr. "The path prefix software testing strategy," *IEEE Transactions on Software Engineering,* vol. SE-13, no. 7, July 1987.

22. Schulmeyer, G. G., and J. I. McManus. *Handbook of Software Quality Assurance.* New York: Van Nostrand Reinhold, 1987.

23. Tausworthe, R. C. *Standardized Development of Computer Software, Part II, Standards.* Pasadena, CA: Jet Propulsion Laboratory, California Institute of Technology, 1978.

24. Taylor, R. N. "Debugging real-time software in a host-target environment," *Proceedings of the Second Software Engineering Conference,* Nice, France, June 4–6, 1984.

25. Thayer, T. A., M. Lipow, and E. C. Nelson. *Software Reliability, A Study of Large Project Reality,* vol. 2." TRW Series of Software Technology, Amsterdam: North-Holland, 1978.

12

Software Configuration Management (Continued)

This chapter builds on the basic Software Configuration Management (SCM) principles covered in Chapter 7 and extends that treatment to include requirements, specification, design, and tools.

To preserve the integrity of a software design throughout its useful life, it must be maintained under SCM control. Most programs have long lives, and many changes are made to correct errors and to make enhancements. When the design is not maintained, these subsequent changes must be made with an incomplete knowledge of the design or the logic behind it. Any relationship of the changed design to the original designers' intent is thus pure coincidence.

Lehman and Belady's "Second Law of Software Evolution" says that the entropy of a software system continually increases unless steps are take to control it.[6] Since increases in entropy mean increasing chaos, system structure thus progressively deteriorates unless efforts are made to preserve it. There are many reasons for this deterioration but they all stem from the need to make changes after the initial design has been completed.

Once the design phase is completed, the implementers are busy with code and test. When they encounter a design problem they therefore attempt to resolve it as quickly as possible. This generally limits their efforts to a quick source code change with an explanatory comment, but no update to the design documentation.

As simple as it may seem to make such updates, this is not a trivial problem. The original designers are rarely available, and it is time-consuming to search through someone else's work and figure out what was meant. With older programs the problem is often much worse. After many changes the design records are hopelessly out of date and the source code looks like a can of worms. If a simple fix gets the test case to work, the implementers would rather let somebody else worry about the design.

The real problem is letting the design deteriorate in the first place. Programs are long-term investments, and if they are to have continuing value, their designs must be maintained. As a program is successively patched, the likelihood of erroneous changes increases. It is thus essential to update the design at the same time that the code is changed.

To make design changes and to provide for their orderly implementation and test, control must be maintained over the following items:[7]

- Operational concept
- Requirements
- Specifications
- Design documents
- Source code
- Object code
- Test plans
- Test cases, test configurations, and test results
- Maintenance and development tools
- User manuals
- Maintenance manuals
- Interface control documents

To control these items and not to constrain early development excessively, design baselines are established at appropriate points.[7] While the baseline selections must be determined by the project's needs, a typical set is:

- *Requirements baseline*   This is established when the requirements are completed and initially approved. It includes the operational concept and the approved requirements documents together with an index to every required function. Subsequent requirements baselines are established for every set of requirements changes.

- *Specification baselines*   These include the program external specifications together with a cross-reference to the requirements and operational concept. Again, a baseline is established for each major approved specification and requirements change.

- *Design baselines*   These are established when the design is initially completed and inspected. They include the design itself, all critical design relationships, and the rationale for all the key design decisions. Again, cross-references are maintained among the design, the specifications, the requirements, and the operational concept.

- *Unit baselines*   As each software unit is completed, inspected, and unit tested, a unit baseline is established. Depending on the organization's prac-

TABLE 12.1
EXAMPLE BASELINE CONTENTS

	Requirements	Specs	Design	Unit Test	Integration Test	Operation
Requirements and Specifications						
Operational concept	X	X	X	X	X	X
Requirements	X	X	X	X	X	X
User needs		X	X	X	X	X
Program specifications		X		X	X	X
Product						
Product design			X	X	X	X
Module design			X	X	X	X
Design logic				X	X	X
Program logic				X	X	X
Source and object code				X	X	X
Information products				X		X
Plans						
Business plan		X	X	X	X	X
Project plan			X	X	X	X
Quality plan			X	X	X	X
Performance plan			X	X	X	X
Usability plan			X	X	X	X
Information plan			X	X	X	X
Test plan			X	X	X	X
Installation plan			X	X	X	X
Service plan				X		X
Distribution plan						X
Maintenance plan						X
Tools, Tests, and Records						
Change records	X	X	X	X	X	X
Tool set used			X	X	X	
Test cases				X	X	X
Test records						X
Quality records						X

tices, this may be done before or after unit test. It is desirable to achieve SCM control early, but this must not impede the implementers in cleaning up their code.

□ *Integration baseline (component and system)*   After initial implementation and unit test, the programs are placed in the integration baseline. This is established when work is started on component or system build, and it is progressively revised with each integration spin.

□ *Operational baseline*   This is established at the time of system shipment. It is the foundation for subsequent shipments, repairs, and enhancements.

An example of the information included in these baselines is shown in Table 12.1. While these items are relevant to the initial software development project, many of them are needed for the subsequent repair and enhancement effort as well.

12.1 The Software Configuration Management Plan

The first step in establishing an SCM system is to develop a Software Configuration Management Plan. This includes objectives, responsibilities, and the approach and methods to be used. Sample SCMP contents are shown in Table 12.2, and a checklist for developing such plans is shown in Table 12.3.[5] Even though this checklist was developed for the military contract environment, it demonstrates the issues that should be considered in developing all such plans.

12.2 Software Configuration Management Questions

Examples of a few of the questions to be answered by a comprehensive configuration management system are:

1. For the requirements phase:

   □ Where is the official requirements statement?

   □ What changes have been made, and have they been approved?

   □ How much change activity has there been, and what is the impact on design and/or development?

   □ How many requirements changes have been made without changes in the contract scope?

2. For the design phase:

   □ Where is this particular requirement covered by the design?

   □ What is the particular requirement that this design element satisfies?

TABLE 12.2
EXAMPLE SCMP CONTENTS [5]
_____

1. Overview
   —SCM objectives
   —System overview

2. SCM Organization
   —SCM responsibilities
   —Configuration Control Board members
   —Configuration Control Board charter
   —Product Assurance relationship

3. SCM Methods
   —Baselines and contents
   —Identification system
   —Control system
   —Auditing
   —Status accounting
   —CM support tools

4. SCM Procedures
   —Procedures manual
   —Forms and records

5. SCM Implementation
   —Personnel plan
   —System support plan
   —Budget
   —Key implementation checkpoints
_____

- What is the current approved specification for this interface?

- Has the format for this data item been specified, where, by whom, and who is using it?

- What is the design impact of this requirements change?

- What tools and methods were used to develop this design?

3. For implementation:

- How has this particular function been allocated to the various implementation areas, and why?

- What is the design logic for this particular code element?

- How is the design affected by this code change?

- What is the implementation impact of this requirements change?

- What compiler version was used to produce this code?

TABLE 12.3
SOFTWARE CONFIGURATION MANAGEMENT PLAN (SCMP) CHECKLIST [5]

General
1. Does the SCMP reflect the documentation identified in the contract?
2. Does it address all questions imposed in the Request for Proposal (RFP)?
3. Do the schedules agree with the phasing identified in the RFP?
4. Does it identify how quality assurance will ensure configuration verification?
5. Does it identify the support necessary for data management to ensure configuration management?

Organization
1. Does the structure adequately define the solid- and dotted-line organizational relationships?
2. Is an organization chart included?

Identification
1. Does the SCMP identify the documentation that will be controlled? Are all contract deliverable items addressed?
2. Does it identify the numbering and marking systems?
3. Does it identify the documents to be used to define the baselines?
4. Is all documentation used for baseline definition shown on the documentation structure?
5. What is the logic in the selection of the software components?
6. Have all deviations from applicable documentation been identified in the SCMP?
7. Is the release system adequate to control documentation?
8. Does it identify any internal programming standards documents used by the developing organization?

Control
1. Are all change definitions adequately identified?
2. At what program milestones is change control introduced and increasingly implemented?
3. Is there a proper procedure for change processing including forms and flow diagrams? Is the method of change proposal, internally and externally, defined?
4. Is the level of control adequate? Will automated libraries be utilized for control?
5. Does the level of control provide for creative freedom in the development process?
6. How will control be exercised over site users? Is prior approval required?

Status Accounting
1. Does the SCMP identify the data required for configuration status accounting and the methods for recording it? Does the contract provide the data?
2. Does it identify the status accounting reports required and state their frequency and distribution?
3. Do the status accounting procedures account for subcontractor data?
4. Are forms, formats, and reports clearly identified and included? Which of these documents are nondeliverable, and is this clearly defined?

Audits
1. Have you indicated when and what kind of audits will be conducted?
2. Have you indicated whether incremental audits will be conducted?
3. Who will make up the audit team? Are all interested/affected areas represented?
4. Have you described the general procedure for conducting audits?
5. What documentation will result from the audit? Is it contractual?

TABLE 12.3 (continued)

6. Have you specifically indicated the customer involvement in the audit? Have you identified the co-chair/chair?
7. Does the SCMP identify any requirement and execution for field audits once the system is declared operational? Are procedures indicating frequency and responsibility clearly identified?

Program Phasing
1. Have you included a time-phased flow diagram of the milestones in the program?
2. Have you shown/described the relationships between:
   a. Reviews
   b. Baselines
   c. Audits
   d. Major document releases
3. Have you shown/described the points at which customer control of changes will occur?
4. Are the major milestones indicated and their relationship consistent with other sections of the RFP/contract?
5. Have you shown any internal milestones? Are they noted as being internal?

Subcontractor/Vendor
1. Have you adequately described your method of ensuring compliance by your subcontractor/vendor?
2. Will you invoke the same SCM requirements on your subcontractor as your customer has invoked on you?
3. Are you preparing an SCM specification to control your subcontractors? Will it be submitted to your customer?
4. Have you indicated your method of ensuring adequate identification, control, and accounting of your subcontractors?
5. Have you indicated how integration of subcontractor technical data will be accomplished?
6. Have you maintained successful control of subcontractors for previous contracts?

Interface Control
1. Does the SCMP identify the procedures to be used to control software/software and hardware/software interfaces?
2. Does the SCMP identify and define the responsibilities and authority of the Interface Control Working Group (ICWG)?
3. Does the SCMP identify any specialized forms and reports to be used in controlling interfaces?
4. Does the SCMP identify what document specifies all the interfaces?

Used by permission of The Electronic Industries Association, 1922 Eye St., N.W., Washington, D.C. 20006

4. For the testing phase:

   □ Where are the tests that verify this functional requirement?

   □ Where is the test data for use with these tests?

   □ Where is the documentation that explains the results to be expected from these tests?

   □ Has this test bucket been updated to reflect the functional content of the latest release or system build?

- What tests have been run on this program version, and what were the results?
- What test tools and support facilities were used for these tests?

If all these questions cannot be answered quickly and accurately, the organization is exposed to serious problems, particularly in final test when finding and correcting them will be most time-consuming and costly. Since SCM is essentially a problem prevention activity, it often is not implemented by organizations that have not lived through at least one project disaster. Those that have, however, know they must establish disciplined methods for handling these issues.

12.3 SCM Support Functions

To support a full range of software engineering activities, a fairly sophisticated set of SCM functions is required. While the following functions may be used in varying degrees during requirements, design, implementation, test, and maintenance, they are all required to provide adequate support and effective control:[1]

- A protected baseline for the operational concept, specifications, design, implementation, test, and tools
- A protected file with a description of all changes and revisions
- Means for each software engineer to read any unlocked element in the baseline
- A private workspace where charged-out designs or implementations can be modified
- Templates that assist in the preparation of new design, implementation, or test descriptions
- A procedure for making approved charge-outs that permits software engineers to obtain any available baseline element for their private workspace and lock out the SCM copy function to prevent anyone else from making simultaneous changes
- A charge-in procedure that:
  1. Verifies that this is the person who charged-out the element
  2. Checks the format of the revision
  3. Checks that the revision has been authorized
  4. Enters a new revision description into the baseline
  5. Creates a change log
  6. Identifies changed items in the new revision
  7. Removes the lock

8. For interface changes, obtains permission from participating module owners before recording the revision

☐ A procedure for making approved deletions of defunct elements

☐ A way to collect, format, and produce consolidated system documents containing the key element descriptions for any given baseline

☐ A way to check that all elements and relevant descriptions have been carried over between baselines

☐ A centralized data dictionary containing the official record of all named items and their formats

☐ A where-used record of every use of every interface and data item in the system

Some of these facilities may be automatically provided by the SCM support system, and some may have to be implemented manually. It is important, however, to ensure that some provision is made for every single item.

The following paragraphs outline additional SCM issues to be faced regarding requirements, design, and implementation.

12.4 The Requirements Phase

The best software practices are useless if they are focused on implementing the wrong functions. The essential role of the requirements phase is to ensure that the users' needs are properly understood before designing and implementing a system to meet them. The requirements also provide part of the basis for system and acceptance testing.

The job of developing software requirements involves gathering relevant information on the users' needs and distilling the critical items. This job is difficult because generally it is hard to distinguish between what is needed and what is wanted. This is further complicated by the fact that users' functional needs are essentially unlimited. The only limitation on requirements content is thus the cost and time needed for system implementation. Requirements will thus continually expand until the project's economic limits have been reached.

Even if the users think they understand exactly what is needed, they rarely do. Not only will their views change when they start to think precisely about the application, but the application itself will change once it is critically examined. There is a requirements uncertainty principle that states that the greater the functional change, the less accurate the requirements.

12.4.1 Requirements Changes

One implication of this requirements uncertainty is that the early design will likely be changed many times. On the other hand, if one tries to delay design until the requirements are firm, a premature requirements freeze will likely result, which leads to ill-informed design decisions and excessive late changes. Either some critical functions will be specified before their implementation consequences are understood or the requirements will be so general that the developers can implement almost anything they want. In either case the results are likely to be unsatisfactory.

If the requirements cannot be completely specified at the beginning of the project, they must be gradually evolved. This places a premium on the means for controlling and tracking requirements changes. As the design evolves, requirements questions will be raised that can only be resolved by the users through requirements refinements. While such changes are difficult to implement contractually, this is the nature of the early requirements work. When the requirements phase is viewed as an evolving part of development, it is obvious that SCM must be a crucial part as well.

Throughout this requirements definition and feedback process, change is constant, and means are needed to control it. As soon as initial requirements agreement is reached, a baseline is established as a design foundation, as a basis for change negotiations, and as a reference point for acceptance testing.

12.4.2 Requirements Baselines and Change Control

Control of changes to the requirements baseline is handled in much the same way as described in Chapter 7. Each change is submitted on a design change request (DCR) form and reviewed, approved, and tracked with the same discipline as design and code changes. All requirements changes are handled in this way, whether submitted by the customer, systems design, development, or test. Without such a discipline, baseline integrity for the entire project is exposed.

The process for controlling all changes is established at project inception and maintained until final delivery.[3] While the SCM organization may not have many items to manage during the early period, this is when they define the project SCM procedures, establish the Change Control Board, draw up the needed forms, and set up the support facilities. The Software Configuration Management Plan is produced at this point and applied to managing requirements changes.

It is also essential to establish project naming conventions. The Software Configuration Identification (SCI) system uniquely identifies every project development item. The SCI definitions are kept under configuration control and expanded as more is learned about the product and its structure. A simplified form of the SCI tree is shown in Fig. 12.1.[3]

A family of forms and procedures is also needed to ensure that every change is recorded, reviewed, and tracked. An example change request form is shown in Table 12.4.[4] The particular forms and their detailed contents must be established by each organization.

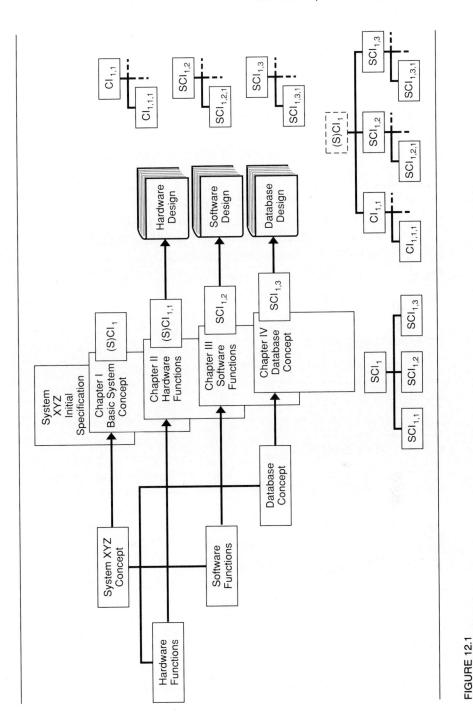

FIGURE 12.1
SCI tree structure.[3]
Bersoff/Henderson/Siegel, *Software Configuration Management: An Investment in Product Integrity*, © 1980, p. 124. Reprinted by permission of Prentice-Hall, Inc., Englewood Cliffs, NJ.

TABLE 12.4
EXAMPLE DESIGN CHANGE REQUEST FORM

DESIGN CHANGE REQUEST

PROJECT NAME _____ DCR NUMBER _____

INITIATED BY _____ DATE _____

CHANGE DESCRIPTION _____
_____
_____
_____
_____
_____

REQUIREMENTS AFFECTED (include identifying numbers) _____
_____
_____
_____
_____

OTHER PROGRAM EFFECTS _____
_____
_____
_____
_____
_____

OTHER SYSTEMS IMPACTS _____
_____
_____
_____
_____

PLANNED START _____ PLANNED COMPLETION _____

RESOURCE EFFECTS:
         PERSONNEL _____
         SCHEDULE _____
         OTHER _____

APPROVALS: SYSTEMS _____ DATE _____
            DEVELOPMENT _____ DATE _____
            SCM _____ DATE _____
            SQA _____ DATE _____
            PROGRAM MANAGER _____ DATE _____

During requirements negotiations the cost and contractual issues must be kept under control. Clever users and creative designers could always add exciting functions if cost and schedule were no object. Many systems get into serious trouble because they do not have adequate control of their requirements.

To facilitate later tracking, every requirement is uniquely numbered. This number is keyed to each paragraph and line of the requirements document and specifies every input, output, file, form, message, and process. These are all identified and tracked in the SCM database. Whenever a requirements change is made, the affected requirement numbers are entered in the DCR form and indexed by the SCM system.

12.4.3 External Specifications

As the project proceeds, detailed specifications are developed for each program component. While these specifications may all be produced at one time, generally some of the component specs are evolved in concert with development.

In DoD contracts the specifications provide the reference point for system design and acceptance testing. They must therefore be carefully verified against the original requirements and the operational concept. Since complex requirements are hard to define through intermediaries, knowledgeable end user representatives should participate in validation to ensure that the product specifications describe what is needed.

The specification uses the same SCI nomenclature as the requirements. Each specification item is identified and is directly traceable to the requirement it satisfies. While it is rarely possible or even desirable to structure the system the way the requirements are written, there must be a clear mapping of each requirement to the one or more specification elements that satisfy it.

The specification is also a reference for developing the functional, system, and acceptance tests. Precise tracking and disciplined change control permits every test to be correlated with both the specifications and the requirements so that every required function is tested.

12.5 Design Control

During design, the Change Control Board (CCB) controls the design changes, and SCM maintains complete records of every change and its rationale. The Software Configuration Identification then connects each design element back to the specifications. This is important because:

1. Design is the creative process of producing a solution to a problem. A good design thus requires a clear problem statement.

2. The design is the template against which the implementers produce the code. It must therefore be clear, unambiguous, and absolutely current.

3. A permanent design reference is required for later repair or product extension. The programmers who do this subsequent work must understand the logic of the original design.

4. A permanent record is needed of the design changes, why they were made, and how they were implemented. Occasionally it is found that a design change had unintended effects and must be backed out. Without a record of what was done and why, this can be very difficult.

5. To maintain control as the design is subdivided into modules, an SCM procedure is required to check the self-consistency of the modules and interface descriptions in each design baseline.

The design phase continues until the smallest structural elements of the system are defined and specified. In this book these smallest elements are called modules, but they are often called by other names, such as packages. The detailed design phase then starts with these module specifications, an example of which is shown in Table 12.5. The module specs now provide the starting point for the detailed design, which is conducted according to the methods adopted by the organization and project involved.

The additional SCM facilities needed for detailed design are:[1]

□ Templates for module specifications and design skeletons

□ Means to ensure, when a module contains multiple routines, that a complete set of these routines is included in the baseline for each module

□ Means to verify that all routines match the module interfaces

□ Means to ensure that all data items are consistent with the data dictionary (the official SCI record of all names, their precise formats and properties, and where they are used)

□ Inclusion of all interfaces and data definitions in the where-used listing

The SCM system must recognize that design is an evolutionary process and that many of the modules, when first identified, will contain little more than a name. These skeletons are progressively refined as the design progresses. Automatic consistency checking of all the names and interfaces will detect many design errors before implementation and test, where correction is much more time-consuming and costly.

Care should be taken not to impose too rigid a control over the design during initial conception. This means that each designer must be able to complete an initial design in a private workspace and include it in the baseline after inspection, test, and approval. Since many SCM functions can assist in this process, its facilities should be available to these private workspaces.

TABLE 12.5
EXAMPLE MODULE SPECIFICATION

MODULE NAME: _____

Purpose: _____
_____
_____

Function: _____
_____

Algorithm: _____
_____

Functional Requirements Addressed: _____
_____
_____

System Environment Constraints:

    Security: _____

    Timing: _____

    Residence: _____

    Hardware: _____

    Portability: _____

    Operating System: _____

Interfaces:

    System Services Provided: _____
_____
_____

    System Services Used: _____
_____
_____

    Preconditions and Inputs: _____
_____
_____

    Postconditions and Outputs: _____
_____
_____

TABLE 12.5 (continued)

Tools and Aids: _____

_____

_____

    Design Language: _____

    Implementation Language: _____

Implementation:

    Standard Routines (Sources and Revisions): _____

    _____

    _____

    _____

Revision History: _____

_____

_____

_____

_____

Designer: _____ Date: _____

_____

12.6 The Implementation Phase

While the SCM tasks for the implementation phase were largely covered in Chapter 7, some additional design-related capabilities are also needed. First, with a fully controlled design, implementation can start on a solid foundation. As implementation proceeds, design problems will be found and design changes will be needed. When such changes are made, the design documentation is updated.

Updating the design documentation may involve changes to system, component, or module specifications, interface definitions, and the data dictionary. While this work is time-consuming, if every design change is not meticulously recorded, the system design will soon become obsolete. The omission of even one simple change will cause a small area of the design to inaccurately represent the code. Over time these inconsistencies will grow, and soon the only way to be sure of the design is to read the code. Even when extensively commented, this is always difficult.

Additional SCM facilities are needed to keep a detailed historical record of all code changes. This typically requires a flagging convention in the comment field to specify when every line of code was added or changed and the reasons for doing so. Because one change may affect many lines within a module, it is usually wise to list the basic data and justification for each change in some designated module header field with a unique change code. Each changed line is then tagged with this change code and a notation of whether it was added or modified. When code is deleted, a notation is made in the previous line that the following N lines were deleted. Typical reasons for such changes are bug repair, customer problem fix, or functional enhancement. When the change identifying number is included, a complete record is available of what code was changed, when, and for what purpose. Without this record it is often impossible to relate program problems to their causes. As is discussed in Chapter 16, this information is needed for effective quality management.

Some special SCM functions needing during implementation are:[1]

□ Source code charge-out and charge-in facilities

□ Read-only access to specifications and object code

□ The ability to compile modules, to link them with baselined object programs, and to use them in private workspaces

□ A procedure for making approved changes to module specifications

□ An SCM procedure to ensure that any new source code is consistent with the module specifications

12.7 Operational Data

In addition to code and documentation, many software systems also require a considerable amount of operational data. For applications such as payroll, for example, this would include the appropriate employee records and tax data. For an aircraft control system this data would have to include aerodynamic, instrument, and engine parameters. Most large-scale software systems generally require large amounts of specialized data that must be specified, produced, tested, documented, and controlled. It is thus essential that SCM provisions be made to handle this data.

12.8 The Test Phase

Once a newly developed program is put in a baseline, all further changes must be controlled. The major concerns are problem incidents, temporary patches, permanent bug fixes, and enhancements. In addition, precise and complete records must be maintained of every test run, the data and test cases used, the configurations on which they were run, and the results. These functions typically can be handled with the SCM facilities already described. In addition, it is essential to have a control system for tracking bug reports. While this may or may not be handled by the SCM organization, it should have the following capabilities:[1]

- ☐ Means for creating new bug reports, logging them, and maintaining status records
- ☐ Means for closing bug reports
- ☐ Periodic reporting of bug status

Finally, for large projects and for all projects during the maintenance phase, procedures are needed to handle the development of simultaneous versions of the same program. This requires:[1]

- ☐ A version description for each deliverable
- ☐ The capability to establish separate baselines for copies of any given modules, as well as their source and object code
- ☐ A means to relate each baseline version with different design descriptions or deltas
- ☐ Separate control over charge-out, charge-in, compile, link, and copy for each version
- ☐ The capability to selectively merge separate developmental deltas into a common program version

A disciplined change process is particularly important during final implementation and test. Changes are so frequent and schedule pressures so intense that the temptation to defer change recording is almost irresistible. If the SCM change procedures are not iron-clad, design control will invariably be lost. This means that once the initial code baseline has been established, all code changes should follow the steps shown in Fig. 12.2. Before the code is placed under configuration control, this same process should be followed, except that change approval is only required for specification and design changes.

12.9 SCM for Tools

One important SCM function that is often overlooked is the need to maintain baseline control over the complete set of tools used to specify, design, implement, and test the software. When a compiler, for example, is modified, it may produce slightly different object code from an identical source program. If this results in a system problem, it may be difficult to find, particularly if the compiler level used is either not known or not available.

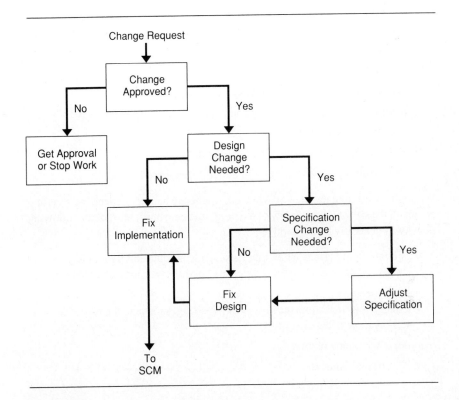

FIGURE 12.2
Implementation Change Control Procedure

One approach is to maintain a standard tool set under configuration control and to establish a new tool baseline whenever any change is made. Each module specification, design, and code record then includes a notation of the tool baseline used in its production. A summary of this data should also be retained with the module revision history.

12.10 Configuration Accounting

The purpose of software configuration status accounting is to maintain a continuous record of the status of all baselined items. This record is not only a useful management tool, but, if old records are routinely archived, it also provides valuable insurance against disaster. The information required for comprehensive status accounting includes:[2]

□ The time at which each baseline was established

□ When each software configuration item and change was included in the baseline

□ A description of each configuration item

□ The status of each software-related engineering change

□ The description of each software change

□ The status of each software change

□ The documentation status for each baseline

□ The changes planned for each identified future baseline

While the need for a detailed SCM record of change activity depends to a certain extent on the size and complexity of the program being built, most of the following items will generally be needed:[7]

□ A configuration item index that lists each configuration item along with its creation date, current released version, and the versions of its component items

□ Change logs that show the history of the changes made to the source files, as well as their release histories

□ All discrepancy reports

□ All change requests

12.11 The Software Configuration Audit

A software configuration audit should periodically be performed to ensure that the SCM practices and procedures are rigorously followed. This audit can be performed directly by the SCM staff or by some independent assurance function. It is generally advisable to have SCM conduct frequent self-audits with an independent party occasionally performing spot checks.

The general ground rules for SCM audits are:[3]

□ They are periodically needed to ensure the integrity of the software baselines.

□ A successful audit is performed before every major baseline change.

□ The audit team consists of qualified technical people who are not involved in the specific tasks being audited.

□ The audit verifies that changes to the baseline are implemented as intended.

□ The auditing function is an integral part of the SCM system.

☐ SCM auditing is continuous, with increased frequency and depth as development progresses.

☐ A documented project SCM plan is used as the basis for all SCM audits.

SCM audits are required prior to key checkpoints in each development phase. As described in Chapter 5, a phase review process then ensures that the proper actions are taken, as follows:[7]

1. *Requirements*   At the requirements phase review, SCM releases the software requirements and operational concept documents and places them under change control.

2. *Functional*   At the specification phase review, SCM releases the software specifications document(s) and places it under change control.

3. *High-level design*   At the preliminary design phase review, SCM reviews the preliminary design documents, assigns configuration items as defined for the software components, and updates the configuration item index. SCM releases the preliminary design document, the software test plan, and the user documents, and places them under change control.

4. *Design*   At the detailed design phase review, SCM reviews the software detailed design documents, assigns configuration items according to the defined plan, and updates the configuration item index. SCM also releases the software detailed design documents and places them under change control.

5. *Product*   SCM reviews the developed software to ensure that all programs are fully updated and have been tested and released to test and evaluation.

6. *Operational*   SCM ensures that all software components are fully updated and have passed appropriate acceptance tests.

12.12 Summary

This chapter continues the discussion of SCM that began in Chapter 7.

SCM control over requirements and specifications is needed to ensure that the product being built and tested is what is wanted. SCM control must also be maintained over the design throughout system life to ensure its integrity and maintainability. To do this, requirements baselines, specification baselines, design baselines, unit baselines, integration baselines, and operational baselines are established and maintained at appropriate points throughout the development cycle.

The first step in establishing an SCM system is to develop an SCM plan. Project naming conventions are established and a family of forms and procedures is provided to ensure that every change is recorded, reviewed, and tracked. The specification is used as a basis for the development work and as a reference for developing the functional, system, and acceptance tests.

During the design phase, SCM maintains control over the design and the rationale for establishing it. As changes are made, the appropriate design documentation is correspondingly updated. Additional SCM facilities are needed to record all code changes. Finally, for large projects and for all projects during the maintenance phase, procedures are needed to handle the development of simultaneous versions of the same program. The tools used to design, implement, test, and maintain the software must also be maintained under configuration control.

The purpose of software configuration status accounting is to maintain a continuous record of the status of all baselined items. A software configuration audit is periodically performed to ensure that the SCM practices and procedures are rigorously followed.

References

1. Babich, W. A. *Software Configuration Management, Coordination for Team Productivity,* Reading, MA: Addison-Wesley, 1986.

2. Bersoff, E. H., V. D. Henderson, and S. G. Siegel. "Software configuration management: a tutorial," *IEEE Tutorial: Software Configuration Management,* IEEE Cat. no. EHO 169-3, October 27, 1980, pp. 24–32.

3. Bersoff, E. H., V. D. Henderson, and S. G. Siegel. *Configuration Management: Investment in Product Integrity,* Englewood Cliffs, NJ: Prentice-Hall, 1980.

4. Braverman, P. H. "Managing change," *Datamation,* October 1976, pp. 111–113.

5. "EIA report of the Ninth Annual Data and Configuration Management Workshop, development of computer program configuration management plans," *IEEE Tutorial: Software Configuration Management,* IEEE Cat. no. EHO 169-3, 1980, October 1975, pp. 40–57.

6. Lehman, M. M., and L. A. Belady. *Program Evolution, Processes of Software Change,* New York: Academic Press, 1985.

7. Tomayko, J. E. "Support Materials for Software Configuration Management," SEI-SM-4-1.0, September 1986, Carnegie Mellon University, Software Engineering Institute.

13

Defining the Software Process

Software development can be exceedingly complex and there are often many alternative ways to perform the various tasks. A defined process can help guide the software professionals through these choices in an orderly way. With an established process definition they can better understand what they should do, what they can expect from their co-workers, and what they are expected to provide in return. This allows them to focus on doing their jobs. A defined software process also provides organizations with a consistent working framework while permitting individual adjustments to unique needs.[1, 7] As Deming says, operational definitions are "something everyone can communicate about and work to."[6]

Software engineering, however, is not a routine activity that can be structured and regimented like a repetitive manufacturing or clerical procedure. We are dealing with an intellectual process that must dynamically adjust to the creative needs of the professionals and their tasks. A trade-off is thus required between the individual need for flexibility and the organizational need for standards and consistency. Some of the factors to be considered are:

1. Since software projects have differences, their software engineering processes must have differences as well.

2. In the absence of a universal software engineering process, organizations and projects must define processes that meet their own unique needs.

3. The process used for a given project must consider the experience level of the members, current product status and the available tools and facilities.

13.1 Process Standards

While the need for project-unique process definitions is clear, there are also compelling reasons for standardization:

- □ Process standardization helps to reduce the problems of training, review, and tool support.
- □ With standard methods, each project's experiences can contribute to overall process improvement.
- □ Process standards provide the basis for process and quality measurements.
- □ Since process definitions take time and effort to produce, it is impractical to produce new ones for each project.

The conflicting needs for customization and standardization can often be resolved by establishing a process architecture, which consists of a standard set of unit or "kernel" process steps with rules for describing and relating them. Customization is then achieved through appropriate interconnections of these standard elements into tailored process models.

13.2 Definitions

Before proceeding further, several terms should be defined. "The term software refers to a program and all the associated information and materials needed to support its installation, operation, repair, and enhancement."[12] This is consistent with Brooks's definition of a programming product as a program together with all those items required to make it intelligible, usable, and extendable.[4] A program, of course, is merely the set of instructions that run on a computer. A program product thus includes all the user and support documentation, as well as any ancillary programs needed to use or support it. With this understanding the term software is used to refer to programming products.

Some definitions of software engineering, the software engineering process, software process architecture, and software process models are:[12]

- □ *Software engineering*   "The disciplined application of engineering, scientific, and mathematical principles, methods, and tools to the economical production of quality software"
- □ *Software engineering process*   "The total set of software engineering activities needed to transform a user's requirements into software"
- □ *Software process architecture*   "A framework within which project-specific software processes are defined"

- □ *Software process model*   "One specific embodiment of a software process architecture"

- □ *Software process*   The set of activities, methods, and practices that are used in the production and evolution of software

Since most software is maintained and enhanced throughout its life, these definitions are intended to encompass new development, enhancement, and repair.

While software process models may be constructed at any appropriate level of abstraction, the process architecture must provide the elements, standards, and structural framework for refinement to any desired level of detail.

13.3 Levels of Software Process Models

Software process models can be defined at any of three levels. The U, or Universal, process model provides a high-level overview. The W, or Worldly, process model is the working level that is familiar to most programmers and managers. The A, or Atomic, process model provides more detailed refinements.

13.3.1 U Process Models

The Waterfall Model, described by Royce in 1970, is still the best known and most widely used overview framework for the software development process.[19] As shown in Fig. 13.1, it describes the basic process steps and provides general guidance on their role and order. While this model has been helpful in explaining the software development process, it has several shortcomings:[3]

- □ It does not adequately address changes.

- □ It assumes a relatively uniform and orderly sequence of development steps.

- □ It does not provide for such methods as rapid prototyping or advanced languages.

To address these concerns, Boehm has proposed the Spiral Model, as shown in Fig. 13.2.[3] This U process model sheds light on some of these issues and can help in identifying several of the key risks in software development.

Unfortunately, the real world of software development doesn't conform neatly to either of these models. While they represent the general work flow and provide overview understanding, they are not easily decomposed into the progressively finer levels of detail that are needed to guide the work of the software professionals.

First, it is important to recognize that a complete model of a complex process must be complex. The operative word is complete. If one wants to use a model for a specific purpose, it can presumably be tailored to that purpose and compromise

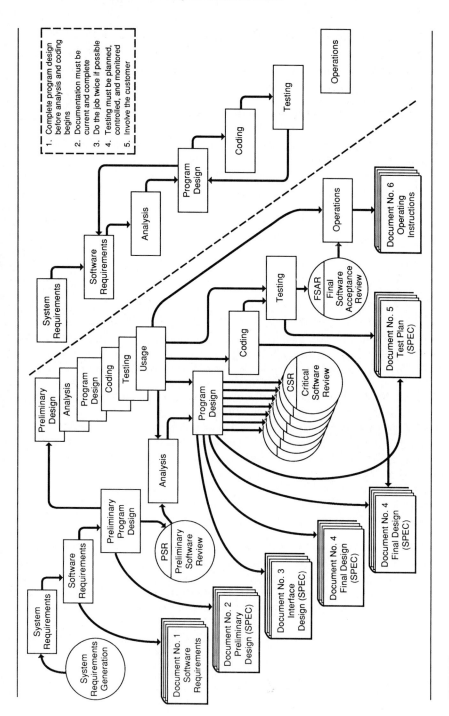

FIGURE 13.1
The Waterfall Process Model.[19]
W. W. Royce, "Managing the development of large software systems," *Proceedings of IEEE WESCON,* August 1970. © 1970 IEEE.

completeness in other respects. These compromises, however, must be made with care, or the resulting simple model representation could easily be misleading.

The fundamental problem with simplistic U-level software process models is that they do not accurately represent what is really done.[13] The reason is that traditional process models are extremely sensitive to task sequence; consequently, simple adjustments can destroy the entire framework. This results from an over-emphasis on modeling tasks. While modeling tasks seems like a natural way to guide task-oriented people, it limits human flexibility and tends to arbitrarily

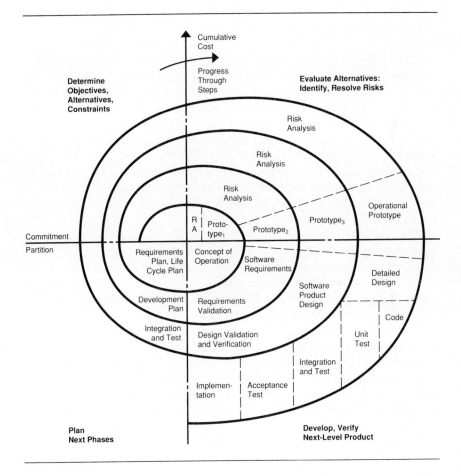

FIGURE 13.2
Spiral Model of the Software Process [3]
B. W. Boehm, "A spiral model of software development and enhancement," *IEEE Computer,* © 1988, IEE.

impose rigidity. With the requirements-design-code-test sequence, decisions to re-examine the requirements during test, for example, cannot be readily accommodated without a complete restructure of the process model. In short, with traditional models it is difficult to adequately address the behavioral aspects of processes.

The traditional task-oriented approach to process models results naturally from our task-oriented view of our work. This, for example, is what led to the Waterfall Model: the need for a general prescription of human activity. While this task structure is quite appropriate and relatively easy to understand when the tasks are simply connected, it becomes progressively less helpful as the number of possible task sequences increases. While it can, in principle, still produce an accurate model, it becomes more difficult to do so and progressively less understandable.

The real danger of attempting to use task-oriented models in such complex situations is that they must be simplified to permit human comprehension, and these simplifications tend to limit flexibility in task sequencing. When there are, for example, ten possible actions that could usefully be performed, a simplified task-oriented process model would presumably only show one or two. While this might be perfectly acceptable under normal circumstances, the other alternatives might then be viewed as abnormal or unauthorized. When such models are used to guide process automation, project management, or contract administration, the resulting process rigidity can cause serious problems. The question, therefore, is not "what is the right way to model the process?" but "what is the most appropriate way to model this process for this purpose?"

A final point concerns actual process execution. When the process model is used to guide or control the detailed performance of the process by people or machines, a comprehensive model is required, and it must include a task-oriented view. Indeed, a complete process model needs to contain functional, behavioral, structural, and conceptual views.[16, 17] For process management purposes, however, a simpler process model is appropriate as long as it does not artificially constrain process execution. There is good reason to believe that task-oriented models are not always the best for this purpose and that an entity view may be more appropriate in many cases. Entity process models are discussed briefly in a later section of this chapter. For this discussion we will deal with the more traditional and easily understood task-oriented process models. As will be noted later, however, many of the same considerations apply to entity process models as well.[13]

13.3.2 A Process Models

At the opposite extreme from U-level models, Atomic- (A-) level process models can be enormously detailed. They are needed by anyone who attempts to automate a specific process activity or use a standardized method or procedure to guide execution of a task. Precise data definitions, algorithmic specifications, information flows, and user procedures are essential at this level. The amount of detail to be included in such models must be determined by their use. For example, an experienced developer who is repeating known manual tasks will not need as detailed a standard as a new trainee. When the task is to be automated, however, a great deal of detail is generally required.

Atomic process definitions are often embodied in process standards and conventions. These can be treated as process abstractions in the higher level W or U process models.

13.3.3 W Process Models

The Worldly (W) process level is of most direct interest to practicing software engineers. It guides the sequence of their working tasks and defines task prerequisites and results. When reduced to operational form, these models generally look like procedures. They specify who does what when. Where appropriate, they reference the A level that specifies standard task definitions or tool usage. For each task, W models define the anticipated results, the appropriate measures, and the key checkpoints.

13.3.4 Examples of Process Models

The three levels of process models can be viewed as embodied in policies at the U level, procedures at the W level, and standards or tools at the A level. Policies establish a high-level framework and set of principles that guide the overall behavior of organizations. They are particularly helpful in unanticipated circumstances where no precedents have been established. Some appropriate policy-level statements on the software process might be:

- All work will be subjected to an inspection before it is incorporated in a baseline.
- The quality of each product, at the time of new shipment, shall be better than its predecessor or leading competitor.
- All commitments for software cost or delivery will be supported by a documented and approved software engineering plan.
- Quality Assurance will review the software development process to assure senior management that the work is done according to established standards and procedures and in conformance with the intent of the stated policies.

At the W level, procedures are established to implement the policies. This W-level process model refers to any available Atomic-level standards that define precisely how tasks are to be performed.

At the W level, for example, a procedure might define the points at which Quality Assurance reviews are to be conducted and how the resulting issues are to be handled. This might specify what percent of the work is to be reviewed, how statistical samples are to be selected, and whether, when, and how SQA independently tests or monitors the software engineering work as it is being done.

Atomic-level standards then serve as the basis for directing the work and for the SQA review. For example, a code inspection standard would specify what code is to be reviewed, when, the methods to be used, the reports to be produced, and the acceptable performance limits. The developers would use this standard to guide their actions, and the SQA people would review their actions and work products against this standard.

13.4 Prescriptive and Descriptive Uses of Models

Process models can be used either to describe what is done or to characterize what is supposed to be done. In a descriptive case, models can provide useful information about the process and its behavior. After such models have been calibrated to reasonably represent actual behavior, they can be used to simulate process performance under varying conditions. This can help identify potential process problems before they occur.

This book uses process models in a prescriptive sense. The approach is to define how the process should be conducted and suggest where appropriate policies, procedures, and standards could help guide the work. As with any standard, process standards must not be overspecified. A coding standard, for example, that precisely specifies commenting rules would probably not be appropriate. While such rules are important, the needs are different for different languages and conditions. If, however, the scope of the standard were constrained to specific languages, it could very well be reasonable.

13.5 A Software Process Architecture

Since most organizations have at least some policies, procedures, and standards, they are also generally following some intuitive U-, W-, and A-level models both prescriptively and descriptively. To be fully effective, however, these process models should be explicit and should relate to each other. The problem of building process models, in fact, is much like that of building software systems. An architectural framework is needed to define the basic elements, how they relate, and how they are decomposed into greater detail.

The process architecture must, therefore, encompass all process levels. U process models permit global understanding and provide a framework for establishing effective policies. W process models guide the daily work, while A process models provide the atomic detail for training and task mechanization. These levels all connect and should be derivable from each other in a consistent and cohesive way. This calls for a family of refineable and relatable process elements that can be coupled to produce the specific models needed to address project needs.

13.6 Critical Software Process Issues

The reason for defining the software process is to improve the way the work is done. By thinking about the process in an orderly way, it is possible to anticipate problems and to devise ways to either prevent or to resolve them. Some of the major software process issues concern quality, product technology, requirements instability, and complexity. In summary, these issues are:

- □ *Quality* Humans are error-prone; they make mistakes. Each error, when found, is a surprise whose correction is both expensive and disruptive. When the organization's quality performance has not been adequate, some process changes are generally required. Examples might be the introduction of design and code inspections, establishing quality plans and measurements, improved testing, or more intensive Software Quality Assurance.

- □ *Product technology* Often with new developments it is not clear how to implement an algorithm, to meet a performance goal, or to pack function into a limited configuration. Since later patching of unsuccessful attempts can be time-consuming and disruptive it is often wise to make process provisions for early experiments to provide this knowledge. Subsequent development can then proceed in a more orderly and effective way.

- □ *Requirements instability* This is probably the most important single software process issue for many organizations. To design, to build, and to test a program the required functions, interfaces, and environments must be stable. While these may change during development, the changes must be temporarily frozen while development proceeds. At planned intervals, batches of changes can be considered and the design adjusted accordingly. If change is not controlled in this way, the development process will become unstable, and productivity and quality will be adversely affected. There are three basic types of requirements changes that can be addressed in different ways by the process:

  1. *Unknown requirements* The users think they know what is wanted, but during initial use they discover that their real needs are not what they had thought. This is the normal consequence of automating a manual process and can be countered by either installing early prototype systems or decomposing the system into small incremental phases that are progressively developed, installed, used, evaluated, and then enhanced.

2. *Unstable requirements*   While the general requirements may be known, the specifics remain fluid. In embedded systems, for which the hardware and the software are often developed simultaneously, hardware changes may affect software requirements. Changing the hardware under a developed program is about as unsettling as changing the foundation while trying to build a house. While the frame may remain, patching all the cracks can be expensive. Here the process approach is to try to anticipate the instabilities and to isolate them. With an ill-defined aircraft flight instrument, for example, an abstraction could represent it to the rest of the program. If done properly, instrument changes could then be contained in the code abstraction that implements them.

3. *Misunderstood requirements*   Even when the requirements are known and stable, the implementers often do not understand them in the detail required to produce a satisfactory product. A typical example is end user interfaces. Here, user tests could be made with interface prototypes, or early versions of the user documentation could be tested in simulated use.

□ *Complexity*   Application programs are often easier to develop than complete systems because their environment is generally more stable. This does not mean the work is less challenging but just that fewer things are changing simultaneously. During development of a new computer operating system, for example, everything is generally in flux: the basic control program, the compilers, the data management system, and often the computer architecture itself. To get anything done at all, special process provisions are required to provide at least intermittent stability.

Typically stability is achieved by establishing a modular design with functional and interface definitions. Disciplined change control then allows each module to have known and stable requirements during the intervals between changes. That is, the system is built in a succession of drivers. The requirements for the modules for driver 1 are defined, and, after it has been designed, driver 2 requirements are established, and so on. As long as the high-level design is well conceived and controlled, the modules can be successively improved, tested, and integrated into a progressively more refined final system.

13.7 A Preliminary Process Architecture

Organizations that face the issues of quality, product technology, requirements stability, and/or complexity need to define ways to address them. A process architecture permits them to represent and manipulate the process at the U level and then selectively to refine it to the W and A levels. This, of course, needs an overall architectural framework and a set of definitions.

The basic element of the process architecture is the unit cell, as shown in Fig. 13.3. Each cell is defined to accomplish a specified task and is uniquely identified. Each cell also has required entry conditions specified for task initiation that include the inputs (one or more with their sources). The task standards, procedures, methods, responsibilities, and required measurements are also defined. Finally, the exit conditions define the results produced, their level of validation, and any other post-task conditions. Cell feedback refers to any data provided to or received from other stages in the process.

As an example of how this cell can be used, Fig. 13.4 shows the full development cycle in one cell. While this abstract U-level model is not terribly informative, it does show the kind of information required for every process cell.

A somewhat more refined U-level model of the development process is shown in Fig. 13.5. Here the development cycle is broken into the basic cells of the Waterfall Model. The E, T, X, M (entry, task, exit, measure) specifications for this cell are shown in Table 13.1.

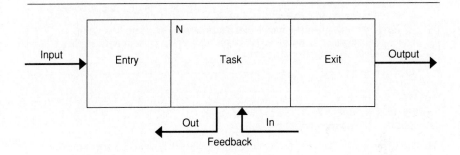

Specifications:
 Entry: The conditions to be met before task initiation.
 Exit: The results to be produced and how embodied.
 Feedback:
  In: Any feedback from other stages.
  Out: Any feedback to other stages.
 Task: What is to be done, by whom, how, and when, including appropriate
  standards, procedures, and responsibilities.
 Measurements: The required task measures (activities, resources, time),
  output (number, size, quality), and feedback (number, size, quality).

FIGURE 13.3
Basic Unit Cell

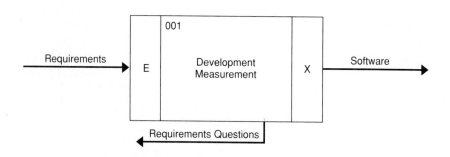

Specifications:
    Entry: Approved requirements document and clarifications from requirements
        organization and requirements changes.
    Exit: Delivered, tested software, including source and object code, design and
        user documentation, and support software.
    Feedback:
        In: User problems.
        Out: Any areas where requirements need clarification from requirements
        organization, as determined in design, implementation, or test.
    Task: The development organization develops the software using specified
        standards, procedures, and methods.
    Measurements: Measurements of the task (changes, programmer time,
        schedule), the product (LOC, pages, defects), and the feedback (require-
        ments issues, user problems).

FIGURE 13.4
The Single-Cell Development Process

13.7.1 Standard Process Elements

When looked at from the highest, or U, level, software processes tend to look much the same. This is because they are described in broad generic terms like "design," "implementation," or "test." When these activities are broken into more detail, however, significant differences show up. For example, the development of a new application program generally involves different activities than the enhancement of a system program. A control program for a new real-time computer or a system support program would also be handled differently. While these efforts could all be represented by the same U model, the actual software tasks are quite different.

With all this variation at the W level, however, many software activities can be relatively standardized across different projects. It is thus possible to establish

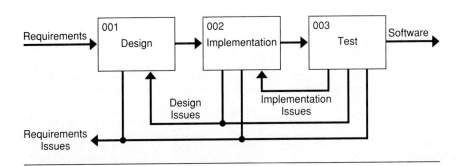

FIGURE 13.5
The U-Level Development Process

some basic process cells that can be interconnected in different ways to meet project-unique needs. The detailed structures of these standard cells are then further defined by A-level models as needed.

13.7.2 Implementation Cells

In defining a standard set of software process cells, we start with some relatively detailed software tasks. The basic implementation cell, C_o, is shown in Fig. 13.6. Since it is not very useful by itself, it is typically augmented with some form of testing, as shown in Fig. 13.7. This is the quick kernel, or K_q, which forms one of the basic elements of the software process. Since K_q often produces poor-quality code, more comprehensive testing or inspection is generally required before useful programs result.

Before modifying C_o to include inspections or testing, however, an inspection operator is established, as shown in Fig. 13.8. With this operator inspections can be applied to any arbitrary process activity (A). The final inspection action is to consider the inspection results and to decide whether to pass the product to the next development stage, to recycle back to A for fixes, or backtrack to a previous stage. Backtracking is often required when an inspection finds problems with earlier work.[5]

The significance of backtracking is that software process actions produce results that depend on them. If, for example, a design decision on some data type specification were later changed, every design and every implementation using this data type must also be examined. This requires knowledge of a growing number of dependencies as development progresses. When a change is made, this

TABLE 13.1
U-LEVEL DEVELOPMENT PROCESS CELL SPECIFICATIONS

Cell:	001	002	003
Entry	Approved requirements, changes, and development plan	Inspected and approved design and changes	Inspected and approved code and changes
Exit	Inspected and approved design and changes	Inspected and approved code and changes	Inspected, tested, and approved software
Feedback In	Design issues	Implementation issues	
Feedback Out	Requirements issues	Requirements and design issues	Requirements, design and implementation issues
Task	Design	Implementation, inspection, and unit test	Testing: Integration, function, system, and acceptance
Measures	Resources, Product: Changes Errors Design Document pages	Resources, Product: Changes Errors Code Document pages	Resources, Product: Changes Errors Code Document pages Test suite

dependency tree must be traced to identify every single resulting design or code change. If an error is not found in the process stage where it was introduced, its consequences can pervade all subsequent work, and correction costs can become quite large. The complexity of this process is one reason why it is so expensive to find and fix errors late in the development process and why abstractions are increasingly used in an attempt to reduce the impact of such changes.

13.7.3 The Unit Implementation Kernel

When the inspection operator is applied to each task in cell C_o, we get the implementation cell C_1, shown in Fig. 13.9. Here backtracking is shown both within C_1 and to prior process stages.

The next step is to add unit test, which results in the unit implementation kernel K_1, shown in Fig. 13.10. This kernel, which is used to implement small program modules, has the following characteristics:

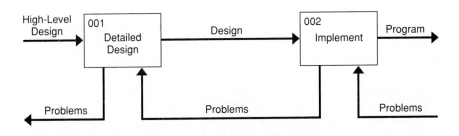

FIGURE 13.6
Basic Implementation Cell C_0

1. Cell 001 uses the implementation cell C_1 to produce code, design, and documentation.

2. The design from 001 is used to define the unit test high-level design in 003. Since this is a white box test of program structure, the tests must be based on the structural design.

3. A C_1 development process is used in 004 to produce the necessary test cases and drivers.

4. At the conclusion of unit test, 002, the results are reviewed to see if the product should be passed to the next development phase or returned for further work.

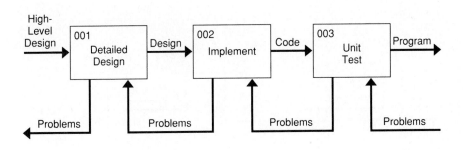

FIGURE 13.7
Quick Kernel K_q

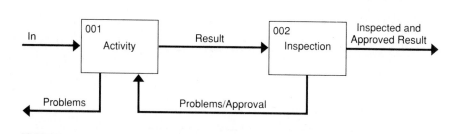

FIGURE 13.8
Inspection Operator

5. Backtracking is possible from cell 001 or 002 and theoretically possible from any cell.

6. The output of unit implementation kernel K_1 is a final unit-tested program module with a documented design.

13.7.4 The Cell Specification

Once the general flow of a process is known, it is important to define each process cell. One approach is to use what is called the ETVX paradigm.[18] This refers to

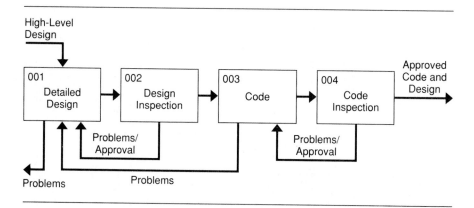

FIGURE 13.9
Implementation Cell C_1

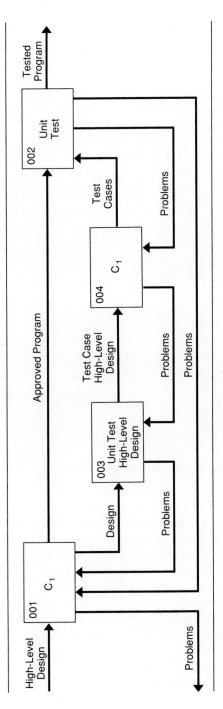

FIGURE 13.10
Unit Implementation Kernel K_1

the explicit characterization of the Entry, Task, Verification, and Exit criteria for each process action. A slightly modified version of this, the Entry-Task-Exit (ETX) specification, is used here for cell definition. The ETX specifications for C_1 are shown in Table 13.2 and the ETX specifications for the unit implementation kernel K_1 are shown in Table 13.3. These process specifications for each project should include explicit responsibilities for task performance and should refer to the applicable standards and procedures.

Such detail may seem unnecessary since all the steps in K_1 are generally handled by a single programmer. Few implementers, however, have the background or training to know how to do every step of K_1 in the most effective way. A defined process can provide them guidance as well as setting the standard for management review and SQA audit.

13.8 Larger Process Models

Once some basic process cells have been defined, it is possible to construct larger process models. This is done by interconnecting these basic cells in various ways. The idea is consciously to design the development or maintenance process to address the anticipated issues and problems. The issues of quality, product technology, unknown requirements, unstable requirements, misunderstood requirements, and complexity generally can be dealt with by such process models. The following sections give examples of how this can be done.

13.8.1 Product Technology Unknowns

In advanced software systems there are often significant technical unknowns. Hardware engineers have long known that initial implementations of novel products rarely work as expected and are never directly shippable. They thus build "breadboards" to test their technical concepts and experiment with alternative approaches. Typically they implement the critical system elements in simplified form and rig the balance of the system in a suitably expedient way.

With software it is also appropriate to breadboard critical, complex, or unusually demanding functions. There are many potential implementation questions, and programmers often are unsure which ones to pursue until they have actually built something and run it. Unfortunately, most such choices are made in a standard product implementation process that does not allow time to try alternatives and throw away early versions.

The quick kernel, K_q, is an appropriate way to produce experimental code. Since such code has a short useful life and is only for use by the implementer, the

TABLE 13.2
ETX SPECIFICATIONS FOR THE IMPLEMENTATION CELL C_1

Cell:	001	002	003	004
Entry	Inspected and approved high-level design	Detailed design and problem fixes	Inspected and approved detailed design and problem fixes	Source and object code and problem fixes
Exit	Detailed design and problem fixes	Inspected and approved detailed design and problem fixes	Source and object code and problem fixes	Inspected software and inspection report
Feedback In	Inspection problems Inspection approval/ disapproval		Inspection problems and inspection approval/ disapproval	
Feedback Out	High-level design problems	Problems found Approval/ disapproval	Detailed design and high-level design problems	Problems found and approval/ disapproval
Task	Produce the detailed design, documentation, and problem fixes	Inspect and approve detailed design and problem fixes	Implement and document detailed design and problem fixes	Inspect and approve code
Measures	Resources expended, work product produced, problems found	Resources expended, work product inspected, problems found	Resources expended, work product produced, problems found	Resources expended, work product produced, problems found

need for documentation, inspection, or testing is minimal. If the code works sufficiently well to prove the concept, the simple K_q process should suffice. Where the implementer concludes that documentation, an informal inspection, or some other provisions are needed they can, of course, be added.

The full experimental kernel, K_e, is shown in Fig. 13.11. The key to this subprocess is the feedback from 002 to 001 that determines whether the experiment should be revised and repeated or if enough has been learned to proceed with a full high-level design (003) and K_1 implementation (004). It is, of course, possible to learn from these steps something that invalidates prior work and causes backtracking to previous stages. The ETX specifications for K_e are shown in Table 13.4.

TABLE 13.3

ETX SPECIFICATIONS FOR THE UNIT IMPLEMENTATION KERNEL K_1

Cell:	001	002	003	004
Entry	Inspected and approved high-level design	Inspected and approved source and object code and test cases	Inspected and approved detailed design	Test case requirements and plan
Exit	Inspected and approved software and inspection report	Unit tested and inspected software	Test case high-level design	Inspected and approved test cases
Feedback In	Unit test problems approval/ disapproval		Test case high-level design problems	Test case problems
Feedback Out	High-level design problems	Unit test problems Unit test approval/ disapproval	Detailed design problems	Test case high-level design problems
Task	Implement and inspect software	Perform unit testing	Produce test case high-level design and plan	Implement and inspect test cases
Measures	Resources expended, work product produced, problems found	Resources expended, work product produced, problems found	Resources expended, work product produced, problems found	Resources expended, work product produced, problems found

13.8.2 The Problem of Complexity

The process kernels described thus far have focused on small tasks that could be performed by one or two programmers. While these kernels provide useful guidance for small tasks, their real value is the insight they can provide for larger projects. Here multiple modules are typically involved, and the work of many professionals must be coordinated.

One effective way to handle the problems of large-scale software process complexity is shown in Fig. 13.12. Here the high-level design (001) establishes the basic requirements for each module, which is then implemented with the appropriate kernel process for that module (002...003). The design is also the foundation for integration planning (005), which produces the integration and test requirements and plan. This in turn defines the required test cases, the drivers, and

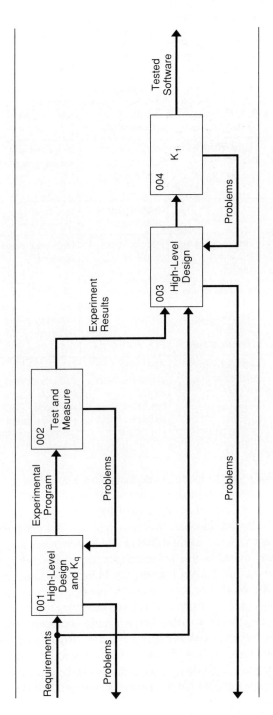

FIGURE 13.11
Experimental Kernel K_e

TABLE 13.4
ETX SPECIFICATIONS FOR EXPERIMENTAL KERNEL K_e

Cell:	001	002	003	004
Entry	Approved requirements	Experimental program design and code Test objectives	Experiment results, inspected and approved requirements	Inspected and approved high-level design
Exit	Experimental program design and code Test objectives	Experiment reslts	Inspected and approved high-level design	Inspected and tested software
Feedback In	Test problems and questions		Implementation problems	
Feedback Out	Requirements problems	Test questions and interim results	Requirements problems	High-level design problems
Task	Develop experimental model	Run experiment, measure, document, and decide if objectives met	Develop and inspect high-level design	Implement, inspect, unit test, and document software
Measures	Resources expended, work product produced, problems found	As specified by test objectives	Resources expended, work product produced, problems found	Resources expended, work product produced, problems found

the stubs to be produced (006). All the modules and facilities are delivered to the integration cell (004), which integrates them together into the final system.

The integration process can be better appreciated by examining a further decomposition (Fig. 13.13). Several modules M_1 through M_i are first integrated (001) to form the basic system nucleus, or initial driver build B_i. While this is a big bang integration, it is kept as limited as possible while still producing a rudimentary driver capability. Once the initial driver is available, additional modules can be incorporated a few at a time. Module test cases then are run against each build to ensure that it was properly incorporated and that it functions according to specifications. These system builds are then made available for use in test or component build.

The build cell is shown in more detail in Fig. 13.14. Here one or more new modules M_j are added to the previous build in spin j (001). The result is tested against the j test cases IT_j in 002, and a decision is made on whether the module passes the integration test criteria and should remain in the spin or if it should be removed. A de-spin (004) is used to remove any troublesome modules.

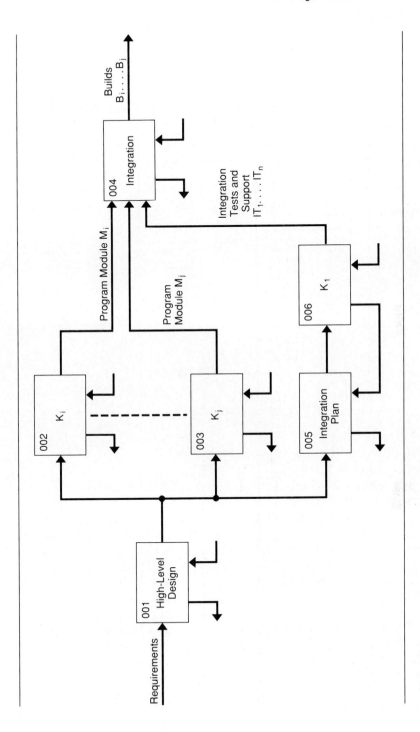

FIGURE 13.12
Integration Cycle

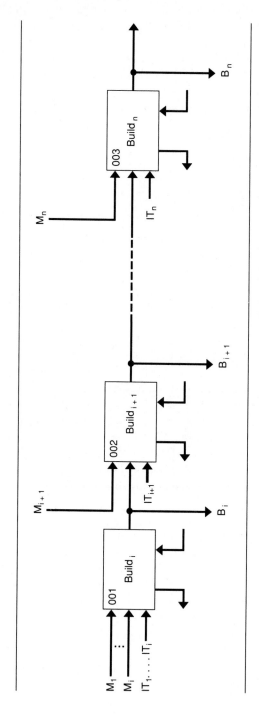

FIGURE 13.13
Integration Cell

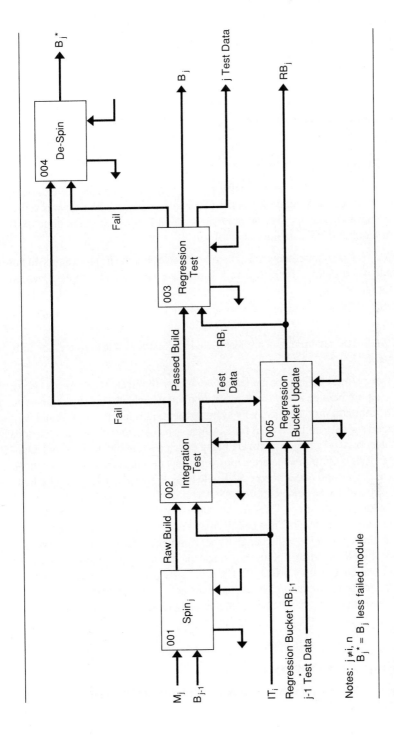

FIGURE 13.14
Build Cell

If the integration decision is passed, regression tests are run (003) to help ensure that the changes in this spin do not invalidate previously integrated functions. Again, the test results are used to decide whether the spin should be accepted. The regression test bucket is updated (005) to reflect the new module and the integration test experience. The regression test data is used in building the next regression bucket, RB_{j+1}.

13.8.3 Requirements Instability

To this point, it has been assumed that the software requirements were known, stable, and understood. Since this is rarely the case, compensating process provisions are needed. The appropriate provisions depend on which of the three basic types of requirements instability is involved:

1. *KSU'* The requirements are known and stable, but the implementers do not understand them sufficiently well to produce an adequate implementation (not U, or U').

2. *KS'U* The requirements are known and understood, but they are not stable (S').

3. *K'SU* The requirements are stable and understood, but they are not fully known (K').

Case 1 seems reasonable, but the other two appear illogical. How, for example, could a requirement be known and understood but unstable? This, unfortunately, is a very common problem. In many systems the requirements are firm and well understood right up until the need for a change is recognized. This often happens when many parts of a large system are being developed simultaneously and unanticipated design or implementation problems in one unit affect several others.

Case 3 was aptly described by Mr. Dooley, Finley Peter Dunne's fictional philosopher, when he said, "It ain't what you don't know that hurts you—it's what you know that ain't so." When software is part of a new application that has yet to be tried, the planners often believe they know the requirements, but they do not. The new application will change its environment, which will change system behavior, modify the user's perceptions, and change the requirements. This is the basic software uncertainty principle: The more an application is changed, the less accurate are its requirements. It is important not to confuse precision with accuracy. Requirements may be very detailed and precise but not accurately represent the real needs of the users.

13.8.4 Prototype Process Models

Prototype programs can be built to learn the potential customers' reactions. These prototypes demonstrate one or more facets of system behavior for test with the intended users. They can then be used to try to reduce the requirements uncertainties. The requirements instability case 1, KSU', can be addressed by using the K_e experimental development cycle in Fig. 13.11. Here the measurement and evaluation step should involve end users or others who understand the application and can spot operational problems. This figure, for example, is the process model that represents a user interface simulation.

The process in Fig. 13.15 deals with requirements that are known and understood but unstable (KS'U). Here the development process is broken into releases, and the requirements changes are batched for periodic introduction. An initial high-level design and K_1 development process (001) are used to develop the initial modules needed for the initial product build B_1. These are integrated in 002, and this initial build is used as the base for integrating the next batch of required function in 004. This process continues until the final build B_n is produced at 006. This incremental development process provides temporary requirements stability while accommodating changing user needs.

The process in Fig. 13.16 is used when the requirements are not known in advance (K'SU). Here the only answer is to install a suitably performing prototype product in the customer's environment for trial use. Once the requirements are known, they are returned to development, where the prior version is updated or a new product is built. The process shown in Fig. 13.16 uses whichever development process, D_1, is appropriate to the situation. For relatively simple systems not requiring integration, high-level design and K_1 kernels could be used. With larger systems, the full integration process of Fig. 13.12 might be used. Here again, the approach is to ensure that the full development process is only used with reasonably stable requirements or with relatively modest incremental requirements changes. With real unknowns, of course, the experimental kernel K_e should be used. With truly revolutionary systems, several rebuild cycles may be needed before the system performs as desired.

The Use of Prototyping.   Each of these prototyping methods could be used at any of the process levels. Instead of using K_1 for implementation, the full integration cycle in Fig. 13.12 could be used, for example. The specific process selected should depend on the problems and risks with the system and each of its modules.

In a large system some modules may require some form of prototyping, while others could be developed directly. With external interfaces, for example, the involved modules should often be prototyped and tested with the end users. Few technical professionals are capable of appreciating the operational details that make systems attractive to their users, though many may think they can. The normal result is a hard-to-use system that is expensive and time-consuming to fix. An appropriate process would ensure that these user interfaces were prototyped and checked before implementation.

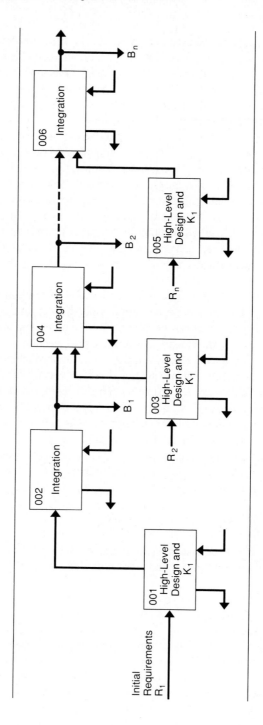

FIGURE 13.15
Requirements Unstable (KS'U)

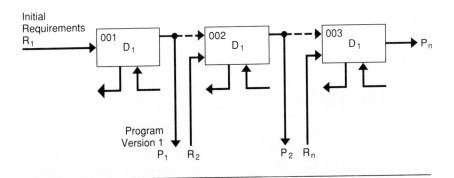

FIGURE 13.16
Requirements Unknown (K'SU)

Prototyping Issues.   Evidence shows that product development through prototyping is substantially faster and less expensive than traditional methods.[2, 8, 9] Some key considerations for using prototypes are:

□ Even if it is only intended as a quick experiment, the prototype's objectives should be clearly established before starting to build it.

□ Define the prototype process in advance. Prototyping does not mean hacking code in any way that comes to mind. The methods used should be appropriate to the specific prototype objectives.

□ The results of the prototyping effort must be documented and analyzed before a decision is made on how to proceed.

□ Complete the initial prototype and analyze the results before starting another prototype iteration. Prototyping is habit-forming, and unplanned iterations can be very expensive.

□ There is no "right" way to prototype. The result may be thrown away, used as a foundation for enhancement, or repackaged as a product. It all depends on the original objectives, the process used, and the desired quality of the result.

□ When the prototype is to be included as part of the final product, the need for design records, service facilities, and user documentation must be recognized at the outset and suitable process provisions made. If these needs are not addressed in the initial implementation, later retrofit is generally more expensive than throwing the prototype away and building a product from scratch. With the knowledge gained, this is often far faster than trying to clear up the undocumented patchwork that often results from prototype enhancements. A carefully developed prototyping plan and process specification are thus of paramount importance.

13.9 Detailed Process Models

While one can say a great deal about knitting without knowing how to make stitches, one can't actually do knitting. The same is true of programming. All the process models in the world will not help to produce programs unless they can be reduced to the level of programming. This is the Atomic process level.

With the A-level process, the detail used in task definition should be appropriate to the knowledge and skill of the professionals. One example is the partial decomposition of the process for building regression test buckets in Fig. 13.17 and Fig. 13.18. In Fig. 13.17, the regression test process starts with the regression test plan (001). The regression bucket is next built (002) using the planning data, the previous bucket, and the test case library, which includes both the prior and new tests. This regression bucket is then run (003) and the results used to decide whether to fail the product or proceed to the next stage.

Regression test planning is further decomposed in Fig. 13.18 as follows:

1. The build schedule and prior build records are examined to determine the new modules that will be included (001).

2. The expect list for these new modules is examined to determine the functions that will be included and the modules they are expected to affect (002).

3. The test records for the impacted modules are examined to identify the test cases available for them (003).

4. The test profiles are examined to determine those test cases that apply to the new functions to be included. A subset of the highest yield functional test cases is also included (004).

5. Previous regression test data and the test histories for each test case and module are examined to determine which of the older tests in the regression bucket should be retained, which should be dropped, and which tests should be added (005).

With this information the final regression bucket can be built for the next build spin. This process could be decomposed into further detail, depending on the specific needs of the project and the experience level of the people.

13.10 Entity Process Models

The process models we have discussed so far are similar to state models of a software system. In simplest terms, the process is either in an idle state before the

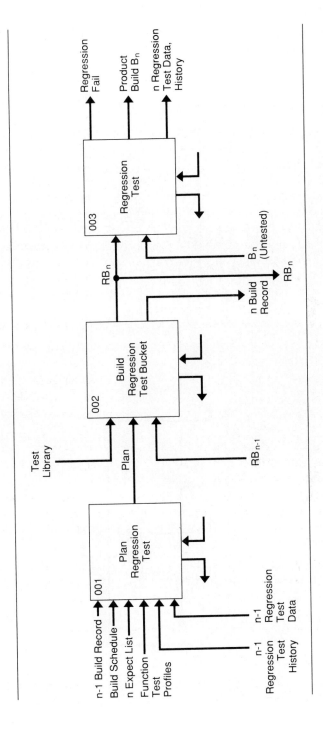

FIGURE 13.17
Regression Test Refinement

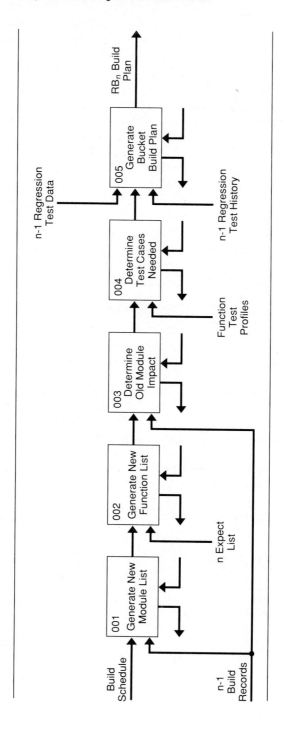

FIGURE 13.18
Regression Test Planning

entry criteria for the first cell are met, or the process is in a state represented by one of the succeeding cells. After the final output from the last cell is produced, the model returns to the idle state, waiting for further requirements. As the implementation tasks become more complex, however, this simplistic picture may provide a less realistic representation of actual task behavior. For example, when a design question is fed back from implementation, implementation work generally proceeds while the design question is being resolved. These small-scale process iterations are thus not visible in the higher-level models.

One alternative is to consider basing process models on entities, similar to those used by Jackson in Jackson System Development.[14] Here one deals with entities and the actions performed on them. Each entity is a real object that exists and has an extended lifetime. That is, entities are living things rather than ephemeral objects that are transiently introduced within the process.

Examples of such entities are the requirements, the finished program, the program documentation, or the design. While these sound like some of the items discussed in the Waterfall Model, they are really quite different. The traditional Waterfall Model deals with tasks such as producing the requirements. This task is then presumed completed before design starts. In reality, the requirements entity must survive throughout the process. While it undergoes various transformations, there is a real requirements entity that should be available at all later times in the process. Exactly the same is true of the design, the implementation, and the test suite.

Entity process models (EPMs) provide a useful additional representation of the software process because they are often more accurate than task-based models for complex and dynamic processes. The reason is that EPMs deal with real objects that persist and evolve through a relatively small and defined sequence of states. The transitions between these states result from well-defined causes, and the relationships of these states and transitions can be relatively invariant to the particular task sequence employed.

For this purpose, entities are real things, not just artifacts introduced to assist in the work. When, for example, the full software product life cycle is considered, a number of "artifacts" produced during development become extremely important. Examples are the requirements, the design, the test documents, the test cases, and the test plans. What is not so clearly recognized, however, is that the traditional view of these items as end products of a development phase can lead to the belief that they are completed and will undergo no further changes. As a result, there are often no official process provisions for keeping the design and requirements documentation up to date throughout implementation and test.

The question then is what are the most appropriate entities to use in modeling the software process. Some obvious entities are:

□ The deliverable code

□ The users' installation and operation manuals

Some other items that should generally be considered as entities that persist after conclusion of the initial software development work are:

- ☐ The requirements documents
- ☐ The design
- ☐ The test cases and procedures

It is clear that each of these entities cycles through a set of states during the software process. By focusing on these states and the actions required to cause state transitions, the process of producing an entity process model becomes relatively straightforward:

1. Identify the process entities and their states.
2. Define the triggers that cause the transitions between these states.
3. Complete the process model without resource constraints (unconstrained process model, UPM).[13]
4. Impose the appropriate limitations to produce a final constrained process model (CPM).[13]

While this procedure is conceptually simple, it can become quite complex when applied to large-scale processes. EPMs provide a useful way to characterize complex and highly fed-back activities at the U or W level, but they must be transformed to a task structure to actually guide the work or its automation. Since they can provide a more accurate high-level representation of the work, however, they provide a useful perspective for planning and tracking purposes.

13.11 Process Model Views

The three basic views of process models are the state view, the organizational view, and the control view. The state view is what we have discussed so far, with the states either representing various stages of the process (tasks) or stages of the product (entities). The state view thus has two complementary representations: task-oriented and entity-oriented. The task-oriented representation explicitly portrays the tasks, while the entity state changes are implied. In the entity-oriented representation, the entity states are explicitly portrayed, while the tasks are implied as causing the transitions between these states.

A view of the development process that defines the responsibilities for each activity is shown in Fig. 13.19. While such a picture is not very informative from a software engineer's point of view, it does identify the essential responsibilities. Again, such a view could be refined to any desired level of detail.

The third view relates to measurement and control. A simplified view of the data gathering and approval aspects of the development process are shown in Fig.

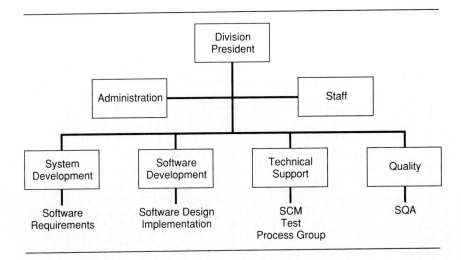

FIGURE 13.19
Organizational View

13.20. The relationships between the management, control, and support activities are shown for data gathering, approval, and reporting. Since these relationships have a critical impact on the behavior of a software organization, they must be clearly defined. This is generally done at the highest level in the organization through organization charts and responsibility statements.

These are different views rather than alternatives. They each present an essential perspective of the process that must be understood, defined, and managed. If any view is not addressed, an important facet of software management will likely be overlooked.

It is possible to produce higher-level models of the software process for use in guiding software engineering activities. While the specific methods are not described here, they are similar to those used in defining traditional administrative procedures, only somewhat more complex.[18] When more detailed process refinements are desired, it is desirable to use automated tools. While there has been only limited experience with such approaches, some techniques and methods have been published.[10, 11, 13, 15, 16, 17]

13.12 Establishing and Using a Process Definition

Each software organization should establish a process architecture and process models tailored to its particular needs. This tailoring is done as follows:

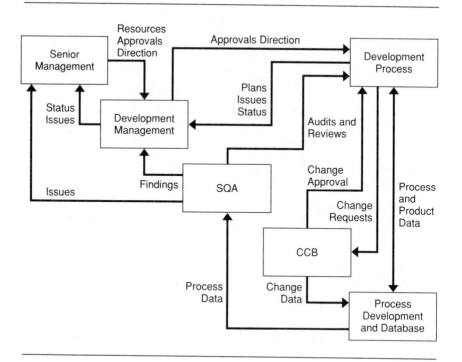

FIGURE 13.20
Control and Measurement View

1. Define a standard process as a foundation for tailoring. It is helpful to identify likely tailoring options in this standard model.
2. Establish the ETX specifications for the standard process model.
3. Make provisions to gather and track the resulting process measurements.
4. Establish checkpoints and standards for SQA review. While such checkpoints have not been illustrated here, they typically involve the review of test and inspection data and the observation of selected tasks. SQA may also conduct independent tests.
5. Incorporate specific measurement and reporting provisions.
6. Instruct the development personnel on the use and value of the process architecture, the standard process models, and when, why, and how they should be tailored.

Since many projects will likely need their own unique process definitions, they should start with the standard process and then take the following steps:

1. Identify the unique project issues, problems, and success criteria:

   □ Knowns and unknowns

   □ Key technical and management risks

   □ Constraints

   □ Measurement, tracking, and review

2. Document the adjustments required to the standard process to produce a basic overall project process. This should address:

   □ The requirements unknowns

   □ The integration and regression issues

   □ The product design and application unknowns

   □ The management and assurance requirements

   □ The staffing and training needs (K_e may be needed just to build an adequate experience level)

3. For each software system component, repeat these definitions.

4. Once each program module has been identified, consider the process definition for it as well and make any necessary adjustments.

13.13 Basic Process Guidelines

Finally, some guidelines are needed for developing and using a process architecture and its process models:

□ Establish objectives for each project's process.

□ Define the basic process architecture, make sure it meets the needs of the projects, and then enforce it as an overall process framework.

□ Remember that each project, component, and module is unique and its process should be uniquely determined. While some combination of the standard process kernels will generally be appropriate, be open to truly new and unique situations and establish process provisions for them when they occur.

□ Establish process definition standards.

□ Change the process model dynamically as the problems change.

□ Require that all deviations for the standard process be documented, reviewed, and approved.

In developing a process architecture and a set of process models, it is important to remember that these can become quite complex. Rather than attempt to establish a fully defined process, it is wisest to create a high-level framework architecture and then refine a few areas at a time. This refinement process should be driven by the needs of the projects. It should also give priority to those areas in which the professionals need the most guidance and should consider the available process skills. Treat process architecture and design much the same as a complex new system development: Start with a high-level prototype and refine it as you gain knowledge and experience.

13.15 Summary

A defined software process provides organizations with a consistent process framework while permitting adjustment to unique needs. The conflicting needs for customization and standardization can be met by establishing a process architecture with standard unit or "kernel" process steps and rules for describing and relating them. Customization is then achieved through their interconnection into process models.

Software process models can be defined at the Universal (U) process level, the Worldly (W) process level, and the Atomic (A) process level. These are typically embodied in policies at the U level, procedures at the W level, and standards at the A level.

When looked at from the U level, software processes tend to look much the same. When one attempts to break these down in more detail, however, significant project differences begin to appear. At the W level, however, many of the tasks are relatively standardized across projects. They may be used in different combinations and sequences, but it is possible to identify some basic process cells that can then be interconnected to meet unique project needs. The detailed structures within these standard cells would then be A-level models.

Each software organization should establish a process architecture and process models that are tailored to its particular needs. The appropriate steps are: identify the unique project issues, problems, and success criteria; establish a basic overall project process; and repeat these definitions for each component and program module.

Some guidelines on developing and using a process architecture are: establish objectives, define the basic process architecture, make sure it meets the needs of the projects, and then enforce it as an overall process framework. Also remember that each project, component, and module is unique and its process should be uniquely determined. Process definition standards are also needed. The process models should be changed as the problems change, and all deviations from the standard process must be documented and approved.

Above all, remember that process definitions can be very complex. They should thus be approached with the same care as the design of a large system; start with a prototype and add enhancements as requirements knowledge and development experience are gained.

References

1. Basili, V. R., and H. D. Rombach. "Integrating measurement into SW environments," *IEEE Proceedings,* Ninth International Conference on Software Engineering, Montery, CA, March 30, 1987.

2. Boehm, B. W., T. E. Gray, and T. Seewaldt. "Prototyping versus specifying: a multiproject experiment," *IEEE Transactions on Software Engineering,* vol. SE-10, no. 3, May 1984.

3. Boehm, B. W. "A spiral model of software development and enhancement," *IEEE Computer,* May 1988.

4. Brooks, F. P., Jr. *The Mythical Man-Month,* Reading, MA: Addison-Wesley, 1975.

5. Chroust, G. "Backtracking in software process models," *IEEE Proceedings,* Third International Software Process Workshop, Breckenridge, CO, November 1986.

6. Deming, W. E. *Out of the Crisis,* Cambridge, MA: MIT Center for Advanced Engineering Studies, 1982.

7. Freeman, P. *Software Perspectives, The System Is the Message,* Reading, MA: Addison-Wesley, 1986.

8. Hekmatpour, S., and D. C. Ince. "Rapid Software Prototyping," Technical Report 86/4, The Open University Milton Keynes, MK76AA, England.

9. Hekmatpour, S. "Experience with evolutionary prototyping in a large software project," *ACM Sigsoft Software Engineering Notes,* vol. 12, no. 1, January 1987.

10. Harel, D. "Statecharts: a visual formalism for complex systems," *Science of Computer Programming* 8, 3, June 1987, pp. 231–274.

11. Harel, D., et. al. "Statemate: a working environment for the development of complex reactive systems," *Proceedings of the Tenth International Conference on Software Engineering,* IEEE, 1988, pp. 396–406.

12. Humphrey, W. S. "Software Engineering Process: Definition and Scope," Fourth International Software Process Workshop, Devin, England, May 1988.

13. Humphrey, W. S., and M. I. Kellner. "Software process modeling: principles of entity process models," *Proceedings of the 11th International Conference on Software Engineering,* IEEE, 1989.

14. Jackson, M. A. *System Development,* Englewood Cliffs, NJ: Prentice-Hall, 1983.

15. Kellner, M. I. "Representational formalisms for software process modeling," *Proceedings of the Fourth International Software Process Workshop,* ACM, 1988, pp. 43–46.

16. Kellner, M. I., and G. A. Hansen. "Software Process Modeling," Technical Report CMU/SEI-88-TR-9, Software Engineering Institute, Carnegie Mellon University, May 1988.

17. Kellner, M. I., and G. A. Hansen. "Software process modeling: a case study," *Proceedings of the 22nd Hawaii International Conference on Systems Science,* IEEE, 1989.

18. Radice, R. A., N. K. Roth, A. C. O'Hare, Jr., and W. A. Ciarfilla. "A programming process architecture," *IBM Systems Journal,* vol. 24, no. 2, 1985.

19. Royce, W. W. "Managing the development of large software systems," *Proceedings of IEEE WESCON,* August 1970.

14

The Software Engineering
Process Group

In approaching the software process it is instructive to examine the way processes are handled in other fields. Consider, for example, the difference between a factory and a machine shop. They both may have similar equipment, but they clearly produce vastly different results. In the machine shop the process depends on who is handling the work, while the process in the factory has been designed. In fact, manufacturing processes are typically designed by process specialists before the tools are even ordered and installed.

While there are vast differences between software engineering and the typical factory, software process development also requires some specialists to do the work. Actually, the problems of software process change are often complicated by the fact that no one is responsible to make it happen. If software process improvement isn't anybody's job, it is not surprising that it doesn't get done! If it is important enough to do, however, someone must be assigned the responsibility and given the necessary resources. Until this is done, software process development will remain a nice thing to do someday, but never today.

14.1 Changing the Software Process

Changing anything as complex as a software process must necessarily involve a host of factors, among which one of the most challenging is the need to change the way the software people do their work. They have typically learned, often through years of experience, how to cope with their many tasks and crises. These professionals must be convinced that changes make sense for them. What is more, software engineering involves complex tasks done under tight schedule pressure. Since change is difficult even without such pressure, it is not surprising that software process change is both painfully slow and haphazard.

Software process improvement is not simple. To achieve tangible results, it needs to be treated like a development task:

1. Identify the key problems.
2. Establish priorities.
3. Define action plans.
4. Get professional and management agreement.
5. Assign people.
6. Provide training and guidance.
7. Launch implementation.
8. Track progress.
9. Fix the inevitable problems.

The task involves a lot of work, which obviously can't be done by any one group. The Software Engineering Process Group (SEPG), however, is the focal point for this total effort. Some of the other people who must be involved are senior management, the line projects, SQA, education, finance, administration, and, most important, the software professionals themselves.

14.2 The Role of the SEPG

The SEPG has two basic tasks that are done simultaneously: initiating and sustaining process change and supporting normal operations. The SEPG may also serve as the spawning ground for other groups such as technology support, education, cost estimating, standards, and possibly even SQA. Large software groups need professional support in all these areas, and, where it is not available, the SEPG can provide guidance until such functions are established.

Change is an essential part of the software process. While projects must not be disrupted with excessive change, the software process should be viewed as continuous learning. Process change involves learning new methods and accommodating to the changing nature and scale of the problems encountered. The products we build in the future will be far larger and more complex than those of today. Without an established software process, projects will not have an organized experience base on which to build and must each learn through painful trial and error. A thoughtfully established software process provides a framework for building on the experiences of others.

Change is also needed to bring current software practice up to the level of current knowledge. We typically know how to do our work far better than we are currently doing. Most software problems are caused not by lack of knowledge but by the lack of the discipline to apply the best known methods and an inability to effectively handle the myriad of associated process and product detail. Building the disciplined practices to do every software task with precise correctness requires a painstaking improvement program.

Changes are therefore a normal and continuous part of software management, and a key SEPG role is to ensure that these changes are effectively implemented. The rate of change should be aggressive but not disruptive, and it should take advantage of available resources and technology. The key need is for a balanced level of SEPG resources that can be sustained on a permanent basis.

The SEPG should also serve as a consolidating force for the changes that have already been made and should support the projects as they use new methods, standards, and technology. This support helps with the adoption of new practices and facilitates their retention in the working fabric of the organization. Without such guidance and support, lasting process improvement is practically impossible.

14.2.1 The SEPG as a Change Agent

A change agent provides the energy, enthusiasm, and direction needed to overcome resistance and cause change.[2] The SEPG fills this role by providing the skilled resources, the creativity, and the management leverage needed to make things happen. The decision to make the changes must rest with line management, but the SEPG should provide the technical guidance on what changes are most important. They must be aware of the state of the software process, appreciate the areas needing improvement, and present practical improvement recommendations to management.

When management approves these action plans, the SEPG takes the lead in launching the required efforts, providing leadership in getting them staffed, and supporting the work with needed information, training, and skills. The SEPG also tracks action plan progress and informs management of status and major problems.

While change is essential, it is also important to control the pace of change. If it is too slow, progress will be limited, while too rapid a pace will be disruptive and self-defeating. No group can tolerate perpetual disruption, and no project can operate without reasonable stability. Change must therefore be carefully planned and coordinated with the status and needs of each project.

14.2.2 The SEPG Sustaining Role

The continuing role of the SEPG can be divided into six categories:

1. Establish process standards.
2. Maintain the process database.
3. Serve as the focal point for technology insertion.
4. Provide key process education.
5. Provide project consultation.
6. Make periodic assessments and status reports.

14.3 Establishing Standards

The SEPG is the focal point for establishing process standards. These include those product-related standards discussed in Chapter 9, as well as the process-related standards described in Chapters 7, 10, 11, 12, and 13.

Since the SEPG staff cannot have sufficient resources or the resident expertise to develop all these standards, it must establish working teams with members drawn from the most involved groups. With configuration management standards, for example, the SCM group should develop the standard, possibly with SEPG help. SEPG can then assist with reviews, approvals, and implementation.

The SEPG standards role involves the following tasks:

1. *The SEPG recommends the priorities for developing standards.* There are many potentially valuable standards, but they must be introduced in an orderly way. New standards efforts should generally not be started until the developed standards have been approved and adopted. The existence of proposed but unapproved standards can be both confusing and disruptive. The SEPG should maintain a prioritized list of standards development work.

2. *The SEPG should ensure that prior work on the subject is reviewed.* With few exceptions, the topics being considered for standardization have been studied by others, and much time and effort can be saved if this work is used as a foundation.

3. *The standards development team should include available experts and users.* Every standard is a balance between what is theoretically desirable and what can be practically implemented. This balance can only be determined through negotiation between the standardization advocates and the people who must use the result. In the absence of a standards development group, the SEPG should coordinate the formation and chartering of these teams.

4. *The final standard review and approval is the most important step.* Even when user representatives have participated in the standards development,

many conflicting opinions and messy details are involved. A comprehensive review by the prospective users will expose these issues and facilitate the thoughtful technical and management debates required to produce a competent result. Since this review process can be time-consuming and complex, the SEPG should ensure that appropriate tracking and control facilities are used for this purpose.

14.4 The Process Database

The process database is the permanent repository for the data gathered on the software engineering process and the resulting products. This data provides the reference for improving estimating accuracy, analyzing productivity, and assessing product quality. It is used by process specialists, project professionals, the quality staff, and management.

The types of information retained in this database are:

□ *Size, cost, and schedule data*   This is data on overall process performance. It is used to validate estimates, to generate estimating factors, and to establish contingencies.

□ *Product metrics*   These provide basic information on the nature, complexity, structure, and quality of the products. The information is used to assess the results produced and to relate these results to process actions.

□ *Process metrics*   These productivity and quality characteristics of detailed process tasks are used to assess task effectiveness and identify the most promising areas for process improvement.

To be most useful, a great deal of information is required for each kind of data. While this is discussed further in Chapter 15, the essential considerations for an effective process database are:

1. *The reason for gathering each piece of data must be stated.* There is so much potentially useful data that any organization could devote much of its time just to gathering it. This is a mistake, however, because data that is not gathered for a specific purpose is generally too loosely defined to be useful.

2. *To define the data, the exact meaning of each field must be specified, together with all the anticipated options and exceptions.* Where data is subject to various interpretations, such as lines of code or programmer months, the items to be included must be specified, together with means to identify them (semicolons, department numbers, and so forth). The data specification must be precise enough so a program could be written to gather and process it.

3. *Simple and easy-to-use procedures are required for gathering the data,* together with tools, forms, training, and assistance.

4. *Means are also required for ensuring that the data is obtained in a timely way. The data gathering must be as complete as practical* because a database that omits relevant data is just as erroneous as one that includes incorrect data.

5. *Means are needed to verify data accuracy.* Since data recorded by practicing programmers has been shown to be as much as 50 percent in error, a verification mechanism is essential.[1]

6. *Resources and procedures are required for entering the data into the database.*

7. *Provision must be made for user access to and analysis of the data.*

8. Finally, *provisions are required to protect and maintain the data.* The database must be updated periodically for format or other changes, old data must be purged, periodic back-ups are needed, and someone needs to enhance and correct the database programs.

14.5 Technology Insertion Focal Point

Technology support for any reasonably large software engineering organization involves seven activities:

1. A process definition is needed to help identify the software tasks that are both widely enough used and sufficiently common to warrant automated support.

2. A set of requirements is then developed for the needed support.

3. These requirements must be approved by the users, the people who will handle installation and support, and management.

4. A search is then made to identify commercially available tools that meet these needs.

5. An overall technology plan is developed that defines long-term technology needs and establishes a strategy for addressing them. This includes an architectural plan for the support environment and a phased introduction plan (see Chapter 18).

6. A technology support group is established to handle tool and environment installation, provide user assistance, and be the interface to the tool suppliers on problems and enhancements.

7. Education, training, and consultation must also be provided before the tools and methods are installed for general use.

In the absence of a technology support group that provides the above services, the SEPG can help coordinate the technology efforts of the various projects. The SEPG should not, however, attempt to provide all the technology support services. This is a large job that could easily consume the entire SEPG's resources. Either a technology group is formed to carry this load or the projects must fend for themselves with SEPG assistance.

14.6 Education and Training

Education could also easily consume all the SEPG resources. The SEPG must serve as the focal point for process education and avoid being saddled with all the teaching responsibilities. Ideally a full-time education group maintains a staff of volunteers, instructors, or consultants to do this job. Where an adequately staffed education group is not available, knowledgeable professionals can generally be found to serve as volunteer instructors.

The SEPG may initially have to teach some of the subjects until qualified instructors can be found or trained. Examples of courses that are often needed are:

- Project management methods: how to plan, estimate, and track projects
- Software design methods: the use of design languages, object oriented design, and prototyping
- Quality management: methods for making quantitative quality estimates and plans
- Design and code inspections

Most of these topics will generally require considerable post-training consultation before the professionals can be suitably proficient. By assigning professionals who have such experience to work for or with the SEPG as consultants, the entire organization can gain from their knowledge and experience. After these methods are better known and a resident knowledge base has been established, the regular education function can generally handle the teaching responsibilities.

14.7 Process Consultation

The key focus of the process group is on improving the practice of software engineering. They do this by working with software practitioners both to provide assistance and to stay current on the projects' problems. If they do not stay current, they will not be able to relate to the practicing professionals.

Another reason for SEPG consultation is that few projects can afford their own SEPG group. For projects larger than about 200 or so professionals, a dedicated process capability might make sense, but even then a central group is required to provide cross-organization standards and awareness.

The SEPG can be most helpful to the project by consulting on:

- □ The process data they should gather
- □ The analyses and interpretation of the data gathered
- □ Tuning the standard process to unique project needs
- □ Assisting with the preparation of quality plans
- □ Serving as experienced inspection moderators
- □ Advising on the priority areas for technology insertion

14.8 Process Status and Assessment

The SEPG is also responsible for understanding the current state of software practice and alerting management to key problems. This includes:

- □ Awareness of how completely each project's process is defined
- □ Knowledge of how the process is implemented
- □ Judgment on when an assessment would be appropriate
- □ Leadership in conducting assessments

Senior management reviews, as described in Chapter 5, are also conducted at least quarterly. These provide an overview of the state of the software process, a summary of process improvement status and plans, and priority items for management attention. The items required to make such reviews effective are:

1. Goals for process improvement
2. A comparison of the actual process state to prior plans
3. The status of the process improvement actions
4. Identified problems and recommended corrective actions
5. Recommended responsibilities for handling these actions

14.9 Establishing the SEPG

The questions to address in setting up an SEPG are:

- □ How big should the effort be?
- □ Where does the staff come from?
- □ Who should head it?
- □ Where should it report?

- What are the tasks for initial focus?
- What are the key risks?
- How is its effectiveness evaluated?

14.9.1 SEPG Size and Staffing

While each organization has its own unique needs, a useful initial guide is to aim at full-time assignments to the SEPG of about 2 percent of the software professionals. For organizations of about a hundred or more software professionals, the typical range falls between 1 percent and 3 percent, with the prime determinants being the ability to recruit suitable candidates and the financial constraints of the organization. For smaller organizations, it is essential to have at least one full-time SEPG professional with the part-time support of other professionals on working groups. When the organization is too small to support a full-time professional, the manager must be the de facto process manager with the support of a committee and special working groups.

Staffing the SEPG with competent and experienced professionals is often the most difficult and time-consuming part of establishing this function. Good people are hard to find, and the projects are never willing to give up their best people. If the process improvement efforts have strong management backing, however, some of the better people will often seek these assignments. These are typically experienced professionals who are convinced that there are better ways to do software and would like to participate in finding and installing them. A respected SEPG manager will often hear of these people through the grapevine. Getting them assigned, however, will generally require management support. If not enough qualified people can be obtained in this way, a "management tax" must be imposed on development. Care is required, however, to guard against getting the lame, the halt, and the tired.

14.9.2 SEPG Leadership and Reporting

The SEPG leader must be a knowledgeable manager with a demonstrated ability to make things happen, the respect of the project professionals, and the support of top management. To select this official agent for process change, the key criteria are:[2]

- Agents should be enthusiastic about leading the change process. Irwin and Langham point out that "enthusiasm can be contagious and people tend to perform better in an optimistic environment than in a won't-work environment."[3]
- Agents must be both technically and politically capable of understanding the problems and ensuring that effective solutions are implemented.

- □ Agents need the respect of the people they are to deal with.
- □ Agents must have management's confidence and support or they will not act with the assurance needed to get wide cooperation and acceptance.

The SEPG must not report to line development management or to the SQA organization. In either case their role would likely become one of taking sides in the traditional SQA/development conflicts and their focus on process improvement would suffer. While there is often no natural reporting point in most organizations, there is usually some technical staff function that could provide a neutral home. The SEPG could, for example, report to the same executive reporting point as SQA, the computing center, SCM, or software technology.

14.9.3 SEPG Priorities and Risks

The SEPG priorities should roughly follow those given in this book, with initial emphasis on project planning and project management. The most important single guideline is for the SEPG to limit its focus to those tasks it can handle reasonably quickly and effectively. It might, for example, focus entirely on installing an inspection program and defer all other work until this is reasonably underway. The danger of superficially addressing many topics is that none will actually get done.

There are, of course, also key risk situations for the SEPG:

- □ It doesn't have enough full-time capable professionals to do competent work.
- □ The SEPG does not have sufficient management support to convince the projects to support the process improvement efforts.
- □ The SEPG manager is not able to obtain the participation of the most knowledgeable software professionals in the process improvement task groups.

With senior management support, these risks can all be handled, but generally none of them can be handled without it.

14.9.4 Evaluating the SEPG

There are many ways to evaluate staff and support groups like the SEPG. Some of the more common methods are to use advisory groups or periodically to poll the users and software professionals for their opinions. While it is probably a good idea to do some of these things, perhaps the best approach is to judge the SEPG on how effectively it applies the software process maturity framework to its own work. This should permit them to present a clear and succinct picture of what they are doing and where they stand against the following criteria:

- □ Level 2: Does the SEPG have a plan for its work, a tracking system, and means to retain and control its work products?

□ Level 3: Have the SEPG professionals established a basic framework for their own work, including standards, procedures, and a review program?

□ Level 4: Does the SEPG measure the productivity and quality of its own work? This, for example, might include workload factors for training, consultation, process development, and administration.

□ Level 5: Do they regularly assess their own activities for improvement opportunities and incorporate them in their working process?

While all of these activities take time and effort to initiate, they will make the SEPG more effective while demonstrating process leadership to the organization. If they are not at least one maturity level ahead of the projects, they may not have the knowledge or conviction to do their job.

14.10 Summary

Software process improvement often receives little orderly attention. If it is important enough to do, however, someone must be assigned the responsibility and given the resources to make it happen. Until this is done, it will remain a nice thing to do someday, but never today.

The SEPG has two basic tasks that are done simultaneously: initiating and sustaining process change and supporting normal operations. Process change requires the professionals to learn new methods and to accommodate to the changing nature and scale of the problems they encounter. The SEPG supports this learning while also serving as a consolidating force for the changes that have already been made. As a change agent, it provides the skilled resources, the organizational focus, and the management leverage to make things happen.

The SEPG is the focal point for establishing process standards, and it maintains the process database as a permanent repository for the data gathered on the software engineering process and products. In its role as a technology insertion focal point, the SEPG helps coordinate the projects' technology efforts, at least until a permanent technology group is established. Further SEPG roles concern education, consultation, and awareness of the current state of software practice.

A useful initial guide is to assign about 2 percent of the software professionals to the SEPG. Staffing the SEPG with competent and experienced professionals, however, is often the most difficult and time-consuming part of establishing this function. This group should not report to line development management or to the SQA organization. The SEPG could, for example, report to the same executive reporting point as SQA, the computing center, SCM, or advanced software technology.

The initial SEPG priorities should roughly follow those given in this book, with initial emphasis on project planning and project management. The most important single guideline is for the SEPG to limit its focus to those tasks it can handle reasonably quickly and effectively. The danger of superficially addressing many topics is that none will actually get done.

The major risks in establishing an SEPG are that it will not be adequately staffed, that it will receive insufficient management support to do its job, or that the SEPG manager will not be able to obtain the participation and support of the project leaders and software professionals. While SEPG performance can be evaluated with the traditional means for judging support staffs, probably the best measure is the SEPG's adherence to the software process maturity framework for their own work.

References

1. Basili, V. R., and Weiss, D. M. "A methodology for collecting valid software engineering data," *IEEE Transactions on Software Engineering,* VSE-10, no. 6, November 1984.

2. Humphrey, W. S. *Managing for Innovation—Leading Technical People.* Englewood Cliffs, NJ: Prentice-Hall, 1987, p. 24.

3. Irwin, P. H., and F. W. Langham, Jr. "The change seekers," *Harvard Business Review,* January–February 1966, p. 75.

Software Engineering Institute

PART FOUR

The Managed Process

Once the topics of Part III are in place, the software organization will have a firm foundation for introducing measurements and statistical management. While the topics from prior sections must continue to be refined and improved, management's attention should now turn to quantitative planning and process control. Appendix A describes the broader spectrum of topics that should be addressed by organizations at this point, but priority should be given to the subjects of Chapters 15 and 16.

Chapter 15 outlines the principles of software process data gathering and discusses the key considerations in establishing a data gathering program. This data meets the basic management needs for quantitative analysis and establishes the foundation for software quality planning and management.

Chapter 16 describes the software quality plan, why it is important, and how it is produced. It also reviews quality measures, quality plans, quality estimates, and the problems of tracking and controlling quality.

Once an organization has effectively introduced the topics in Part IV, it will have the quantitative foundation needed for orderly process analysis, process improvement, and technology investment. These are the topics of Part V.

15

Data Gathering and Analysis

We gather and analyze software data to help us improve the software engineering process. As we face increasingly demanding software projects, we need to understand more precisely what we are doing and how to improve our effectiveness. This chapter first outlines the principles of data gathering and then discusses the data gathering process. The balance of the chapter is then devoted to examples of software data gathering and analysis.

Data gathering is expensive and time-consuming. It affects the busiest people and may even be viewed as personally threatening. There is also considerable confusion on what data to gather and how to use it. While all these factors must be considered, there is no way to learn how to gather and analyze data without gathering and analyzing data.

15.1 The Principles of Data Gathering

In summary, the principles of effective data gathering are:

- □ The data is gathered in accordance with specific objectives and a plan.
- □ The choice of data to be gathered is based on a model or hypothesis about the process being examined.
- □ The data gathering process must consider the impact of data gathering on the entire organization.
- □ The data gathering plan must have management support.

The following paragraphs discuss each of these points.

15.1.1 The Objectives of Data Gathering

Data gathered without a clear objective is unlikely to be useful. Since any complex process involves a host of parameters, the chance of accidentally gathering the right information is remote. Unlike research, in which data gathering may not have a clear purpose, data gathered for process improvement should have a specific objective. There are four basic reasons for collecting software data:

1. *Understanding*   As part of a research or development study, data can be gathered to learn about some item or process.

2. *Evaluation*   The data can be used to study some product (or activity) to see if it meets acceptance criteria.

3. *Control*   The data can be used to control some activity.

4. *Prediction*   The data can be used to develop rate or trend indicators.

While software process data can be used in a wide variety of ways, it is essential to clearly define the primary reasons for obtaining it.

15.1.2 Data Gathering Models

To measure the software process successfully, one must almost start by knowing the expected results. With a poorly understood process, it is hard to be precise about the data that is needed. After some study and evaluation, however, assumptions can usually be made about the key process events and their relationships. Data is then gathered to verify these assumptions. These measures are related to this conceptual model, the variations are examined, and changes are made to the process or the model to bring them into closer agreement.

Without a process model data gathering is like searching for the proverbial needle in a haystack. There are so many possible measures in a complex software process that some random selection of metrics will not likely turn up anything of value. While it could be argued that a little data is needed to gain understanding, such undirected searches must be viewed as research. As psychologist George Miller once said: "In truth, a good case could be made that if your knowledge is meager and unsatisfactory, the last thing in the world you should do is make measurements. The chance is negligible that you will measure the right things accidentally."[8]

Kearney et al. wrote a thought-provoking paper on software complexity measurement in which they point out the difficulties of making statistical studies of the software process.[15] They note that, given enough measurements, one can always find apparently statistically significant results and correlations from random events. These, however, generally have no predictive value. Examples are the relationships found between election outcomes and football scores or between stock market prices and astronomical events. For example, it has been determined that the likelihood of a recession is far greater in a year that contains three Friday the 13ths.[22] Similarly, from William Henry Harrison in 1840 up to Ronald Reagan in 1980, no president elected in a year ending with a "0" has survived his presidency. While such relationships may have impressive historical correlations, they have no predictive value at all.

Without a clear cause-and-effect connection, such statistical studies are not very useful. Even when high correlations are found, it is necessary to establish a likely reason for what is happening before any useful conclusions can be drawn. This is what we mean when we say that a model is required as a basis for any useful data gathering program.

15.1.3 The Impact of Data Gathering on the Organization

There are two fundamental issues that data gathering plans must consider: the effects of measurement on the people and the effects of the people on the measurements. First, since software engineering is largely a human process, the measurement activity will change it. The reason is that when people know they are being observed, their performance will generally change. When measurements are used for people evaluation, for example, they will give top priority to improving the measure, almost regardless of anything else. Any improvement in the quantities measured must then always result in an improvement in the results desired.[15] This is why such pay systems as piece work or sales quotas must be managed so carefully. With the software process, unless it is continually emphasized that the process measures will not be used to evaluate their performance, the software people will often go to great lengths to make the numbers "look good."[12] Since personal motivations are extraordinarily difficult to anticipate, all software process measures must be nonthreatening and nonevaluative.

In a sense the second data gathering issue is the inverse of the first. It concerns the impact of people's attitudes on the data. The actual work of collecting data is tedious and must generally be done by software professionals who are busy with other tasks. Unless they and their immediate managers are convinced that the data is important, they either won't gather it or will not be very careful when they do. There is also a natural tendency to defer such work until project completion. When data gathering is delayed, however, the results are invariably inaccurate or incomplete.

It is thus essential to motivate the professionals to gather the needed data in a timely way. If professionals are shown how the data could help them, they will more likely be interested in the results and exercise greater care. It also helps to first give them the results that relate to them. Obviously, nothing that they produce must be used in any way to embarrass or evaluate them.

For reasons of objectivity and cost it is important to automate as much of the data gathering as possible. Special data gathering instrumentation can be expensive, so it is wise to make data collection a part of the existing software engineering processes wherever possible. If portions of the SCM function are automated, for example, they can usually provide key data with relatively little added effort.

15.1.4 Management Support

Because it is so expensive and because there is often considerable delay before the benefits of data gathering are apparent, data gathering must be viewed as an investment. As with any other investment, senior management support is essential to keep the needed resources in place. Once useful results have been produced, however, the project managers generally will be more willing to support the work.

To start, management agreement is needed on a data gathering plan. Since few software groups have experience with quantitative management it is hard for them to agree on the data to be gathered or to accept precise metrics definitions. Finally, the most difficult job is to obtain the resources needed to do the job. If senior management does not actively support all these steps, there is no chance of success.

15.2 The Data Gathering Process

Because of the issues of resources, cost, and accuracy, people often see data gathering as an expensive waste of time. Project managers are reluctant because they do not see the direct value to their projects and are hesitant to insist on any long-term efforts that may affect immediate priorities. This is why the data gathering program must start with management support and be thoroughly planned and carefully validated. These topics are discussed in the following sections.

15.2.1 Managing the Data Gathering Process

The Software Engineering Laboratory at the NASA Goddard Space Flight Center has gathered software engineering data for a number of years. Their experience shows that data gathering can be expensive, particularly if it is done as part of a research program. As shown in Table 15.1, they spent approximately 15 percent of their development costs just gathering and processing some 747 different measures on a number of projects.[16, 21]

The reason it is so expensive to gather and analyze software data is that this is manual work by people who are inexperienced at data gathering. The effort of

TABLE 15.1
COST OF DATA COLLECTION [16, 21]*

	SEL Experience
Overhead to tasks (experiments)	3–7%
Forms	
Meetings	
Training	
Interviews	
Cost of using tools	
Data processing	10–12%
Collecting/validating forms	
Archiving/entering data	
Data management and reporting	
Analysis of information	Up to 25%
Designing experiments	
Evaluating experiments	
Defining analysis tools	

*As a percentage of tasks being measured

recording time spent per task, results produced, or defects found is time-consuming. With increasing experience and improved tools, however, these costs can be reduced. They will, however, never become insignificant.

Since data gathering is expensive its process must be carefully planned and managed. The data must be precisely defined to ensure that the right information is obtained and it must be validated to ensure that it accurately represents the process. Finally, the data must be retained by someone who owns and maintains the process database.

A great deal of data gathering experience has been accumulated with data processing application studies, and much of it is directly applicable to software engineering. Alter's summary of typical data gathering problems is shown in Table 15.2.[1]

15.2.2 The Data Gathering Plan

The data gathering plan should be produced by the Software Engineering Process Group with the help of the projects and the participation of some of the professionals who will gather the data. It should cover the following topics:

1. *What data is needed, by whom, and for what purpose?* The plan must clearly and precisely state how the data is to be used. To guard against any hint that it will be used for personnel evaluation, the plan should emphasize the use of the resulting data to assess the product and to support the professionals in process improvement rather than providing management with status and control information.

TABLE 15.2
SUMMARY OF DATA GATHERING PROBLEMS [1]

Problem	Typical Cause	Possible Solutions
Data is not correct	Raw data was entered inaccurately	Develop a systematic way to ensure accuracy of raw data
	Data was generated carelessly	Carefully monitor data values and gathering
Data is not timely	Method of generating data not rapid enough	Modify system for generating data
Data not measured or indexed properly	Raw data not gathered consistently with purposes of analysis	Develop a system for rescaling or combining the improper data
Too much data needed	Volume of raw data needed to calculate coefficients in detailed model	Develop efficient ways to extract and combine data
	Detailed model has so many coefficients that it is difficult to develop and maintain	Develop simpler and more highly aggregated models
Needed data does not exist	No one has retained data currently needed	Where practical and justified, store data for future use
	Required data never existed	Reevaluate the need and/or attempt to generate the data

Steven Alter, *Decision Support Systems.* © 1979, Addison-Wesley Publishing Co., Inc., Reading, Massachusetts. Fig. on page 130. Reprinted with permission.

2. *What are the data specifications?*   These include the definition of the initial data to be gathered and the plan for defining any additional data that will likely be needed. The definitions must be reviewed and accepted by all the involved parties and all issues resolved before data gathering begins.

3. *Who will gather the data?*   The people who will gather the data are identified, they agree to do the work, and they understand what to do and when to do it.

4. *Who will support data gathering?*   A training program is provided, and a support group is available to answer questions.

5. *How will the data be gathered?*   Appropriate forms and data entry facilities are made available, and suitable procedures are established and documented. It is also wise to do some trial data gathering before broader implementation.

6. *How will the data be validated?*   Since software process data is error-prone and volatile it should be validated as rapidly as practical. Data that is not validated should be flagged and used with caution.

7. *How will the data be managed?*   One can gather enormous amounts of data on software projects. A professional staff and suitable system facilities are needed to ensure timely and accurate entry., periodic update, and retrieval support.

The management of data is crucial. On the IBM system 370, the central software process database contained quality and cost estimate data on over a billion dollars of software development.[9, 11] The Software Engineering Laboratory at NASA Goddard Space Flight Center amassed 21,000 forms of data on only 40 projects.[16] Such a database is a valuable asset and must be treated as such.

15.2.3 Data Validation

Basili has found that software data is highly error-prone and that special validation provisions are generally needed.[2] He found that often as much as 50 percent of the raw error data was incorrect, even when it was recorded by the programmers at the time they first found the errors. This suggests that the data must either be gathered automatically or extensively validated.

The way data is validated depends on the data involved. With time measures, for example, the total elapsed time can be compared to the total of the elements. Product volumes (like defects or lines of code) can be recorded at several points in the process and compared. Spot checks can also be used for error category classification or other judgmental items.

When people have been trained on the definitions and data gathering methods, periodic spot checks will generally suffice. Without such training the initial validation efforts generally turn into distributed training. The people who do this validation must be able to explain the data definitions, the data gathering methods, and the program's objectives. In the long run, a brief training program covering these items is probably more economical and effective.

15.3 Software Measures

With this background we next look at some specific software measures. First, the characteristics of several useful software measures are outlined, and then several examples of software data are discussed. Since there is considerable literature on this subject, only a few examples are provided.[5, 6, 10]

15.3.1 Data Characteristics

To be of most value, software process measures should have the following characteristics:[15]

□ *The measures should be robust.*   That is, they should be repeatable, precise, and relatively insensitive to minor changes in tools, methods, or product characteristics. When this is not the case, it is hard to tell whether the variations are caused by process or measurement anomalies.

□ *The measures should suggest a norm.*   With defect measures, for example, a lower value is better while zero is best.

□ *The measures should relate to specific product or process properties.*   That is, they should relate to errors, size, or resources expended, for example.

□ *The measures should suggest an improvement strategy.*   Measures of complexity, for example, imply an objective of complexity reduction.

□ *They should be a natural result of the process.*   While special measurement provisions will generally be required, it must be remembered that the intent of the process is to produce a product, not to make measurements. Wherever possible, therefore, the measures should be a by-product of the normal development work, with only a modest additional effort needed for data gathering.

□ *The measures should be simple.*   Complex measurements are generally hard to explain, apply, and interpret, and they often indicate an overly intricate process model.

□ *They should be both predictable and trackable.*   Measures are of most value when they are projected ahead of time and then compared with actual experience. Project personnel can then better see how to change their behavior to improve the result.

Software measurements can be classified in several ways:[21]

□ *Objective/subjective*   This distinguishes between measures that count things and those involving human judgment.

□ *Absolute/relative*   Absolute measures are typically invariant to the addition of new items. The size of one program, for example, is an absolute measure and is independent of the sizes of the others. Relative measures change, as with an average or a grading curve. Objective measures are often absolute, while subjective measures tend to be relative.

□ *Explicit/derived*   Explicit measures are taken directly, while derived measures are computed from other explicit or derived measures. An example of an explicit measure would be programmer months expended, while a derived measure would be productivity or lines of code per programmer month.

□ *Dynamic/static*   Dynamic measures have a time dimension, as with errors found per month. Here, the values tend to change depending on when the measures are made in the product cycle. Static measures, however, remain invariant, as with total effort expended or total defects found during development.

□ *Predictive/explanatory*   Predictive measures can be obtained or generated in advance, while explanatory measures are produced after the fact.

The software engineering objective for data gathering and analysis is to use an increasing number of objective, absolute, explicit, and dynamic measures to control and improve the way the work is done. Over time, prediction accuracy based on these measures should gradually improve until they closely parallel actual experience.

15.3.2 Software Size Measures

Size measures are important in software engineering because the amount of effort required to do most tasks is directly related to the size of the program involved. Unfortunately, there is no generally accepted measure of program size that meets all the previously described criteria. This is not a serious problem, however, as long as the measurement limitations are recognized and appropriately addressed.

One problem is lack of simplicity: There are no simple measures of software size because software size is not a simple subject. For example, one must consider new, changed, deleted, reused, and modified code. There are also differences depending on whether one is dealing with high-level language, assembly code, job control, object code, comments, data definitions, or screen presentations. Also, in addition to the products themselves, one must consider temporary patches, test programs, and support programs.

Lines of Code.   As stated in Chapter 6, the line of code (LOC) measure is probably most practical for measuring program size. The major risk is that its unthinking use can motivate maximization of LOC counts. For example, if people were paid by line of code produced, one could expect every macro to be expanded, all reusable code to be rewritten, or iterative loops to be coded as serial in-line tests. Even though inefficient programs would likely result, the added work would be trivial and, with a simplistic measure, would look highly productive.

There is no measure of software size that will guard against mindless maximization. The only solution is to use size measures as guides and not for evaluation of people or organizations. In any case they must be used carefully and with judgment.

Jones has described some alternative ways of counting lines of code:[14]

- ☐ Executable lines
- ☐ Executable lines plus data definitions
- ☐ Executable lines, data definitions, and comments
- ☐ Executable lines, data definitions, comments, and JCL
- ☐ Physical lines on an input screen
- ☐ Logical delimiters, such as semicolons

Even with these definitions, one must also decide what kinds of lines to count:[14]

- □ Only new lines

- □ New and changed lines

- □ New, changed, and reused lines

- □ All delivered lines plus temporary scaffold code

- □ All delivered lines, temporary scaffolding, and support code

While any of these combinations can be used, the particular choices that IBM has found most useful for its commercial software work are the last alternative for counting lines of code (logical delimiters, such as semicolons) applied to the second and third possibilities of what kinds of lines to count (new and changed lines or new, changed, and reused lines.[9, 11] These alternatives have the advantage of being relevant for both development and maintenance and the disadvantage of not properly recognizing several other important software engineering activities. For example, test case development often involves a great deal of code. Similarly, particularly with maintenance or enhancement, code deletion may be as time-consuming and complex as code addition. Finally, the reuse of previously developed code is generally desirable because it is usually more productive than rewriting the same functions from scratch. On one hand, if no productivity credit is given for such work, the modest effort of identification and possible adaptation is not recognized. Conversely, if full credit is given for all reused code, excessive credit will be allowed for small modifications of very large programs.

Normalized LOC Measures.   Another problem with LOC counts is that with high-level languages they do not recognize the increased functional content of the source lines of code. Some organizations compensate for this by using factors to generate equivalent assembly language.[9] To be truly representative, such factors must reflect both the source and assembly languages being used, as well as the particular program functions involved. Often, however, these factors are picked without an adequate foundation. This then changes an objective, explicit measure to a subjective derived one. It is therefore generally wise not to use such adjustment factors at all.

An important reason to use a simple measure is to make it machine-countable. With IBM System/370 commercial software, LOC counts are made with a common measurement program. Since the IBM developers use the same counting tool there is no doubt about the measurement definition or how to obtain it. While there were many debates when this measure was initially introduced, they have largely been forgotten. Once it was clear that management insisted on measures and that these measures would not be used to evaluate individual programmer performance, they were readily accepted and widely used.[9, 11].

15.3.3 Error Data

Johnson, Draper, and Soloway note that the determination of what constitutes an error depends largely on what the programmer intended to do.[13] For example, in one experiment the error count was made by counting the changes required to correct the program. In one case there were two possible corrections, depending on the programmer's original intentions. One alternative took eight different changes and the other took only three. Both resulting programs were correct! We clearly must distinguish between errors made by programmers and defect corrections. To do this, a set of definitions is required:

□ *Errors*   These are human mistakes, and their quantification often depends on an understanding of the programmer's intentions. In the case of typographical or syntactic errors their causes are generally clear, but the nature and cause of design errors is much harder to establish precisely, particularly after the fact.

□ *Defects*   These are improper program conditions that are generally the result of an error. Not all errors produce program defects, as with incorrect comments or some documentation errors. Conversely, a defect could result from such nonprogrammer causes as improper program packaging or handling.

□ *Bugs*   A bug (or fault) is a program defect that is encountered in operation, either under test or in use. Bugs result from defects, but all defects do not cause bugs (some are latent and never found). With widely used software, the defects may be found many times, resulting in duplicates or multiple bugs per defect.

□ *Failures*   A failure is a malfunction of a user's installation. It may result from a bug, incorrect installation, a communication line hit, a hardware failure, and so forth.

□ *Problems*   Problems are user-encountered difficulties. They may result from failures, misuse, or misunderstanding. Problems are human events as opposed to failures, which are system events.

These definitions are summarized in Table 15.3 and shown diagramatically in Figure 15.1. Starting with programmer error, one can trace down this figure to get to problems or one can start with problems and trace back up to find causes.

The Process of Problem Analysis.   Basically the software error measurement problem is one of distinguishing between causes and effects. Since our intent is both to correct and to prevent the errors that programmers make, we must work our way up this chain of possible measurable events. In testing or operation, the problems encountered must be analyzed to see if they result from failures, whether the failures are due to software bugs, and whether these bugs are caused by defects in the program. In the traditional maintenance situation these defects are repaired

TABLE 15.3
ERRORS, DEFECTS, BUGS, FAULTS, AND PROBLEMS

Category	Items Measured	Causes
Errors	Human actions	Programmer mistakes
Defects	Program properties	Errors
Bugs	Program malfunctions	Program defects
Failures	System malfunctions	Bugs and other malfunctions
Problems	Human perceptions	Failures, human errors, human misconceptions

and operational use is resumed. In both development and maintenance it is desirable to trace the bugs to find the specific defects and errors that caused them. Finding errors in this way involves a long chain of analysis, starting with the operational behavior of a complete system. In some widely used commercial systems, unique defects represented only about 3 percent to 5 percent of the software problems encountered by the users. This after-the-fact process of identifying software defects and the errors that caused them can thus be quite expensive and time-consuming.

The process of problem analysis demonstrates a fundamental distinction between tests and inspections. With testing, problems are encountered during operation and are analyzed to determine their causes. One can thus directly measure the problem data, but one must, through analysis, derive or deduce the data for the number of failures, bugs, defects, and errors. This demonstrates an interesting advantage of the software inspection process: The errors are directly identified. Direct identification saves time, and the error measures obtained from inspections are inherently more valid than the data derived from operational testing because fewer judgments are required.

Classes of Defect Measures.   Since software defects are a major concern in both testing and operation, it is natural to use them as one key process measurement. Software defects (and the bugs that identify them) can be categorized as follows:

1. *Severity*   Measures the actual or anticipated impact of a defect on the user's operational environment. Typically such measures are valuable in establishing service priorities.

2. *Symptoms*   This category refers to the observed system behavior when the defect was found.

3. *Where found*   Defects can be categorized by the system location where they were identified. This is often the program segment actually being executed at the time the bug was encountered.

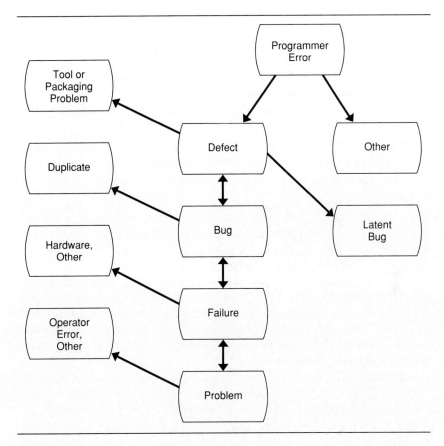

FIGURE 15.1
Errors, Defects, Bugs, Failures, and Problems

4. *When found*   This counts defects by when they are found in the software life cycle, as in unit test, function test, system test, acceptance test, installation, or operation.

5. *How found*   This relates to the operations being performed when the defect was found, such as design inspection, implementation, diagnostic test, and so forth.

6. *Where caused*   Often the system element causing the problem is not apparent at the time a bug is encountered. Examples are checking routines that identify mistakes in the outputs of other programs. While the checking routine was being executed at the time the problem arose, it was not the problem cause.

7. *When caused*   This often requires considerably more analysis. Generally it identifies defects as introduced during high-level design, detailed design, implementation, defect correction, and so forth.

8. *How caused*   Counts of the errors that caused the defects can be most useful in improving the software process. Such errors are typically categorized as logical, data definition, syntax, interface, and so forth.

9. *Where fixed*   This is a record of where changes are made when installing fixes.

10. *When fixed*   While this is not a primary development measure, it can be helpful for evaluating and improving the maintenance and enhancement process.

11. *How fixed*   Here one is concerned with how the change is designed and applied.

These are all perfectly valid ways to categorize bugs and defects. In software engineering one is most interested in getting to the where-caused, when-caused, and how-caused data as quickly and accurately as possible. This permits more effective product and process improvement.

Buckland has described a study of errors reported during the development and use of Deep Space Network/3.[4] The categories he used are shown in Table 15.4. As can be seen, the first category, Time of Occurrence, is a type 4 defect measure, Criticality Levels are type 1, and the Error Category is type 8. A considerable amount of additional data was also gathered on these errors to facilitate subsequent analysis and repair, as shown in Table 15.5.

A statistical breakdown of error cause categories was supplied by Rubey, as shown in Table 15.6.[18] His paper provides further detail on each of these categories. Pettijohn has abstracted Schneidewind's earlier categorization as shown in Table 15.7 and Table 15.8.[17, 19] While many other categorization systems have been reported, there is no single system that meets all needs. Each organization should thus develop its own classifications based on its own particular situation.

15.3.4 Productivity Data

Productivity data is gathered to answer some of the following questions:

- □ How much effort is spent in each task of the software process? These task classifications are defined in the process architecture.
- □ For each product element, what effort was devoted to each process task?
- □ What is the relative cost of defect removal by the various tests and inspections and by each major error category?
- □ How effective are various methods and technologies in improving the productivity of each process task?
- □ What is the resource history by major process task, and how should the planning factors be adjusted for subsequent projects?

TABLE 15.4
ERROR CATEGORIES [4]

Time of Occurrence
    D = Development—design, coding, and unit test
    V = Verification—integration and testing of subsystem
    A = Acceptance—formal testing and acceptance of subsystem
    T = Transferred—software subsystem operational
    U = Unknown

Criticality Levels
    A = Critical   C = Minor
    B = Dangerous   U = Unknown

Error Category
    CO = Computational Error   OP = Operational Error
    LO = Logic Error   RI = Requirements Incorrect
    DH = Data Handling Error   DE = Design Error
    IN = Interface Error   CL = Clerical Error
    DB = Data Base Error   OT = Other

Software engineering productivity measures are difficult to gather and even trickier to use. There is an almost childlike belief that programmers' performance can be measured by some simple productivity metric like lines of code per programmer month. No one would dream of applying such simple measures as pounds per person week or rooms per worker year to masons, factory workers, architects, or house painters. When managers or executives seek simple, one-dimensional measures of software, software people are reluctant to provide any numbers in the not unreasonable fear they will be misused.

TABLE 15.5
PROBLEM DISCOVERY AND RESOLUTION DATA [4]

Data required at problem discovery time:
1 - Who found the problem?
2 - When was the problem found?
3 - What happened?
4 - What was being used?
5 - Is this a recurrence of a previously closed problem?
6 - What is the level of criticality?

Data required at problem resolution time:
1 - Why did the program fail?
2 - What was the solution?
3 - Who supplied the resolution?
4 - When was it closed?

TABLE 15.6
FREQUENCY OF ERROR OCCURRENCE [18]

Error Category	Total		Serious		Moderate		Minor	
	#	%	#	%	#	%	#	%
Incomplete/erroneous specification	340	28	19	11	82	17	239	43
Intentional deviation from specification	145	12	9	6	61	13	75	14
Violation of programming standards	118	10	2	1	22	5	94	17
Erroneous data accessing	120	10	36	21	72	15	12	2
Erroneous decision logic or sequencing	139	12	41	24	83	17	15	3
Erroneous arithmetic computations	113	9	22	13	73	15	18	3
Invalid timing	44	4	14	8	25	5	5	1
Improper handling of interrupts	46	4	14	8	31	7	1	0
Wrong constants and data values	41	3	14	8	19	4	8	1
Inaccurate documentation	96	8	0	0	10	2	86	16
Total	1202	100	171	14	478	40	553	46

R. J. Rubey, J. A. Dana, and P. W. Biché, "Quantitative aspects of software validation," *IEEE Transactions on Software Engineering,* vol. SE-1, no. 2, June 1975. © 1975 IEEE.

Productivity data can be useful at the task level, but it becomes progressively less pertinent as the tasks are combined into larger work units. Every project team faces many unique conditions. Since no two projects are comparable in any gross sense, no simple measures can usefully compare them. Unfortunately, when managers hear that one project produced 1000 lines of code per programmer month and the other only 200, they want to "fix" the one with the low productivity. The fact that one was a prototype and the other was for distribution to 10,000 customers is ignored. The use of a common standard for two such different projects is like comparing the construction of a sand castle with the building of Windsor Castle by counting tons of sand used per labor hour. Both projects involved castles and they both used sand and labor, but the magnitude and complexity of the work was vastly different, and no sets of comparative numbers can provide any useful insights on either project.

Organizational Productivity.   Productivity measures are most prone to misuse when they are applied at the highest project and organizational level. It is, however, desirable to have some measure of how the organization is performing over time. For software, unfortunately, the only simple measures available are lines of code and effort expended. IBM has used total lines of code shipped per programmer year as a measure of each software laboratory.[9, 11] This measure has the

TABLE 15.7
TYPES OF DESIGN ERRORS [17]

Percent of total	Description
7	Communication error
20	Forgotten cases or steps
10	Timing problems
2	Initialization error
12	Inadequate checking
17	Extreme conditions neglected
8	Sequencing error
12	Misunderstanding of problem specifications
12	Other

advantage of being objective and easily computable but the disadvantage of not being very robust. A slight change in the actual shipment of a major project from December to January dramatically changes a laboratory's perceived performance. Since this was the only available measure, however, management decided to use it to gain insight into historical trends rather than to focus on year-to-year variations or cross-laboratory comparisons.

To use the LOC productivity measure, it was essential to define the terms used precisely. For lines of code a counting tool was provided for all the laboratories to use. The labor counts included all software professionals and support personnel including management. Maintenance and Quality Assurance were not

TABLE 15.8
TYPES OF CODING ERRORS [17]

Percent of total	Description
14	Misunderstanding of design
4	Initialization error
29	Inadequate or forgotten checking
4	Case selection error
20	Inconsistent use of variables or data
7	Sequencing error
4	Loop control error
7	Language usage problems
4	Incorrect subroutine usage
7	Other

included, but technology support, process groups, documentation, and test development were. While the measure had many faults, no one had proposed a better one.

The value of such gross productivity measures is debatable. While the trends provide useful insight, it is hard to explain all their important qualifications to executives who are not versed in software. I have found that the most useful productivity data is that obtained as a basis for project planning, as described in Chapter 6. Since this data is in relatively fine detail, it more closely represents the actual activities performed. It also provides essential validation of the estimating parameters used for project planning.

Sensitivity of Productivity Measures.   I once ran a brief study to see why software productivity numbers varied so widely among several companies. There turned out to be significant differences among the organizations' definitions of lines of code and labor expended. The differences among the line of code definitions could easily account for variations of at least two orders of magnitude in productivity:

☐ The difference between counting only new and changed lines versus counting all lines shipped accounted for a factor of over ten. For follow-on product releases some organizations counted all program lines shipped, even though only a small percentage of them involved significant development work.

☐ When code was reused many times, some organizations counted every reuse, some only counted the first reused version, and others only counted the changes required for each adaptation. These considerations apply equally well to modules, macros, library routines, and so forth. The variations observed ranged as high as ten or more times.

☐ Language variations are often compensated for by calculating equivalent assembler code. As previously noted, arbitrary factors are generally used that may be as high as six or more—unfortunately, with little justification.

For labor expended, the variations are not quite as great, although they can be large. Defining labor as only including direct development programmers as opposed to all involved labor categories can cause productivity variations of three to five or more times.

It is clear that productivity data can be highly misleading unless all the parameters are strictly defined and controlled. If this is not done and if management uses such measures for evaluation purposes, the numbers can often be "adjusted" to look good. Programmers have the very best equipment for generating and manipulating data so they can be expected to produce whatever management wants to see.

15.4 Data Analysis

A few published examples of software engineering data analyses are described in the following sections. While many kinds of analyses are possible, these few indicate some ways data can be used to support software development and maintenance. As software organizations gather data and begin to use it, they will find many more ways to apply it.

15.4.1 Error Data Analysis

Endres has reported an exhaustive study of data analysis on the IBM DOS operating system.[7] This study identified the types of errors made during DOS development and provided insights on detecting and preventing them. The questions addressed by this study are shown in Table 15.9. The particular project studied was a large modification of the existing 522 module DOS operating system. It resulted in 190,000 instructions and 60,000 lines of comments, of which 86,000 instructions were changed or added.

During the study a total of 740 problems were encountered in test, with 432 classified as unique programming errors. The balance were operator errors, machine errors, improvement suggestions, documentation difficulties, or duplicates. The effects of these errors on the 422 changed modules are shown by the distributions in Table 15.10 and Table 15.11. Endres noted that the three largest modules also had the largest numbers of errors. They were each over 3000 instructions, while the average module size was 360 instructions. In all, only 48 percent of the modules had any errors at all, while the 21 percent of the modules that had more than one error accounted for 78 percent of the total errors.

Table 15.12 shows the error density of the new and the modified DOS modules. The numbers at the bottom of this table show that the changed code had a 60 percent higher error rate than new code (7.8 versus 4.8). Endres's paper also includes considerable detail on their error cause analysis results.[7] He concluded from this data that only about half of the mistakes can be avoided with better programming tools and techniques. To address the rest, better means are needed for problem definition, improved training, and better availability of previous solutions to known problems. He found that an important benefit of gathering and analyzing such data is the focus it provides on the areas with the greatest likelihood of causing problems.

15.4.2 Test Data Analysis

Many different analyses can be made of test data. Here, typically, one is looking at defect data rather than examining the error causes for programming defects. Some examples of the kinds of questions that can be addressed are:

TABLE 15.9
QUESTIONS TO BE ANSWERED BY IBM
DOS ERROR STUDY [7]

1—Where was the error made?
2—When was the error made?
3—Who made the error?
4—What was done wrong?
5—Why was the particular error made?
6—What could have been done to prevent this particular error?
7—If the error could not be prevented, by which procedure can this type of error be detected?

A. B. Endres, "An analysis of errors and their causes in systems programs," *IEEE Transactions on Software Engineering*, vol. SE-1, no. 2, June 1975. © 1975 IEEE.

□ What is the relationship between test coverage by program module and the number of defects detected and remaining in the program?

□ What is the effectiveness of each type of test at finding the major defect types, and how is this effectiveness changing over time?

□ What is the cost of finding each defect type by each test category?

□ How effective are the individual test cases?

□ How does the effectiveness of testing and inspection compare for each defect type?

□ What is the defect history of a given product, and where should attention be focused for most effective improvement?

TABLE 15.10
NUMBER OF MODULES AFFECTED BY AN
ERROR [7]

Number of Errors	Number of Modules Affected
371	1
50	2
6	3
3	4
1	5
1	8
432	

A. B. Endres, "An analysis of errors and their causes in systems programs," *IEEE Transactions on Software Engineering*, vol. SE-1, no. 2, June 1975. © 1975 IEEE.

TABLE 15.11
NUMBER OF ERRORS PER MODULE [7]

Number of Modules	Errors per Module*
220	0
112	1
36	2
15	3
11	4
8	5
2	6
4	7
5	8
3	9
2	10
1	14
1	15
1	19
1	28
422	

*That is, 220 modules had no errors, 112 had one error, and one
module had a total 28 errors.

A. B. Endres, "An analysis of errors and their causes in systems
programs," *IEEE Transactions on Software Engineering,* vol.
SE-1, no. 2, June 1975. © 1975 IEEE.

With a little experience many other profitable areas of study will be suggested.
Since test data can be obtained relatively easily, testing is one of the best places to
start gathering and analyzing the software engineering process.

15.4.3 Analysis of Inspection Rates

Wenneson has published an interesting analysis of inspection data.[23] He describes using statistics for tracking, estimating, planning, and scheduling development and QA work. For FORTRAN design and code inspections, he gives the
norms shown in Table 15.13. Significant deviations from these values were cause
for review of the way the inspection was conducted.

It is customary to count preparation time as the sum of the preparation times
for all the individuals involved. Conversely, inspection time is the time spent by
the entire team in the inspection process. For a five-person inspection group,
therefore, one inspection hour equals five programmer inspection hours, while one
preparation hour equals one programmer preparation hour. Although it is not
entirely clear from Wenneson's paper, he appears to have used an average of the
individual preparation times rather than a sum.

As a result of his studies, Wenneson has drawn some interesting relationships, as shown in Fig. 15.2 and Fig. 15.3. From Fig. 15.2 it is clear that the errors

TABLE 15.12
FREQUENCY OF ERRORS [7]

| | Code Origin of Module | | |
	New Only	Old + New	Total
Total number of modules	169	253	422
Number of modules with errors	81	121	202
Percentage of modules with errors	48	48	48
Number of errors	254	258	512
Errors per module	1.5	1.0	1.2
Size of new code	53K	33K	86K
Errors per 1K of code	4.8	7.8	6.0

A. B. Endres, "An analysis of errors and their causes in systems programs," *IEEE Transactions on Software Engineering*, vol. SE-1, no. 2, June 1975. © 1975 IEEE.

found per KLOC decline with increasing inspection rate. While it is true that code with a large number of errors is harder to review, this effect probably tails off at about 400 LOC per hour. It appears, therefore, that a rough upper limit of 300 to 400 LOC/hour (0.3 to 0.4 KLOC/hr) was probably about optimum for these FORTRAN programs.

From Fig. 15.3 it appears that inspection preparation time should roughly equal review time. In Fig. 15.4, however, Wenneson plots the upper and lower limits of inspection rates with various preparation times. For code, at a preparation rate of 7 hours per person per KLOC, the inspection rate ranges from a low of 100 to a high of about 330 lines per hour. This equates to a range of 3 to 10 hours of inspection per KLOC plus 7 hours of preparation time, or a total range of 10 to 17 hours per KLOC. For this preparation rate, the LOC per hour of inspection plus preparation is thus between 60 and 100.

TABLE 15.13
NOMINAL INSPECTION RATES [23]

Design Inspections	
Hours/KLOD*	23
Errors/KLOD*	
Major	83
Minor	143
Code Inspections	
Hours/KLOC	3 to 10
Major Errors/KLOC	10 to 80

*Lines of design defined as:
    Preliminary design: 1 LOD = 15 to 20 LOC
    Detailed design: 1 LOD = 3 to 10 LOC

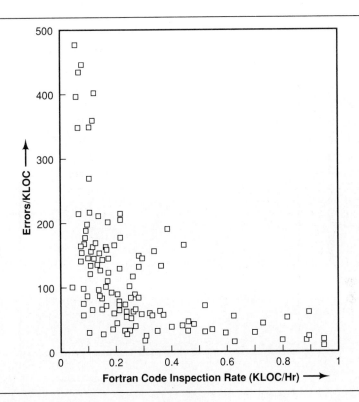

FIGURE 15.2
Errors Detected Versus Inspection Rates [23]

15.4.4 Inspection Data Analysis

Schulmeyer and McManus have provided some data on design and code inspections that can be analyzed with statistical techniques.[20] Table 15.14 shows some
selected data from their work. This data is taken from one large project with seven
major components. Each component had many modules, some of which were
inspected. This data is the average of the module inspections for each component.
While it is generally preferable to use the module level data directly, this average
data serves to demonstrate the statistical techniques involved.

As described in Chapter 10, various rate and error data can be gathered on
each inspection. The data in Table 15.14 is: the total lines of code inspected per
programmer hour, the errors found per programmer hour, and the errors found per
KLOC. In addition, average data was provided by the authors for the total project

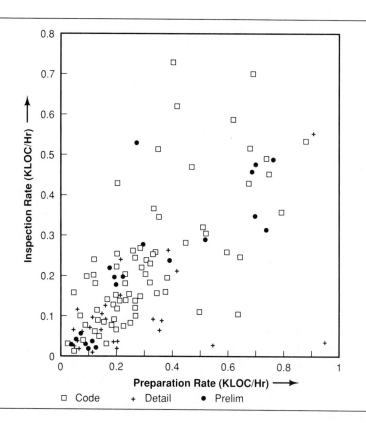

FIGURE 15.3
Inspection Rate Versus Preparation Rate [23]

(component 8) and for those modules judged poor enough to be reinspected (component 9). This composite data, however, is not included in the following statistical calculations. The additional items at the bottom of this table are explained further in the following paragraphs.

Constructing Statistical Control Charts.   To facilitate analysis, the statistical control charts of Fig. 15.5, 15.6, and 15.7 are next constructed.[3] This is done by plotting the data from Table 15.14 together with the average value and the upper and lower control limits (UCL and LCL). To find these control limits, the calculations shown in Table 15.14 are made: The average is the simple mathematical average of the values for components 1 through 7, the standard deviation is calculated using the formula shown in the footnote, and the UCL and LCL are established at two standard deviations above and below the average. In instances in which these calculations would give a negative LCL, zero is used.

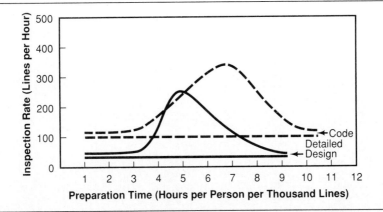

FIGURE 15.4
Upper and Lower Ranges of Inspection Rates Versus Preparation Times [23]

These control limits are established as a guide to help determine which results are likely due to random statistical variation and which probably represent unusual behavior. For example, if one were sampling the precise weight of "one-pound" objects, there would be small statistical variations around the nominal value of one pound. If the calculations were made of the average value and standard deviation, the actual weight values would be randomly distributed around the average with about 68 percent falling within one standard deviation (SD) of the average and 95 percent within two standard deviations. Table 15.15 shows the percentages of values that would fall within various numbers of standard deviations of the average. This assumes, of course, that the process was behaving in a purely random manner.

Using Control Charts.   The reason these UCL and LCL values are important is that we need to identify unusual conditions and control them as we try to improve our processes. It is thus important to screen out those values that are probably due to purely random variation and examine the rest. If, for example, we set the UCL and LCL at one SD above and below the average and then examined every case that fell outside these limits, we could do a lot of nonproductive work. On average, even with a well-controlled process, 32 percent of the values would fall outside these limits, just due to random causes.

The data in Fig. 15.5, 15.6, 15.7, and 15.8 provides a useful example of how such analyses can be done. Figure 15.8 has been added because it provides additional insight into the inspection process. Its data is also derived as shown in Table 15.14. First, the variations shown in these figures are unusually large, indicating a

TABLE 15.14
SELECTED DESIGN INSPECTION DATA

Component	LOC PH	LOC IH	LOC TH	ERRORS TH	ERRORS KLOC	PH IH
1	161	171	83	1.1	12.7	1.5
2	144	347	102	.5	4.7	2.4
3	108	50	34	1.1	31.3	2.2
4	764	788	388	2.0	5.2	1.0
5	102	149	60	.4	6.5	1.5
6	191	257	110	2.1	19.4	1.3
7	547	523	267	1.2	4.5	1.0
Average	288	326	149	1.2	4.7	1.5
SD	241	236	120	1.0	9.3	.5
UCL	770	798	389	3.2	30.7	2.6
LCL	0	0	0	0	0	.4
Total product(8)	178	245	103	1.4	13.2	1.4
Worst modules(9)	62	230	49	2.0	40.6	3.7

LOC: lines of source code
PH: preparation hours
IH: inspection hours
TH: total inspection and preparation hours
SD: standard deviation: [average of (values)^2 − (average of values)^2]$^{1/2}$
UCL: upper control limit = average + (2 × SD)
LCL: lower control limit = average − (2 × SD) (0 if negative)

process that is under tenuous statistical control at best. The total inspection rates have a ten to one variation and the errors per KLOC vary by over seven to one. Clearly, the first step should be to understand the reasons for these extreme swings and to address them. This problem is generally resolvable with an inspection training program and management emphasis on the importance of performing good inspections.

Next, even with these wild swings, some conclusions can be drawn about the individual inspections. The inspections for component 1 appear to be near average in every respect. For component 2, the errors found per hour and per KLOC were relatively low, while the total inspection time was about normal. Here, Fig. 15.8 provides added insight: A great deal of preparation time was required per hour of inspection. This could be interpreted in several ways: (a) a very well-prepared and thorough inspection, (b) a normal inspection of complex code, or (c) an inexperienced group struggling to understand the program. In situation b or c, some further examination might be warranted.

Component 3 is an altogether different matter. Here the preparation time was large, the inspection rate was low, and a very large number of errors were found. This looks like a careful inspection of a low-quality product. Component 4 again tells a different story: a high inspection rate, low preparation time, a high number

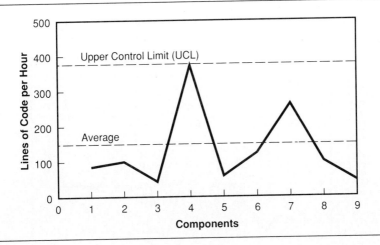

FIGURE 15.5
Inspection Control Chart—Lines of Code Inspected per Hour

of defects found per hour, but a low number of defects found in the product. This looks like a poorly prepared and conducted inspection.

A similar analysis can be made for each of the components. It is interesting to note, however, that the modules identified by the project as being particularly troublesome have very unusual control charts (labeled as component number 9 in the figures). They had the lowest inspection rates, the highest number of errors found per inspection hour, the highest error density, and the highest preparation rates. On balance it looks as if these inspections were rather well done and that they found some of the worst quality code.

Data of this sort can be extremely valuable, particularly when it is accumulated over a period of time on a large number of projects. With a little experience one can readily spot inspections that should be repeated and product elements that need closer attention. By later analyzing such data against product performance during test and field use, it is possible to set informed standards for those key relationships that indicate potential product or process problems. If the control limits exceed these standards, then the inspection process itself needs attention. Conversely, if the control limits are within the acceptable standards, the focus should be on the individual inspections that fall outside these limits. Finally, test and inspection data should be continually examined to see if the standards need adjustment. Because of the large variations among organizations and among software products, such data should be gathered by each organization for its own use.

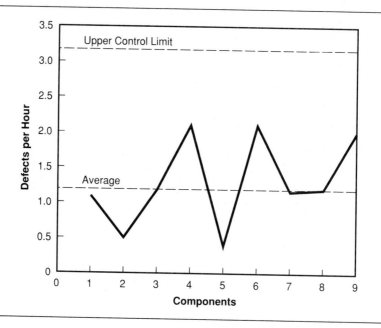

FIGURE 15.6
Inspection Control Chart—Defects per Total Inspection Hours

It is also most useful to gather this data and use it to monitor project performance. This provides an ongoing indication of process performance and a timely
indication of process problems. A steady trend in one or more parameters, for
example, might provide early indication of a problem. Even if the values were all
within established control limits, a trend could indicate nonrandom behavior that
should be addressed.

15.4.5 Statistical Analysis of Test Data

Card has reported an example of how these same statistical techniques can be
applied to test data.[5] In Fig. 15.9 he shows the test rates for seven consecutive
releases of two products that were each several hundred thousand lines of code in
size. Project D was judged under statistical control, while project Z appeared to
have gone out of control in the seventh release.

In these figures the top line (testing efficiency) is the percentage of all defects
found during system testing. In effect it measures the quality of the testing activity.
The next curve, total defect rate, shows all noncosmetic defects reported during

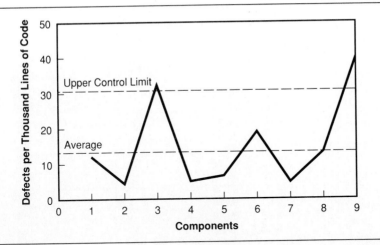

FIGURE 15.7
Inspection Control Chart—Defects per Thousand Lines of Code

system testing, acceptance testing, and operation. In evaluating the seventh release, the control limits were computed from the first six releases.

In this example the data for calculating these charts was not available until
after acceptance test and a period of field operation. Similar charts could have been
made, however, from data available during development and test. This would then
permit judgments on the adequacy of each module, each inspection, and each test.
With such data, those modules that appeared out of control could be reinspected
or retested. Any offending inspection or test step could also be examined to see
what caused it to deviate and to make the indicated process corrections or improvements.

15.5 Other Considerations

Since it is easy to draw erroneous conclusions from poorly conducted measurements, it is important to remember some key points:[2]

   □ Since data can generally be interpreted in many ways, listen to what the data
     is saying rather than using it to reinforce preconceived opinions. If the data
     appears to support your prior views, be suspicious. Having a model is essen-
     tial, but believing it too implicitly can be a mistake.

TABLE 15.15
PERCENTAGE OF VALUES
WITHIN CONTROL LIMITS

N	Percentage within the Range Average $+/-$ (N × SD)
.25	19.74
.50	38.29
.75	54.67
1.00	68.27
1.25	78.87
1.50	86.64
1.75	91.99
2.00	95.45
2.25	97.56
2.50	98.76
2.75	99.40
3.00	99.73

UCL = Average + (N × SD)
LCL = Average − (N × SD)
SD = [average of (values squared) −
(average of values) squared]$^{1/2}$

□ Provide resources to validate and analyze the data. Validation is often over-looked, and its cost is almost always underestimated. As expensive and valuable as data is, it is almost worthless if not validated.

□ *Make sure that process data is never used to evaluate people!*

□ The simple act of gathering data will change the process. After a reasonable period, the programmers will become accustomed to data gathering and the results will stabilize, but in the meantime remember that the process is changing while it is being measured.

□ Start carefully and don't attempt to do too much at one time. Wherever possible, integrate data collection into the existing process tasks and auto-mate as much of it as practical. Data collection is work, and the programmers will resist if too much is attempted too quickly.

□ Seek the views of the data collectors on the data collection process and any modifications, enhancements, or support they need. Don't promise more than you can deliver, however, for tool support is also expensive.

□ Provide the initial results to the people the data concerns before giving it to anyone else.

□ Start with a comprehensive plan. This should include data definitions, forms or protocols for recording the data, a system for collecting the information, a validation system, and plans for analyzing and distributing the results.

□ The debates on data definitions and formats can be endless. Up to a point these are helpful, but once all the issues have been aired, little further can be

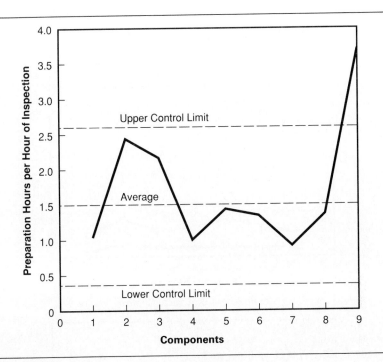

FIGURE 15.8
Inspection Control Chart—Hours of Preparation per Hour of Inspection

gained from study and debate. The only way to find out what data should be gathered and analyzed is to gather and analyze data. With that experience, the debates can generally be settled quickly.

Finally, get the resources and get started.

15.6 Summary

Software process data is gathered to learn how to make process improvements. The principles of successful data gathering are: The data is gathered with a specific objective; the choice of data is based on a model of the process being examined; the data gathering process itself is defined and managed, it is tailored to the needs of the organization, and it must have management support.

The data gathering plan specifies who will use the data and how it will be used. It covers why the data is needed, the data specifications, who will gather it and how, and how it will be validated and managed.

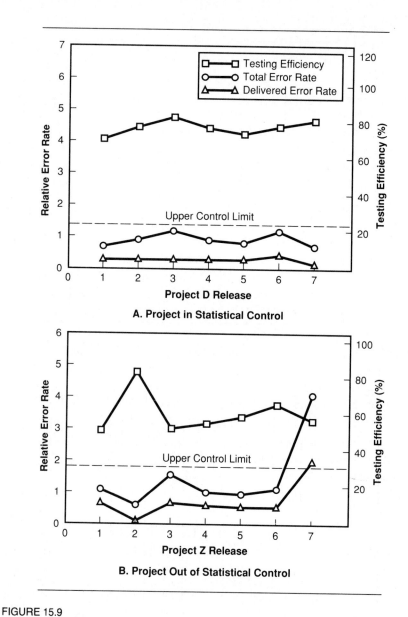

FIGURE 15.9
Process Control Results [5]
First published in "Improving software quality and productivity" by D. N. Card, T. L. Clark, and
R. A. Berg in *Information and Software Technology,* vol. 29, no. 5, June 1987.

To be of most value, software process measures should be robust, suggest a norm, relate to specific product or process properties, suggest an improvement strategy, be a natural result of the process, be simple, and be capable of projection and tracking.

Measurements can also be objective or subjective, absolute or relative, explicit or derived, dynamic or static, and predictive or explanatory. The objective in software engineering is to use an increasing number of objective, absolute, explicit, and dynamic measures to control and improve the way the work is done. As several examples of software measures demonstrate, data can be gathered and analyzed in varying ways, and the resulting knowledge can be applied to improve the products and the process.

Some key things to consider in data gathering and analysis are: Listen to what the data is saying, provide adequate resources, and don't use the data to evaluate people. Since the debate on data definitions and formats can be endless, the only way to find out how to gather and analyze software data is to gather and analyze software data. So get the resources and get started!

References

1. Alter, S. L. *Decision Support Systems, Current Practice and Continuing Challenges.* Reading, MA: Addison-Wesley, 1980.

2. Basili, V. R., and D. M. Weiss. "A methodology for collecting valid software engineering data," *IEEE Transactions on Software Engineering,* vol. SE-10, no. 6, November 1984.

3. Berger, R. W., and T. Hart. *Statistical Process Control—A Guide for Implementation.* New York: Marcel Dekker, ASQC Quality Press, 1986.

4. Buckland, D. E. "Error taxonomy, what can be gained?" *Proceedings of the Seventh Annual Software Engineering Workshop,* Goddard Space Flight Center, December 1, 1982.

5. Card, D. N., T. L. Clark, and R. A. Berg. "Improving software quality and productivity," *Information and Software Technology,* vol. 29, no. 5, June 1987.

6. Conte, S. D., H. E. Dunsmore, and V. Y. Shen. *Software Engineering Metrics and Models,* Menlo Park, CA: Benjamin/Cummings, 1986.

7. Endres, A. B. "An analysis of errors and their causes in system programs," *IEEE Transactions on Software Engineering,* vol. SE-1, no. 2, June 1975.

8. Fairley, R. E. *Software Project Management,* ACM Tutorials for Professional Development, undated.

9. Flaherty, M. J. "Programming process productivity measurement system for System 370," *IBM System Journal,* vol. 24, no. 2, 1985.

10. Grady, R. B., and D. L. Caswell. *Software Metrics: Establishing a Company-Wide Program,* Englewood Cliffs, NJ: Prentice-Hall, 1987.

11. Humphrey, W. S. "The IBM large-systems software development process: objectives and direction," *IBM Systems Journal,* vol. 24, no. 2, 1985.

12. Humphrey, W. S. *Managing for Innovation, Leading Technical People.* Englewood Cliffs, NJ: Prentice-Hall, 1987.

13. Johnson, W. L., S. Draper, and E. Soloway. "Classifying bugs is a tricky business," *Proceedings of the Seventh Annual Software Engineering Workshop,* Goddard Space Flight Center, December 1, 1982.

14. Jones, Capers. *Programming Productivity.* New York: McGraw-Hill, 1986.

15. Kearney, J. K., R. L. Sedlmeyer, W. B. Thompson, M. A. Gray, and M. A. Adler. "Software complexity measurement," *Communications of the ACM,* vol. 29, no. 11, November 1986.

16. McGarry, F. E. "What have we learned in the last 6 years, measuring software development technology," *Proceedings of the Seventh Annual Software Engineering Workshop,* Goddard Space Flight Center, December 1, 1982.

17. Pettijohn, C. L. "Achieving quality in the development process," *AT&T Technical Journal,* vol. 65, issue 2, March-April, 1986.

18. Rubey, R. J., J. A. Dana, and P. W. Biché. "Quantitative aspects of software validation," *IEEE Transactions on Software Engineering,* vol. SE-1, no. 2, June 1975.

19. Schneidewind, N. F. and H. Hoffman, "An Experiment in Software Error Data Collection and Analysis," *IEEE Transactions on Software Engineering,* vol. SE-5, no. 3, May 1979.

20. Schulmeyer, G. G. and J. I. McManus. *Handbook of Software Quality Assurance.* New York: Van Nostrand Reinhold, 1987.

21. Software Engineering Laboratory Series, *Evaluation of Management Measures of Software Development, Volume 2: Data Description,* Goddard Space Flight Center, SEL-82-001, September 1982.

22. *The Wall Street Journal,* November 13, 1987.

23. Wenneson, G. "Quality Assurance software inspections at NASA Ames: metrics for feedback and modification," *Proceedings of the Tenth Annual Software Engineering Workshop,* Goddard Space Flight Center, December 1985.

16

Managing Software Quality

One of the best ways to evaluate a software organization is to examine the quality of its products. Product quality is thus a key measure of the software process. It provides a clear record of development progress, a basis for setting objectives, and a framework for current action. As we strive to improve the quality of our software products, it is instructive to examine the experiences in other fields. While the methods are not directly relevant to software, Agresti has pointed out that the principles of industrial engineering can be effectively applied to software.[1] He concludes that of all the lessons of industrial engineering the most important involve quality measurement and the impact of such measurements on the performance of the people who do the work.

In any human-intensive process, motivation is the key to good work.[11] To consistently achieve superior performance, management must establish challenging quality goals and strive to meet them. Conversely, if senior management tolerates poor work, sloppiness will pervade the entire organization. This is true not just for complex software products but for all aspects of a business. When meetings are perpetually late, status reports are inaccurate, or management's memos have typographical errors, the programmers realize that quality is not a priority. It should then hardly be surprising if some of them are not as careful with inspections or tests. They know that in a pinch management will likely take the quick and easy way out. With software, however, the quick and easy solutions rarely pay off in the long run. The key question for management is: Do you intend to do anything about software quality? If you do, then your organization must live by four basic quality principles:

1. Unless you establish aggressive quality goals, nothing will change.
2. If these goals are not numerical, the quality program will remain just talk.
3. Without quality plans, only you are committed to quality.
4. Quality plans are just paper unless you track and review them.

16.1 The Quality Management Paradigm

The basic principles of software quality management are much like those for cost management: You set goals, make plans, track performance, and then adjust the plan.[10] This cycle is the foundation for industrial engineering, and it applies equally well to software. This chapter starts with some examples of successful software quality management and then discusses the motivational force of a quality measurement program. After reviewing several potential quality measures, the techniques for planning and tracking quality are outlined. This then provides the foundation for establishing quantitative quality plans and managing to meet them.

16.2 Quality Examples

Quality programs really work. Poston and Bruen describe the Leeds and Northrop experience with a real-time process monitoring program of 27,719 lines of source code.[18] By rigorously following a quality plan, failure density rates were reduced from 1.3 to 0.072 defects per 1000 lines, or a 95 percent improvement. Their typical productivity rates had averaged about 7 lines of source code per staff day on previous projects, but following the plan they produced 29, an enormous productivity improvement as well.

While they attribute these results to a combination of many management and technical actions, the quality and productivity improvements resulted from finding and fixing essentially all the errors early in the program. Only one bug was found in system test, and that had to be forced by driving the system beyond its rated capacity. In several months of use all eight customers found only 11 problems. The authors conclude that this resulted from a measured and planned quality program.

Grady, of Hewlett-Packard, describes the use of measurements to improve software maintenance.[8] By tracking defects found in development and customer use, they made significant process improvements. In four successive releases of one product, the percent of defects found after release "dropped from 25 percent of the total for the first two releases to less than 10 percent in the third and to zero in the fourth." While many factors contributed to this improvement, Grady concludes that "without such measures for managing software maintenance, it is difficult for any organization to understand whether it is successful."

16.3 Quality Motivation

The purpose of a quality program is to motivate action. To ensure that this action results in better products, the measurements must reasonably represent "goodness" in customer terms.

When considered as a motivational program, quality measurements take on special meaning. For example, many different metrics can be used to characterize software systems. In one report no less than 72 parameters are described for measuring some 29 desirable program characteristics.[3] While some of these might be used as design standards, few can have any conceivable motivational value. This does not mean that they are not useful. One reason for such measures was shown by a study that correlated a total of 15 software characteristics with the views of several experienced software professionals. Eight of the characteristics had high correlation with their perceptions of program quality.[2] The characteristics that ranked highest were device independence, self-containedness, accuracy, robustness, and consistency.

Even though it is hard to see how such characteristics could be included in a quality measurement program, their potential value should not be ignored. By including these characteristics in the product standards and telling the professionals what is wanted and why, there is a good chance that the right work will get done.

16.3.1 Measuring Quality

A different approach is needed to motivate an aggressive quality effort. Since people can only respond to a few motivational drives at a time, the measurement and tracking for the quality program must be tightly focused. The need is to establish a small number of specific, numerical quality measures. Typical examples are defects found at various stages of the process, inspection efficiency, or test coverage.

If numerical quality measures are not used, only one measure of development performance remains: schedule. Unfortunately, when adherence to schedule is the only visible sign of progress and there is no indication of the adequacy of the product being produced, all energies are directed toward meeting the deadline. This has historically motivated actions that tend to reduce product quality. A single-minded focus on schedule diverts attention from the results and, without some quality measures, anything shipped can count. Since any sensible schedule measures must have quality qualifications, these qualifications are the foundation for the quality program.

Since no single measure can adequately characterize a complex product, a focus on one product element will likely maximize this single indicator at the expense of the rest. On the other hand, too many measures can be even more confusing. This conundrum can best be resolved by using a few carefully selected measures as quality indicators while insisting that all applicable standards and specifications be met. Since the simplistic use of any numerical criteria can easily cause unnatural efforts to maximize that one measure, close management attention and informed judgment must always be the final guide.

16.3.2 Classes of Quality Measures

Quality measures fall into the following general classes:

- □ *Development*   Defects found, change activity
- □ *Product*   Defects found, software structure, information (documentation) structure, controlled tests
- □ *Acceptance*   Problems, effort to install, effort to use
- □ *Usage*   Problems, availability, effort to install, effort to use, user opinions
- □ *Repair*   Defects, resources expended

As shown in Table 16.1, these measures are characterized as follows:

- □ *Objective*   Can the measure be repeatably produced by different people?
- □ *Timely*   Is it available in time to affect the development or maintenance process?
- □ *Available*   How hard is it to obtain?
- □ *Representative*   To what degree does it represent the customer's view of "goodness?"
- □ *Controllable*   To what extent can its value be changed by development or maintenance actions?

Clearly, measures are desired that are readily available, easy to gather, representative of the customer's needs, and directly controllable by development or maintenance. Unfortunately, no single known measure meets all these criteria. For example, defect data is readily available early in the project, reasonably objective, and relatively inexpensive to gather but it does not always represent the customer's quality perceptions. Conversely, those measures that best represent the customer are often not available until late in the program, are very expensive to gather, or are subjective.

16.4 Measurement Criteria

In deciding what measures to use it is essential to consider the objectives of the measurement program. If the measures will be used to manage software develop-

TABLE 16.1
CLASSES OF QUALITY MEASURES

	Objective	Timely	Available	Representative	Controllable
Development					
Defects	yes	yes	yes	moderate	yes
Change activity	yes	yes	yes	poor	no
Product					
Error seeding	moderate	yes	difficult	doubtful	moderate
Software structure	depends	yes	moderate	doubtful	yes
Controlled tests	moderate	yes	difficult	good	yes
Acceptance					
Problems	no	late	yes	good	moderate
Install effort	moderate	late	difficult	good	yes
Usage					
Problems	no	late	yes	good	moderate
Operating effort	moderate	late	difficult	good	yes
Surveys	no	late	difficult	very good	no
Availability	yes	late	moderate	very good	yes
Repair					
Defects	yes	late	yes	moderate	yes
Repair effort	moderate	late	moderate	moderate	yes

ment, they should be objective, timely, available, and controllable. While they should also have some reasonable relationship to the customer's needs, if they cannot be obtained during development, they will not be used.

On the other hand, if the quality measures are to support decisions on product acceptance, they must reasonably represent user needs and be available before the acceptance decision. While defect measures may be of some value, better results can generally be obtained with controlled tests. If the quality measures used during development are available, they can help in acceptance decisions, but the prime criteria should be based on more representative measures. The next few sections discuss the suitability of these measures.

16.4.1 Defect Measures

Defect counts only moderately represent the customer's view of product quality. While it is generally true that programs with large numbers of bugs have poor customer satisfaction, once a base level of quality is reached, defect measures no longer predict customer satisfaction.

This was demonstrated by a study one software supplier made of six programs. These programs were subjectively ranked by a panel of users according to their opinions of overall program quality. This data, together with the relative data on user-reported program errors and overall user problem activity, is given in Table 16.2. It shows that the program that ranked best according to the panel members' subjective opinions ranked worst in defects per 1000 lines of code. The problem rankings, on the other hand, were somewhat closer to these subjective views. The relative correlations of the various columns show that the panel members' opinions actually had a slight negative correlation with program defect rates.

These negative and weak correlations with problem and defect data seem to indicate that, beyond a certain point, problem and defect activity is less important than other factors such as usability, performance, and functionality. Clearly, determining what truly represents quality in the customer's eyes is not a simple task.

16.4.2 Change Activity

Change activity can be a useful measure of development quality. When change activity remains high late in a development program, it is a good indication of overall quality problems. Unfortunately, this measure is generally not directly controllable by the development group but is a consequence of such factors as defect rates or requirements stability. It is thus generally wise to use more direct defect measures for quality planning and to track change activity by program module as an added indicator of development progress.

Change activity data can be useful if it is properly recorded. The reasons for each change must be noted, together with its size. For example, for changes due to defect corrections the LOC change count is often a more objective measure than the defect count itself. The reason is that the scope of a single defect is often a subjective decision. If, for example, an eight-line change can be counted as one defect in one case and two in another, the measure is clearly not repeatable. Another problem concerns the handling of defects that span several modules. Is each module credited with a single defect, a fraction of a defect, or is the defect only assigned to one of the modules? Counting the LOC changes resolves this confusion.

A similar benefit can result from counting LOC changed due to requirements changes. By tracing this activity throughout the project the cost impact of requirements instability can be graphically demonstrated.

16.4.3 Error Seeding

Error seeding is a potentially interesting way to evaluate program quality.[4, 6] The idea is to inject a known number of "dummy" defects into the program and then to track how many of them are found by the various tests or inspections. If, for

TABLE 16.2
USER QUALITY RANKINGS

	Rankings		
	Panel Opinion	Defect Density	Problem Activity
Product #			
1	1	6	3
2	2	5	1
3	3	1	5
4	4.5	2	2
5	4.5	4	6
6	6	3	4
Correlation		−0.55	0.38

example, 60 percent of the seeded defects are found, the presumption is that 60 percent of the other bugs have been found as well.

While there is increasing evidence that the seeding idea is promising, it must still be viewed as an experimental technique.[16] The key problem is creating defects that suitably represent the natural defects remaining in the program. While various approaches have been tried, seeding remains more an art than a science.

16.4.4 Software Structure

Various complexity measures have been proposed for evaluating software designs. The available evidence suggests, however, that complexity is no better a guide to likely defect levels than is LOC.[19]

16.4.5 Controlled Tests

With controlled tests the product is subjected to a simulated work environment, and an evaluation is made of its operational suitability. Human factors tests, for example, are typically used to determine the adequacy of user interfaces and documentation; a special test environment is established with the documentation and system facilities required to demonstrate specific aspects of operational behavior. This differs from system testing in that some system functions may not be needed or may be supplied through simulation or prototypes.

16.4.6 Problem Measures

Problem activity data provides a potentially useful measure of program quality. After program installation and cut-over, records can be kept of user-reported problems. While these problems typically do not all relate to software defects, those that do are passed on to the maintenance organization for correction. The remainder generally concern user errors, hardware problems, duplicate defects, suggested improvements, and unknown causes. For large systems with many users the number of problems due to software defects is typically less than 3 to 5 percent of this total.

Problem measures, however, do have moderate correlation with user product satisfaction. This is quite understandable because problems waste the user's time and money and generally cause much inconvenience. Problem counts are a potentially attractive measure of software quality because they include software defects as well as installation and operational issues. The two biggest disadvantages with problem counts are that they are only available after development is over and they are subjective. Their subjectivity relates to the human nature of problems, which can be caused by a lack of human comprehension, a simple human mistake, or by a system malfunction. When conducted properly, controlled tests can sometimes address these disadvantages and provide valuable information before the development work is completed. But such tests are generally only possible late in the development cycle.

16.4.7 Installation and Operational Effort

While the effort required to install and operate the system is a good indicator of customer satisfaction, such measures are again not available until after completion and customer delivery. They also require the customer to do a lot of work. In this case, however, the factors that make installation and operation expensive can be usefully examined early in program development. The general approach is to define the step-by-step procedures for installing and operating the system and then actually measure the time and effort required to perform them. When such tests are conducted by qualified human factors professionals, much can be learned about training needs, documentation adequacy, interface problems, and even issues with the physical layout. With this knowledge, plans can be developed to improve these factors, the plans can be reviewed with knowledgeable users, and further controlled tests can be conducted. While there has been little experience with such quality plans, a few limited trials suggest it is a promising area for further attention.

16.4.8 Customer Satisfaction Surveys

To understand the customer's view of their products, some organizations use customer satisfaction surveys. IBM, for example, periodically conducts mail or telephone surveys to determine their customers' views of certain key products and support services. They include in the questions a request for suggestions on where the products or services could be improved. Such surveys, if properly conducted, can provide an informed view of product quality. Unfortunately, this measure again is not available until substantially after development completion.

16.4.9 Reliability and Availability

For some programs the customer is most concerned with the system's ability to perform the intended function whenever needed. This is called *availability*. Such measures are particularly important for system and communication programs that are fundamental to overall system operation. These generally include the control program, database manager, job scheduler, user interface, communication control, network manager, and the input-output system. The key to including any program in this list is whether its failure will bring down the critical applications. If so, its availability must be considered.

Availability cannot be measured directly but must be calculated from such probabilistic measures as the mean time between failures (MTBF) and the mean time required to repair and restore the system to full operation (MTTR). Assuming the system is required to be continuously available, availability is the percent of total time that the system is available for use:

$$\text{Availability} = \left(1 - \frac{\text{MTTR}}{\text{MTTR} + \text{MTBF}}\right) \times 100$$

Clearly, if the system could be repaired instantaneously then, barring operational disruption, availability would be 100 percent, regardless of how often it failed. It is thus important to use this measure in conjunction with others that relate to defect levels or failure rates.

Availability is a useful measure of the operational quality of some systems. Unfortunately, it is very difficult to project prior to operational testing. Since many products, operational factors, and service facilities are generally involved, it also is difficult to allocate availability goals to the system elements.

16.4.10 Selecting Quality Measures

While the most appropriate quality measures depend on their intended use, they also must depend on the kinds of data available. Since defect data is all that most software development organizations can obtain before system shipment, it should be used. While this properly emphasizes the need to reduce the number of delivered defects, it does not consider many other important quality attributes.

When no quantitative measures are available for such things as functionality, performance, and human factors, other steps must be taken to ensure that these important topics are given adequate attention. Some practical steps are to include selected customer representatives in specification reviews, conduct laboratory usability tests, do benchmark testing of customer programs, and conduct customer surveys. In addition, it is almost always worthwhile to do some early testing in either a simulated or real operational environment prior to final delivery. Even with the most thorough plans and a highly capable development team, the operational environment always seems to present some unexpected problems. These tests also provide a means to validate the earlier installation and operational plans and tests, make early availability measurements, and debug the installation, operation, and support procedures.

16.5 Establishing a Software Quality Program

The software quality principles stated at the beginning of this chapter can be expanded into the following steps:

1. Senior management establishes aggressive and explicit numerical quality goals. Without numerical measures, the quality effort will be just another motivational program with little lasting impact.

2. The quality measures used are objective, requiring a minimum of human judgment.

3. These measures are precisely defined and documented so computer programs can be written to gather and process them.

4. A quality plan is produced at the beginning of each project. This plan commits to specific numerical targets, and it is updated at every significant project change and milestone.

5. These plans are reviewed for compliance with management quality goals. Where noncompliance is found, replanning or exception approval is required.

6. Quality performance is tracked and publicized. When performance falls short of the plan, corrective action is required.

7. Since no single measures can adequately represent a complex product, the quality measures are treated as indicators of overall performance. These indicators are validated whenever possible through early user involvement as well as by simulated and/or actual operational testing.

In implementing such a program, a quality plan is produced during the initial project planning cycle. The plan is documented, reviewed, tracked, and compared to prior actual experience. Based on these comparisons, one of three situations will occur:

□ *The actual results will track just about on plan.*   As the plan meets management's goals and the goals are suitably aggressive, this is the optimum result.

□ *The actual results are significantly worse than the plan.*   This means that either the plan was more aggressive than the organization's current capability or the organization is not doing as well as it should. In either case the project should establish an action plan to bring performance as close to the original plan as practical. The revised plan is then reviewed and approved as before. In no case should the project merely change its plan without incorporating significant improvement actions.

□ *The actual results are significantly better than the plan.*   From a motivational point of view this can be the worst case. For example, the project team may be playing it safe with a plan they know they can meet. This can be corrected by revising the plan to present a challenge and then establishing action plans to meet these new goals.

It is important, however, to distinguish a situation of playing it safe from the aggressive team that made a truly dramatic improvement. They deserve a celebration. In every situation, however, when performance exceeds the plan, a newer and more aggressive plan is required. Quality improvement does not come from sprinting and resting; it is a continuous effort that builds on success. Each achievement is thus both cause for celebration and an opportunity to establish more aggressive goals for the future.

The process of quality control is not a new one but one that has been successfully used in many fields.[14, 15] It also closely parallels the project planning process described in Chapter 6, in which historical data are used to assist in making size and resource estimates that are then tracked against actual experience. After a few cycles of plans, tracking reviews, and improvement actions, the organization will learn how to make reasonably accurate quality plans. The real value of this process, however, is the ability to define increasingly effective software quality improvement actions. Good planning skills derive from an appreciation of the forces that affect the result. With this knowledge one is able to establish progressively more effective ways to improve the process. Progressive improvement, of course, is a key objective of the quality program.

16.5.1 Development Plan Quality Measures

When the objective is to motivate superior development or maintenance performance, defects are the most practical quality measure. This is because there is little other data that can reasonably be gathered and used during development. Further, if defects are not measured, it is hard for the software professionals to take any other measures very seriously. They know from experience that the program has defects that must be identified and fixed before the product can be shipped. Everything else will thus take second priority.

The specific defect measures must be selected by each organization based on the data they can gather. Generally they are classed much as described in Chapter

15, but the prime emphasis should be on those that are likely to cause customer problems. Many organizations restrict the definition of valid defects to those that require code changes. If clear criteria can be established, however, documentation changes also should be included.

Once the defect types have been established, normalization for program size is generally required. Defects per 1000 lines of source code is generally the simplest and most practical measure for most organizations. This measure, however, requires that the line-of-code definition be established (again as described in Chapter 15).

The next issue is determining what defects to measure and over what period of time. This again depends on the quality program objectives. If the focus is on managing the development process, measures are needed during development, test, and customer use. The development measures provide a timely indicator of performance, the test measures then provide an early validation, and the customer use data completes the quality evaluation. With this full spectrum of data it is possible to calibrate the effectiveness of development and test at finding and fixing defects. This requires long-term product tracking during customer use and some means to identify each defect with its point of introduction. Errors can then be separated by release and those caused by maintenance activity can be distinguished.

When such long-term tracking is done, it is possible to evaluate many software process activities. By tracking the inspection and test history of the complete product, for example, it is possible to see how effective each of these actions was at finding and removing the product defects. This evaluation can be particularly powerful at the module level, where it provides an objective way to compare task effectiveness using the statistical analysis methods described in the previous chapter.

16.5.2 Portraying Software Quality During Acceptance Test and Use

For tracking customer-found defects, Inglis suggests a set of cumulative defect curves, starting with system test.[12] These curves are normalized per 1000 lines of code and plotted as shown in Fig. 16.1. Here, the cumulative number of defects are plotted each month as received. For a three-release product, as in this figure, the actual release 1 experience is plotted at the top, with the life-of-product (LOP) cumulative goal shown at the right. The plan and actual to date for each of the succeeding releases are shown below. For release 2, an action plan was required at month 12, as indicated by the circled x. This same data can be plotted as a monthly defect rate, as shown in Fig. 16.2. Here, the defects found each month are shown for the release 2 plan and for actual experience. When normalized by program size, such historical data can provide a helpful reference in producing new quality estimates.

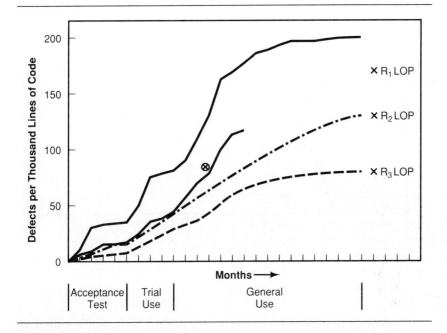

FIGURE 16.1
Plan Versus Actual—Three Product Releases

16.6 Estimating Software Quality

In making a software quality estimate it is important to remember that every project is different. While all estimates should be based on historical experience, good estimating also requires an intuitive understanding of the special characteristics of the product involved. Some examples of the factors to consider are:

□ *What is the anticipated rate of customer installation for this type of product?* A high installation rate generally causes a sharp early peak in defect rate with a rapid subsequent decline. Typically programs install most rapidly when they require minimal conversion and when they do not affect overall system operation. Compiler and utility programs are common examples of rapidly installed products.

□ *What is the product release history?* A subsequent release may install quickly if it corrects serious deficiencies in the prior release. This, of course, requires that the earliest experience with the new version is positive. If not, it may get a bad reputation and be poorly accepted.

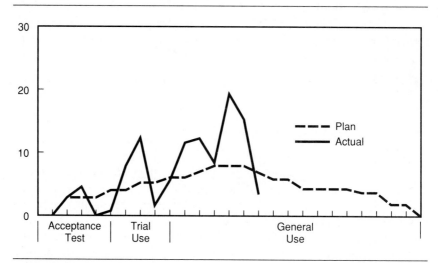

FIGURE 16.2
Defect Rates—Release 2

□ *What is the distribution plan?*   Will the product be shipped to all takers immediately, will initial availability be limited, or is there to be a preliminary trial period?

□ *Is the service system established?*   Regardless of the product quality, will the users be motivated and able to submit defect reports? If not, the defect data will not be sufficiently reliable to validate the development process.

16.6.1 Making a Software Quality Estimate

An estimate of program quality is made as follows:

1. Recent programs completed by the organization are reviewed to identify the ones most similar to the proposed product. Where the data warrants, this is done for each product element.

2. Available quality data on these programs is examined to establish a basis for the quality estimate.

3. The significant product and process differences are then determined and their potential effects estimated.

4. Based on these historical data and the planned process changes, a projection is made of anticipated quality for the new product development process.

5. This projection is then compared with goals and needed process improvements are devised to meet the goals.

6. The project quality profile is then examined to determine the areas for potential improvement, and a desired quality profile is produced.

7. A development plan is produced that specifies the process to be used to achieve this quality profile.

These steps are discussed further in the following sections.

16.6.2 Software Quality Models

To make an accurate quality estimate it is essential to have a quality model. While this need not be an explicit mathematical model, it should identify the basic assumptions behind the estimates. The reason most mathematical software models are not helpful for estimation purposes is that they make some highly restrictive assumptions about the software process. While such assumptions are generally needed to make the problem mathematically tractable, they do lead to serious problems when trying to make accurate projections. Examples of some of these typical assumptions are:[7, 17]

- The failures are independent.
- The number of failures is constant.
- Each failure is repaired before testing continues.
- All failures are observed.
- Testing is of uniform intensity and representative of the operational environment.
- The failure rate at any time is proportional to the current number of remaining defects in the program.
- The times between failures are independent.
- The different types of errors are of equal importance.
- Each error exhibits the same failure rate.
- No errors will be introduced during the testing and repair process.
- The failure rate will decline during debugging and operation.

Since these assumptions are clearly inappropriate for most projects, it is not surprising that development groups do not generally use quality models in their work.

16.6.3 Intuitive Quality Models

One of the special challenges of software engineering is that it is an intellectual process that produces artifacts that do not obey the laws of nature. The models needed for estimation purposes must reflect the way people actually write programs. The fact that such models have not yet been reduced to neat mathematical form is not a serious problem as long as we are not trying to build an algorithmic mechanism for generating estimates. It is, in fact, just these unique, nonuniform characteristics that make the software engineering process tractable. Some of these characteristics are:

1. Program module quality will vary, with a relatively few modules containing the bulk of the errors.
2. The remaining modules will likely contain a few randomly distributed defects that must be individually found and removed.
3. The distribution of defect types will also be highly skewed, with a relatively few types covering a large proportion of the defects.
4. Since programming changes are highly error-prone, all changes should be viewed as potential sources of defect injection.

While this characterization does not qualify as a model in any formal sense, it does provide a framework for quality planning. Each organization should assess its own product experience to determine the degree to which this model fits its situation. It is helpful, for example, to establish typical Pareto distribution profiles of module defect densities or defect types, as shown in Fig. 16.3.[9] This Pareto distribution is a ranking of the number of defects by cause, starting with the most prevalent on the left. In this data from four Hewlett-Packard programs, over one third of the defects were in the three highest categories. By focusing their process improvement efforts on the most prevalent defect categories from Table 16.3, Hewlett-Packard was able to achieve significant quality improvements.[9]

16.6.4 The Quality Estimate

In comparing the components and modules of the new product with similar elements of prior products, each program's unique design and implementation characteristics must be considered. As a consequence the quality profiles for each program will also probably be different. A hypothetical example of a defect profile is shown in Table 16.4.[13] Here, the defect injection and removal efficiencies are calculated by starting with the high-level design phase (HLD) in the left column. The anticipated number of errors to be injected is entered, together with the number expected to be found during HLD, desk checking, and HLD inspection. The number remaining is then entered, together with the injection rate and the removal efficiency. This is done for each phase, and each injection and removal rate is calculated. The injection rate refers to the errors injected in that phase, and removal efficiency refers to the percent of all errors present at that point that are removed in that phase.

The final figure at the bottom of Table 16.4 is the inspection efficiency. This is the percent of those defects found during development that are found by inspection. This is a good indicator of a high-quality development process. The 63.8

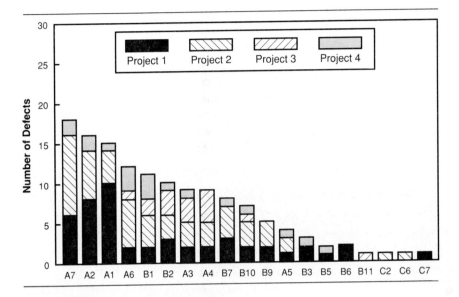

FIGURE 16.3
Pareto Analysis of Software Defects [9]
Robert B. Grady and Deborah L. Caswell, *Software Metrics; Establishing a Company-Wide Program,* © 1987, 125. Reprinted by permission of Prentice-Hall, Inc., Englewood Cliffs, New Jersey.

percent figure shown here is respectable but not particularly impressive. Inspection efficiencies below 50 percent generally indicate a development process that is highly test-oriented and probably not too effective at defect removal. One advantage of using inspection efficiency as a development measure is that the required data is available at the end of development and does not require a defect reporting system for the usage phase.

When historical data on these rates and efficiencies is available for a family of previously developed programs, the estimator can make highly informed judgments about the next project.[20] Analysis of this data also will suggest where to focus the development effort to produce better results.

By reviewing the quality profiles and deciding which are most representative of the product elements being estimated, a projection can be made for the new product, assuming nothing changed in the process. Next, the organization doing the work should decide what changes they will make in their process and what the resulting injection and removal efficiencies will likely be. The new rates are then estimated and a plan produced for the new product, as shown in Tables 16.5 and 16.6. (The generation of these figures is described in the next section.) Since the rates shown are in defects per 1000 lines of code, the actual rates should be factored to represent the size of the planned program.

TABLE 16.3
CATEGORIES OF SOFTWARE DEFECTS [9]

User Interface/Interaction
1. User needs additional data fields
2. Existing data needs to be organized/presented differently
3. Edits on data values are too restrictive
4. Edits on data values are too loose
5. Inadequate system controls or audit trails
6. Unclear instructions or responses
7. New function or different processing required

Programming Defect
1. Data incorrectly or inconsistently defined
2. Initialization problems
3. Database processing incorrect
4. Screen processing incorrect
5. Incorrect language instruction
6. Incorrect parameter passing
7. Unanticipated error condition
8. Operating system file handling incorrect
9. Incorrect program control flow
10. Incorrect processing logic or algorithm
11. Processing requirement overlooked or not defined
12. Changes required to conform to standards

Operating Environment
1. Terminal differences
2. Printer differences
3. Different versions of systems software
4. Incorrect JCL
5. Incorrect account structure or capabilities
6. Unforeseen local system requirements
7. Prototyping language problem

Robert B. Grady and Deborah L. Caswell, *Software Metrics; Establishing a Company-Wide Program,* © 1987, 124. Reprinted by permission of Prentice-Hall, Inc., Englewood Cliffs, New Jersey.

16.7 Removal Efficiency

One indication of the overall efficiency of the development process is the cumulative removal efficiency, which indicates the cumulative percent of the previously injected errors that have been removed by the end of each project phase. Since defect removal costs can be expected to roughly double with each project phase, attention should be focused on early removal. By comparing Tables 16.4, 16.5, and 16.6, one can see that the new product is expected to have substantially higher quality than its predecessor. This was accomplished in this case by improving the effectiveness of code inspections and unit test. This then results in increased inspection efficiency.

TABLE 16.4
DEVELOPMENT DEFECT PROFILE*

Defects	HLD	DLD	Code	U/T	I/T	S/T	Usage
Residual	0	4	13	34	19	13	9
Injected	10	21	63	5	2	2	3
Removed	6	12	42	20	8	6	12
Remaining	4	13	34	19	13	9	0
Injection rate	10	21	63	5	2	2	3
Removal efficiency	60%	48%	55%	51%	38%	40%	100%
Cumulative efficiency	60%	58%	64%	81%	87%	91%	100%
Inspection defects	6	18	60				
Development defects	6	18	60	80	88	94	
Inspection efficiency						63.8%	

*Per 1000 LOC
HLD - high-level design
DLD - detailed level design (module level)
U/T - unit test
I/T - integration test
S/T - system test
Injection rate - errors injected in the phase per 1000 LOC
Removal efficiency for a process phase: 100 × (removed)/(residual + injected)

It is interesting to note that a 20 percent improvement in inspection efficiency (from 63.8 percent to 76.3 percent) has resulted in a three times improvement in the resulting shipped product quality (91 percent to 97 percent, or 9 percent versus 3 percent of the errors being left in the product). Inspection efficiency is a very sensitive indicator of shipped program quality.

The determination of these actual defect removal efficiencies requires that each defect be evaluated to determine the process phase where it was injected. Since this must be done through the development, test, and field maintenance phases, each line of code must include some identification of when and why it was entered or changed. It also means that each defect must be returned to development for analysis. This is particularly important with multi-release products to permit separation of the residual defects from newly injected ones. Also, those made in maintenance must be separated from those made in development, and these must all be related to the specific release where they were injected.

16.8 Quality Goals

The quality goals of every development, manufacturing, or service organization must be established by senior management.[10] The senior managers are the only ones who can set such standards and they are the ones who best appreciate the full benefits of an aggressive quality program. This means that senior management

TABLE 16.5
PLANNED INJECTION RATES AND REMOVAL EFFICIENCIES

Defects	HLD	DLD	Code	U/T	I/T	S/T	Usage
Prior Project:							
Injection rate	10	21	63	5	2	2	3
Removal efficiency	60%	48%	55%	51%	38%	40%	100%
Cumulative efficiency	60%	58%	64%	81%	87%	91%	100%
New Project:							
Injection rate	10	21	63	1	1	0	1
Removal efficiency	60%	48%	70%	65%	41%	40%	100%
Cumulative efficiency	60%	58%	76%	92%	95%	97%	100%

must establish quality goals and clearly state them to their people. Without such guidance, the product managers will give top priority to schedule and cost issues because that is where their management's interest generally is focused.

While every organization must establish its own quality goals, a reasonable starting point would be:

1. Every new product or product release must have better quality than its predecessor.

2. The corporate quality organization, with the assistance of the software groups, will establish the quality measures to be used.

3. Each product manager is responsible for producing a documented quality plan to meet these goals.

4. Product quality performance will be judged by:

TABLE 16.6
PLANNED DEFECT PROFILE

Defects	HLD	DLD	Code	U/T	I/T	S/T	Usage
Residual	0	4	13	23	8	5	3
Injected	10	21	63	1	1	0	1
Removed	6	12	53	16	4	2	4
Remaining	4	13	23	8	5	3	0
Injection rate	10	21	63	1	1	0	1
Removal efficiency	60%	48%	70%	65%	41%	40%	100%
Cumulative efficiency	60%	58%	76%	92%	95%	97%	100%
Inspection defects	6	18	71				
Development defects	6	18	71	87	91	93	
Inspection efficiency						76.3%	

□ The degree to which quality plans show improvement

□ The effectiveness of the action plans to address areas of deficient performance

□ Product management's willingness to establish more aggressive goals when performance exceeds plan

5. The quality organization will periodically report to senior management on product and organizational performance against these goals.

Aggressive quality goals are tough to live with. They demand extraordinary actions, but they can also produce extraordinary results. The key is to measure the managers on how aggressively they set their quality goals and on how effectively they respond with action plans when performance falls short. If the emphasis is on meeting the goals, the project managers likely will make quality plans that are as safe as they can get by with. Goals and plans should be sufficiently aggressive so that a reasonable percentage of the products come in over target and require remedial action.

16.9 Quality Plans

The quality plan documents the quality actions management intends to implement. It includes the derivation of the quality measures, the identification of the planned process changes, and the anticipated quality improvements. Some examples of typical improvement actions that could have produced the improvements shown in Tables 16.4, 16.5, and 16.6 are:

□ Improve code inspection coverage from 39 percent to 100 percent. This is expected to improve removal efficiency of the coding phase from 55 percent to 70 percent, resulting in a cumulative removal efficiency at code exit from 64 percent to 76 percent.

□ Augment module unit test (UT) to include 100 percent test of all parameters both within and outside their expected bounds. This is expected to improve removal efficiency of UT from 51 percent to 65 percent and cumulative removal efficiency at UT exit from 81 percent to 92 percent.

□ Increase the inspection of code changes from 35 percent coverage to 100 percent. This is expected to reduce the probability of defective changes from 25 percent to 5 percent, resulting in reduced error injection rates and an overall process removal efficiency of 97 percent at S/T exit.

While these numbers are hypothetical, they are not unreasonable. Even though each of these reductions looks relatively modest, in total they result in an improvement factor of three in shipped defects from 9 to 3 per KLOC. It should also be noted that each level of improvement becomes progressively more difficult as the quality of the product is improved. A change from 99.5 percent to 99.7 percent in cumulative removal may seem relatively modest, but it reduces residual errors from 0.5 to 0.3, or by 40 percent. As can be seen, relatively small process changes can result in enormous product improvements.

There are many actions that can be taken to improve quality, and the most effective generally concern defect prevention rather than removal. Some such actions would include use of advanced design methodologies, a new design or implementation language, early prototyping, or improved requirements planning. The quality plan should thoughtfully consider both defect removal and error prevention strategies. Prevention methods are discussed further in Chapter 17.

By quantifying the plans and by making explicit estimates of the removal efficiencies at each process stage, it is possible to track performance and determine the impact of each process change. Tracking not only assists the development team in improving its performance but also provides improved planning data. If, for example, it was found that unit testing of all parameters resulted in removal efficiency of 75 percent, such testing would likely be more widely implemented. As pointed out in Chapter 11, there is evidence that such improvements are possible.

The outline of a typical quality plan, together with some explanatory comments on each of the major sections, is given in Table 16.7.

16.10 Tracking and Controlling Software Quality

The critical elements of a software quality management system are:

1. A responsible authority is named to own the quality data and the tracking and reporting system.

2. Quality performance is tracked and reported to this authority, during both development and maintenance.

3. Resources are established for validating the reported data and retaining it in the process database.

4. Actual product and organizational performance data is periodically reviewed against plan:

   □ Results are initially reviewed with responsible line management and any discrepancies resolved.

   □ Performance against targets is determined, and, if worse than plan, line management prepares an action plan for review with higher management.

TABLE 16.7
QUALITY PLAN OUTLINE

Product Introduction
- — A general product description, including the product's intended market, use, and current competitive or replacement quality expectations
  - — Objectives
  - — Planned market
  - — Competitive/predecessor product quality

Product Plans
- — The approach to be taken with the product, by whom, and when
  - — Critical dates, responsibilities, and checkpoints
  - — Release plans
  - — Distribution plans
  - — Service plans
  - — Operating environment

Process Description
- — The development and service processes to be used
  - — The development process
    - — Description of any process elements that deviate from the organization standard
    - — Explanation of the reasons and anticipated results of any deviations
  - — The assurance process
    - — Identification of those process actions and product elements to be reviewed
    - — Definition of the sampling methods to be used and the review techniques to be applied
  - — The service process
    - — Description of any process elements that deviate from the organization standard
    - — Explanation of the reasons and anticipated results of any deviations

Quality Plan
- — The quality goals and plans for this product
  - — Quality goals
  - — Prior relevant quality experience
  - — Quality actions planned
  - — Quality commitments

Risks and Exposures
- — A listing of the key risks and exposures and the actions to be taken to address them
  - — Risks and exposures
  - — Responsibilities
  - — Checkpoints

□ If actual performance is substantially better than plan, product management establishes more aggressive targets.

5. Quality performance is published, and a highlight report is provided to senior management.

6. Overall performance is periodically reviewed with senior management.

The purpose of the quality plan is to motivate action, not to evaluate people. When aggressive targets are not met, action plans are initiated to improve performance. That is exactly the desired result. Conversely, when an organization always meets its quality plans, it is not as motivated to develop and implement improvements. This likely is an ineffective quality program, since there is always room for improvement.

16.11 Summary

Product quality is one of the best measures of a software development project. Quality measures establish a clear record of progress, represent a powerful vehicle for setting objectives, and provide a graphic framework for current action.

To consistently achieve superior performance, management must establish challenging quality goals and strive to meet them. This requires senior management involvement, numerical quality goals, quality plans, quality tracking, and management review.

The five classes of quality measures are: development, product, acceptance, usage, and repair. These measures are characterized by being objective, timely, available, representative, or controllable. Measures are desired that are readily available, easy to gather, representative of the customer's needs, and directly controllable by development or maintenance.

During initial project planning, a quality plan is produced. This plan is documented, reviewed, and compared with actual experience. By quantifying the plans and making explicit estimates of the defect removal efficiencies at each process stage, it is possible to track quality performance and thus to determine the quality effects of each improvement in the software process.

The purpose of the quality plan is to motivate action, not to evaluate people. When aggressive targets are not met, action plans are initiated to improve performance. That is exactly the desired result. Conversely, when an organization always meets its quality plans, it has little motivation to develop and implement improvements. This indicates an ineffective quality program—there is always room for improvement.

References

1. Agresti, W. W. "Applying industrial engineering to the software development process," *Proceedings,* IEEE 23rd COMPCON Conference, 1981.

2. Boehm, B. W., J. R. Brown, and M. Lipow. "Quantitative evaluation of software quality," *Proceedings, Second International Conference on Software,* IEEE, San Francisco, CA, Oct. 13–15, 1976, pp. 592-605.

3. Bowen, T. P., C. B. Wigle, and J. T. Tsai. "Specification of Software Quality Attributes," RADC-TR-85-37, Rome Air Development Center, February 1985.

4. DeMillo, R. A. "Hints on test data selection: help for the practicing programmer," *IEEE Computer,* April 1978.

5. Deming, W. E. *Out of the Crisis,* Cambridge, MA: MIT Center for Advanced Engineering Study, 1982.

6. Gilb, T. *Software Metrics,* Bromley, England: Winthrop, 1977.

7. Goel, A. L., V. R. Basili, and P. M. Valdes. "When and how to use a software reliability model," *Proceedings of the Seventh Annual Software Engineering Workshop,* NASA Goddard Space Flight Center, December 1, 1982.

8. Grady, R. B. "Measuring and managing software maintenance," *IEEE Software,* September 1987.

9. Grady, R. B., and D. L. Caswell. *Software Metrics: Establishing a Company-Wide Program.* Englewood Cliffs, NJ: Prentice-Hall, 1987.

10. Humphrey, W. S. "The IBM large-systems software development process: objectives and direction," *IBM Systems Journal,* vol. 24, no. 2, 1985.

11. Humphrey, W. S. *Managing for Innovation—Leading Technical People.* Englewood Cliffs, NJ: Prentice-Hall, 1987.

12. Inglis, J. "Standard software quality metrics," *AT&T Technical Journal,* vol. 65, issue 2, March–April 1986.

13. Jones, T. C. "Measuring programming quality and productivity," *IBM Systems Journal,* vol. 17, no. 1, 1978.

14. Juran, J. M., and F. M. Gryna, Jr. *Quality Planning and Analysis, from Product Development Through Use.* New York: McGraw-Hill, 1980.

15. Klippel, W. H., ed. *Statistical Quality Control.* Dearborn, MI: Society of Manufacturing Engineers Publications Department, 1984.

16. Knight, J. C., and P. E. Ammann. "An Experimental Evaluation of Error Seeding as a Program Validation Technique," Software Engineering Laboratory, NASA Goddard, December 1985.

17. Mellor, P. "Software reliability modeling: the state of the art," *Information and Software Technology,* vol. 29, no. 2, March 1987.

18. Poston, R. M., and M. W. Bruen. "Counting down to zero software failures," *IEEE Software,* September 1987.

19. Shen, V. Y., S. D. Conte, and H. E. Dunsmore. "Software science revisited: a critical analysis of the theory and its empirical support," *IEEE Transactions on Software Engineering,* vol. SE-9, no. 2, March 1983.

20. Shooman, M. L. *Software Engineering: Design, Reliability, and Management.* New York: McGraw-Hill, 1983.

Software Engineering Institute

PART FIVE

The Optimizing Process

Once an organization has established process measurements and quality plans, it can use these capabilities to make process improvements. The professionals can now precisely assess their tasks, learn from their experiences, and use this knowledge to make improvements. This is why Level 5 is optimiz*ing* rather than optimiz*ed*. Process improvement is a way of working rather than a destination.

Although all the topics previously discussed should continue to receive attention, the priority areas at this stage are those covered in Chapters 17, 18, and 19.

Chapter 17 describes defect prevention, why it is important, and how it is done. It also describes how defect prevention can be used to motivate continuing process improvement, how a defect prevention program can be established, and some of the potential benefits.

Chapter 18 discusses automation of the software process, how it relates to process management, and how such investments can be justified. The crucial role of tools and environments are also covered, together with their role in software process improvement.

As software organizations mature, the most effective management techniques also change. Chapter 19 discusses the general software management problem and outlines the way management philosophy should change with increasing process maturity.

17

Defect Prevention

Based on a detailed review of the errors in the IBM DOS operating system, Endres concluded that errors result when the difficulty of the problems exceeds the power of the methods used to solve them.[7] While this is not a terribly surprising finding, it does clearly identify the importance of using powerful software methods. Many approaches to defect prevention have been devised, such as formal specifications, improved design techniques, and prototyping, and these and other innovations will continue to improve our ability to produce quality software. This chapter, however, concentrates on the techniques for error cause analysis and defect prevention. Error cause analysis involves finding the major causes of errors, and defect prevention concerns the steps to prevent them. This process approach complements improvements in software technology and can help advance a software process (almost) regardless of the technologies used. The best process management techniques cannot be fully effective, however, unless they are used in conjunction with effective technologies.

While the concepts of error cause analysis and defect prevention seem almost too simple to bear discussing, they are not easy to implement because they require that a precise process discipline be used by everyone in the software organization. As difficult as it is, however, it is the essential element of the optimizing process.

17.1 Defect Prevention Not a New Idea

The concept of defect prevention is not new. W. E. Deming and J. M. Juran played key roles in introducing the concepts of statistical quality control to Japanese industry shortly after World War II.[6, 13] An important element of the Japanese success was the production workers' involvement in improving their own working processes. These techniques became known as quality circles, and they are still being used with great success in Japan.[3, 14, 16] While the success of quality circles in the United States has not been as widespread, there are many cases in which they have been used effectively in manufacturing organizations.[3, 10] With different details, these same principles can work for software engineering.[1, 12]

The logic for applying such methods to software is:

1. To meet the escalating needs of society, progressively larger and more complex programs will be needed.

2. Since these programs will be used in increasingly sensitive applications, software defects will likely become progressively more damaging to society.

3. For the foreseeable future, programs will continue to be designed by error-prone humans.

4. This means that, with present methods, the number and severity of bugs encountered by systems users will increase.

Thus, unless we do something differently, errors will be progressively more likely and progressively less acceptable. This generally means that software organizations must start on defect prevention. This can be highly beneficial because:

□ The costs of finding and repairing defects increase exponentially the later they are found in the process.

□ Even early in the process, preventing defects is generally less expensive than finding and repairing them.

17.1.1 Why Defect Prevention Is Crucial to the Software Process

Finding and fixing errors accounts for much of the cost of software development and maintenance. When one includes the costs of inspections, testing, and rework, as much as half or more of the typical development bill is spent in detecting and removing errors. What is more, the process of fixing defects is even more error-prone than original software creation. Thus with a low-quality process, the error rate spiral will continue to escalate.

In describing Hewlett-Packard's experiences with defect prevention, Grady notes that more than a third of the errors were due to poor understanding of the users' interface requirements.[8, 9] By establishing an extensive prototyping and design review program, the number of defects found after release was sharply reduced. Their experiences on three classes of defects for four successive releases are shown in Fig. 17.1. The percentage of defects found after release dropped from 25 percent of the total for the first two releases to less than 10 percent for the third release and to zero in the fourth.

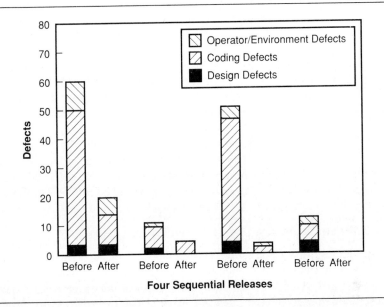

FIGURE 17.1
Number of Defects Found Before and After Release [8]
R. B. Grady, "Measuring and managing software maintenance," *IEEE Software*, September 1987, © 1987 IEEE.

A development project at another company used defect prevention methods to achieve a 50 percent reduction in defects found during development and a 78 percent reduction in errors shipped. This is a factor of two improvement in injected errors and a four to one improvement in shipped quality. While it might seem surprising that shipped product quality improved more rapidly than the error injection rate, this is the normal result. First, with a stable process the shipped errors will generally decline at least in proportion to the defect injection rate. Second, when total error content is reduced, the test and review processes can be more effective. When a program contains a large number of trivial errors, the reviewers will likely be distracted by the volume of detail and overlook more serious problems. This is why it is important to analyze data on defect distribution and repeat inspections with too high a proportion of trivial errors. Preventing the volume of simpler errors reduces these distractions, and the review process can be more efficient. As seen in Chapter 16, modest improvements in review efficiency can dramatically improve shipped quality.

While I know of no data to support this, I suspect that similar improvements are possible in testing, for much the same reasons. As the number of errors is reduced, the test cases can be designed to focus on the more sophisticated problems. What is more, undetected bugs may lurk behind the ones that were found. This focus on more complex problems should both reduce the required amount of testing and improve its effectiveness.

Finally, the most important single reason for instituting defect prevention is to provide a continuing focus for process improvement. While everyone will agree that process improvement is important, unless some mechanism drives process change, it will not happen in an orderly or consistent way. A defect prevention program focuses on those process areas that are the greatest sources of trouble, whether methods, technology, procedures, or training. When the developers become sloppy in reporting their data, when the SCM group makes build mistakes, when the test team uses the wrong regression buckets, or when defect corrections introduce new errors, these causes can be identified and corrective actions taken.

17.1.2 When Errors Are Life-Threatening

Perhaps the best way to look at defect prevention is to consider how you would act if a single error could threaten your life. This is the situation in nuclear submarines. If the personnel who operate and maintain the nuclear power plant make serious mistakes, the ship and its entire crew are in mortal danger. While the details of the nuclear propulsion safety program are classified, the essential elements are not. In brief, it is as follows:

1. All personnel, from the lowest-rated seaman to the commanding officer, are trained in the details of their own and their shipmates' jobs.

2. All personnel are required to know and periodically to demonstrate satisfactory performance to their job standards.

3. Audit groups frequently inspect each ship and each operation to ensure that every procedure and method is properly understood and executed.

4. When deviations are found, they are reported directly to the admiral in charge of the Navy Nuclear Power Program, and the commanding officer must promptly report on the corrective actions.

5. With even the most trivial operational error, an investigation is conducted to determine what went wrong, why, and what is required to correct and prevent it.

6. The results of such investigations are reported to the admiral, and a tracking system ensures that the commanding officer personally guarantees successful action implementation.

During the reviews, an objective, fact-finding attitude is maintained. All problems are divided into materiel, procedure, or personnel, depending on their cause. The materiel causes can generally be handled quite easily, while the procedure and personnel situations usually require more attention. All individuals are trained to report precisely what they did and why. If they made a simple error, they say so and work with those conducting the investigation to understand why they made the mistake and what steps are required to prevent a repetition.

It is instructive to think about our software problems as if they were highly critical.[15] How would we behave if we knew that any single software error could result in our being marooned at 200 fathoms with an exploding nuclear reactor? I suspect that an objective and impersonal defect prevention program would be the order of the day.

17.2 The Principles of Software Defect Prevention

The fundamental objective of software defect prevention is to make sure that errors, once identified and addressed, do not occur again. Defect prevention cannot be done by one or two people, and it cannot be done sporadically. Everyone must participate by faithfully executing the process—almost as if their lives depended on it. As with any other skill, it takes time to learn defect prevention well, but if everyone on the project participates, it can transform an organization.

Most software professionals spend much of their working lives reacting to defects. They know that each individual defect can be fixed but that its near twin will happen again, and again, and again. . . . The poet Rita Mae Brown has said that insanity is doing the same thing over and over and expecting different results.[2] To prevent these endless repetitions, we need to understand what causes these errors and take conscious action to prevent them. We must then obtain data on what we do, analyze it, and act on what it tells us. We will then begin to see what we can change and what might result. With time we will learn to address the fundamental causes of our problems and thus to prevent them. We must also remember one of Deming's fundamental principles:[6]

> In the state of statistical control, action initiated on appearance of a defect will be ineffective and will cause more trouble. What is needed is improvement of the process, by reduction of variation, or by change of level, or both. Study of the sources of product, upstream, gives powerful leverage on improvement.

While this viewpoint may seem radical, it worked for the Japanese with watches, radios, steel, shipbuilding, automobiles, televisions, and cameras. There is no apparent reason why it will not work for software as well.

The principles of software defect prevention are:

1. *The programmers must evaluate their own errors.* Not only are they the best people to do so, but they are most interested and they will learn the most from the process.

2. *Feedback is an essential part of defect prevention.* People cannot consistently improve what they are doing if there is not timely reinforcement of their actions.

3. *There is no single cure-all that will solve all the problems.*   Improvement of the software process requires that error causes be removed one at a time. Since there are at least as many error causes as their are error types, this is clearly a long-term job.[7] The initiation of many small improvements, however, will generally achieve far more than any one shot "breakthrough."

4. *Process improvement must be an integral part of the process.*   As the volume of process change grows, as much effort and discipline should be invested in defect prevention as is used on defect detection and repair. This requires that the process be architected and designed, inspections and tests be conducted, baselines established, problem reports written, and all changes tracked and controlled.

5. *Process improvement takes time to learn.*[6]   When dealing with human frailties, we must proceed slowly. A focus on process improvement is healthy, but it must also recognize the programmers' need for a reasonably stable and familiar working environment. This requires a properly paced and managed program. By maintaining a consistent, long-term focus on process improvement, disruption can be avoided and steady progress will likely be achieved.

17.2.1 The Steps of Software Defect Prevention

As Deming has said, every quality program must start with a clear management commitment to quality.[6] This commitment must be explicit and all members of the organization must know that quality comes first. Until management delays or redirects a project to meet quality goals, the people will not really believe it. Even then, the point must be reemphasized and the software engineers urged to propose quality improvement actions, even at the potential cost of schedule delays. In spite of what the schedule says, when quality problems are fixed early, both time and resources are saved. When management really believes this and continually reinforces the point to the software professionals, the right quality attitudes will finally develop.

Beyond management commitment, the implementation steps for a defect prevention program are:

1. *Defect reporting*   This includes sufficient information to categorize each defect and determine its cause.

2. *Cause analysis*   The causes of the most prevalent defects are determined.

3. *Action plan development*   Action teams are established to devise preventions for the most prevalent problems.

4. *Action implementation*   Once the actions have been determined, they must be implemented. This generally involves all parts of the organization in a concerted improvement effort.

5. *Performance tracking*   Performance data is gathered, and all action items are tracked to completion.
6. *Starting over*   Do it all again, only this time focus on the most prevalent of the remaining defects.

17.2.2 Defect Reporting

To implement defect prevention, a significant amount of information must be gathered at the time a defect is identified. Tables 17.1 and 17.2 show Jones's lists of the data IBM gathered from the inspections of a number of communications products.[12] Table 17.3 is the form used for collecting such information. Here, for problems found in test, the person who finds or fixes the problem is often not the same as the one who originally made the error. In this case some of the required information may not be available until a subsequent causal analysis review.

17.2.3 Error Cause Categories

When one embarks on defect prevention, one thinks about defects in a new way. Previously the emphasis was on how to fix them and, occasionally, on how to find them more effectively. This causes one to think about defect categories in terms of symptoms or repair actions. The need now is to understand what caused the problems. As Spohrer and Soloway have pointed out, this often requires one to understand what the programmer originally intended.[17] Since the originator is generally the only person who knows this, the original programmers are an essential part of any cause analysis effort. Soloway's research with novice programmers, however, suggests that only a few error categories need be examined to cover a large percentage of the problems. As shown in Table 17.4, for three of his students' programs, somewhere between 10 percent to 20 percent of the bug categories included about half of all the errors.[17]

From his experience with the IBM DOS operating system, Endres has also found that relatively few categories will cover most of the errors in a software system.[7] The six categories of errors that he suggests for defect prevention analysis are:

1. *Technological*   Definability of the problem, feasibility of solving it, availability of procedures and tools
2. *Organizational*   Division of workload, available information, communication, resources
3. *Historic*   History of the project, of the program, special situations, and external influences
4. *Group dynamic*   Willingness to cooperate, distribution of roles inside the project group

TABLE 17.1
DATA GATHERED AT THE TIME A DEFECT IS FOUND [12]

DEFECT ENTRY #	A unique entry identification number
PRODUCT	Product name
RELEASE	Release identifier
DRIVER	Driver identifier (a small subset of the release)
LINE ITEM	Functional item being developed
STAGE DETECTED IN	Process stage where error was detected
STAGE CREATED IN	Process stage where error was created
QIT* DEPARTMENT	For QIT suggestions, the QIT department number
PROBLEM REPORT #	For miscellaneous problem suggestions, the problem number (example, test problem number)
CREATE DATE	Date the defect was entered into the system
ANALYST	Programmer who should be contacted for questions
TYPE OF ANALYSIS	Inspection, test problem, field problem, QIT, miscellaneous
CHECKPOINT DATA	Current entry status—attentioned, screened, being investigated, closed

*QIT = quality improvement team

5. *Individual*   Experience, talent, and constitution of the individual programmer

6. Other causes and inexplicable causes

It is wise to limit the amount of information required during defect analysis to the absolute minimum needed to permit the causes to be determined and corrected. In most cases the details of each specific bug will have to be considered in any event, so any more sophisticated categorization should be aimed at identifying defects that can be prevented with a common action.

17.2.4 Cause Analysis

Cause analysis should be conducted as early as possible after a defect is found. Some delay may be necessary, however, to assemble the people required to do an effective job. Also, to be most efficient, a modest backlog is required for each analysis session. Since many software defects generally stem from a relatively few causes, this grouping tends to make the cause analysis sessions much more efficient.

For a given product, some useful guidelines on holding these sessions are:

1. Shortly after the time all product modules have completed detailed design, cause analysis sessions should have been held for all problems identified during the design inspections.

TABLE 17.2
DATA GATHERED AT THE TIME A DEFECT IS CLOSED [12]

CLOSE DATA	Closing/reason codes, answer text, programmer identification, and date
CATEGORY OF CAUSE	Communications breakdown Inadequate education—New function Inadequate education—Base function Inadequate education—Other Oversight—Did not consider all cases Transcription error—Mistake
DEFECT/PROBLEM ABSTRACT	A short description of the defect
DEFECT CAUSE ABSTRACT	A short description of defect cause
ASSIGNED ACTIONS (list of associated actions)	Action numbers assigned to prevent this defect
PROBLEM DESCRIPTION (and suggested actions)	A full description of the problem and actions
LOG OF ACTIVITIES (against the database)	A track record of all activities checkpointed against this defect

2. Shortly after the last module has completed each test phase, cause analysis meetings should have been held for all defects found during that test phase for these modules.

3. To be of most value to the later modules, cause analysis meetings should be held for all problems found for the first few modules as soon as possible after they have completed each development inspection or test phase.

4. Cause analysis reviews should be held on a product after a reasonable number of user problems have been found after customer release. Such reviews should be held at least annually after release, even if the defect rate is relatively low. These reviews should be continued until no significant number of new defects is reported.

5. The cause analysis meetings should be held often enough to permit completion in one and a half to two hours. Longer meetings will be less effective and harder to schedule. Short cause analysis meetings are generally most productive.

The objective of the cause analysis meeting is to determine the following:

1. What caused each of the defects found to date?
2. What are the major cause categories?
3. What steps are recommended for preventing these errors in the future?
4. What priorities are suggested for these actions?

The result of the cause analysis meeting is a report on each defect, much like that shown in Table 17.5.[12]

TABLE 17.3
PROBLEM REPORT FORM [12]

PROBLEM REPORT FORM			Page ____ of ____
circle one: PRODUCT COMPONENT MODULE CODE OTHER: _____			
circle one: INSPECTION PEER REVIEW TEAM LEADER REVIEW			
Product	Release	Driver	Line Item
Component	Module/Macro	Developer	Reviewer
Date Submitted for Review	Date Reviewed	Hours	# Major Errors
Person raising issue:		Problem Description:	
Answer Date:	Answered by:	Ans. Review Date:	Reviewed by:
Solution:			

Abstract of defect (50 char max):

PHASE where error was CREATED (check one)

____ PRODUCT DESIGN   ____ FUNCTIONAL TEST
____ COMPONENT DESIGN   ____ PRODUCT TEST
____ MODULE DESIGN   ____ SYSTEM TEST
____ CODE   ____ PACKAGING TEST
____ UNIT TEST   ____ POST-SHIP

Cause Category (check one):

____ Education: Didn't understand new
____ Education: Didn't understand base
____ Education: Other
____ Communications
____ Oversight: Didn't consider all cases
____ Transcription: Simply made a mistake

Abstract of cause of error (50 char max):

How can error be avoided the next time?

What action is needed?

17.2.5 The Cause Analysis Meeting

Cause analysis meetings are similar in many ways to inspections. They have a leader and a recorder and include the involved programmers and some of their peers. The meeting should not be too large (five to eight professionals at most) and should not include managers. The result of the meeting is a report on each defect, as

TABLE 17.4
PERCENTS OF PROBLEMS BY TYPES [17]

Percent of Types	Cumulative Percent of Total Problems		
	Program 1	Program 2	Program 3
10	44	46	32
20	55	64	46
25	62	69	56
50	80	84	77

described above, and a report on the meeting itself. This report should include the basic data on the meeting, such as preparation time, meeting time, defects handled, and number of actions recommended. Also, a summary cross index should be prepared of the defect report numbers with the action recommendation numbers.

After the cause analysis meeting leader has been identified and the team selected, preliminary data on each defect is provided to the team members. They review this data in advance to become familiar with each defect and to list questions to ask the implementers during the meeting. Where practical, these questions are given to the implementers ahead of time. Jones has suggested an agenda for cause analysis meetings, as shown in Table 17.6.[12]

Occasionally, when actions to prevent a particular defect or defect class cannot be established at the meeting, more work is needed. Typically one of the programmers on the cause analysis team is asked to study the problem and prepare a brief report. This should be circulated to the team members before the next meeting. An example of such a report is shown in Table 17.7.[12]

At the conclusion of the cause analysis meeting the leader summarizes the findings in a report to all members, including the action recommendations and the defects addressed by each. The final step is to turn over the recommended action list to the action team.

Grady and Caswell report an interesting example of the cause analysis process.[9] Figure 17.2 shows the major defect types for a compiler project; the design defects are detailed in Fig. 17.3. Finally, the register allocation defects are further analyzed by use of a cause/effect diagram as shown in Fig. 17.4.

17.2.6 The Action Team

Up to this point the main concerns have been with understanding problem causes and how they might be fixed. Next, the actual preventative actions are initiated. This is no longer a study by a small team of technical professionals. Managers are involved, responsibilities are assigned, and implementation progress is tracked.

The first question in forming an action team is deciding on its role and composition. Key action team responsibilities are:[12]

TABLE 17.5
DEFECT ANALYSIS REPORT [12]

PRODUCT: _____ RELEASE: _____
ANALYST NAME: _____ DEPARTMENT: _____
TYPE OF ANALYSIS: INSPECTION   TEST-PROBLEM   FIELD-PROBLEM
                      DESIGN-CHANGE   QIT   MISC   POSTMORTEM

If Inspection: If Test: If Field:
Release #:   _____   Release #:   _____   Release #:   _____
Driver #:   _____   Lineitem #:   _____   Change #:   _____
Lineitem #:   _____   Problem #:   _____   Fix #:   _____

Stage where error was detected:
_____ PRODUCT DESIGN   _____ FUNCTIONAL TEST
_____ COMPONENT DESIGN   _____ PRODUCT TEST
_____ MODULE DESIGN   _____ SYSTEM TEST
_____ CODE   _____ FINAL PACKAGE TEST
_____ UNIT TEST   _____ AFTER SHIPMENT
                                         _____ OTHER

For Inspection, Test-Prob., Field-Prob., Design-Change:
Abstract of defect (50 char max):

Process Stage where created: (check one)

_____ PRODUCT DESIGN   _____ FUNCTIONAL TEST
_____ COMPONENT DESIGN   _____ PRODUCT TEST
_____ MODULE DESIGN   _____ SYSTEM TEST
_____ CODE   _____ FINAL PACKAGE TEST
_____ UNIT TEST   _____ AFTER SHIPMENT
                                         _____ OTHER

Category of Cause (check one):

____ Education: Didn't understand new
____ Education: Didn't understand base
____ Education: other
____ Communications
____ Oversight: Didn't consider all cases
____ Transcription: Simply made a mistake

Abstract of cause of error (50 char max):

How can error be avoided the next time?

For QIT, Postmortem, or Misc. Entry:

QIT Dept. #: _____   Postmortem—Release #: _____

Abstract of Problem (50 char max.):

Abstract of Cause of Problem (50 char max):

TABLE 17.6
CAUSAL ANALYSIS MEETING AGENDA [12]

1—Compare release goals, team goals, and actual results.

2—Causal analysis:

    a. Evaluate all errors. That is, read through each error, discussing the defect and the cause. Make sure that all team members understand why the error occurred.

    b. Create an action list after all errors have been discussed by quickly reviewing the errors and placing their preventive actions in a list. Several defects may contribute to the same action, and several actions may be required for a given defect.

3—Process stage evaluation—When all causal analysis is complete, do the following:

    a. Ask the following questions:

       (1) What was done by this team that worked well and should be recommended or pointed out to the next team going through this stage?

       (2) What could be done to improve the process?

       (3) What tools could help detect the errors while still in this stage?

    b. Create additional action items based on discussions in the process evaluation part of the session.

---

1. Prioritize all action items.

2. Establish an implementation plan for the highest-priority items.

3. Assign responsibilities.

4. Track implementation.

5. Report to management on progress.

6. Ensure that all success stories are recognized and the responsible individuals identified.

7. Continue with the next-priority items.

The members of the action team should include the following:

- The manager responsible for action implementation, often the process group leader
- A process group representative
- The education manager
- A tools and methods specialist
- One or more management representatives from the involved product groups
- Quality Assurance
- Configuration management

Since the action team will be a long-term assignment, it is wise to occasionally rotate its membership. The product members also will change periodically as new product programs are established and previous ones are completed.

TABLE 17.7
ACTION PLAN ANALYSIS [12]

PRODUCT: _____

PROGRAMMER NAME: _____

PRIORITY (circle one): 1   2   3   4

COMMITTED TARGET DATE: _____

PROJECTED COST (persons-days): _____

ABSTRACT OF ACTION ITEM (50 char max):

DETAILED DESCRIPTION OF ACTION ITEM:

LIST OF DEFECT ANALYSIS ENTRY IDS:

Action Team Meetings.   The action team meeting starts with an initial review of the recommendations made to date and a decision on the priority of the items to be addressed. Since there are probably many more items than can be reasonably handled at one time, the most important areas are addressed first, and actions are promptly launched to handle them. As success is achieved with these initial actions, additional items can be handled.

The action priorities should be based on historical data as well as future plans. For example, even if design problems have historically been most prevalent, if no projects are entering the design phase, perhaps implementation or test actions would be most pertinent at this time. These decisions must consider the lead times for action implementation so they will be completed in time to meet project needs.

The action team initially should meet at least once a week and reduce meeting frequency as the workload permits. They also should review the performance of the cause analysis teams and track the implementation progress for each action item. Based on these reviews, they should make periodic reports to management on progress and key item status.

One of the most important action team duties is to ensure that progress is publicized and that all key contributors are recognized. While most people will voluntarily make extra efforts to solve important problems, their enthusiasm will cool quickly if they are not recognized. Continued reminders of the importance of the work and the progress being made help to maintain enthusiasm.[11]

Example Actions.   While defect prevention has been used in various branches of manufacturing and engineering for many years, few realize how much it has driven the field of software. In the earliest days of computer programming many programs were entered by hand in octal machine code on Flexowriter paper tape.

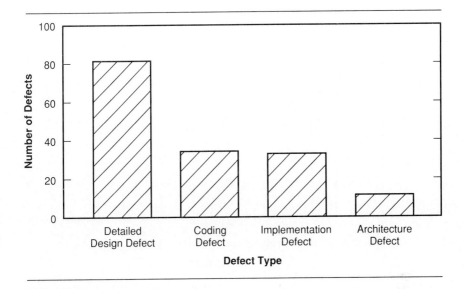

FIGURE 17.2
Compiler Defects [9]
Robert B. Grady/Deborah L. Caswell, *Software Metrics: Establishing a Company-Wide Program,* © 1987, 126. Reprinted by permission of Prentice-Hall, Inc., Englewood Cliffs, New Jersey.

The use of absolute addresses and the recoding of standardized functions were both time-consuming and error-prone activities. Many steps have been taken over the intervening years to replace or better support these and other such manual tasks. Defect prevention has thus been a significant force behind many software developments, starting with assembly languages, subroutines, high-level languages, compilers, editors, and many other widely used tools. Many current software practices are also intended either to prevent or detect errors early in the process. Examples are change control, file protection, standards, and inspections.

Some of Jones's examples of errors and their preventive actions are shown in Table 17.8.[12] As these demonstrate, some actions are simple and can be implemented quite quickly. Others, such as initiating or modifying a training program, might take more effort. The development or modification of tools or support facilities is also often a larger job that requires time, management support, and funding. Since there is generally wide variation among the action items, large organizations may find it helpful to establish a hierarchy of action teams. The items requiring major long-term effort are referred to the higher-level teams, while the simpler and more immediate items are handled at the working level.

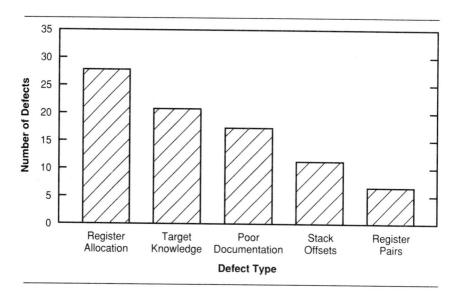

FIGURE 17.3
Compiler Design Defects [9]
Robert B. Grady/Deborah L. Caswell, *Software Metrics: Establishing a Company-Wide Program,* © 1987, 126. Reprinted by permission of Prentice-Hall, Inc., Englewood, New Jersey.

17.2.7 Tracking Action Progress

While we think nothing of establishing systems to track bugs to closure, no one thinks much about tracking the process changes required for defect prevention. This, however, is exactly what is needed. Every action must be logged and tracked and its status periodically reported. There should be follow-up reports, aging statistics, open item lists, and priority hot lists. Every delay in prevention action permits more errors to be made. Once a prevention action has been approved, it thus should be instituted with all possible speed.

A typical action record is shown in Table 17.9.[12] Such records should be maintained for all actions, starting on the date they were originally suggested by the cause analysis teams. Actions are only removed from this record by being implemented or superseded by other actions or by the action team's decision that they are no longer pertinent.

The periodic status reports show the action item identification, its priority, the products involved, the date the item was submitted, the person responsible for implementation, the date assigned, and the planned completion date. Other pertinent information is the planned cost, the expected quality impact, intermediate checkpoints, a summary of the actions to be taken, and a record of the error types

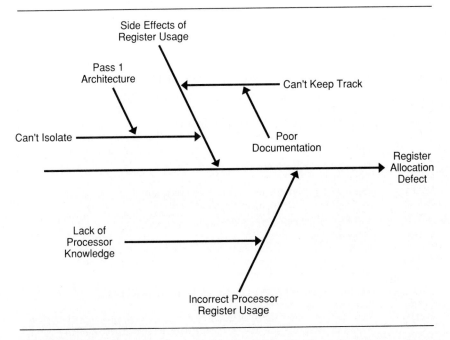

FIGURE 17.4
Cause/Effect Diagram [9]
Robert B. Grady/Deborah L. Caswell, *Software Metrics: Establishing a Company-Wide Program,* © 1987, 127. Reprinted by permission of Prentice-Hall, Inc., Englewood, New Jersey.

and quantities that would have been prevented by the action. This report should highlight those actions that have not yet been assigned for implementation by suggested priority, and listed in aged sequence.

17.2.8 Prevention Feedback

Perhaps the most important single action to come out of any defect prevention program is the awareness effort. This ensures that all software professionals are aware of the major error categories and the actions they can take to prevent or detect them at the earliest possible time. The awareness effort should involve training programs for the new tools and methods and special seminars on the most recent prevention experiences and plans.

One particularly effective action is the project kick-off meeting held at the beginning of each project phase.[12] This involves the full project team and covers the following items:

TABLE 17.8
EXAMPLE DEFECTS AND PREVENTIVE ACTIONS [12]

Error:	WXTRN was coded when an EXTRN was needed.
Categ.:	Education—base code/other.
Cause:	EXTRN statement not understood.
Action:	Create an entry for the project notebook on EXTRN statements.
Error:	Several program error conditions were overlooked.
Categ.:	Oversight.
Cause:	Last-minute additions caused multiple errors.
Action:	Add item to common error list to warn people that late changes are more prone to error.
Error:	Program abnormally ended.
Categ.:	Transcription.
Cause:	Wrong register label typed in (assembler program).
Action:	Write a tool to trace registers during unit test.
Error:	Program functions were coded in incorrect order.
Categ.:	Communications.
Cause:	Communications failed between high-level and low-level designers.
Action:	Change the process to include regularly scheduled communication sessions to be attended by the designers.
Error:	Function would not work as designed in the low-level stage.
Categ.:	Education—new function.
Cause:	Low-level designers were not aware of a high-level design implication. (The low-level designers and high-level designers are in separate groups.)
Action:	Institute education sessions involving both design groups.
Action:	Make sure that low-level designers are assigned in time to attend all education sessions.

1. The key phase activities are reviewed, including the inputs required, the outputs to be produced, and the key methodologies to be used. Any input problems are identified and resolved.

2. The error checklists are reviewed to ensure that all team members are aware of the errors most common to this phase and the actions recommended for their prevention.

3. Goals are set for the phase. This includes the entire team's commitment to defect injection and removal targets for the phase. While these goals are the team's property and are not for publication, they should be consistent with or better than the project's quality plan for that phase. This is rarely a problem, however, since teams will typically set more challenging goals for themselves than management would dare to impose.[11]

The kick-off meeting is an ideal forum for raising any questions and discussing issues and concerns. The team manager should conduct the meeting and ensure that it is cooperative and nonthreatening. The intent is for everyone to understand what is to be done, to be aware of the pertinent defect prevention actions, and to be committed to the common quality effort.

TABLE 17.9
ACTION RECORDS [12]

ACTION #	A unique number to identify the action.
PRODUCT	The product name or identifier.
PROGRAMMER	Programmer submitting the action.
CREATE DATE	Date action item was entered into the system.
PRIORITY	1, 2, 3, or 4.
AREA CODE	Where the implementation occurred (process, tools, etc.)
LINE ITEM	Specific item within the area.
CHECKPOINT INFO	Current status of the entry—attentioned, screened, being investigated, closed.
COST ESTIMATE	Number of programmer days expected for implementation.
TARGET DATE	Date of expected completion.
CLOSE DATE	Closing reason codes, programmer identification, date.
FINAL COST	Number of programmer days implementation actually took.
ABSTRACT OF ACTION	A short description of the action.
ASSOCIATED DEFECTS	List of all defects linked to this action.
ANSWER TEXT	A full description of the action that took place.
LOG OF ACTIVITIES AGAINST THE DATABASE	A track record of all activities checkpointed against the action.

17.3 Process Changes for Defect Prevention

The process changes required to incorporate defect prevention are shown in Fig. 17.5. In summary, the new elements are:[12]

1. Kickoff meeting—the entire team meets to review the work to be done, the goals, and any defect prevention methods that are pertinent such as check lists, review guidelines, or new tools and methods.

2. The data from the process task is entered in the process database.

3. A cause analysis review meeting is held as part of task exit to examine the problems and recommend any improvements.

4. A cause analysis team periodically reviews the process database to determine any cross-project problems that need special attention.

5. All improvement suggestions are retained in the action tracking system.

6. An action team decides on priorities, selects the items for immediate implementation, and assigns implementation responsibility. They then track progress to ensure effective and timely implementation.

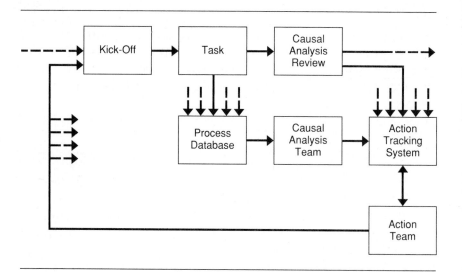

FIGURE 17.5
Defect Prevention Process [12]

7. A feedback system is established to ensure that the results are communicated to the professionals and that their contributions are recognized.

With defect prevention there are several process levels to consider. The first is the actual work of developing the software. Above this is the process model that provides the framework for project analysis and control. At a third and higher level, the defect prevention process is used to change the software development and maintenance process. As this third level process achieves the discipline and structure of the others, it will ensure steady and consistent process improvement.

17.4 Defect Prevention Considerations

Some questions frequently asked about defect prevention are: Where should one start, what is the role of tools and technology, what does it cost, and what is management's role? The following sections briefly discuss these topics.

17.4.1 Where to Start?

While there is no magic answer to the question of where to start, there is compelling evidence that software modification is the most fruitful area for improving software development and maintenance. Collofello and Buck, for example, point out that 62 percent of the defects in their systems were due to incorrectly implemented changes.[4] While most of these were caught through testing, they estimated that many more such errors were not even reported. The data in Table 17.10 shows that 52 percent of the errors were regressions to functions that had previously worked. The defects due to new work were only 21 percent for new features and 17 percent that were latent defects discovered late in the process.

Clearly, the change process is a fruitful one for initial exploration. This question, however, should be thoughtfully considered before launching a program. To verify the situation in any particular organization, data is required on the most likely sources of errors and how they are found and fixed. If such data is not available, it is likely that software change is the most profitable area for initial focus by the defect prevention activity.

17.4.2 The Role of Tools and Technology

While the subject of tools and technology is covered in more detail in the next chapter, cause analysis provides an informed way to select parts of the software process for automation. This approach requires a precise definition of the tasks to be automated, why they are important, and their current problems. When this work is done in the context of a structured and quantified process, the resulting tools are more likely to be effective in assisting the professionals to do their jobs.

17.4.3 The Costs and Benefits of Defect Prevention

Crosby points out that most organizations worry about the cost of defect prevention. While this is a reasonable concern, it only makes sense when considered in light of the costs of not preventing them. For software, much as with hardware, this generally includes the costs of testing, repair, customer dissatisfaction, and warranty and field service. Unless one considers both sides of this equation, it is impossible to make an intelligent decision on the matter. In fact, in every field Crosby examined the costs of testing and repair so far exceeded the costs of prevention that he asserted that "quality is free." While his book does not specifically address software, his list of actions for prevention, detection, and repair are instructive. A summary is given in Table 17.11.[5]

Jones asserts that the costs of a defect prevention program are not as high as one might think:[12]

- □ The kick-off session typically only lasts one to one and a half hours.
- □ The added cost of gathering the needed data must be considered, but if the programmers do it as part of their normal work, it is not excessive, particularly if on-line data recording facilities are available.

TABLE 17.10
DISTRIBUTION OF DEFECT ORIGIN [4]

Defect	Percent
Defects induced by corrective changes	10
Residual product defects	17
Defects to new features	21
Defects to existing features resulting from new features	52

- A typical cause analysis meeting lasts about one and a half hours. If there are too many errors to be covered in this time, a second meeting should be held.

- The action team meetings can be brief, particularly after the program is established. They should only last half an hour to an hour.

- The only new staffing needs are for the action team, which can be relatively small. For an organization of 100 to 150 people, Jones suggests four or five full-time members with a manager. If defect prevention is made the responsibility of the SEPG, they could carry the full-time load, with the project and other members serving on a rotating or part-time basis.

TABLE 17.11
HARDWARE PREVENTION, APPRAISAL, AND FAILURE COSTS [5]

Prevention Costs

Design reviews	Product qualification
Drawing checking	Engineering quality orientation
Make Certain program	Supplier evaluations
Specification review	Supplier quality seminars
Tool control	Process capability studies
Operation training	Quality orientation
Acceptance planning	Zero Defects program
Quality audits	Preventive maintenance

Appraisal Costs

Prototype inspection and test
Production specification conformance analysis
Supplier surveillance
Receiving inspection and test
Product acceptance
Process control acceptance
Packaging inspection
Status measurement and reporting

Failure Costs

Consumer affairs	Engineering change order
Redesign	Purchasing change order
Rework	Corrective action costs
Scrap	Warranty
Service after service	Product liability

□ A database system is needed to assist in tracking and reporting.

□ Some new tools will be needed to address some of the action recommendations. These can be justified more readily once the facts are known.

□ Process training and documentation must be updated to incorporate defect prevention.

While the costs are generally obvious, the benefits are not. We all know that a large portion of software development is devoted to testing. If defect prevention can make a significant dent in test time, it must pay off. Further, it often costs as much as 20 programmer hours to find and fix a single software bug through laboratory testing. Field repair costs are generally two to ten times higher. These costs are large and measurable, but the costs of customer dissatisfaction due to poor product quality are often impossible to measure and are generally far more important to an organization's continued success.

There is, however, no absolute economic proof that defect prevention is cost-effective. The automobile industry faced a similar situation, but they chose to wait until they lost a third of their market before reacting. Unfortunately for the watch, camera, steel, shipbuilding, and television industries, they too did not react in time. While it is not clear that software faces an equivalent challenge, there is no convincing proof that our situation is any different. While the threat of unemployment may seem remote to most U.S. programmers, it once did to automobile and steel workers as well. Even if there were not a national need, it would thus be prudent to strive for superior software quality, and this requires that we start to do defect prevention.

17.5 Management's Role

Table 17.12 gives Crosby's list of questions for managers and supervisors to help them understand their quality situation and whether they are prepared to take action.[5] While these questions were developed for hardware manufacturing, they apply equally to software. Software managers should answer these questions and then, unless satisfied with the result, proceed to implement the actions discussed in this chapter.

Assuming you decide to move ahead with defect prevention, the next steps are:

1. Meet with your team and make a joint commitment to defect prevention.
2. Select a trial project area and develop an introduction plan.
3. Appoint an action team manager and assist in staffing the action team.
4. Develop kick-off packages for the pilot project.
5. Install any needed tools and support.
6. Conduct appropriate seminars and training.

TABLE 17.12
QUALITY IMPROVEMENT SELF-EVALUATION [5]

The supervisor who wonders how to effect quality improvement in his or her area should ask the following questions:

Do I really understand the cause of the defects that occur?

What are the most frequent defects occurring in my area?

What of these defects are the most expensive to repair?

Do I feel that any of them are the fault of my people or myself?

If so, which ones?

If not, who do I feel is responsible?

Have I talked with the other departments involved about the defects that concern me?

What was their reaction?

If I could eliminate three problems, what would they be?

Do I feel that I am personally responsible for causing any of these three problems?

Suggestion: Select one of these three problems and analyze it in depth. Guideline questions:
  How do I know the problem exists?
  What is the apparent cause of the problem?
  What do the other people involved say the apparent cause is? (Does it agree with your answer?)
  Have I asked anyone not directly involved to look at it?
  What did this person say?

---

7. Launch a pilot defect prevention program.

8. Monitor progress, and take corrective action as needed.

9. After some initial experience, modify the program to correct deficiencies.

10. If the changes are modest, prepare for broad introduction. If the changes are substantial, conduct another pilot.

Defect prevention takes time. Stick to it until the benefits are apparent. If you don't see results in about six months, seek help—you are probably doing something wrong. While defect prevention requires the whole-hearted participation of everyone involved in the organization, it can only be initiated and maintained by management.

Finally, defect prevention is not a modest change in the software process; it is an entirely new way of life. It will transform your software organization.

17.6 Summary

Finding and fixing errors accounts for much of the cost of software development and maintenance. When one includes the costs of inspections, testing, and rework, more than half the typical development bill is spent in removing errors. In addition to cost and schedule savings, the most important reason for instituting defect prevention is to provide a continuing focus for process improvement. While everyone will agree that process improvement is important, unless some mechanism motivates process change, it will not happen in an orderly or consistent way.

The fundamental objective of defect prevention is to make sure that errors, once identified and addressed, do not occur again. Like any other skill, defect prevention takes time to learn, but if everyone on the project participates, it will improve over time.

The basic principles of defect prevention are: The programmers must evaluate their own errors, feedback is essential, there is no single cure-all, it must be an integral part of the process, and learning to be proficient at defect prevention takes time.

The first steps call for a clear management commitment to quality. Following this, the implementation steps are: defect reporting, cause analysis, action plan development, action implementation, tracking performance, and starting over.

Defect prevention takes time. Stick to it until the benefits are apparent. If you don't see results in about six months, you are probably doing something wrong. Defect prevention is not a modest change in the software process; it is an entirely new way of life that will transform your software organization.

References

1. Agresti, W. W. "Applying industrial engineering to the software development process," *Proceedings,* IEEE Computer Society 23rd International Conference (Fall COMPCON), 1981.

2. Brown, Rita Mae. Private communication.

3. Cole, R. E. "A Japanese management import comes full circle," *Technology Review,* May/June 1983.

4. Collofello, J. S., and J. J. Buck. "Software Quality Assurance for maintenance," *IEEE Software,* September 1987.

5. Crosby, P. B. *Quality Is Free: The Art of Making Quality Certain.* New York: Mentor, New American Library, 1979.

6. Deming, W. E. *Out of the Crisis.* Cambridge, MA: MIT Center for Advanced Engineering Study, 1986.

7. Endres, A. "An analysis of errors and their causes in system programs," *IEEE Transactions on Software Engineering,* vol. SE-1, no. 2, June 1975.

8. Grady, R. B. "Measuring and managing software maintenance," *IEEE Software,* September 1987.

9. Grady, R. B., and D. L. Caswell. *Software Metrics: Establishing a Company-Wide Program,* Englewood Cliffs, NJ: Prentice-Hall, 1987.

10. Humphrey, W. S. "Japanese management: perspectives for U.S. engineering," *Manufacturing Engineering,* April 1982.

11. Humphrey, W. S. *Managing for Innovation—Leading Technical People.* Englewood Cliffs, NJ: Prentice-Hall, 1987.

12. Jones, C. L. "A process-integrated approach to defect prevention," *IBM Systems Journal,* vol. 24, no. 2, 1985.

13. Juran, J. M. "Product Quality—A Prescription for the West," European Organization for Quality Control, Paris, June 9–12, 1981.

14. Lawler, E. E. III, and S. A. Mohrman. "Quality circles after the fad," *Harvard Business Review,* January–February, 1985.

15. Leveson, N. G. "Building safe software," in *Software Reliability.* Boston: Blackwell Scientific Publications, 1987, pp. 1–18.

16. Mohr, W. L. *Quality Circles: Changing Images of People at Work.* Reading, MA: Addison-Wesley, 1983.

17. Spohrer, J. C., and E. Soloway. "Novice mistakes: are the folk wisdoms correct?" *Communications of the ACM,* vol. 29, no. 7, July 1986.

18

Automating the Software Process

Our attempts to automate the software process are motivated by our need to improve the quality and productivity of our work. When we can reduce a task to a routine procedure and then mechanize it, we not only save labor but also eliminate a source of human error—which, it turns out, is the most effective way to improve productivity. One software organization studied the potential benefits of various software tools and found that the greatest productivity improvements came from eliminating error causes. This is a good general rule: Greater productivity improvement will come from eliminating mistakes than from performing tasks more efficiently.

Since such improvements will not happen quickly or easily, organizations need an automation strategy to guide them. Framing this strategy requires knowledge of what is needed, awareness of what is feasible, and a long-term commitment to investment in software process improvement. Since the subject of software automation is too large to treat comprehensively in one chapter, the emphasis here is on the considerations involved in producing and implementing a software process automation strategy and plan.

18.1 The Need for Software Automation

If history is any guide, we face a long-term, insatiable demand for larger and higher-quality software systems. To this point, this book has dealt with the problems of improving the way people implement the software process. Once all these improvements are in place, however, what then? There will always be potential procedural improvements, but progress will likely grow more difficult with each step.

At present, software development is a human-intensive process with all the limitations that implies. For example, people can only do things so fast. We accept the four-minute mile as near the limit of human capability and see the three-minute mile as beyond human aspiration. There are similar limits with software, but they are not as clear. While human capabilities do seem to improve with time, such improvements are only gradual. Clearly, our hopes must rest on some new conceptual view of our tasks or on the use of more powerful tools.

In sum, once we remove the basic frictions and human inefficiencies in our process, we will still be faced with inherent human limitations. To make continued improvements, therefore, we must increasingly rely on technology. Improved tools and methods have been helpful throughout the history of software, but once we reach Level 5 (Optimizing Process), we will be in a far better position to understand where and how technology can help.

In advancing from Level 1 (Chaotic Process), major improvements were made by simply turning a crowd of programmers into a coordinated team of professionals. Perlis put it best in 1968 when he said that:[13]

> We kid ourselves if we believe that software systems can only be designed and built by a small number of people. If we adopt that view this subject will remain precisely as it is today, and will ultimately die. We must learn how to build software systems with hundreds, possibly thousands of people.

This is the key challenge faced by chaotic software organizations: how to coordinate the creative work of their professionals so they support rather than interfere with each other.

Software process management provides a framework for progressively improving the orderliness of our work. By moving from the Initial (Level 1) to the Repeatable (Level 2) and then the Defined (Level 3) process, we have established the commitment framework needed to coordinate large operations. By using a structured, managed, and planned process, our professionals will better understand their roles and their interrelationships. The defined software process will then facilitate more rational reactions to surprise.

Once such orderly performance has been achieved, improvements will continue, but they only will be incremental. At some point the professionals will be using the process about as effectively as they know how to, and yet we will still need further quality and productivity improvements. When this point is reached, how can we expect to make further improvements, and what limitations will we ultimately face?

In the next decade quality demands will increase by not just 2 or 3 or even 10 times but by closer to factors of 100 or even 1000. For productivity, we will need factors of 10 to 100 times, with demands for much more. While quality improvements alone will yield greater productivity, history suggests we will need improvements of these levels just to match society's demands for added software capability.[7]

While it does not now seem likely that such enormous quality and productivity improvements can be achieved, the demand will likely grow far more rapidly than our capability. Even though there is no clear best strategy on how we should proceed, it appears that the greatest likelihood for major improvement will come through a combination of approaches. By progressively automating more and more of those tasks that are now done manually, we will not only increase productivity and quality but we will also enrich the roles of the professionals, free them from much of their current drudgery, and make more of them available for more creative work.

While automation of our current process will help, it is unlikely to get us very far by itself. We will also need to couple automation with improved process concepts for managing our work and our work products. Through the power of automated environments, we should be better able to relate to and to capitalize on the work of others. The need is for better ways to characterize software objects, better processes for controlling and relating them, and more powerful ways to access and manipulate them. This combination of method, process, and automation should enable software professionals to finally start down the same path that has fueled four centuries of scientific progress. While reuse has long been more of a hope than a promise, the greatest opportunity for dramatic productivity and quality improvement will be through improved ways to build new software on the progressively richer foundation of previously produced products. We will then, to paraphrase Isaac Newton, be able to build our products on the achievements of our predecessors.[8] Making this dream a reality will require a creative combination of method, process, and technology.

There is also the potential for significantly improving the way the software process is supported. By making current tools more consistent and integrating them into a common environment, we will move beyond task support to supporting the full life cycle. As these environments grow more sophisticated, we can expect substantial improvement in their ability to manage and guide the execution of individual tasks so they each better relate to the total. Any large software project is performing a complex process, and it is often difficult to know which steps are most appropriate at any point. Data gathering and analysis also require support both to make them more economical and accurate but also to assist in process management. While automated support for these needs will come only gradually, organizations should take early steps to develop a software process support strategy. This will provide a framework for orderly and steady improvement.

18.2 What to Automate?

Much has already been done to provide automated support for individual software development tasks. This classical approach has produced many tools that effectively support parts of the software process. Henderson and Notkin have described several ways that computers can help with these problems:[5, 14]

- □ Automating the menial tasks, such as ensuring that object code compilation includes the right contents, prerequisites, and conditions
- □ Maintaining consistency among the requirements, the design, and the code
- □ Providing a full range of interactive tool capabilities for the programmers
- □ Providing environmental support for project management, version control, and incremental programming

These basic capabilities are needed and should help, but they don't reach as far as Freeman and Winograd suggested in their prescient articles in the early 1970s.[3, 17] Winograd suggested attacking the software problem by developing an "Intelligent Assistant." This facility would draw inferences from accumulated process and product data to perform tasks such as the following:

- □ *Error checking* By being aware of language context, the system would identify errors as they were made. This would permit the programmer to react in real time rather than waiting possibly hours or even days for a compiler or test to indicate errors.
- □ *Question answering* Anticipating the impact of possible actions, such as what modules would be affected by a change, or what objects of this type have been created.
- □ *Trivia* Programmers today are forced to handle many details that should not concern them, such as completing standard command sequences.
- □ *Debugging* Again, an Intelligent Assistant could provide substantial help by finding the routine that set a value or tracking the execution sequence just prior to an event.

While we cannot expect to replace creative programmers and managers by automated tools, we certainly can develop far more capable support systems. There are many opportunities for such intelligent assistance that are well beyond the level of mere task support. Some examples are:[1, 9, 10]

- □ Defining the conditions that must be satisfied before some action is taken. For example, have all unit test fixes been incorporated before entry into integration test?
- □ Forward or backward chaining to maintain implementation consistency. One such situation is the identification of all program versions to which a fix applies.
- □ Checking and exposing the side effects of potential actions. A change in message format, for example, could affect all programs that must interpret the message.
- □ Building logs and data records of process transactions. This involves the tracking of time spent, defects found, or changes made, for example.

□ Providing symptomatic assessments of software process data. It would be helpful, for example, to have a ready summary of the error or change history and trends for every module as well as detailed status against plan.

Such sophisticated support extends beyond individual tasks and recognizes that the management and coordination of the software process are generally at least as complex as the design, implementation, and test. As Perlis points out, the problems of large-scale software development are not task-oriented.[13] They stem from software complexity and large numbers of human interactions. As shown on the left side of Fig. 18.1, the software process is traditionally viewed as a single thread of tasks. With today's larger systems, however, we are dealing with the situation on the right. At the highest design level, the system is subdivided into multiple components that are further subdivided into modules. These modules are then individually implemented, unit tested, and progressively integrated into larger aggregations leading up to a final system test.

If every decision made in this process were completely correct, and if all of these elements could be truly independent of all the others, the software process would be relatively simple. Unfortunately, that is rarely the case. Design decisions are frequently changed, interfaces are incomplete, requirements are modified, test corrections affect the design, and so forth. Because of this hierarchy of interrelationships, the number of interactions among tasks can be enormous. The problem of tracking all these items and ensuring that they are completely and properly handled can rapidly exceed the capacity of any manual system. When it is necessary to maintain consistency between every requirement, design, and implementation element, the job approaches the superhuman.

18.3 Development Environments

A software environment is the full set of facilities that support the programming process. Stenning describes the fundamental role of an environment as supporting the effective use of an effective process.[15] Installing an environment is thus not the way to establish an effective process but it can serve to make an effective process more efficient. As our systems grow larger, these environments will more completely integrate the support for each separate task into a support framework for the entire process. Since an increasing number of software tasks span multiple development phases, these separate activities must be handled in a consistent way. Environments should thus have certain basic characteristics:[15]

□ The environment must be convenient to use. Among other things, convenience requires consistent user interfaces.

□ We must be able to customize the environment to provide support for entire organizations as well as specific projects.

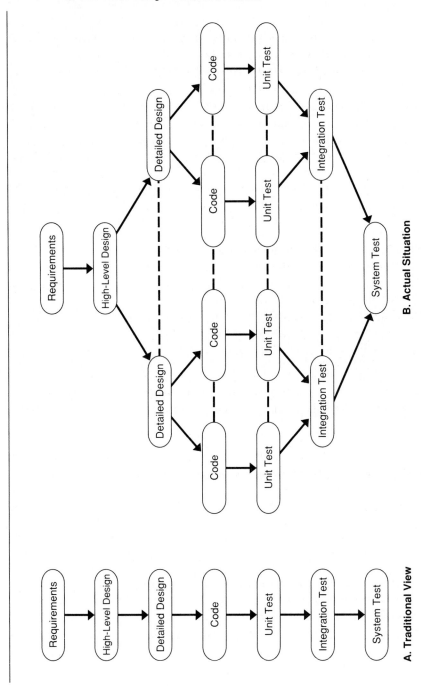

FIGURE 18.1
The Large System Development Process

- ☐ The environment architecture must be open and capable of evolving with the needs of the projects and the advent of new tools and methods.
- ☐ It must support technical development, project management, configuration management, and Quality Assurance.
- ☐ While the environment may be implemented incrementally, its overall architecture must provide for longer-term needs.
- ☐ The environment should provide for strict enforcement of a liberal process. That is, while the programmers need considerable latitude in what they do, the environment motivates a disciplined way to do it.
- ☐ The environment must have a comprehensive conceptual schema that encompasses the database, process data, tool interfacing, and environment evolution.

The environment is thus a comprehensive system of facilities and tools that share a data model and user facilities.[4, 6, 16] This has a number of implications:

1. Such comprehensive environments will likely be very large, possibly rivaling or even surpassing the largest current operating systems.
2. They will thus be so expensive to build and support that their development must evolve through many incremental versions.
3. This implies concurrent development by multiple vendors and suggests multiple de facto levels of structural and interface standardization.
4. Because of their evolutionary nature, environments will develop gradually, there will be many false starts, and premature standardization could easily constrain innovation.
5. When standardized environments become generally available, individual tools will be greatly simplified, thus accelerating more rapid software process automation. Since tools need no longer provide their own databases, user interfaces, system interfaces, and process controls, they can support smaller and simpler micro functions. These micro tools can then be used more generically throughout the software life cycle.

18.4 Organizational Plans to Automate

The automation of an organization's software process must start with an understanding of the current process and its support status. Improvement plans and goals are then established. In developing these automation plans, certain basic principles should be observed:

1. Determine the support time frame for the planned environment (e.g., it will handle the operation for at least five years).

2. Build this environment on commercially available tools and methods.

3. Do not use any tools or methods that are not proven to be at least as robust as the products they are to support.

4. Place highest priority on those activities that people do least well. Put lowest priority on those things that currently are being handled most effectively.

5. Start with the currently installed environment (even if it is manual) and develop a plan to evolve.

6. Establish a detailed plan that includes training, installation, conversion, and support.

7. Commit sufficient resources to do the entire job.

There are many different ways to plan for process automation, as well as a number of conflicting forces. Historically, attention has been largely focused on automating the middle of the software process. There is thus less need to provide additional support for implementation. It is, however, not uncommon for an organization to have generally adequate implementation tools but to find a few projects struggling with archaic facilities. This can happen, for example, if they are developing for a specialized target machine, using a poorly supported development system, or working on fixes and enhancements to a previously developed system. These undersupported groups can best be identified by making an inventory of the support tools used by every project in the organization.

The front end of the process is one area where early attention can produce important benefits. Tools and methods can be used for precisely representing requirements and specifications and simple labeling techniques can help in tracking requirements through the development cycle. With the strong research and advanced development interest in analyzers, simulators, and prototyping methods, these areas should be explored to identify potentially useful tools and methods. The quality of the early work in the software process often limits the success of the total project, so tools to help this phase can pay big dividends. Tool support for the front end of the process should consider the following three general areas of need:

- Assistance in ensuring that each requirement is understood. This can involve improved representation methods as well as prototyping.

- Means to understand the implications of a given requirement. Here, analyzers, simulators, and prototypes can be helpful.

- Ways to ensure that some requirement is not forgotten and either not implemented or not tested. This can be done by tracking the allocation of each requirement throughout development and ensuring the traceability of every function and test case back to its source requirement.

As systems grow larger, it is easy for people to become confused, misunderstand, or forget. Since such problems with the requirements can have disastrous consequences for the rest of the program, even simple tool support for the initial process phases can pay big dividends later.

The back end of the process needs automatic support because it typically involves the highest costs and has the greatest risk of lost control. While library management systems are generally used for code control, broader support for testing, packaging, maintenance, and documentation is urgently needed. This area should receive high priority both because it is so critical to product quality and because large resources are typically involved. As more tools and aids are used to support the development environment, it is also important to apply the same configuration management rigor to them, both to protect the tool assets themselves and to permit later determination of problem cause and prevention.

An overriding need for most projects is tool and environment support for process management. For maturity Level 1 (Initial) and 2 (Repeatable) organizations, this involves the traditional planning, estimating, and tracking functions of typical project management tools. At higher maturity levels, there are additional needs for instrumentation and database support (see Chapter 15). Because even modest-sized projects can generate large amounts of data, automated data acquisition, management, and analysis facilities are essential.

18.4.1 The Long-Term Automation Plan

The basic steps required to establish a long-term automation plan are:

1. Establish an Automation Focal Point. This involves naming an individual to lead the study and planning efforts. Where possible, this responsibility should be in a group with the requisite skills and resources to assist in the work. It is often wise initially to establish this responsibility within the Software Engineering Process Group (see Chapter 14).

2. Next, define current automation status, establish immediate priority needs, and gather information on pertinent available tools and methods. The information gathering should involve a comprehensive inventory of the tools currently used by the projects. In defining status and establishing priorities, a structured assessment methodology such as that proposed by Firth et al. can help to clarify the similarities and differences between projects.[2]

3. An orderly assessment is next made of the most promising available environments and tools.

4. Establish a strategic plan for environmental support. This plan should typically focus at least five years in the future and identify both the host and target systems to be supported and the environment that is tentatively selected. If an environment is not visible several years in advance of the planned need, it is

unlikely to be sufficiently robust or comprehensive to be of much value to the development groups.

5. Define a migration plan to take the organization from its current support systems to the strategic environment. This plan should identify the key transitions and support capabilities over a period of five or more years.

6. While this long-term planning will require considerable time and effort, it is needed to provide a clear framework for selecting suitable interim tool sets and migration plans. Without such preparation, frequent environment changes and tool conversions are likely.

18.4.2 Implementing an Automation Plan

Following acceptance of these planning recommendations, the needed steps are:

1. An implementation support group is established to handle the ordering, vendor negotiations, installation, conversion, operation, and support for the environment. These tasks are typically an expansion of the normal data processing department's role.

2. A more detailed automation plan is developed. This is done by the implementation support group under the guidance of the Automation Focal Point and it includes the same level of detail and sign-off required for a product plan.

3. Next, specific project automation objectives and plans are developed, consistent with this overall plan. The need is to get each project's commitment to the direction rather than to start them on immediate implementation. At least one major project must start implementation immediately, however, or the automation plan will never happen. If some of the shorter-term projects choose not to migrate, they should at least establish follow-on plans. If none of the longer-term projects is willing to convert, however, the automation plan should be reexamined and possibly revised with stronger project participation.

4. Each project then develops a specific migration plan with agreed responsibilities and milestones for each key transition step.

5. As part of this plan, conversion is treated as the single most important issue. If the automation plan cannot safely and efficiently move each project to the new environment, it will never be implemented. Implementation will generally require gradual conversion and parallel operation. Often many special facilities or ad hoc implementations are required to ensure that no project is seriously at risk. While these steps may not be architecturally attractive, they are often the price required to obtain agreement from the major users. When project managers have millions of lines of code on old systems, they will not willingly make any changes that even slightly risk the integrity of their systems.

6. The new environment will require the programmers to change the ways they work. Since usability is akin to familiarity, the system will not initially appear usable to anyone, particularly if it is not properly introduced. Successful introduction requires orderly training and hands-on practice sessions, knowledgeable instructors, and expert assistance.

18.4.3 Advanced Environment Planning

In preparing for migration to a more comprehensive development environment, two additional topics should be handled by the central focal point group. These concern a common data model and a common user interface.

The common data model for the software environment defines the naming conventions and notations used by the entire organization. If these are not thoughtfully established to cover the needs of all the key projects and activities, it will later be difficult to make the changes needed to accommodate new projects or to relate their data to all of the rest. The development of a common data model for the organization must be a continuing effort, and interim results must be documented, circulated, and maintained under baseline control. An organizational owner must also be established to handle conflicts and answer questions and concerns. These latter are best handled with an architectural review committee that meets periodically to handle issues and to document changes and clarifications.

A common user interface is required so that the various tools and facilities are consistently represented to the users. If the current environments consist of collections of stand-alone tools, there are likely many different command languages, screen formats, function key assignments, and help facilities. While it is probably not possible to make sense out of all these disparate facilities, it is important to establish a direction and to gradually converge on a reasonably coherent and convenient interface strategy. The development of a common user interface is again a continuing activity that includes basic system procedures and protocols as well as the traditional command structures, naming conventions, and screen formats. While some of this work will have to wait until the initial environment and tool set have been selected, an early start helps in the environment selection and migration planning. Interface development is handled in much the same way as the data model, except that interface prototyping may be needed to reach final agreement on some items. Even then, the interface will generally be inadequate when first used and will have to be revised periodically. With experience these revisions will be progressively less drastic.

18.5 Technology Transition

In all this planning, it is essential to recognize the natural inertia in the organization. Not only are people generally reluctant to change their working habits, but the projects typically face challenging schedules that leave them little room to do studies or to migrate to new tools or environments. While many of these issues were discussed in Chapter 2, it is important to reemphasize the need to involve the technical professionals and their managers. They must agree that a change is needed, that the strategy makes technical sense, that the plan meets their needs, and that they are willing and able to do the required work. While senior management backing is essential, so are extensive planning, persuasion, training, and support.

18.6 Special Considerations

Within these broad guidelines, there are several special considerations for planning, installing, and using support environments. For example, should a standard environment be purchased, or would custom tailoring make more sense? And, since newer and better environments will be available in the future, why focus on this issue now? Many organizations also face skill shortages and are properly concerned about their ability to handle such sophisticated systems. Without adequate skills, there is also the risk of making a mistake. Finally, several factors should be considered in determining the scope and operational practices for such systems. These questions are discussed further in the following sections.

18.6.1 Commercial Systems

An important special consideration is the use of commercial systems. Regarding environments, software organizations are of two types: those that have to deliver products and those that do not. These latter groups typically have a research or advanced development charter that allows them the time and resources to develop experimental environments and to pioneer their early use. This is the only way adequate prototypes and early experience can be obtained. On the other hand, *organizations that must deliver products must stick to proven commercially available supported environments.*

Environments will likely become the largest, most sophisticated, and most expensive facilities to be developed by the software industry. Because of their enormous functional range and their extreme requirements for performance, security, usability, portability, flexibility, and capacity they may ultimately dwarf the largest operating systems in both scope and complexity. Organizations that are not in the business of developing and enhancing large-scale operating and support systems should thus not attempt to develop and maintain their own environments. While they may have some initial successes, they will soon become trapped by the limited capability of their own special system and be faced with the need for large resources to continue enhancing their own system or to migrate to a commercial one.

To achieve the widest use, commercial software environments will be designed to be as general purpose as possible. This implies facilities that are independent of the host and application systems. Once these systems are installed, their users' software operations will become totally dependent on them. This means they will have long useful lives and that their development and maintenance costs will be substantial.

18.6.2 Timing

Special timing considerations must be taken into account by each organization contemplating automation. Even when a suitably robust general-purpose commercial environment is identified, each organization must plan for gradual installation, conversion, and migration. This does not mean that they should wait for the commercial development and introduction of appropriate facilities before they start planning. The longest lead time items in moving to a comprehensive environment are planning, skill development, and migration. As more is learned about the software process and its support needs, a growing volume of increasingly suitable facilities can be expected. Without a sound long-term plan organizations will have no way to know which will best meet their overall needs.

Automation, of course, includes a wide spectrum of considerations. The organization's automation plan should start with the current facilities and migrate through a sequence of gradual changes. This sequence involves developing the necessary skills, planning the conversions, and supporting the migration of each project. By starting with an assessment of the organization's current automation status and reviewing commercially available facilities, a series of intermediate automation stages can be defined.

Other early steps include detailing the initial protocols and procedures to be supported and defining the major elements of the organization's data model. These steps require the involvement of many skilled people from all parts of the organization over a period of many months. Organizations with no prior experience with such work, however, could require several years to build the needed expertise and to do the work. Since these actions must be taken before any commercial environment can be sensibly procured and installed, they should be started as early as possible.

18.6.3 Skills

The biggest single problem for most organizations is the lack of suitably experienced professionals to do this technical planning work. This lack is compounded by the fact that very few such people exist and even fewer are being trained. Organizations thus generally have to develop their own skills.

While skill development is a substantial job, a few experienced professionals with suitable software engineering or computer science backgrounds can rather quickly assess the current state of an organization's software support facilities. Within the constraints of the current projects and the installed computer systems there will likely be relatively few available environments or tool sets to consider. Using a suitable evaluation method, they can then assess these options to see which best meet their needs.

After this background assessment, it is wise to install an early environment on an experimental basis both to learn about the product itself and to gain experience with the installation, training, conversion, and support issues. This will both provide detailed knowledge of the proposed system and help the organization develop the skills to intelligently plan for full conversion and support.

18.6.4 Caveat Emptor

Buyer beware! The first environment you buy will not work, and the second won't do what you want or need! It is essential to move toward automation, but at least until this business matures, blind leaps will be expensive. While these assertions are pure speculation, experience with prior software disasters suggests the following general guidelines for obtaining and installing a software support environment:

□ If you don't have the skill to understand it, you are not ready to buy it!

□ If the organization selling the environment is not using it for its own work, don't even think about trying it!

□ Once you have found the best available system for your needs, install it on an experimental basis.

□ Until you have actual experience using the environment to build and test experimental software, don't rely on it for a committed product.

While these guidelines may seem conservative, it is wise to act as if a serious problem with your environment will shut you down. *It will!*

18.6.5 Tool Complexity

By permitting reduced tool complexity, environments offer some exciting opportunities. The most powerful advantage of general-purpose environments is process flexibility. At present the software process is constrained by the blunt instruments we use for tools. While we think of compiling, testing, and editing as individual tasks, each of them is really a composite of several micro tasks. A compiler, for example, might be viewed as doing lexical processing, syntax processing, semantic processing, optimization, and code generation.[11] Because each of our current tools typically provides its own operational facilities, data model, and user interface, it is impractical to build tools that merely handle a code update, parse a small code fragment, or optimize a code segment. What this means is that, in spite of our interactive computing systems, many of our software tools continue to constrain us to batch thinking.

With the advent of integrated environments we will finally be able to move to interactive software engineering. Rather than being forced to execute an entire string of operations, for example, we can dynamically execute the particular micro tasks required. For example, instead of recompiling a program just to check its syntax, we can syntax check individual program segments or changes. This has several important consequences:

1. A fully functional development environment must include a common data model, standard intermediate representations, standard user interfaces, standard system interfaces, and standard system protocols and procedures. While each organization must develop many of these context definitions to meet its own needs, the architectures of commercially supported environments should guide and facilitate this work.

2. Within this context, tasks are handled as individual entities with clean external couplings.

3. The definition and automation of these micro tasks is far simpler than for the larger entities of today.

4. This simplicity enables programmers to implement private aids far more economically than with typical current support facilities.

5. Because these individual aids will be relatively self-contained and somewhat further removed from unique operating and computer system characteristics, they will likely be easier to port to other applications and environments.

6. Where today the creative energies of software professionals are spent producing special aids for their private use, standard environments will permit us to capitalize on this work for the benefit of the organization and even the entire industry.

This means that the advent of such large-scale, architected, general-purpose environments will unleash a level of software innovation that will likely surpass our wildest dreams.

18.6.6 Control Versus Support

A final special consideration is the issue of control versus support. Stenning points out that "most of the processes used in the software industry would be completely unworkable were it not for human ingenuity and flexibility."[15] In implementing software process environments we must recognize that no one is smart enough to define precisely what should be done in even relatively small parts of the software process. We must be careful that the imposition of constraints and controls always leaves room for exceptions and escapes. Strong facilities are needed for such items as protection, recovery, change authorization, and promotion control, but even these will need management-authorized escapes. Within these fundamental constraints the system should permit wide latitude on what tasks are performed, when, and how.

Regarding individual tasks, considerable flexibility should again be allowed, as long as the basic constraints are observed. An example is the measurements required before a task can be completed. All such items must be examined periodically to ensure that process automation assists the people rather than unduly constraining them.

This flexibility issue also extends to the projects. At least for the foreseeable future, every project will have its own variant process that is supported by a customized environment. Some process options will be established by the organization, some by the project, some by the programming team, and some by the individual programmers. If automated process environments are to be fully effective, they must permit individual programmers to set many of their own private parameters. After some experience with a quantified process, the professionals will best understand those guides, constraints, hints, and facilities that are most helpful to each of them. Since these will change with the tasks and with the programmer's experience, they must be readily adjustable. Ultimately, perhaps, such systems will heuristically adapt to individual demands, but for the near term, personal manual control is essential.

18.7 Productivity

In studies at the Software Engineering Laboratory of the NASA Goddard Space Flight Center, McGarry has measured the value of software technology support.[12] He used a technology index to correlate the degree of modern tool and method usage with project productivity and quality. As shown in Fig. 18.2, he found a high correlation between quality and the technology index but no correlation with productivity.

On reflection, this result should not be too surprising. First, there is an undoubted impact of quality on productivity, but so many other factors are involved that this impact is hard to isolate. This is particularly true when organizations have relatively low process maturity, since there are wide variations in their management and technical methods. As the software process matures, these variations will likely decrease and the economic factors will be easier to distinguish.

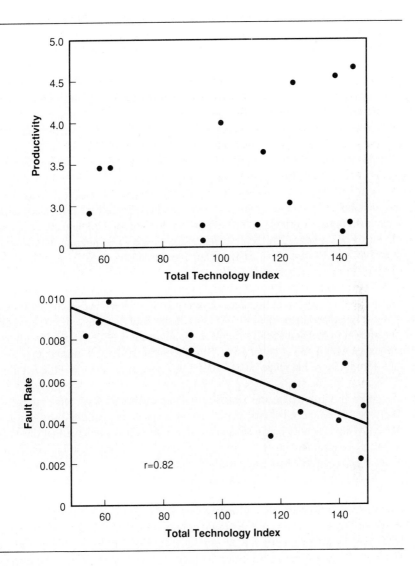

FIGURE 18.2
Technology Index Versus Productivity and Quality [12]

McGarry's inability to demonstrate the productivity advantages of tools and methods is disappointing to those of us who must justify their acquisition. This, however, is not a new problem. Using productivity data to justify tools is a "what if" exercise. We are trying to demonstrate how productive the organization is by comparing it to how it would have been without the particular new tool or method.

In the absence of statistically valid data from a large number of controlled experiments, we must always compare a fact with an opinion. Unfortunately, when dealing with senior executives, it is their opinions that count the most.

With complex processes such statistical studies are often futile. They are like trying to economically justify rear wheels on an automobile. Since one can clearly demonstrate that the car would be useless without rear wheels, the entire value of the automobile could be apportioned to the rear wheels. The same could also be done for the gas tank, steering wheel, and brake pedal. Essential facilities interact, and their values can not be separated. Since there is no way to use the automobile without any one of them, the only valid approach is to use one's best judgment to make an economic allocation.

With the software process the problem is similar. There are far too many interdependent factors to permit controlled studies. Even if we used the identical team to do the same job in two different ways, their second implementation would obviously be influenced by the first. So, unless we are willing to run a large number of carefully measured statistical tests, any measurements we take can only provide support for our own best judgment.

This problem of economic justification can best be illustrated by considering the case with high-level languages. Even though we have had such facilities for many years, there are no definitive studies demonstrating their value. Why is this? The answer is that statistically sound economic studies of the value of high-level languages would be very expensive. Since it could easily cost more than learning and introducing a language and buying a new compiler, there is little economic motivation for the study.

With environments, the situation will be different. Over time, these will likely be the single most expensive capital investments software organizations make. While it is not clear what such systems will cost, I believe that ultimately software environment costs will exceed the costs of the organization's other software, computing systems, and terminals combined.

Most software professionals can generally obtain approval to purchase a software package for a few hundred dollars. While they may have to answer some questions, a little arm waving and technical mumbo jumbo generally suffice. When the costs mount to a few thousand dollars, a manager's approval is required, but again, as long as he or she agrees, arm waving will generally win the day. When the costs rise much beyond this, hard data will be required. The question then becomes what data and how can it be presented to win approval?

There are several ways to get large expenditures approved in dollar-conscious industrial organizations:

□ Use the testimony of a recognized outside expert. This is not a very reliable method and will not alone suffice when the costs reach a million dollars or more. Since it will be some time before environments reach that financial stratosphere, the expert route will likely be adequate for the near term.

- ◻ The leading competitor has one. This is almost foolproof. Unfortunately, it requires a competitor who is willing and able to be first. At least for that competitor, this returns us to the previously unsolved problem.

- ◻ The contract requires it. Here the odds favor agreement to get an environment. If history is any guide, however, the environment will be provided as government furnished equipment (GFE) and it will not be ready at contract start time. Unfortunately, this also often means that a reliable and fully functional environment will not even be ready at contract completion.

- ◻ Develop an economic justification.

The last method requires work, but it can be brought off. Some of the steps to do this successfully are:

1. Develop a task map for the technology currently being used and another task map for the planned technology.

2. Identify the current resource expenditure profiles for each task. These numbers must be reviewed and accepted by the leading project managers.

3. Assemble a team of experts to determine the resource impact of the new environment and its associated support tools and methods. This determination considers the likely quality consequences at each process stage, using the techniques outlined in Chapter 17. It should also be done in the same level of detail as the task maps. When completed, these are also reviewed with the project managers and their leading technical people. Their comments and suggested changes are incorporated before proceeding.

4. Review each project's migration plan to determine the accrual rate of these savings.

5. Obtain each project's commitment to this savings schedule, together with their agreement to adjust their project plan accordingly. This will not be easy, but it is the only way to convince finance that this investment is worthwhile.

6. Establish a new schedule of estimating factors for project planning, as described in Chapter 6.

7. Construct a composite savings schedule for the organization as a whole.

8. With this justification, request management approval for the plan.

This work is impossible without the support of the project managers. Even with their support, it will be hard to sell cost-conscious senior managers on a major investment that does not directly increase revenue. With enough support and persistence, however, the case can be made.

18.8 Justification Considerations

In generating an economic justification, some special considerations should be kept in mind:

- □ *Don't get too far out on a technological limb.*   Stick to practical and achievable improvements. It is essential to have conservative plans within an aggressive strategic framework. It may be helpful to describe the entire strategy, but only request approval and funding for the initial steps, emphasizing that early successes will form the foundation for succeeding funding requests.

- □ *There is no way to absolutely prove the economic value of a software environment.*   This, however, is generally true of any other capital investment.

- □ *Involve the financial people.*   A professional financial story takes a lot of work, but it will be far more convincing to the intended audience than a technical presentation.

- □ *Do the work in detail.*   While the detail will not be presented, a well-structured summary of the detailed results should be brought as back-up. Although it is rarely needed, a thick pile of back-up material builds the presenter's confidence and deters the most detail-minded financial executive.

- □ *Without line management's agreement and savings commitments, no approval is likely.*

- □ *It takes time to do it right,* but there is no shorter way.

18.9 Summary

The reason for automating the software process is to improve the quality and productivity of our work. Organizations need an automation strategy to guide their use of new methods and techniques. This requires knowledge of what is needed, awareness of what is feasible, and development of an orderly plan.

A software environment is the full set of facilities that support the efficient use of an effective process. It must be convenient to use, support customization, have an open architecture, and have a comprehensive conceptual schema that encompasses the database, process data, tool interfacing, and environment evolution.

The basic steps required to establish a long-term automation plan are: establish an Automation Focal Point, understand current automation status, make an orderly assessment of the most promising available environments and tools, start work on a common data model for the software environment, and establish a common user interface.

Next, develop an economic justification, starting with a task map for the technology currently being used and another for that planned. Then identify the resources currently expended by each task and assemble a team of experts to determine the resource impact of the new environment and its associated support tools and methods. Review each project's migration plan to determine the accrual rate of these savings, and get each project's commitment to this savings schedule, together with their agreement to adjust their plans accordingly. Establish a new schedule of estimating factors for project planning and construct a composite savings schedule for the organization as a whole. With this justification, request management approval for the plan.

Above all, involve the financial people, and do the work in detail. Without line management's commitment to these savings, no approval is likely. It takes time to do it right, but there is no shorter way.

References

1. Dart, S. A., R. J. Ellison, P. H. Feiler, and A. N. Habermann. "Software development environments," *IEEE Computer,* vol. 20, no. 11, November 1987.

2. Firth, R., V. Mosley, R. Pethia, L. Roberts, and W. Wood. "A Guide to the Classification and Assessment of Software Engineering Tools," Technical Report CMU/SEI-87-TR-10, Software Engineering Institute, Carnegie Mellon University, August 1987.

3. Freeman, Peter. "Automating software design," *Computer,* April 1974.

4. Haberman, A. N. "Tools for software system construction," *Software Development Tools,* Springer-Verlag, May 1979.

5. Henderson, P. B., and D. Notkin. "Integrated design and programming environments," *IEEE Computer,* vol. 20, no. 11, November 1987.

6. Hoffnagle, G. F., and W. E. Beregi. "Automating the software development process," *IBM Systems Journal,* vol. 24, no. 2, 1985.

7. Humphrey, W. S. "The IBM large-systems software development process: objectives and direction," *IBM Systems Journal,* vol. 24, no. 2, 1985.

8. Humphrey, W. S. *Managing for Innovation—Leading Technical People.* Englewood Cliffs, NJ: Prentice-Hall, 1987.

9. Kaiser, G. E., and P. H. Feiler. "Intelligent assistance without artificial intelligence," *Proceedings of COMPCON, Spring 87,* February 23–27, 1987, San Francisco, CA.

10. Kaiser, G. E., and P. H. Feiler. "An architecture for intelligent assistance in software development," *Proceedings, Ninth International Conference on Software Engineering,* March 30, 1987, Monterey, CA.

11. Lewis, P. M. II, D. J. Rosenkrantz, and R. E. Stearns. *Compiler Design Theory,* Reading MA: Addison-Wesley, 1978.

12. McGarry, F., S. Voltz, and J. Valett. "Determining software productivity factors in the SEL," *Proceedings of the 11th Annual Software Engineering Workshop,* NASA Goddard Space Flight Center, December 3, 1986.

13. Naur, P., and B. Randell. "Software Engineering," NATO Science Committee, October 1968.

14. Notkin, D. "The GANDALF project," *Journal of Systems and Software*, 5, p. 91–105, 1985.

15. Stenning, V. "On the role of an environment," *Proceedings, Ninth International Conference on Software Engineering*, March 30, 1987, Monterey, CA.

16. Wasserman, A. I. "The ecology of software development environments," in C. Jones, *Programming Productivity: Issues for the Eighties*, IEEE Tutorial EHO186-7, COMPSAC 81.

17. Winograd, T. "Breaking the complexity barrier (again)," *Proceedings ACM SIGPLAN-SIGIR*, Gaithersburg, MD., November 1973.

19

Contracting for Software

This chapter considers the issue of contracting for software. By thinking of the software process as a management contract, we can better differentiate its two fundamental parts: defining what is wanted and managing its development. Freeman suggests we assume a machine that will automatically produce a program once it is told what is wanted.[1] When viewed in this light, it is obvious that a precise specification is an essential prerequisite to effective software management. In the absence of such programming machines, we are also left with the task of ensuring the work is properly done.

19.1 Software Contracting

We can also view software contracting in terms of trust. How would buyers behave if they did not trust their vendors, doubted their competence, and believed in their own? Under these conditions, they would probably do the following:

1. Start with a very precise statement of what was wanted.

2. Insist on rigid standards and detailed documentation of every process step.

3. Require that each step be completed and approved before the next was initiated.

4. Demand a firm commitment at the outset.

411

This is essentially the Waterfall development process. While there is little question that the generally abysmal historical performance on many software contracts has led to such arm's-length relationships, this management system has been demonstrably ineffective. As process maturity improves, we should thus reexamine our management paradigm.

19.1.1 The Issue of Trust

Consideration of the issue of trust should not imply that software organizations are dishonest or that their managers or contracting officers suspect them of lying, cheating, and stealing. Trust, however, is a fragile attitude. It is established slowly and carefully and can evaporate quickly. The necessary conditions required for trusting someone sufficiently to become dependent on them are:

- □ *History*   They have either never done anything to cause you to distrust them, or, if they have, your most recent experiences are sufficiently positive to supplant these earlier concerns.
- □ *Understanding*   They know what you want them to do and you know that they know.
- □ *Awareness*   You know their work plan and are aware of their progress. Furthermore, they make sure that you know.

With software contracts these conditions rarely all exist at the same time. First, because of software's prior history, many managers and contracting agencies intuitively fear that things will go wrong. Even without supporting evidence, experience with software development has been so poor that we are all tarred with the same brush. Software managers or contracting agencies thus often start with at least a subconscious fear that the developers cannot be trusted to perform without close supervision and control.

During the contract, trust is established through effective performance. This, of course, involves the issue of awareness. To really trust people to perform, you must be aware of their progress. When you know their precise status against their plan, you can be reasonably comfortable the work is progressing satisfactorily. With software such status information is rarely available. One of the fundamental benefits of establishing a mature software process is that you can know precisely where you stand and you can keep your management properly informed.

19.1.2 The Trusting Software Contract

Trust is the foundation for an effective contract. Any good lawyer will tell you that if you can't trust your vendor, don't deal with him. Contracts that are not built on mutual trust rarely succeed. Even if you do trust your vendor implicitly, however, always keep one hand on your wallet. While trust is important, blind faith is not. There is, however, an enormous difference between an adversarial contract and one with a reasonable level of arm's-length protection.

Protection is at least as important with software development as with most other fields. First, so many variables and subtleties are involved that an unscrupulous vendor can deliver incompetent work with little risk of being caught, at least contractually. Second, most software tasks involve many requirements uncertainties, and a vendor with a sharp pencil can often make an exorbitant profit on the changes.

While there are a few untrustworthy operators in every field, it is unwise to base all contractual relationships on the assumption of vendor cheating. Some will surprise you, but the vast majority will not. If, however, the entire process is designed to block the few miscreants, it will be so badly warped that the honest shops will be hamstrung by constraints.

When a trusting relationship is assumed, the development process has a new degree of freedom. Requirements can be handled more rationally, and much expensive documentation is now unnecessary.

19.1.3 Auditing

Regardless of the level of trust, however, every project should be audited to ensure honest and competent performance. Without some kind of independent review, projects rarely perform with the discipline required. This is not because people are dishonest or slovenly but because the day-to-day pressures of software work are so enormous and the apparent efficiency of most shortcuts is so seductive. A policing system is thus needed to keep us consistently on our toes.

This auditing activity can also be used to check for unscrupulous behavior. This requires that the auditors be skeptical and ask to see clear evidence of project performance. As long as they behave this way, however, no one else needs to, and the contracting relationship can be a trusting one.

A higher level of software process maturity can greatly simplify this auditing process. The SQA organization, for example, can now largely focus on data analysis and interpretation. They can provide management with a precise picture of how the process is working and help in identifying potential trouble spots. They must, of course, continue to spot check the process data to verify that it accurately represents the work being performed.

19.1.4 Buyer and Vendor Competence

Once the issue of trust is resolved, the relative competence of the parties must be considered. The four basic cases are:

1. Both the vendor and buyer are technically competent.

2. The vendor is technically competent and the buyer is not.

3. The buyer is technically competent and the vendor is not.

4. Neither is technically competent.

When both the vendor and buyer are technically competent, a truly cooperative partnership is possible. The buyer can concentrate on defining needs, while the vendor focuses on implementing them. Both recognize the necessity of continually validating their work as the buyer's installation, conversion, training, servicing, and operational plans are progressively refined. Similarly, as design progresses, many product-related questions in these same areas must be considered. With an effective partnership, these improving levels of buyer and vendor knowledge support each other in producing a well-researched set of requirements. This means, of course, that the requirements are not completed until the design work is done and possibly not even until the system is installed and operational. The buyer here is clearly responsible for requirements but recognizes the need for their validation as more development knowledge is gained. The vendor is likewise responsible for development but also ensures that the evolving product continues to match the buyer's needs and that the buyer is regularly apprised of status and plans.

The case of a technically competent vendor and an incompetent buyer is more normal in professional situations. Buyers who are incompetent at software development are presumably competent about their own needs. When dealing with a surgeon or an architect, for example, we may be very concerned with the outcome, but few of us feel competent to direct their work. Once we find people we can trust we work closely with them to determine what needs to be done but we generally trust them to do their work their way.

With software this second case can be treated much the same as with case 1. The buyer again focuses on requirements, while the vendor supports this work by identifying those areas needing further definition before design can proceed. Again, complete buyer awareness of plans and status is essential.

The worst situation with case 2 is when the incompetent buyer directs the way the software job is done. Since most vendors have learned not to argue too strenuously with their customers, this generally results in much unnecessary vendor work and a buyer who is distracted from the essential job of requirements validation.

When the buyer is technically competent and the vendor is not, the first choice is to get a better vendor. If one cannot be obtained, the need is for a contract management process that ensures that each task is done precisely as the buyer directs. While this is not a desirable relationship, it is practical for simple tasks, even in software. It is not recommended, however, when much vendor ingenuity is required or when poor initial quality is unacceptable.

When neither the vendor nor the buyer is technically competent, the only practical choices are to either get a different vendor, get professional help, or defer the job.

19.2 Negotiating a Software Contract

With software it is rare to know in advance precisely what functions are wanted. There are exceptions, of course, as with small enhancements to existing programs, well-known technologies like sorts and compilers, or systems built to model existing entities, such as aircraft simulators. More typically the user wishes to implement some new function and doesn't know precisely how it will behave in actual use.

This lack of precise foreknowledge means that the functions, the operational procedures, and the interactions with other systems must all be worked out in detail. This is a crucial phase of the software process that is often given inadequate attention. The need is to establish an agreed upon conceptual description of how the system will actually be used in operation. If this operational concept is not developed at the outset, it is unlikely that the buyer and vendor can have an informed agreement on the requirements. The development of this operational concept can be a challenge because it involves people's habits, preferences, and capabilities. Few professional programmers, for example, can design an easy-to-use system for nontechnical users because they cannot conceive of the problems and confusions they will face. Any programmer knows, for example, that the command "EXECUTE" means to run the program. Few untrained operators, however, will select such a command without at least a tremor of concern.

The job of precisely defining the needed software functions is rarely simple, even if the system itself is. It is therefore generally impractical to start by contractually specifying every requirements detail. Some period of mutual exploration is needed before the buyer and vendor should even try to agree on the details of what is wanted.

Here is where the issues of trust and competence are most critical. When both sides operate at arm's length, their mutual desire for protection changes what should be a creative design process into a wary negotiation. This generally causes insistence on a premature commitment: unreasonable schedule demands, firm specifications, and strict acceptance criteria. A fixed-price contract for something that is not well understood either includes large safety factors or is an enormous gamble.

When such high-risk situations are mixed with competitive bidding, technical factors have less impact on the contract value than the relative desperation and competence of the bidders and the buyer. As long as the buyers can recognize technically incompetent bidders, the risks of an unrealistic proposal are reduced.

When they can't, however, the technical competence of the best suppliers often excludes them from the competition: They know too much to submit a low enough price to win.

19.3 The Principles of Effective Software Contract Management

In summary, the key criteria for successful software contracting are:

- ☐ The vendor must be trustworthy and technically competent.
- ☐ The buyer must be capable of identifying technically competent vendors.
- ☐ The contract presumes mutual trust.
- ☐ SQA and audit ensure honest and disciplined performance.
- ☐ Initially the highest-priority task is to arrive at agreement on what is to be produced, a plan to produce it, and acceptance criteria.
- ☐ It is recognized that the operational concept and the product requirements will evolve throughout the contract and that appropriate provisions will be made to handle the resulting scope and plan changes.

When the vendor is technically competent and can be trusted, the need for a technically proficient buyer is reduced. The one essential need, however, is the buyer's capability to recognize vendor competence. One need not be a software expert to do this, however, as long as competent advice is available and a well-structured evaluation method is used.[2] With this caveat, the principles of software contract management are essentially the same regardless of the buyer's technical competence:

1. *The basic system objectives are established at the outset.* These might deal with performance, reliability, function, compatibility, cost, size, usability, training, or service, for example. Without clear "goodness" criteria, it is almost impossible to make intelligent requirements trade-offs.

2. *Where specific functional requirements are known, they are stated.* When possible this is done in an operational concept document. Since the greatest danger is overstating requirements, poorly understood functions should be stated conceptually and not defined in detail until they are known with certainty. The most serious system development failures can generally be traced to incorrect requirements. The resulting system must then be scrapped or modified to produce a cobbled-up interim patchwork. This is the most expensive way to define requirements. To again quote Mr. Dooley, with requirements "it ain't so much what you don't know that hurts you as what you know that ain't so."

3. *A documented plan is produced for establishing and validating requirements against the stated objectives.* This includes, for example, prototypes, tests, reviews, experiments, surveys, or demonstrations. The plan answers the question: What must I do to *know* the requirements are correct before the system is completed.

4. *A joint requirements effort defines the system tasks with sufficient precision to permit design to start.* The key is to recognize that the requirements will not be completed until the design and development work is done.

5. *Before any prototype, model, or test is implemented, its objectives are clearly stated.* For example, what design decision am I validating against what requirement or objective, what will denote success, and how will it be determined?

6. *The full development process is defined,* including those process indicators that ensure contract performance.

7. *The project is implemented, tracked, audited, and assured.*

19.4 Managing Software Contracts

Assuming you have selected a capable vendor and you have worked out an appropriate understanding of what is to be done, you are left with the question of awareness. This is where software management typically breaks down, and there are several steps one can take to address this problem. Since the specifics of these steps depend on the maturity of the vendor's process, however, we first discuss the principles involved and then generally describe the management process for various maturity levels.

The key to effective software contract management is to focus on what is done rather than on the product being built. While the product design is certainly important, that is what vendors are paid to do. Since it is also their area of presumed expertise, your concern must be to ensure that they use due skill and diligence. If, however, you focus on analyzing their work products, you will waste everyone's time. The contractors are presumably more technically skilled than you, have more resources, and already know the design in detail. Your review of their specifications, design, or code will thus take an enormous amount of time and accomplish very little. Typically such "reviews" turn into "dog and pony shows" that have either of two results:

1. The vendors put on a dazzling display of competence and everyone leaves with a warm feeling that the product will be a success.

2. There are enough user representatives present to debate the details of the system's operational characteristics. The meetings then degenerate into long

discussions of specific user-related parameters. Often these issues are too many or too complex for resolution at the meetings, so follow-up reviews are scheduled.

The first result may be satisfactory, but more often it is a superficial "snow job" that papers over unresolved questions and concerns. The second case is actually preferred because it results in a better understanding of the needed system functions. The interesting point, however, is that neither case actually involves reviewing the design. All these debates generally concern external system characteristics.

While a better requirements definition is always desirable, there are better ways to achieve it than by specification, design, or code reviews. These are usually done too late in the program to permit simple changes anyway, and much time and effort have generally been wasted in detailing the wrong functions.

19.4.1 Developing Software Requirements

As discussed in Chapters 6 and 13, requirements development is both a negotiating and a creative process. This means that three parties should be involved:

- □ *The developers*   They know the technical issues, will generally know what is feasible, and can estimate the required development time and cost.

- □ *The users*   They know what is needed and how it is supposed to behave. As they debate alternative approaches with the developers, they will gain new insights on their problems and often completely change their views.

- □ *The contracting agency*   Since many software requirements are inherently unlimited, such creative debates must be tempered with the realism of affordability. While it is not wise to continually inject such concerns, each potential requirement must be reviewed to ensure it can be produced within available time and money.

The point is that as development proceeds, new information is gained that will likely affect the compromises already made. A desired function may turn out more costly than anticipated, an operational requirement may no longer appear critical, or the financial situation may change. If these changing trade-offs are not examined periodically, an optimum system solution is highly unlikely.

The next questions concern the form of these debates. Here, of course, the nature of the problems and the mix of skills and experience must be considered. There are several situations with different approaches:

1. *Experienced users and developers*   The most tractable situation is when an installed and operational system is being enhanced by the team that originally built it. It is, of course, also desirable to have the requirements negotiations involve users, designers, and contracting people who know and have experience with this specific system. Here, a relatively straightforward process of

producing and documenting traditional requirement statements, estimates, and plans will generally suffice.

2. *Inexperienced designers*   When either the users or the designers are not intimately familiar with the existing system, it is necessary to be more specific on the desired functions. With designers who are inexperienced with the application, a first draft of the user's manuals and installation and operational procedures will probably suffice. This set of operational concept documents should always be produced, reviewed, and agreed to before the full-scale development work starts. Prototypes or test implementations may, of course, be required to try a particular implementation approach. Since requirements reviews and approvals typically produce many surprises and changes, it is wise to defer major development investments until there is reasonably informed agreement on what is wanted.

3. *Inexperienced users*   When the users do not have detailed operational knowledge with the specific application being considered, paper requirements will no longer suffice, even for relatively modest enhancements. Here, in addition to the operational concept documents, it is absolutely essential to produce an operating prototype of the end user functions and conduct operational tests. While some form of simplified table-driven displays may be adequate, it is important to conduct a planned and instrumented series of simulated operational tests. These must be extensive enough to clearly demonstrate the usability of all the critical new functions in the anticipated environment.

19.4.2 Prototypes

The options are relatively clear in the case of enhancement to existing systems, but the choices are somewhat more complex for entirely new systems. Here, it is often necessary to build an operational prototype of the complete system and install it for trial use. While it might be argued that the time and cost of this prototype will delay the final system, experience shows that the actual lead time to a fully operational system is generally much less. When the users and designers really know what is wanted and the designers have already built a simplified operational version, a full development program is generally much less expensive and time-consuming. What is more, the product is much more likely to perform as desired when it is initially delivered!

While prototyping was discussed in some detail in Chapter 13, it is important to point out why prototypes are substantially easier to develop than full products:

□ *The amount of code is substantially less,* often only one-tenth as much. It is normal, for example, to build only the mainline code and ignore the unusual and pathological cases. Special provisions for error recovery, peak period demands, special checking, service aids, and help screens, for example, must be considered, but their implementation can often be deferred until full product development.

□ *The documentation needs are substantially less.*   While it is important to document the prototype's functions as well as the test and evaluation plan, the users of the prototype are known in advance, so documentation can be tailored to their unique needs. Similarly, there is no need for maintenance documentation, and the design documentation can be limited to that needed by the designers and implementers. Since software developers do change jobs, however, enough design documentation is needed so the prototype knowledge will not be lost or forgotten. Since the product of a prototype effort is knowledge, a new prototype effort is often required when an entirely new development team is involved.

□ *Testing can be tailored to the specific prototype environment and operational needs.*   This reduces the testing load by a large factor.

□ *Training can generally be limited to those people who will actually operate the prototype in the operational tests.*

Each prototype effort should conclude with a written report that states what was done, the results, their implications, and the degree to which the prototype's original objectives were met.

19.4.3 Managing the Software Process

Once agreement is reached on requirements, it is necessary to agree on a plan for the work and then to track progress against it. This plan may include documentation and approval of the requirements and it must include the needed verification that the work is properly done. For example, are steps taken to ensure that the requirements really meet the user's needs? Are there adequate provisions to ensure that the requirements are implemented in the design? Finally, on such parameters as performance, usability, maintainability, and recoverability, what steps will demonstrate that the product performs as desired?

The key to good development is knowledge. Unsubstantiated guesses made by the development team are almost invariably wrong. Insist on a plan that demonstrates the actual characteristics needed, and insist that this demonstration be made during design, when timely corrections are still possible.

A good example of the need for a demonstration plan is performance. Programmers often argue that they can't predict performance, but not to worry. Programmers who say this are almost always wrong. Performance degradations of 1000 times or more are common, and they come from poor design decisions. If performance is even a moderate concern, early fast-path prototypes or simulation models are essential. These can be built without excessive effort, and the knowledge they provide for subsequent design and validation is priceless.

These same considerations apply to all aspects of the development process. Unless the plan includes sufficient provisions for early prototypes or independent technical reviews that focus on the key parameters, they will invariably be inadequate, and expensive retrofit efforts will be needed.

19.4.4 Project Tracking Considerations

Once an agreed-upon development plan is in place, one needs to track performance against it. This involves several key considerations:

□ *The items being tracked should be a natural result of the development process.*   Software development is so complex that any effort to impose arbitrary measures will seriously impede the work. A mature development process produces many progress indicators, so there should be no need for specially generated measures, at least if the development plan suitably considers progress tracking.

□ *Tracking must be distinguished from reviewing.*   For tracking one wants clear evidence that a planned item is 100 percent complete. The successful completion of reviews is an important tracking indicator.

□ *The particular items to track and review depend on the plan.*   There is no magic set, other than what is needed to do the job correctly.

□ *The specific items to track and review depend on process maturity.*   With a mature process, one can increasingly rely on precise numerical measures.

19.4.5 Technical Reviews

Technical reviews should focus on how well the job is being done. Initially the most important reviews are for the requirements, the operational concept, and the development plan. The requirements and operational concept focus is to ensure that the right work is being done, and the plan review is to ensure that it is being done right. Some review examples are:

□ *Plan reviews*   Is the plan complete and signed off by all involved parties? Does it include adequate requirements and operational concept verification, and are the end users directly involved? Are all key parameters and functions validated early in the design phase or are steps taken to ensure that they can be adjusted later? Do these reviews include sufficiently knowledgeable people to ensure that the work is properly done? Does the plan identify a sufficient number of 100 percent completion checkpoints and progress measures to permit rate charting and tracking (see Chapter 6)?

□ *Have appropriate steps been taken to validate the requirements and operational concept?*   This may include functional documentation, early user's manuals, or prototypes, but it must involve knowledgeable end users who *know* what is needed.

□ *The high-level design must be reviewed to make sure that it properly represents the requirements and that structural issues have been adequately considered.* If the structural design of the software system is not competently architected, performance, maintainability, and testability will likely be adversely affected. The high-level design decisions will also determine the work allocation to development groups, the interfaces between product elements, the degree of functional interdependence, the ease of future modifications, and the isolation of bugs and fixes. The high-level design thus largely determines the cost, quality, and performance of the system. The development plan must allocate sufficient time, resources, and skills to high-level design and specify appropriate technical reviews and inspections.

□ *Reviews of detailed design, implementation, and test are all handled in much the same way.* The key is to ensure that adequate inspections are conducted and that suitable audits are held.

While the design and code inspections involve only technical people, the validation reviews must also include SQA and user representatives or outside experts. The resources and schedules for these reviews are also part of the development plan. The management concern is whether the inspections and reviews were done on time and involved the right people, and not with the technical details, which are best left to the inspection, review, and audit experts.

19.4.6 Quantitative Process Tracking

Quantitative process tracking is based on the rate charting approach described in Chapter 6. Each checkpoint must be a 100 percent completion indicator, with no credit for a partial job. Each item must also have a value measure that can be used to calculate its fraction of the total job. One way to do this is to break the total job into phases and allocate percents to each phase on the basis of planned programmer months. Within each phase some more detailed tracking can be done, using, for example, some of the following measures:

□ *Code size* An LOC measure can weight the value of each module completing design inspection, code inspection, or unit test. The total number of planned LOC is the base and the planned LOC for each module are used to determine the fraction of the job it represents. These weights, however, do not change as LOC estimates change, unless a new plan and schedule are produced. While the LOC or other counts indicate the relative scale of the work completed, it is the tests and inspections that ensure that the intended task was actually completed.

□ *Planned resources*   This measure uses programmer months planned for each task. This is the most appropriate measure when several activities have no common parameter like LOC or document pages. As with LOC, this measure is used to set a percentage value for each task and this value is not changed unless the project is completely replanned.

□ *Planned schedule*   The planned calendar time can be used in much the same way as programmer months.

□ *Number of modules completed*   It is generally wise to weigh this crude measure with the LOC for each module unless they are all roughly the same size.

□ *Tests successfully completed*   This is a valuable measure, but it must be used carefully. The definition of a test can be tricky, as can the measure of test success. A compiler test, for example, is only passed when the generated code executes properly, not when the compilation is completed without error. This measure is also of little value unless care is taken to ensure that a comprehensive set of tests is used as the basis for establishing the 100 percentage value.

□ *Number of defects found*   This is not a useful rate chart measure since it is not a known quantity in advance. While tracking the number of defects against the quality plan is important, it takes some analysis to determine whether a low number represents good product quality or poor inspections or tests.

19.4.7 Quality Tracking

While the specific quality indicators must be determined by the process definition and the quality plan, the approach for tracking quality is:

1. As described in Chapter 16, a quality plan is produced showing planned defect injection and removal rates, inspection coverage, and inspection efficiency.

2. Inspection coverage and removal rates are tracked for the entire product and for each of its components and modules (see Chapter 10).

3. Data on defect injection rates for each phase is accumulated as each defect is found and analyzed (see Chapters 16 and 17).

4. The number of modules falling outside of injection or removal rate control limits is identified and corrective actions initiated and tracked (see Chapters 15, 16, and 17). For example, if an excessive number of design problems are found during unit test, the module design inspection data are reexamined. If warranted, new design inspections are held.

5. Cumulative module inspection efficiency is tracked, and action plans are implemented for the out-of-limit cases. Examples are reinspections or retests (see Chapters 10, 15, 16, and 17).

6. At the conclusion of each test phase, the modules with excessive problems are noted. Depending on system criticality and module size, the reinspection and retest trigger point could be set at one or more system test defects (see Chapters 15, 16, and 17).

While these steps appear to involve many reinspections and retests, this is rarely the case. First, the mere existence of a quality plan results in more care at every process step. Second, when each module is reinspected or retested as soon as its problems are noted, code quality improves far earlier in the process, actually reducing total test time. Third, when every design and code change is inspected, total test problems are further reduced.

19.5 Process Certification

With improving process maturity it is possible to increasingly trust the development organization to follow an effective process. At maturity levels 4 and 5, for example, one can consider process certification:

1. The process is maintained under tight and well-defined statistical control limits.

2. All key process parameters are measured and tracked.

3. There is a sound and documented statistical foundation for sampling these process measures, conducting analyses, and generating reports.

4. In the event of a process "yield bust," aggressive action is taken to restore the process.

5. Records are retained of all yield busts and the actions taken to prevent their recurrence.

When such a yield bust occurs, a crisis team is formed to find and fix the problems. Sufficient data is retained so that process actions can later be devised to prevent their recurrence. This is also done whenever an out-of-limits error trend appears, either at design or code inspections or in test. But if several modules are out of the planned statistical range, special action is required. Until the problems are understood and fixed, the best development and SQA people should be devoted to the crisis team. Neither SQA nor the process group can possibly be staffed to fix all yield busts or to develop preventive actions for all problems. They can, however, be responsible for alerting management to the problems and leading the crisis action teams.

19.5.1 Managing the Low-Maturity Process

As stated earlier, the appropriate way to manage a software process depends on its maturity. For the Level 1 process, management essentially pushes them toward

Level 2. If they are at the bottom of the Level 1 scale with no established planning or management methods, it is best to find another development group. If this cannot be done, it is essential to impose discipline through contract or management edict. The critical steps are:

1. Install a management review system as described in Chapter 5. This involves senior management and ensures that plans are produced, approved, and tracked in an orderly way.

2. Insist on a comprehensive development plan. This must follow the basic outlines described in Chapter 6, including code size estimates, resource estimates by key Work Breakdown Structure items, and a schedule.

3. Set up a Software Configuration Management (SCM) function, as described in Chapter 7. This is crucial to maintaining control and must be in place and operational before completion of detailed design. As soon as possible, these functions are expanded to include requirements and design, as covered in Chapter 12.

4. As described in Chapter 8, ensure that a Software Quality Assurance (SQA) organization is established and sufficiently staffed to review a reasonable sample of the work products. Until there is evidence that the work is done according to plan, this is essentially a 100 percent review. With successful experience the sampling percentage can be reduced.

5. Following the principles outlined in Chapter 6, establish rate charts for tracking the plan, using the key plan milestones with their anticipated resource expenditures. Typical milestones are: requirements completed and approved, the operational concept reviewed and approved, high-level design completed and reviewed, percent of modules with detailed design completed, percent of modules through code and unit test. Similar rate charts can be established for each phase of test.

Until Level 1 organizations demonstrate their ability to perform to a plan, the traditional management systems should be retained, whatever they are. It is essential to ensure that any new management system is working before abandoning the old one.

19.5.2 Managing the Level 2 Maturity Organization

At the Level 2 maturity stage, the management process motivates the organization to improve its process maturity. The reason for motivating improvement rather than imposing it is that the organization is reasonably sophisticated and has many sound practices in place. In addition to the basic items already discussed for the low-maturity organization, the following items should be considered:

□ *Review SQA staffing to see that it is adequate to handle the anticipated review workload.*   While many software organizations have SQA functions, these are often so sparsely staffed that they can only review a miniscule percentage of the work. In one case a large and fairly competent military software contractor had an SQA group chartered to perform all the proper tasks, but it only had resources to review 3 out of approximately 300 detailed design records against standard. Not surprisingly, inconsistent detailed design was a source of later trouble.

☐ *Ensure the SCM function is used, not only to monitor contract deliverables but also for the ongoing development work.*   Many organizations are contractually required to establish an SCM function, but only to control final deliverable items. This is like locking the barn after the horse is gone. Loss of development control can often occur during development as well as during system and acceptance test (see Chapters 7 and 12).

☐ *Establish some key process and product standards,* such as design, coding, test, and inspection. The approach is as described in Chapters 9, 11, and 13.

☐ *Ensure that design and code inspections are instituted,* as described in Chapter 10.

☐ *Establish a Software Engineering Process Group (SEPG)* to lead this work, as described in Chapter 14.

Until the SEPG is established, the traditional management methods should be retained, at least in most cases. Once some of these key standards and methods have been introduced and are being monitored by SQA, it is wise to discontinue many of the prior control and review mechanisms and base the management tracking system on the approved development plans. While traditional specifications and reviews serve a useful purpose in low-maturity organizations, the combination of an SEPG, standard procedures and methods, SQA review, and rate tracking provide far better assurance that an effective job is being done.

19.5.3 Managing Organizations at Level 3 and Higher

At Level 3 and beyond, the organization is effectively managing its own process, and the basic oversight need is to ensure status awareness and to maintain an emphasis on further process improvement. The prime areas for focus are:

☐ Establish a comprehensive program of process measurement and analysis. This data is retained in the process database and used by SQA, the SEPG, and the project managers to monitor product and task quality.

☐ Ensure that suitably aggressive quantitative quality plans are established and tracked. When these plans are not being met, remedial action plans are required, as described in Chapter 16.

☐ Initiate a comprehensive defect prevention program, as described in Chapter 17.

□ Establish a strategy and plan for process environmental support, as described in Chapter 18.

19.6 Technical Leadership

With improving process maturity it is increasingly important for the managers and contracting officers to provide technical leadership. "A technical leader's most important role is to set goals and drive unswervingly to meet them."[3] The key to continually improving the software process is to have managers and contracting officers who set aggressive goals and stay actively involved in reviewing performance against them. Dr. Arthur Anderson, a retired IBM vice-president, used to say, "There is always room for improvement."[3] That is the way to manage the mature software process.

19.7 Summary

It is instructive to view the software process as a contract between management and the development organization. The principles of software contract management are essentially the same regardless of the buyer's technical competence: The basic system objectives are established at the outset; where specific functional requirements are known, they are stated. A documented plan is then produced for establishing and validating the requirements and the operational concept against these objectives, and a joint requirements effort defines the system tasks with sufficient precision to permit design to start.

Once an agreed-upon development plan is in place, performance is tracked against it. While the particular items to track and review depend on the plan as well as on process maturity, they should result naturally from the development process itself. With a mature process, one can increasingly rely on precise numerical measures.

Quantitative process tracking is based on rate charting, in which each checkpoint is a 100 percent completion item with no credit for partial completion. The quality indicators are determined by the process definition and the quality plan, and they are also tracked. With improving process maturity, it is possible to increasingly trust the development organization to follow an effective process. At maturity levels 4 and 5, for example, one can consider process certification.

With improving process maturity the need for technical leadership is increasingly important. "A techical leader's most important role is to set goals and drive unswervingly to meet them."[3] The key is to recognize that there is always room for improvement. That is the way to manage the mature software process.

References

1. Freeman, Peter. "Automating software design," *Computer*, April 1974.

2. Humphrey, W. S., and W. L. Sweet. "A Method for Assessing the Software Engineering Capability of Contractors," SEI Technical Report SEI-87-TR-23, September 1987.

3. Humphrey, W. S. *Managing for Innovation—Leading Technical People*. Englewood Cliffs, NJ: Prentice-Hall, 1987.

20

Conclusion

To make major process improvements software organizations need an overall plan, some dedicated process people, clear goals, and management's commitment to these goals. This chapter summarizes the basic prerequisites for changing an organization's software process and then discusses several of the questions groups often face in doing this work. Finally, several examples describe some actions organizations have taken to address many of these same issues.

20.1 A Framework for Software Process Change

The six requirements for software process change are:

1. *Sell top management*   Significant change requires new priorities, additional resources, and consistent support. Senior managers will not provide such backing until they are convinced that the improvement program makes sense.

2. *Get technical support*   This is best obtained through the technical opinion leaders. Every organization has a few technical professionals whose opinions are widely respected. When they perceive that a proposal addresses their key concerns, they will generally convince the others. On the other hand, when the technical community is directed to implement something they don't believe in, it is much more likely to fail.

3. *Involve all management levels*   While the senior managers provide the resources and the technical professionals do the work, the middle managers

make the daily decisions on what is done. When they don't support the plan, their priorities will not be adjusted, and progress will be painfully slow or nonexistent.

4. *Establish an aggressive strategy and a conservative plan*   While senior management will be attracted by an aggressive strategy, the middle managers will insist on a plan that they know how to implement. It is thus essential to be both aggressive and realistic. The strategy must be visible, but the plan must provide frequent achievable steps toward the strategic goals.

5. *Stay aware of the current situation*   It is essential to stay in touch with current problems. Issues change, and elegant solutions to last year's problems may no longer be pertinent. While important changes take time, the plan must keep pace with current needs.

6. *Keep progress visible*   People easily become discouraged if they don't see frequent evidence of progress. Advertise success, periodically reward the key contributors, and maintain enthusiasm and excitement.[5]

20.2 Managing Resistance to Software Process Change

Resistance to change is normal and can be handled by the methods outlined in Chapter 2. It is also wise to anticipate the common questions that concern managers and professionals. Many of these may be simple requests for information, but some are almost unanswerable and are often intended to derail the change effort. Regardless of the motivation these questions should not be ignored or brushed off. The next several paragraphs discuss the following questions:

- □ What makes the process maturity model right?
- □ Why should we have an SEPG?
- □ Why can't Software Quality Assurance do the SEPG job?
- □ As my process improves, do I need to retain SQA?
- □ Why is defect prevention so important?
- □ What is the financial return from this investment?
- □ Why do this work right now?

It is hoped that these discussions will help you address the special concerns of your organization.

20.2.1 What Makes the Process Maturity Model Right?

The question "What makes the process maturity model right?" is a logical one that deserves a thoughtful answer. The maturity model has been found to reasonably represent the issues that many software organizations face at various stages in process improvement. While many of these organizations have found it helpful in establishing improvement priorities, this does not make it right and all other models wrong. There are many possible improvement paths, and each organization must pick the one that best matches its needs.

If the maturity model gives some actions high priority while thoughtful local opinion selects others, discard the model. The model is only a guide, and when those closest to the problems have a better vision, they should follow their instincts. The world changes, and software is too dynamic for any canned criteria to meet all needs forever.

Orderly process improvement, however, does require a model of the evolutionary stages. It is therefore not wise to discard this method without a new one to replace it. Software people are often prone to strike out on their own instead of building on prior results. When experimenting is appropriate, go ahead, but first make sure you really have a new problem and a defined improvement paradigm that addresses your needs.

20.2.2 Why Should we Have an SEPG?

The reasoning behind having an SEPG is another thoughtful question that must be answered. Fortunately, there are a number of reasonable answers. First, once there is agreement to improve the software process, someone must be assigned to do the work. Regardless of whether they are called a Software Engineering Process Group (SEPG) or not, these people are performing the SEPG function.

The true skeptics will still not be convinced. They will wonder why anyone needs to be assigned at all. Why not just tell everybody to do it the right way? This is a little like expecting a football team to win without giving them time to develop and practice their plays. If the software professionals could do better work by just being told to, they would probably have done so already. The need is not for sweeping directives but for skilled professionals to look at the organization's problems and to devise and implement solutions. If no one is assigned this work, it will not get done.

A few doubters may still raise objections. Why change the process when we can buy a few new tools to solve the problems? While this is a valid question, it stems from a fallacious view of software process improvement. As Brooks has said, "There is no silver bullet."[1] Some magic tool or method will not by itself make a significant improvement. It must be designed into the process and coupled with all other facets of the work. If a new tool doesn't fit smoothly into the current operation and precisely match the existing formats, languages, and procedures, something must change or it will not be used. Someone is needed to figure out what changes are needed, get them made, tested, and introduced, and then provide continuing support. New tools can be a great help, but only if they are thoughtfully selected, properly introduced, and fully supported. The mere introduction of tools will not make an ineffective process effective; it can only make an effective process more efficient. If your current process is not suitably effective, you will need an SEPG to improve it.

For engineering-oriented managers, the previously mentioned analogy to manufacturing can be helpful. Ask them to consider the difference between a machine shop and a factory. Both may have the same machines, but the process in the machine shop is determined by the people who happen to handle each job. On the other hand, a factory is not designed as the work is done or by buying machines. In software, too, we will be most successful if we first design our process and then select and install tools to support it.

20.2.3 Why Can't SQA Do the SEPG Job?

The possibility of assigning SQA the process group tasks is a reasonable question that indicates three things: confusion about the SQA role, growing agreement that something needs to be done about improving the software process, and concern about where to obtain the needed resources. First, as discussed in Chapters 8 and 14, the roles of SQA and the SEPG are quite different. Software Quality Assurance is concerned with auditing the process to ensure proper implementation. At least from a parochial development viewpoint, they are thus often viewed as the enemy, or at least as an unnecessary annoyance. Since the development groups must be held responsible for the quality of their own work, this attitude is not entirely unreasonable. The SEPG, on the other hand, is responsible for devising process improvements, installing them, and supporting the projects in their use. To be effective the SEPG must work cooperatively with the project teams and get their participation in the task groups that devise, plan, and implement the process improvements. Clearly, if both functions are assigned to the same group, one responsibility or the other will suffer.

20.2.4 As My Process Improves, Do I Need to Keep an SQA Group?

This question indicates a growing appreciation of the benefits of a managed software process. While some audit activity will be needed even with the most mature software process, its scope and focus can change. First, at levels 4 (Managed) and 5 (Optimizing) the software professionals and managers will generally do their own quality assurance. They will measure their work, assess trends, and take corrective action. The size of the SQA staff can thus be reduced significantly, but they must retain these key tasks: Statistically sample the software engineering work to ensure it is performed to standard, sample the data to assure that it represents the work being done, and analyze the data and alert management to any out-of-line trends or conditions.

20.2.5 Why Is Defect Prevention So Important?

Unless the organization is fairly advanced, the importance of defect prevention will not be questioned except rhetorically. The reason is that there is an obvious contradiction with general software practice: Defect prevention is clearly beneficial but is rarely practiced.

Defect prevention is essential to software process improvement because it provides an orderly way to make consistent progress against the most important problems. The definition of insanity fits here so aptly that it is worth repeating: "Someone is insane if they do the same thing over and over and expect a different result."[2] Defect prevention is the conscious way to change what we do to get a better result. Even though it may not be recognized, defect prevention is behind many of the software improvements made in the last 30 years. Practicing software engineers, however, have yet to adopt defect prevention as a common daily practice.

It is often convincing to cite the Japanese experience with quality circles.[3, 4, 7, 8] Remarkable success has been achieved by having factory workers make process improvements through defect prevention. A quality circle examines the problems the members face and recommends changes to solve or prevent them. As described in Chapter 17, these methods have been successfully tried by some software groups.

20.2.6 What Is the Financial Return from This Investment?

This question is the classic coup de grace. When managers don't want to do something, they ask for a financial justification. Because most complex business issues involve many unquantifiable factors it is rarely possible to make accurate financial projections. Most senior management decisions are thus based on intuition with a seasoning of financial judgment. Since technical intuition rarely carries enough weight to overcome financial resistance, however, the financial justification question cannot be brushed off, particularly when substantial amounts of money are involved.

One possible approach is to point out the costs of the status quo. These involve test and defect correction costs, lost revenue from delayed product deliveries, and lost sales due to customer dissatisfaction. There are also often indirect costs from lost new product opportunities or a delay in anticipated cost savings. While such data helps establish the need to change, it often has the dangerous side effect of emphasizing the poor prior performance of the software organization. This argument is thus best made by a newly appointed manager.

Next, of course, is the need to demonstrate that the proposed investment will actually solve the problems. Since there can be no single answer to all the problems of any complex organization, the only logical approach is to start by attacking the highest-priority items. Generally, even a 10 percent improvement in the most important cost exposures will produce enough savings to easily cover most software investments.

This approach, however, contains another potential trap. Finance will often agree with such plans as long as the software managers commit to reducing their budgets in accordance with the planned savings. There is no easy answer to this except to agree to a date by which such a schedule will be produced. Then work must be started to make a reasonable estimate of a new cost profile that the software managers will accept. As described later in this chapter, these improvements must then be included in the factors used for planning future projects.

20.2.7 Why Do This Work Right Now?

This is the final knock off. While it might be prudent to agree to a delay in return for a promise of funding next year, putting a project on the shelf is an almost certain way to kill it. One answer is to argue that competition is ahead, but that may be hard to prove. One could argue that the Japanese are coming or that IBM is already doing it, but without proof however such rejoinders are rarely convincing.

For DoD contractors, the Software Engineering Institute's work on contractor evaluation may provide convincing justification.[6] In this work branches of the Army, Navy, and Air Force are examining the quality of the software processes used by potential contractors. Their intent is to avoid doing business with organizations that have poor software management practices. This could well mean that competitors with more mature processes will be more likely to win contracts. This argument has a factual basis and is therefore likely to be more convincing. Even those organizations not doing military contracting might reflect that many of their competitors do and that their improved software processes are applicable to their commercial work as well.

20.3 What Do I Do Next?

Now that management is convinced (we hope) that this work is worth doing, the time has come for action. While the most appropriate next steps must depend on the organization's special needs, some examples of successful approaches to common problems may be helpful. The ones treated in the following paragraphs are:

- □ Staffing a laboratory process group
- □ Staffing process groups in a large corporation
- □ Initiating project estimating and scheduling
- □ Establishing quality measurements

□ Starting to track and report software quality

□ Facilitating data analysis

□ Estimating improvement benefits

Each of the following examples is based on one or more actual cases, but some of the details have been altered to protect confidentiality.

20.3.1 Staffing a Laboratory Process Group

Our first example involves staffing a laboratory process group. The assessment of a large software shop concluded by recommending the establishment of a Software Engineering Process Group (SEPG) with an initial staff of five professionals. Larry, the laboratory manager, accepted the recommendation and put Phil in charge of the SEPG. Phil's first step was to go to the various department heads to request the transfer of five of their best people.

No department head agreed with the selections, each countering with names that were unacceptable to Phil. While these negotiations continued, Larry decided to hold a monthly review. He was not pleased with the lack of staffing and directed each department head to identify one good candidate.

By the next monthly review two people had been selected and one had already started work. This time Larry applied more pressure and two more were selected by the next meeting. The fifth manager asked for a three-month delay to meet a critical product deadline, but then he promised to provide an acceptable candidate. Larry agreed and the SEPG was soon fully staffed.

The lesson from this case is that, even with top management support, staffing takes time. Without such support the task is almost impossible. Periodic senior management review is thus essential to getting the job done.

20.3.2 Staffing Process Groups in a Large Corporation

Bill, the software staff manager, had concluded that each of the division's five major software departments should have their own process group. The laboratory managers agreed, but their resources were so tight they could not provide any resources and did not expect to be able to next year either. Since the total required staffing was only 28 out of the 1600 programmers in these laboratories, the division staff was unwilling to provide all the money. After some negotiation, headquarters finally agreed to fund some of the effort, but only if the laboratories paid for the rest. With this as a start, Bill persuaded each laboratory director to agree to pay for half the people if he could obtain funding for the rest. Headquarters agreed, and the plans were approved for full staffing in the following year. By the end of that year the groups were funded, staffed, and busily at work on software process improvement.

The lesson here is that most software managers are anxious to improve their processes, but they generally need senior management help. Given half the chance, they will put the right actions in place, even at some sacrifice to their other needs. When senior management is unwilling to contribute anything, however, the software managers rightly question their conviction to process improvement and will not make the entire investment themselves.

20.3.3 Staffing a Process Group in a Small Organization

Fred managed a small software group that was primarily involved in contracting for maintenance and enhancement of older military software packages. While this work was quite stable, they were starting on some new product development, and Fred recognized the need for process improvements. Since he did not have the resources to establish a full-time process group, he formed a management steering committee that would set up and manage the work of several part-time process working groups. To coordinate this work and ensure continuity, one full-time professional was assigned to work for the committee chairman. While this arrangement did not make as rapid progress as Fred had wished, it did provide a focal point for process change and served to maintain a continuing focus on improvement.

20.3.4 Initiating Project Estimating and Scheduling

Project estimating and scheduling are important tasks that should be addressed early in the process, as this example demonstrates. Because he had successfully managed an engineering group and knew something about software, Jim was put in charge of a large software development organization. The vice-president told him his top priority was to "straighten out this software mess." Jim understood this to mean that they were to start delivering products on schedule and at or near their projected costs.

Jim's first action was to call a meeting of the six project leaders to plan an early review of their operations. He started the review by asking for a copy of the official project schedule and estimate. Each organization had notes or memos supporting the original project proposal, but no one had a current documented schedule and plan showing the entire project from start through test and delivery. When Jim asked for size and resource estimates, nobody even knew what he meant. In the ensuing discussions every manager agreed that such documents were desirable but nobody had ever had the time to produce and maintain them. These items had never been demanded before and resources were so short that they had never taken the time to produce them on their own.

Jim knew that no hardware or software development project could work effectively without current schedules and estimates. After getting the vice-president's agreement, he told the project leaders that they henceforth must produce and maintain documented schedules and estimates. He would personally review every new program proposal, plan change, or product delivery, and none would be approved without such supporting documentation.

The project managers were shocked. Such detailed planning had never been required of them, and they didn't know how to start. They asked Jim to delay this edict to give them time to prepare, but he insisted that it take effect immediately. He arranged for a one-week management course on estimating and scheduling, as well as for the help of two engineering cost estimators.

After a three-month delay the first estimates and plans were produced. Though crude, they did help the projects plan their work. To improve schedule performance, Jim added a modest contingency on every delivery schedule but insisted the projects drive for the original dates. Over the next two years no project missed any of its newly committed dates.

The lesson here is that detailed estimates and schedules must be required by management and there is no better time to start than right now. As long as they are optional, they won't be done. In hardware the discipline of release-to-manufacturing forces the necessary detailed planning, but with software the only discipline is that imposed by management or the professionals themselves. Any management edicts must, however, be supported by senior management, a training program, and suitable support facilities.

20.3.5 Establishing Quality Measurements

In this case corporate headquarters had issued a policy that each new product was to have measurably better quality than its predecessor. Since the software groups did not know how to demonstrate improvement, the technical staff held meetings with people from all the software groups and soon learned what measures were available and their shortcomings. Unfortunately, every measure had serious faults, and nobody would agree on any single set. The staff thus developed their own recommendations. They then negotiated with the two programming directors they felt were most likely to agree. After several meetings one programming director agreed, and after some minor changes the second one did. The staff head then decided to issue the new measures in a letter to all the laboratories and ask for comments. While most of them reluctantly agreed, one was adamantly opposed. After a hearing with senior management, this last manager also finally agreed, and the new quality standard was adopted.

The lesson here is that groups are generally reluctant to accept a set of metrics that will be used to measure them. The key is to take the time and effort to understand the issues and then get management's backing to put a reasonable set of measures in place. There will likely be some initial problems, but if some measures are not adopted and used, no progress will be made. In sum, the only way to learn how to measure is to measure.

20.3.6 Starting to Track and Report Software Quality

Once an organization adopts quality metrics, it is necessary to establish formats and procedures for quality plans and tracking. One organization used the general format shown in Fig. 20.1. The cumulative defects were plotted from product introduction and general acceptance to end of life, which was typically assumed to be four years. Each successive product version was to be better than its predecessor, as described in Table 20.1. While the specific improvement goals were established by each product manager, the emphasis was on steady improvement.

When the product managers started to make these plans, they did not appreciate the effects of customer installation rates, field testing programs, total installation quantities, and interim release schedules. The first product was a compiler, and its plan and early experience looked like Fig. 20.2. As can be seen, actual experience was substantially worse than plan during the first six months. It was not initially recognized, however, that compiler programs are relatively easy for customers to install, so problem occurrence rates would peak early, as shown in Fig. 20.3. Some products, like communications control programs and file systems, require more preparation and conversion effort, so their error reporting rates will typically spread over a more extended period. Each product has a characteristic error discovery curve, and with experience the product managers soon learned to accurately project these defect discovery profiles. With this insight the compiler manager was able to establish action plans and more accurately project their effect. The product ultimately did meet its original end-of-life goals.

A final point concerned motivation. Performance against the quality plans was periodically reviewed with the senior corporate executives. When a product did not perform as planned, a division president or corporate vice-president would call to see what actions were planned to address the problem. While this system could easily have caused the product managers to make safe plans, the approach adopted put as much emphasis on aggressive plans as on meeting them. When product managers met all their plans, they were likely to be viewed as playing it too safe. On the other hand, when a plan was missed, they were expected to respond with action plans to address the problems and to bring the products up to plan. This put the emphasis where it belonged: on devising actions to aggressively improve product quality.

The lesson here is that visibly tracking quality performance versus plan motivates the entire organization to improve quality. While these measures must relate to business needs, numerical plans and public quality reporting are an essential part of an effective product quality program.

20.3.7 Facilitating Data Analysis

One organization started gathering data on the defects found during customer use of its products. Every line of code had been flagged with the date it was added or

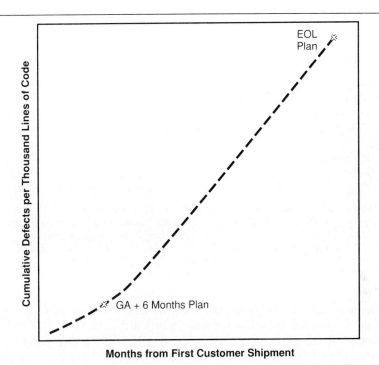

FIGURE 20.1
Software Quality Tracking

changed and why. The problem reporting system thus was able to trace each problem to determine whether it was introduced during code modification, new development, subsequent enhancement, or maintenance.

Fred, a thoughtful software assurance professional, wanted to see how module error rates varied between newly produced and subsequently enhanced code. As shown in Table 20.2, he found that changes were more than ten times as error-prone as new code. He also found that the error rate for the smallest changes was nearly 40 times greater than that for new code. This finding was a surprise to the developers and was largely responsible for increasing the emphasis on the inspection and test of small development and maintenance changes.

The lesson here is that an occasional highly motivated professional will look at whatever data is available to see what it means. While it is risky to gather data without a clear plan for its use, data is powerful, and curious people will often find important and unanticipated ways to use it.

In another software organization management was increasingly concerned with the cost of maintaining a large communication control program. They asked Pete, a consultant, for advice, and he requested their maintenance data. Even

TABLE 20.1
EXAMPLE SOFTWARE QUALITY MEASURES

1—The basic quality measure (BQM) is cumulative defects per 1000 lines of source code.
   a—The defects counted are customer-reported, valid, unique code or documentation errors. Defects found in development or field test, duplicate defect reports, user errors, or other invalid reports are not counted.
   b—The line-of-code count is all noncomment, nonblank source instructions obtained by use of a specified standard counting program.
   c—The line-of-code count includes all instructions shipped with the product, whether new, modified, or reused.

2—The end-of-life (EOL) measure requires that the BQM of the new product or release planned for EOL be less than the actual or planned value for its predecessor. Where not otherwise specified, EOL is assumed to be 48 months from first customer shipment.

3—The two early-life target criteria are:
   a—The new product BQM at six months from first customer shipment must be less than the predecessor product at six months from its first customer shipment.
   b—The new product BQM at six months from first customer shipment must be less than the predecessor product BQM for its most recent six months.

---

though management didn't know they had any data, Pete found a maintenance professional who did. In fact, he had three years of data on the errors found in each of the approximately 1600 modules. After getting the line-of-code counts from the developers and doing a few calculations, Pete showed that nearly 50 percent of the errors came from only 3 percent of the code. As a result, management started a special inspection and test effort for these few modules and was soon able to significantly reduce maintenance costs.

The lesson here is that when faced with a problem, look at the data. If data is not readily available, look deeper, as some gems are likely hidden in somebody's desk drawer. If there really isn't any data, insist that work start on defining and gathering it. If you have no clear idea on where to start, it is probably wise to start by gathering data on the defects found by module during inspection, test, and customer use.

20.3.8 Estimating Improvement Benefits

Our final example demonstrates the steps involved in estimating improvement benefits. Mark, the manager of technology development for a large software group, was in charge of developing a software support environment and a set of tools. This was becoming a more expensive program than anyone had expected, and questions were being raised about its financial return. The finance people argued that a cost/benefit analysis was needed for any expense of this magnitude. Up to now Mark had successfully argued that this was modern technology and all

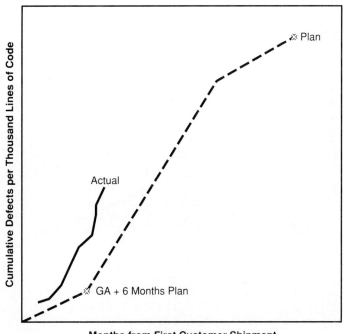

Months from First Customer Shipment

FIGURE 20.2
Compiler Quality Plan

their competitors were using it. This time, however, the budget request was too big
for such arm waving to work.

After talking to the manufacturing engineers about how they justified capital
equipment, Mark met with several senior software managers. They agreed to form a
committee of experts to estimate their potential savings. The group was to be given
the cost profile for the current process and the new support plan and asked to assess
each major task to determine the anticipated savings. They were then to produce a
projected new cost profile and a transition schedule by product. This would allow
each project to estimate its new cost pattern, leading to a total annual savings figure.

This plan was reviewed with the programming managers, and the committee
began work. They soon learned that this estimating job was not as simple as it first
appeared. The methods used in each stage affected the work in many others, so the
analysis had to consider the effects of new defect injection rates, reduced change
activity, and new inspection and testing strategies. They found that the single most
important factor in determining the cost savings was a reduced rate of defect

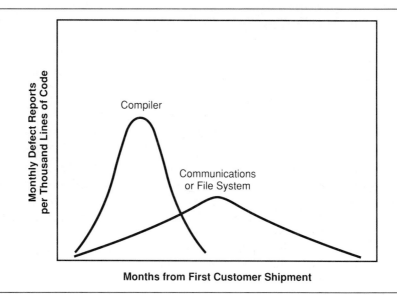

FIGURE 20.3
Defect Rate Curves

injection. They thus gave highest value to any tools or methods that would reduce this rate and second highest value to those that improved early defect removal efficiency. The tools and methods that merely saved labor were generally found to have lower cost reduction potential.

The committee started by estimating the defect injection and removal profiles for every step of the old and new environments. They next projected the labor content of each phase and then calculated the new cost profiles. These profiles, together with the anticipated new level of product quality, permitted them to project savings in development, field support, and maintenance.

The initial savings estimates were so high that Mark decided they were unrealistic. On close examination it was found that the work had not been done in sufficient detail. For example, the documentation savings from reduced changes were much too high. The savings ratios had been applied to the total writers' time. While improved quality would clearly reduce overhead, it would be hard to justify cutting such items as training, planning, meetings, phone calls, and personnel administration.

The appropriate changes were made in all the task projections and the figures looked much more reasonable. When the financial people reviewed the results, they were impressed by the thoroughness of the work and agreed to support the budget request. It was quickly approved.

TABLE 20.2
RELATIVE DEFECT RATE VERSUS
PERCENTAGE OF MODIFICATION

Newly written code	1.0
All modified programs	11.1
Large modifications (more than 5% of the LOC)	4.5
Small modifications (less than 5% of the LOC)	37.8

The lesson is that effective software process support will become increasingly expensive. These large investments will have to be justified and financially sound estimates will be required. The estimates should be based on data on the current process and must represent the best judgment of the software managers and technical professionals. If the numbers hold up under critical financial examination, the required capital funds will more likely be provided.

20.4 Final Remarks

While the preceding are only a few examples of approaches that have worked, they are all relatively straightforward and logical. The key point is that the problems addressed are not new. While their software context adds some new elements, it is generally possible to talk to people in other disciplines to see how similar questions, objections, or stumbling blocks were handled.

The methods described in this book have all been used and proven to be effective. They are not, of course, the end of the line. As the software process evolves, new methods and better approaches will undoubtedly be found. If we assign some of our best people to process improvement, they will generate a host of ideas that will provide the best possible road map for improvement. We can, however, no longer muddle through on intuition; the process is too complex and the products too important. To make progress, we must assign some capable people to the job and get started. It is my hope that this book will help.

References

1. Brooks, F. P. "No silver bullet, essence and accidents of software engineering," *IEEE Computer*, April 1987.

2. Brown, Rita Mae. Private communication.

3. Cole, R. E. "A Japanese management import comes full circle," *Technology Review*, May/June 1983.

4. Humphrey, W. S. "Japanese management: perspectives for U.S. engineering," *Manufacturing Engineering,* April 1982.

5. Humphrey, W. S. *Managing for Innovation—Leading Technical People.* Englewood Cliffs, NJ: Prentice-Hall, 1987.

6. Humphrey, W. S., and W. L. Sweet. "A Method for Assessing the Software Engineering Capability of Contractors," SEI Technical Report SEI-87-TR-23, September 1987.

7. Lawler, E. E. III, and S. A. Mohrman. "Quality circles after the fad," *Harvard Business Review,* January–February, 1985.

8. Mohr, W. L. *Quality Circles: Changing Images of People at Work.* Reading, MA: Addison-Wesley, 1983.

APPENDIX

A Software Process Maturity Framework

This appendix is an overview of the key activities judged necessary at each level of software process maturity. This maturity framework was developed at the Software Engineering Institute (SEI) of Carnegie Mellon University. It is based on the extensive software experience of the SEI staff, and it has been found to reasonably represent the status and key problem areas of many software organizations. As the practice of software evolves, however, and as our knowledge improves, we can expect this framework to evolve as well. It is presented here to provide a broader perspective on the improvement needs of software organizations.

Software process improvement actions are divided into 15 categories, which are further grouped into 4 major topics. In summary, these topics are:

- □ *Organization* This deals with management leadership of software organizations. This leadership is typically exercised through policies, resource allocation, management oversight, communications, and training. Policies state the basic principles of organizational behavior. The organization structure establishes basic responsibilities and allocates resources. Management oversight concerns management awareness of organizational performance. Communication deals with the means to ensure available knowledge to support timely action. Training ensures that the software professionals are aware of and capable of using the pertinent standards, procedures, methods, and tools.

- □ *Project management* Project management deals with the normal activities of planning, tracking, project control, and subcontracting. Planning includes the preparation of plans and the operation of the planning system. The tracking and review systems ensure that appropriate activities are tracked against plan and that deviations are reported to management. Project control provides for control and protection of the critical elements of the software project and its process. Subcontracting concerns the means used to ensure that subcontracted resources perform in accordance with established policies, procedures, and standards.

☐ *Process management*   With improving organizational maturity, a process infrastructure is established to uniformly support and guide the projects' work. This involves process definition, process execution, data gathering and analysis, and process control. The process definition provides a standardized framework for task implementation, evaluation, and improvement. Process execution defines the methods and techniques used to produce quality products. Analysis deals with the measurements made of software products and processes and the uses made of this data. Process control concerns the establishment of mechanisms to assure the performance of the defined process and process monitoring and adjustment where improvements are needed.

☐ *Technology*   This topic deals with technology insertion and environments. Technology insertion covers the means to identify and install needed technology, while environments include the tools and facilities that support the management and execution of the defined process.

In the following, some specific techniques or methods such as prototyping or reuse are described. While these particular techniques might not be appropriate for every organization, their inclusion here offers some points to consider in adopting these or similar methods.

Actions Performed at Level 2—the Repeatable Process

At the Repeatable Process Level the organization has achieved stable performance by initiating rigorous commitment, cost, schedule, and change management. This stability typically involves a range of actions designed to achieve control over cost and schedule. These actions involve organization, project management, process management, and technology.

Organization

A policy statement requires a commitment and tracking system to ensure that commitments are only made after senior management review and approval. Appropriate review mechanisms verify that established policies, procedures, methods, and standards are followed, and where they are not, a contention system ensures that issues are escalated and resolved. A training organization is established, and standard courses are offered on estimating, scheduling, the commitment process, and change management. These basic actions are:

- □ *Policy*

    Senior management issues a policy statement requiring that project and unit managers identify their commitments, have them reviewed in advance by senior management, and be held accountable for meeting them.

- □ *Resources*

    A software management structure is established.

    Software Quality Assurance (SQA) has a reporting channel independent of the development organization, and it is allocated sufficient resources to monitor development performance.

    The system design organization has sufficient software skills and/or resources to ensure adequate coverage of software issues.

- □ *Oversight*

    No commitment is made without senior management review and approval.

    SQA tracks development performance and informs management whenever established policies, procedures, methods, or standards are not followed.

    A contention system ensures that issues are escalated to the appropriate management level to resolve them.

- □ *Communication*

    Steps are taken to ensure that the software designers fully understand the software requirements.

- □ *Training*

    A training organization is established.

    Standard courses are offered on estimating, scheduling, the commitment process, and change management.

Project Management

A planning process is implemented by the projects, monitored by SQA, and periodically reviewed by senior management. A similar subcontract management organization is established to track subcontractor performance against plan. These actions are:

- □ *Planning*

    All projects produce and document their plans, including projections of product size, resource estimates, staffing levels, schedules, and key checkpoints.

- □ *Tracking*

    The planning process is monitored against approved standards and procedures by SQA.

Quarterly management reviews are held to track project size, staffing, schedules, and key checkpoint performance against plan.

□ *Project Control*

Mechanisms are established to monitor and control requirements changes and ensure piecewise stability for the development process.

A change control and configuration management system is established for requirements, code, and test.

□ *Subcontracting*

Responsibilities and resources are established to track subcontractor performance against plan.

Subcontractor standards and procedures for estimating, planning, and change management are reviewed.

Subcontractor SQA resources, procedures, and standards are periodically reviewed to ensure they are adequate to monitor subcontractor performance.

Process Management

Procedures, standards, and methods are produced for developing and approving product plans, conducting management reviews, and tracking performance. The actions are:

□ *Definition*

Documented standards are produced for software size estimates, resource projections, schedules, and product plans.

Product style guides are developed to guide the design and coding activities.

Documented procedures are produced for developing and approving product plans; approving and making changes to requirements, designs, or code; conducting audits; and holding management reviews.

□ *Execution*

Basic software design, code, and test methods are defined and documented.

Software design feasibility studies are conducted of each requirement baseline before it is established.

Standard methods are developed for project estimating and planning.

□ *Analysis*

Measurements and analyses are made of staffing versus plan, code size versus projections, and resources expended versus plan.

Historical data is retained on code and test errors; actual versus planned units designed, coded, tested, and integrated; and release content versus plan.

□ *Control*

Mechanisms and responsibilities are established to ensure that plans are produced and tracked for all projects, the plans are endorsed by the implementing teams, all plans are reviewed prior to commitment, audits are conducted when specified, change control is rigorously implemented, and SQA and Software Configuration Management (SCM) are performing effectively.

Procedures, methods, and responsibilities are established to ensure that the developers understand both the requirements and the user's application environment.

Technology

Steps are taken to ensure awareness of available technology and to install appropriate tools and methods.

☐ *Insertion*

Means are established to provide awareness of available tools and methods.

Actions Performed at Level 3—the Defined Process

At the Defined Process Level the organization has established a standard process that is customized to meet the needs of each project. This provides an informed basis for handling process contingencies, allows orderly improvement, and facilitates the introduction of supporting technologies. In moving from Level 2, the Repeatable Process, to Level 3, the Defined Process, organizations typically institute a range of practices and methods that codify the most effective means for addressing anticipated contingencies. Key actions are required in organization, project management, process management, and technology.

Organization

A management policy requires that a standard software development process be used and a Software Engineering Process Group is established to do this work. Periodic management reviews are held of process improvement status, and a training plan is established for a required set of standard courses.

☐ *Policy*

A policy is issued requiring that a standard software development process be used as the foundation for each project's activities and that deviations be documented and approved.

☐ *Resources*

A Software Engineering Process Group is established to lead the process improvement activities and to ensure awareness of effective process management methods.

A software-knowledgeable system design organization is maintained for each project from initial requirements through final test and delivery.

A separate test and integration capability is established.

□ *Oversight*

Periodic management reviews are held on training, technology insertion, software process status, and process improvement plans.

□ *Communication*

Means are established to ensure close coupling between system and software design.

Mechanisms are established for identifying system and software design issues and promptly resolving them.

□ *Training*

Standard courses are offered on quality management, managing software professionals, basic software methods, and inspections.

A training plan is produced defining the required courses for each job function.

Project Management

Project risk management plans are developed, project performance is tracked against the defined process, and formal procedures are established for dealing with subcontractors.

□ *Planning*

Resources are estimated for each key activity in the defined software process.

Contingencies are established for all estimates based on historical experience.

Project risk management plans identify technical and business exposures and define process means to address them.

Project staffing plans address needs for special skills and application domain knowledge.

□ *Tracking*

Project performance is tracked and reviewed by key activity in the defined standard process.

Design and code inspection items are tracked to resolution.

The development and documentation of process standards and methods are tracked and reviewed.

□ *Project control*

The development tools and methods for each project are maintained under SCM control.

The process definitions and standards for each project are maintained under SCM control.

□ *Subcontracting*

Formal procedures are established for selecting subcontractors.

Mechanisms and resources are established for tracking subcontractor performance against plan.

SQA monitors subcontractor SQA performance.

Process Management

A standard process framework is established, and mechanisms are instituted to ensure that it is used. Basic measurements are initiated, and documented methods are established for design, inspection, and test. The actions involved are:

□ *Definition*

Documented standards are produced for the process framework, project cost records, testing methods, and product quality reports.

Organization-wide style guides are developed for the design and coding activities.

Documented procedures are established for producing and approving product and process standards.

Process definitions are customized to dynamically address the contingency needs of each project.

□ *Execution*

Documented methods are developed for design, coding, inspection, and test.

Methods are established to trace and relate all design and code items from requirements through test.

□ *Analysis*

Measurements are made of errors found and costs incurred by process activity.

□ *Control*

Mechanisms and responsibilities are established to ensure that each product requirement is testable.

Mechanisms and responsibilities are defined for ensuring the production of process standards and cost tracking.

Mechanisms are established to ensure that the process standards are thoroughly reviewed and that their adoption is endorsed by the technical community.

Mechanisms and responsibilities are established for reviewing the effectiveness of the SEPG.

Process mechanisms are established to ensure validation of the design approach against the user's needs.

Technology

Technology insertion plans are developed and an initial software engineering environment is obtained and installed. The actions are:

□ *Insertion*

A technology insertion plan is established.

□ *Environments*

A software development environment framework is established and installed.

A standard set of compatible tools is defined and available.

Actions Performed at Level 4—the Managed Process

At the Managed Process Level, the organization has initiated comprehensive process measurements and analyses. The resulting precise knowledge of the process provides the foundation for significant and continuing product quality and productivity improvement. In moving from Level 3, the Defined Process, to level 4, the Managed Process, an organization typically institutes key actions in the areas of organization, project management, process management, and technology as described in the following sections.

Organization

A policy requires that each new or improved product release be measurably better than its predecessor or leading competitor. An organizational focal point is established to monitor quality planning and track quality performance, and periodic management reviews are held of quality performance against plan. Standard courses are offered on quality and process methods. The actions are:

□ *Policy*

A policy is established requiring that each new or improved product release be measurably better than its predecessor or its leading competitor.

A policy statement is issued requiring that all projects establish plans to move to the established standard methods and tools or obtain exception approval.

□ *Resources*

An organizational focal point is established for quality planning and tracking.

Resources are provided to support technology introduction.

□ *Oversight*

Each major organizational entity is required to periodically conduct or obtain an assessment (at least once every two years, for example).

Periodic management reviews are held of performance against quality plans and quality improvement actions.

□ *Communication*

Means are established to ensure that software process and environmental support issues are identified and promptly resolved.

□ *Training*

Standard courses are offered on quality planning, quantitative process management, advanced development methods, prototyping, and technical career planning and development.

Project Management

Each project produces quality plans, and a quality improvement action plan is produced whenever a project does not meet its committed quality plan. The actions are:

□ *Planning*

Quality plans are produced for each project.

Quality improvement action plans are produced whenever a project does not meet its committed quality plan.

□ *Tracking*

Performance is tracked against quality plans and quality improvement actions.

□ *Project control*

Process customizations of the standard process for each project are retained under SCM control.

The process metric definitions are maintained under SCM control.

□ *Subcontracting*

Means are established for coupling with the subcontractor's development environments.

Standard subcontractor quality metrics are established and tracked.

Subcontractor SQA performance is tracked and reviewed.

Process Management

Documented standards are produced for key technical activities, and procedures are defined for quality planning and tracking. The process database is centrally maintained and suitably protected, and comprehensive measurements and analyses are made of the products and the software engineering process. The actions are:

□ *Definition*

Documented standards are produced for inspections, tools and methods, quality plans, and quality tracking by process task.

Documented guidelines are produced for process and environment customization.

Documented procedures are developed for quality plans and tracking, inspections, and process and environment customization.

□ *Execution*

Documented methods are established for prototyping and quantitative design.

Prototypes are developed to demonstrate the feasibility of critical requirements before they are baselined.

□ *Analysis*

Measurements and analyses are made of product defect levels, inspection and test coverage and efficiency, error distribution, task productivity, and tools and methods effectiveness.

A process database is established.

The process database and quality reporting system are centrally maintained and suitably protected.

□ *Control*

Mechanisms and responsibilities are established for ensuring the definition and use of standard metrics, the production and tracking of quality plans, and the appropriate insertion of new technologies.

Mechanisms and responsibilities are defined to ensure that the project technical professionals endorse the product quality plans and are personally committed to meeting them.

Technology

Technology insertion and support resources are established, a basic support environment is installed, and the environment is instrumented to provide process data. The actions are:

□ *Insertion*

Technology support facilities are established, including support for tools installation and use, new methods assistance, and environment customization.

□ *Environments*

Key elements of the basic tool set are integrated into the environment framework.

Process instrumentation automatically records key process data.

Actions Performed at Level 5—the Optimizing Process

At the Optimizing Process Level the extensive data on the software process is used to evaluate process effectiveness and make regular adjustments. This provides a foundation for continuing process improvement and orderly and planned productivity improvement. In moving from Level 4, the Managed Process, to Level 5, the Optimizing Process, the organization concentrates on building the projects' and the professionals' skill and commitment to continuing process improvement. This typically requires the actions discussed in the following sections.

Organization

A policy calls for productivity improvement plans and periodic management reviews of performance against them. Standard courses are offered on economic justification and advanced technical methods. The actions are:

- *Policy*

  A policy is issued requiring each development group to demonstrate a steady productivity improvement trend.

  A policy calls for each development group to use the officially established tools and methods.

  A policy calls for each development group to use the available reuse components or obtain exception approval.

- *Resources*

  An organizational focal point is established with the necessary resources to obtain or develop, introduce, and support reusable components in accordance with the organization's needs.

- *Oversight*

  Periodic management reviews are held on performance against productivity plans.

- *Communication*

  Means are established to ensure that software process and environmental support improvement actions are objectively evaluated, recognized, and rewarded.

- *Training*

  Standard courses are offered on economic justification, advanced design, reuse methods, and error prevention methods.

Project Management

Process improvement plans are produced and tracked for each project, and productivity improvement plans are produced and tracked for each software organizational unit. Subcontractor monitoring mechanisms are established for quality and productivity improvement. The actions are:

□ *Planning*

Process improvement plans are produced for each project.

Productivity improvement plans are produced by each software organizational unit.

□ *Tracking*

Performance is tracked against process improvement and productivity plans.

□ *Project control*

The reuse components and their definitions are maintained under SCM control.

□ *Subcontracting*

Subcontractor process improvement mechanisms are reviewed, approved, and tracked.

SQA monitors subcontractor focus on process improvement and productivity improvement actions.

Process Management

Documented productivity measures and statistical limits are established, and mechanisms and responsibilities are defined for tracking against them. Measurements and analyses are made of economic effectiveness, and defect cause and prevention analyses are conducted. The actions are:

□ *Definition*

Documented standards are produced for each task productivity measurement and its statistical limits.

Documented guidelines and standards are produced for component reuse, including standard interfaces and definitions.

Documented procedures are developed for productivity planning and tracking, reuse requirements generation, reuse component customization, and reuse support.

□ *Execution*

Documented methods are developed on designing for reuse, defect prevention analysis, and defect extinction.

Economic and technical trade-off studies are conducted during the project requirements and design phases to decide where existing, modified, or newly developed reusable components should be used.

❑ *Analysis*

Measurements and analyses are made of the economic effectiveness of tools, prototyping methods, and reuse by component.

Defect cause analyses are conducted.

❑ *Control*

Mechanisms and responsibilities are defined for productivity tracking, technology integration, and reuse effectiveness tracking.

Mechanisms and responsibilities are established to ensure that the project professionals are trained and capable of performing defect prevention and are personally committed to process improvement.

Technology

Technology support analyses are made of each process task to determine required support, the economics of that support, and the need for prototyping potential support enhancements. The actions are:

❑ *Insertion*

The technology support activities include analysis of each process task to determine required support, the economics of that support, and the prototyping of potential tools and methods.

❑ *Environments*

The tool set is progressively enhanced to include the use of new technologies and methods.

B

APPENDIX

Software Engineering Institute Assessment Agreement

This Agreement is entered into by and between the Software Engineering Institute (SEI) and _____ (hereinafter referred to as Affiliate) with its principal office located at _____. This Agreement will be effective when executed by both parties. Its duration will be limited by the nature and scope of the undertakings set forth in the Agreement. Certain commitments will survive completion of the basic tasks set forth.

The SEI is a federally funded research and development center (FFRDC) owned and operated by Carnegie Mellon University pursuant to contract with the Department of Defense (DoD). Included in the SEI Charter is a requirement that the SEI shall establish standards of excellence for software engineering practice. In furtherance of that requirement, the SEI is conducting assessments of software engineering practice with individual companies and studying industry-wide practices of software engineering (the Assessment Program). Affiliate has a vested interest in assessing its level of software engineering practice on both an absolute and comparative basis.

Therefore the parties hereto agree as follows:

1. Affiliate agrees to participate with the SEI in an assessment of the Affiliate's software engineering practices.

2. The specific results of the Affiliate assessment shall be proprietary to Affiliate to be used by Affiliate as it chooses (with appropriate credit to the SEI) subject to the right of the SEI to use such results as hereinafter described.

3. Confidentiality is essential to the success of the SEI Assessment Program. The SEI will not release or otherwise identify the results of any organization's assessment.

4. The SEI is free to use assessment data and conclusions to be derived therefrom for statistical, analytical or reporting purposes provided that the confidentiality requirement can be honored and that the information can be used without attribution to its source either directly or by inference.

5. The SEI will not publish collective data externally unless such data is based upon information from not less than 10 different organizations.

6. The senior manager of the segment of Affiliate to be assessed will actively participate in the assessment by agreeing to be present (on mutually acceptable dates) for the opening on-site assessment briefing and the on-site review of final findings and recommendations. This level of participation is critical to the success of the project.

7. The SEI will provide four to six professionals as assessment team members.

8. The Affiliate will provide one or two professionals as assessment team members. It is expected that one of these professionals will, in addition, be assigned the following responsibilities:
   a. participate in a one or two day working session at the SEI shortly following the on-site assessment period to prepare the final assessment report.
   b. develop the organization's action plan based upon the final assessment report.

9. There will be two days of pre-assessment training at the SEI for the entire assessment team.

10. The assessment by the SEI/Affiliate team at the Affiliate site will be done in three or four days.

11. Typically, three to five projects will be reviewed during the on-site assessment period. The Affiliate will ensure that none of the projects selected for review is involved in a competitive phase of a procurement during the on-site assessment period.

12. The SEI as soon as practicable thereafter will provide to Affiliate a final assessment report which will include recommended actions. The SEI does not represent any U.S. Government procurement agency; therefore, the recommendations made by the SEI are not to be construed as contractual directions or constructive changes to contracts which may exist between the Affiliate and the U.S. Government.

13. The Affiliate will within 60 days thereafter provide a review for the SEI of its action plan based on the final assessment report. The Affiliate is the sole determinant as to the extent that recommended actions are implemented through its action plan. It is expected that the review will cover the reasons for

rejection of any final assessment report recommended actions not incorporated into the action plan.

14. The SEI, at its option, and with the consent of the Affiliate, may continue periodic interaction with the Affiliate during implementaton of the action plan.

15. Each participating organization will be responsible for its personnel and their expenses. Each will provide to the other reasonable working space and support services for assessment team activities.

16. If Affiliate discloses identified proprietary information to the SEI, such information should be disclosed pursuant to a separate nondisclosure agreement. The execution of such agreement notwithstanding, the parties agree to respect the confidential nature of this Agreement and all exchanges of information hereunder. All confidential and proprietary information shall be treated with at least the degree of care with which each party treats its own such information.

17. When Affiliate has received an assessment report from the SEI and has in turn reviewed its action plan with the SEI, the basic assessment tasks will be complete and this Agreement will have served its primary purpose. However, any commitments which by their nature are intended to survive termination of the Agreement (such as nondisclosure) will survive.

18. This agreement shall not constitute, create, give effect to, or otherwise imply a joint venture, partnership or formal business organizaton of any kind. Each party to this Agreement shall act as an independent contractor and not as an agent for the other, and neither party shall have any authority to bind the other except to the extent, if any, specifically provided herein or by other written mutual agreement of the parties.

Software Engineering Institute

By _____

Date _____

Affiliate

By _____

Date _____

APPENDIX
Conducting Software Inspections

Inspections are detailed technical peer reviews of software designs or implementations. They should be conducted at every point in the development or maintenance process at which such products are produced. Because they are time-consuming, involve people from several groups, and generally use scarce resources, they should be carefully planned. In addition to inspections of new product elements, every change should be inspected, and reinspections of an entire product element are needed when there is substantial change activity or when inspection and test results indicate unusual problems. As pointed out in Chapter 15, there are several ways to determine inspection effectiveness and when parts of a product have not been adequately inspected. Suggested reinspection criteria are discussed in Chapter 10 and later in this appendix.

Inspection Participants

The inspection participants include the following people:[4]

- *The moderator* (or inspection leader) The person responsible for leading the inspection expeditiously and efficiently to a successful conclusion.

- *The producers* The person or persons who did the work that is being inspected. When several producers are involved, they are all present. If this involves too many people, the inspection is attempting to cover too much material and it should be broken into several smaller inspections.

☐ *Reviewers* (or inspectors)   These are generally people directly concerned and aware of the work being inspected. They may share common data, receive or provide services, or share common facilities. In the case of a detailed design inspection, the reviewers could include some of the following: the high-level designers, the implementers, the documentation people, and the test developers. If the inspection team does not include at least three to five objective technical participants, some other peers of the producing group should be added to ensure impartial coverage of the material.

☐ *Recorder* (or scribe)   Someone who records the significant inspection results. Every issue is clearly noted, together with the name of the person who raised it and the person responsible for resolving it. The recorder is also responsible for ensuring that all the relevant data on the inspection is gathered and given to the moderator.

While many more people may be interested in the inspection results, the purpose of the inspection is to assist the producers in improving their work. This can best be done by limiting attendance to five or six reviewers. Larger groups are harder to manage and are much less efficient. If more people need to learn about the results, the producers should probably conduct a separate walk-through for this purpose. Inspections must not be used for education. Every participant should be technically competent and fully involved, even when being trained as a review moderator.

The key point of this attendance list is that *only technical peers attend.* The moderator is not the manager of the work being reviewed, and neither are any of the other participants. The inclusion of managers changes the inspection process and distorts the participants' objectivity. Regardless of the manager's behavior, the participants will feel that it is they who are being reviewed rather than the product.[10]

Managers who are producers can participate in inspections as long as they recognize that any of their subordinates who are involved may have trouble being completely objective. If enough outside reviewers are used, this may not be a problem. Similarly, managers who have expertise in particular fields can usefully participate in inspections, but it is not wise for them to do it for their subordinates' work. It is usually more effective for them to hold these discussions in private as part of their normal supervisory duties and preserve the inspection process for objective technical peer discussions.

Freedman and Weinberg have published some helpful rules for reviewers and managers. These are shown in Tables C1 and C2.[6]

Managers are properly interested in the results of every inspection. For example, they should ensure that the identified action items are completed, examine the data on inspection effectiveness, require that all product results are inspected, and respect the reviewers' judgments on troublesome product areas.

The managers' use of inspection data can be a source of concern. Some programmers feel that by reporting data on an inspection they are exposing them-

TABLE C1
SUMMARY OF HELPFUL RULES FOR REVIEWERS [6]

Be prepared
Be willing to associate
Watch your language—be polite and objective
One positive—one negative—compliment good work
Raise issues; don't resolve them
Avoid discussions of style
Stick to standard—or stick the standard
Only technically competent people attend reviews
Record all issues in public
Stick to technical issues
Remember education
Do not evaluate the producers
Distribute the report as soon as possible
Let the producers determine when the product is ready for review

Daniel P. Freedman and Gerald M. Weinberg, *Handbook of Walkthroughs, Inspections and Technical Reviews.* © 1982, 1979, Scott Foreman and Company. Reprinted by permission.

selves to personal evaluation. While managers can use such data in this way, they must be careful not to do so. Inspection data is gathered to see how well the project is progressing, not to evaluate the people. Since reviewers are human, however, they are subject to error, and managers need to study the inspection data to see where improvements are needed. Specific criteria and techniques for making such studies are discussed in Chapters 15 and 17.

Planning for the Inspection

The full inspection process consists of a preparation phase, the inspection itself, and then some post-inspection activity. Since several people are involved, a plan is needed. This is typically the producers' responsibility.

As a first step, the producers and their manager decide that the product is ready for inspection and agree on the inspection objectives. Typical code inspection objectives are shown in Table C3. Next, the inspection participants are identified. The manager, with the producers' agreement, first selects the moderator. With the moderator's agreement, the other participants are selected and invited to participate. Management's assistance may be required if the desired participants are not available.

The inspection entry criteria are next prepared and the supporting materials produced for the opening meeting. The producers must ensure that the product is ready for inspection and that all pertinent standards have been met or appropriate waivers obtained. A design specification standard, for example, would generally

TABLE C2
SUMMARY OF HELPFUL RULES
FOR MANAGEMENT [6]*

Show a commitment to the inspection process
Budget time for the inspection process
Be prepared to assign qualified people to the inspection task
Encourage the participants to prepare
Help out with the physical arrangements
Don't be penny wise and pound foolish
Reward good inspections of bad products
Discourage poor inspections of any product
Discourage poor inspection behavior
Override an inspection judgment only at your peril

*Slightly edited with the meaning essentially unchanged.
Daniel P. Freedman and Gerald M. Weinberg, *Handbook of Walkthroughs, Inspections and Technical Reviews.* © 1982, 1979, Scott Foreman and Company. Reprinted by permission.

call for a design overview, the shared data structures, a list of lower-level design units, integration guidelines, and a listing of those areas most likely to change during implementation or subsequent enhancement.[7] Sample code inspection entry criteria are shown in Table C4.

Inspection Preparation

The next step is to hold a meeting of the entire inspection group. The moderator opens with a brief statement of the subject to be inspected, the inspection objectives and, if needed, an overview of the inspection process. The producer(s) then provides a brief tutorial on the area being addressed, including an overview of the design, an outline of the implementation approach taken, and a summary of any special considerations or areas that might be particularly difficult to understand. The moderator then provides a copy of the inspection package to each of the participants. Example inspection package contents for code inspections are shown as part of the inspection entry criterion in Table C4. The criteria and inspection packages are, of course, tailored to the particular inspection type and product involved.

Following this introductory meeting, the reviewers individually prepare for the inspection. They first review the pertinent checklists, guidelines, standards, and available data on typical errors. Then, for code inspections, for example, they each familiarize themselves with the design and read through the code. Where the implementation is confusing or appears in error, they so note, together with a sufficient explanation so the producers can understand the problem or the reason for confusion.

During preparation the reviewers record their time and the errors identified on the error log form. They then submit it and the completed entry preparation form to

TABLE C3
EXAMPLE CODE INSPECTION OBJECTIVES

Identify all the design errors in the product

Identify any cases in which the code does not implement the design as intended

Identify any improper use of interfaces

Inspect for adherence to usability considerations

Inspect for appropriate implementation of maintainability provisions

Inspect for adherence to appropriate style guidelines and to any required standards or constraints such as:
  Naming
  Commenting
  Flagging
  Compiler restrictions
  Size constraints
  Performance limitations

Verify that previously identified issues have been resolved

the inspection moderator before or at the opening of the inspection meeting. A copy of the error log should also be given to the producers as early as possible to permit time for study and consolidation of the several reviewers' findings. Examples of the appropriate forms are shown in Tables C5 and C6.[1]

During preparation the reviewers generally find it helpful to know the types of errors most commonly found in the class of product being inspected. Such checklists are not only needed for each type of inspection, but they should be continually updated. People tend to repeatedly make the same kinds of errors, and a record of their prior experience can be very helpful. In fact, with experience professionals can substantially improve their own performance by tracking, recording, and compensating for their personal error propensities.

Experience has shown that about three-quarters of the errors found in well-run inspections are found during preparation. Good preparation is thus essential.

Conducting the Inspection

The inspection meeting is conducted as follows:

1. The moderator first checks to see if all reviewers are prepared and obtains copies of any preparation reports not already submitted. This includes a brief examination of the data and error logs to verify adequacy of preparation. When preparation is not adequate, the inspection is deferred until all participants are fully prepared. If this happens often, management must be informed.

TABLE C4
EXAMPLE CODE INSPECTION ENTRY CRITERIA

The producer(s) certifies that the program is ready for inspection:
—it has compiled
—all text has been spell-checked
—all pertinent specifications have been met or copies of waivers are included in the inspection package

The inspection package includes
—a program source listing
—any pertinent detailed design, high-level design, or requirements documentation
—copies of any pertinent specifications or common facilities definitions, such as interfaces, macros, services, shared data, or message formats
—a description of any machine or system constraints
—copies of the inspection entry and exit criteria
—blank copies of all required forms and reports

Prior to conducting the inspection:
—all reviewers must have completed their preparation and submitted their error logs to the producer(s) in the established format
—all reviewers must have recorded their preparation time and the major and minor errors found on the inspection preparation form and furnished copies both to the moderator and the producer(s)

2. The moderator next checks to see if the producer is fully prepared. For example, have the reviewers' error logs been analyzed, duplicates consolidated, and discussion notes prepared?

3. The producer then reviews each major error either to clarify why it is not an error, to understand what the reviewer(s) meant, or accept it.

4. Pertinent data on each error is recorded. This includes error location, a brief description, the error category, and the error cause if readily apparent.

5. After discussing all major errors, the product is briefly reviewed to identify any other areas of confusion or concern. Data on errors identified in this process is also recorded.

6. Throughout the meeting the moderator keeps the discussion focused on identifying and explaining the errors and not on resolving them, placing blame, or other extraneous topics.

7. At the conclusion the moderator checks that all participants have voiced their concerns and questions, that all action items are clearly defined and understood, and that the responsibilities and planned resolution dates are established. All the necessary forms are reviewed to ensure that all required data has been obtained. The basic forms are the error logs (Table C5), the preparation form (Table C6), the inspection report (Table C7), and the inspection summary (Table C8).

TABLE C5
EXAMPLE CODE INSPECTION ERROR LOG

Project: _____   Reviewer: _____   Date: _____
Moderator: _____   Producer: _____

Review Type: _____

Location	Defect Description	Category XYZZ
_____	_____	_____
_____	_____	_____
_____	_____	_____
_____	_____	_____
_____	_____	_____
_____	_____	_____
_____	_____	_____
_____	_____	_____
_____	_____	_____
_____	_____	_____
_____	_____	_____
_____	_____	_____
_____	_____	_____
_____	_____	_____
_____	_____	_____
_____	_____	_____
_____	_____	_____
_____	_____	_____
_____	_____	_____
_____	_____	_____
_____	_____	_____
_____	_____	_____
_____	_____	_____
_____	_____	_____

Defect Categories: X: 1 - major*, 2 - minor*
Y: M - missing*, W - wrong*, E - extra*
ZZ: FN - function, IF - interface, DA - data, LO - logic,
IO - input/output, PF - performance,
MT - maintenance, ST - standards,
DC - documentation, HF - human factors, SN - syntax,
OT - other

*Major = a defect that would likely cause a problem in program operation.
Minor = all other defects.
Missing = required code is not present.
Wrong = the code includes some errors.
Extra = unneeded code is included.

TABLE C6
EXAMPLE INSPECTION PREPARATION FORM

REVIEWER: _____ DATE: _____

PROJECT: _____ UNIT: _____

MODERATOR: _____ ROOM: _____ PHONE: _____

MEETING TYPE:

    OVERVIEW: _____   REINSPECTION: _____

    REQUIREMENTS: _____ DESIGN: _____ CODE: _____

DATE RECEIVED REVIEW PACKAGE: _____

	DATE	TIME
PREPARATION LOG:	_____	_____
	_____	_____
	_____	_____
	_____	_____
	_____	_____

ERRORS FOUND:

	MAJOR ERRORS*				MINOR ERRORS*			
	M	W	E	TOTAL	M	W	E	TOTAL
FUNCTION								
INTERFACE								
DATA								
LOGIC								
I/O								
PERFORMANCE								
MAINTENANCE								
STANDARDS								
DOCUMENTATION								
HUMAN FACTORS								
SYNTAX								
OTHER								
TOTALS								

Distribution: Project Manager
              Quality Assurance
              Process Group
              Producer(s)
              Review Coordinator

*Major = a defect that would likely cause a problem in program operation.
Minor = all other defects.
M: Missing = required code is not present.
W: Wrong = the code includes some errors.
E: Extra = unneeded code is included.

TABLE C7
INSPECTION REPORT [7]
_____

PROJECT: _____ DATE: _____

SYSTEM NAME: _____ UNIT: _____

MODERATOR: _____ ROOM: _____ PHONE: _____

MEETING TYPE:

      OVERVIEW: _____   REINSPECTION: _____

      REQUIREMENTS: _____   DESIGN: _____ CODE: _____

NUMBER OF THE INSPECTION: _____   INSPECTION DURATION: _____

TOTAL NUMBER OF REVIEWERS: _____   INSPECTION PREP TIME: _____

TOTAL LINES INSPECTED: _____   PAGES OF DIAGRAMS: _____

DISPOSITION: ACCEPT: _____ CONDITIONAL: _____ REINSPECT: _____

ESTIMATED REWORK EFFORT: _____ (HOURS)

REWORK TO BE COMPLETED BY: _____

REINSPECTION SCHEDULED FOR: _____

REVIEWERS:

_____   _____

_____   _____

_____   _____

PRODUCER(S):

_____   _____

RECORDER:

_____

MODERATOR CERTIFICATION: _____ DATE: _____

ADDITIONAL COMMENTS: _____

_____

_____

Distribution: Project Manager

              Quality Assurance

              Process Group

              Producer(s)

              Inspection Coordinator

TABLE C8
INSPECTION SUMMARY [7]

PROJECT: _____ DATE: _____

SYSTEM NAME: _____ UNIT: _____

MODERATOR: _____ ROOM: _____ PHONE: _____

MEETING TYPE:

    OVERVIEW: _____   REINSPECTION: _____

    REQUIREMENTS: _____ DESIGN: _____ CODE: _____

ERRORS FOUND:

	MAJOR ERRORS*				MINOR ERRORS*			
	M	W	E	TOTAL	M	W	E	TOTAL
FUNCTION								
INTERFACE								
DATA								
LOGIC								
I/O								
PERFORMANCE								
MAINTENANCE								
STANDARDS								
DOCUMENTATION								
HUMAN FACTORS								
SYNTAX								
OTHER								
TOTALS								

Distribution: Project Manager
             Quality Assurance
             Process Group
             Producer(s)
             Review Coordinator

*Major = a defect that would likely cause a problem in program operation.
Minor = all other defects.
Missing = required code is not present.
Wrong = the code includes some errors.
Extra = unneeded code is included.

8. Based on the inspection results, and after asking the reviewers for their views, the moderator decides whether a reinspection is required. Sample reinspection criteria are shown in Table C9.

9. The moderator then closes the meeting by summarizing the actions to be taken and thanking the participants for their support.

Post-Inspection Actions

Following the inspection the producer fixes the identified problems and either reviews the corrections with the moderator or in a reinspection. After examining these changes the moderator may decide that a reinspection is needed, even if the previous decision had been not to hold one. It is generally wise to have a reinspection if the changes are more extensive than expected. Even if the entire module is not completely reinspected, every individual change should always be independently reviewed.

As the final inspection action, the moderator ensures that the inspection results and data are inserted in the process database and that management is informed that the inspection has been successfully completed.

TABLE C9
SAMPLE REINSPECTION CRITERIA

Inspection rates unusual:
    Inspection time per LOC too short
    Inspection time per LOC too long
    Too many errors per programmer hour
    Too few errors per programmer hour

Error data out of line:
    Too many minor errors, and too few major errors (preoccupied with details)
    Too many major errors
    Unusual error distribution
    Too low a percent of errors found during preparation

Other:
    Any module with more than *N* errors (*N* set in project plan)
    Any module with persistently high error rates
    The reviewers suggest a reinspection
    The moderator suggests a reinspection
    The testers suggest a reinspection
    The module contains uninspected changes

Inspection Responsibilities

The moderator has a key role in the inspection process. A capable moderator will generally produce an effective inspection, while an inexperienced or poorly qualified one often will not do so. An inspection is an interpersonal activity, and the moderator's role is to ensure that the people constructively interact to produce the proper result. In so doing it is often helpful to provide the reviewers with some guidance on appropriate ways to review other people's work. Druffel has provided the following helpful thoughts on this subject:[3]

> Those who wish to achieve excellence must submit their work to the scrutiny of others. Likewise, an organization that seeks excellence must necessarily undergo self-scrutiny. . . . Since each of us must assume the role of critic, it is worth a moment to reflect on the appropriate conduct of that role.
> Criticism is the action of passing judgment upon the qualities or merits of anything; especially, the passing of unfavorable judgment; fault finding, censure. A critic is one who pronounces judgment on any thing or person; especially, one who passes severe or unfavorable judgment; a censurer, fault finder. . . . Most of us would probably prefer not to be viewed as a critic in this sense. Certainly none of us likes to receive criticism. However, we do willingly submit drafts or incomplete work to the review of our peers. We do so, not because we wish to be the object of censure, but because we recognize that to submit our work to review will help us improve its quality. The Oxford English Dictionary gives a second definition of critic, one that describes a constructive critic: one skillful in judging the qualities and merits . . . a professional. . . . Properly applied, criticism makes us think more carefully, often from a different perspective.

The moderator's primary responsibility is to maintain this kind of constructive and impersonal attitude throughout the inspection. This is not a technical job, although technical skill is needed. While management may occasionally ask the most qualified technical person to be the moderator, it is often wiser to use such a person's talents on the technical issues rather than the interpersonal ones. Not everyone has the skills and aptitudes to be a good moderator, so people with such talents should be carefully identified and developed.

The Moderator's Role

The desired attributes of a good moderator are:[2]

- ☐ The technical ability to understand the area under review
- ☐ Ability to lead the group in effective discussions

□ Ability to mediate disagreements

□ Understanding of the organization and how to assign responsibilities

□ Ability to identify the key issues and maintain the group's focus on them

□ An unbiased view of the topics under review

The basic tasks of the moderator are to:

1. Obtain a good inspection or report to management on why one was not held.

2. Assist the producer in selecting the reviewers and arranging for their participation.

3. Ensure that the reviewers do not have other reviews scheduled for the same day or have any other involvement that would impair their objectivity.

4. Conduct a pre-inspection session for all participants and ensure that they understand both their responsibilities and the inspection process.

5. Ensure that the entry criteria are met.

6. Make sure that the scheduled participants are present and that no managers or observers are in attendance.

7. At the opening of the inspection, ensure that all participants are prepared or reschedule the inspection.

8. Conduct the inspection in an orderly and efficient manner.

9. Ensure that the inspection starts and ends on time.

10. Ensure that all identified problems are recorded and resolution responsibility is assigned.

11. Track each problem to resolution or ensure that it is tracked by someone else.

12. Gather the required inspection data and enter it into the process database.

13. Communicate the inspection results to all interested parties.

A checklist for inspection moderators is shown in Table C10.[6]

Recorder Responsibilities

The recorder's job is:

1. To be generally aware of the subject matter being reviewed.

2. To record all issues raised and ensure that the persons raising them agree with the way they are recorded.

3. To record any required data on the inspection and its preparation and provide it to the moderator.

4. To produce the final inspection report, listing all issues, the responsible party for resolving each, and the schedule for resolution.

TABLE C10
CHECKLIST FOR INSPECTION MODERATORS [6]

Your Qualifications
Do you understand the purpose of inspections in general?
Do you understand why this particular inspection is being held?
Can you be objective on the subject of the inspection?
Have you ever participated in an inspection as reviewer or reviewee?
Do you have any personal difficulties with any of the reviewers that might interfere with your ability to lead the inspection?

Preinspection
Is the product ready for inspection?
Are all relevant materials in your possession?
Have all relevant materials been distributed on time?
Have all the reviewers received the materials?
Have the reviewers confirmed their acceptance of the schedule?
Has the conference room been scheduled?
Have arrangements been made for the necessary equipment?

During the Inspection
Are all participants well prepared?
Is there agreement on the objectives of the inspection?
Are all the participants contributing?
Is the inspection well paced?
Is interest waning?
Has everyone been heard?
Has anyone tuned out?
Has someone (such as the producer) swayed people with emotional arguments or smooth presentation?
Is there agreement on the outcome of the inspection?
Is that agreement truly understood by all participants?

Postinspection
Was the inspection successful?
Did it reach a workable conclusion?
Was anybody responsible, if the inspection was not successful?
Is the report prompt and accurate?
Are all participants satisfied with the outcome?
Did the product get a fair and adequate treatment?
Does the producing group have a reasonable basis for clearing up the issues?
Have all relevant people received the appropriate information?
Have the producers and participants profited from the inspection?
What can you do to make the next inspection better?
Has the required inspection data been gathered and recorded?
Have all identified problems been resolved or management informed?

TABLE C11
CHECKLIST FOR RECORDERS [6]

Your Qualifications
   Do you understand the purpose of inspections in general?
   Do you understand why this particular inspection is being held?
   Do you understand the jargon used and the formats used in this
      material?
   Are you able to communicate with the type of people who will be in the
      inspection?
   Can you be objective on the subject of the inspection?
   Have you ever participated in an inspection as a reviewer or as a
      reviewee?

Preinspection
   Can you identify, by name, the inspection leader and other participants?
   Have you arranged your schedule to allow time for the inspection?
   Have you allowed time for the work you will have to do after the
      inspection?
   Do you have the materials necessary for keeping an accurate record in
      the proper formats?
   Do you have the resources available to carry out your job, during and
      after the inspection?

During the Inspection
   Do you understand what an issue is?
   Are you recording all issues?
   Are you recording things that aren't really issues?
   Are your notes accurate reflections of the comments?
   Are you making a flip chart or other visible record of the issues?
   Do your detailed notes actually correspond to the flip chart
      abbreviations?
   Do you have copies of any supplementary material introduced as a part
      of any issue?
   How much of your report consists of editorial commentary?
   Is the outcome stated explicitly and unambiguously?
   Are the issues recorded in neutral language?

Postinspection
   Was the report promptly prepared?
   Was it accurate?
   Was the report properly reviewed and signed?
   Was it distributed to all relevant people, including participants?
   Was a complete copy of the inspected material and the report placed in
      the historical record?
   If there were related issues raised, was a related issues report prepared?
   Was all pertinent data on the inspection and its preparation gathered and
      provided to the moderator?

A checklist for recorders is shown in Table C11.[6]

Reviewer Responsibilities

The reviewers, in some respects, have the easiest job. They need only focus on the technical issues, and, when the inspection is over their work is done. The reviewers' particular responsibilities are:

1. Be prepared for the inspection.
2. Be objective; focus on issues and not on the people.
3. Concentrate on problems, and offer suggestions on style or problem solutions before or after the inspection.
4. Address major issues and submit minor items separately.
5. Insist on understanding issues and proposed explanations. When something is not clear, do not hesitate to stop progress until you understand.
6. When you are shown to be wrong, forget it.
7. Support the moderator.
8. Do not hesitate to praise good work.

Producer Responsibilities

The producers are the ones the entire review is aimed at supporting, and they should behave accordingly. The only reward for the reviewers, the moderator, and the recorder is the satisfaction of helping someone do a better job and the implied promise that they will be helped in return. In spite of the critical nature of the inspection process, the producers must remember that all these people are giving their valuable time to help them.

The producer's responsibilities are thus:

1. To ensure that the work is ready to be reviewed
2. To make the preparatory material available on time for all the participants
3. To support the moderator in making the meeting arrangements, providing copies for the inspection package, and helping to establish schedules
4. To promptly resolve all the identified issues
5. To check with the participants whenever issues are not clear or when ideas and suggestions have been offered
6. To be objective and avoid becoming defensive

As simple as the last point sounds, it is probably the most difficult responsibility of all. After working for months on a task the producers will have already thought through and addressed many of the issues. It will therefore seem like an enormous waste of time to have to explain them all over again. This, however, is a necessary cost of conducting an inspection, and it invariably pays enormous dividends.

Inspection Checklists

For each of the major inspection types some special considerations are appropriate. Freedman and Weinberg have published several checklists for common inspections, and Kernigan and Plauger have produced a useful guide to programming style.[6, 8] Slightly edited copies of these are provided in Tables C12 through C16.

While such guides are useful as a start, each organization should establish its own, building on available guides where appropriate. Experience with such guides should be periodically monitored to see what items are no longer pertinent and what should be added or modified. Style guides and checklists that are appropriate for one programming language or environment may not be proper for another. It is not a good idea, for example, to include in such a checklist any items that will be caught by the compiler.

TABLE C12
REQUIREMENTS INSPECTION CHECKLIST [6]*

1. All items needed to specify the solution to the problem have been included.
2. Each item is free from error.
3. Each item is exact, there is a single interpretation, the meaning of each item is understood, and the specification is easy to read.
4. No item conflicts with another item in the specification.
5. Each item is pertinent to the problem and its solution.
6. During program development and acceptance testing, it will be possible to determine whether the item has been satisfied.
7. Each item can be traced to its origin in the problem environment.
8. Each item can be implemented with the available techniques, tools, resources, and personnel and within the specified cost and schedule constraints.
9. The requirements specifications are a statement of the requirements that must be satisfied by the problem solution, and they are not obscured by proposed solutions to the problem.
10. The requirements specifications are expressed in such a way that each item can be changed without excessive impact on other items.
11. Changes to the completed requirements specifications can be controlled, each proposed change can be traced to an existing requirement, and the impact of the proposed change can be assessed.

*Slightly edited with meaning unchanged.

Daniel P. Freedman and Gerald M. Weinberg, *Handbook of Walkthroughs, Inspections and Technical Reviews.* © 1982, 1979, Scott Foreman and Company. Reprinted by permission.

TABLE C13
DESIGN MISFIT CHECKLIST [6]

1. Boundary Oversights
   a. Is anything going to fall between the cracks of "mine" versus "yours?"
   b. Is anything going to be claimed by two or more parties?
   c. Is each input, function, and output addressed by a specific, identifiable part of the system? Can you prove it?
   d. Is there any misinterpretation of the person-machine interface—either by a person or machine?

2. Overadaptation
   a. Has any portion of this design received more emphasis than it seems to deserve? Can you explain why that happened and what effects it has had?
   b. Is the design overly constrained, perhaps by paying too much attention to one part at the expense of others?
   c. If you could relax any single constraint, which would it be? How would the design be affected?

3. Afterthoughts
   Examine the last three things added to the design and answer the following questions for each:
   a. What has been crammed in?
   b. Could someone tell that the change was not part of the original conception—that is a patch to the design?
   c. What wasn't considered when this change was made?
   d. What would happen if this change were undone and left out of the final design?

4. Vestiges
   a. What things are in the design because "we've always done it that way?" Why are you doing it that way?
   b. Does the design reflect the machine on which it will operate? If so, why?
   c. Is your design independent of the programming language that will be used? If not, why not?
   d. Do you have a place to hold the buggywhip?

5. Mistakes
   a. What have you forgotten?
   b. What has been done wrong?
   c. Did you dot the *i*'s?
   d. Did you ever go back and correct that problem you found when you were busy with something more important?
   e. Do you have any notes on scraps of paper?

6. Insensitivity
   a. Have you remembered the people who will have to use this system?
   b. Have you remembered the people who will have to operate it?
   c. Have you remembered the people who will have to repair it?
   d. If you were one of these people, what one thing would you change in the design to make your life easier? Why wasn't that change made?

Daniel P. Freedman and Gerald M. Weinberg, *Handbook of Walkthroughs, Inspections and Technical Reviews.* © 1982, 1979, Scott Foreman and Company. Reprinted by permission.

TABLE C14
QUESTIONS TO KEEP IN MIND WHEN INSPECTING CODE [6]

Function
1. Is there a concept, an underlying idea, that can be expressed easily in plain language? Is it expressed in plain language in the implemented code?
2. Does the function of this part have a clear place in the overall function of the whole, and is this function clearly expressed?
3. Is the routine properly sheltered, so that it may perform its function reliably in spite of possible misuse?

Form
1. Whatever style is adopted, is it clean and clear when taken as a whole?
2. Is it meaningful to all classes of readers who will see it?
3. Are there repeated code segments, whether within or between routines?
4. Are comments useful or are they simply alibis for poor coding?
5. Is the level of detail consistent?
6. Are standard practices used?
7. Is initialization properly done, and does the routine clean up after itself?

Economy
1. Are there redundant operations for which there is no compensating benefit?
2. Is storage use consistent, both internally and with external specifications?
3. How much will it cost to modify? (Consider the three most likely future modifications.)
4. Is it simple?

Daniel P. Freedman and Gerald M. Weinberg, *Handbook of Walkthroughs, Inspections and Technical Reviews.* © 1982, 1979, Scott Foreman and Company. Reprinted by permission.

Inspection Training

Moderator training courses are absolutely essential. The moderators need a complete grounding in the principles and methods of inspections before they can be expected to do a competent job. Training gives them the basic skills and helps to provide the self-confidence needed to lead such a potentially contentious activity.

A few of the key guidelines for moderator training are:

1. Get a good instructor, preferably someone who has moderated inspections. If no such person is available, the selected instructor should attend a commercially available course if one can be found or, at the minimum, read the key references and lead one or two practice inspections before the first class.[1, 5, 6]

2. The value of inspections and management's commitment to them are an important part of the course. A senior manager should open each class with some brief comments emphasizing support for the inspection program.

3. The psychology of inspections should be discussed, including exposure to the key literature on the subject.[6, 9]

4. Guidance should be given on handling problem personalities, resolving disputes, and reaching agreements.[5]

TABLE C15
GUIDELINES ON CODING STYLE [8]

Write clearly—don't be too clever.

Say what you mean, simply and directly.

Use library functions.

Avoid temporary variables.

Write clearly—don't sacrifice clarity for "efficiency."

Let the machine do the dirty work.

Replace repetitive expressions by calls to a common function.

Parenthesize to avoid ambiguity.

Choose variable names that won't be confused.

Avoid the FORTRAN arithmetic IF.

Avoid unnecessary branches.

Don't use conditional branches as a substitute for a logical expression.

If a logical expression is hard to understand, try transforming it.

Use data arrays to avoid repetitive control sequences.

Choose a data representation that makes the program simple.

Write first in an easy-to-understand pseudo-language; then translate into whatever language you have to use.

Use IF . . . ELSE IF . . . ELSE IF . . . ELSE . . . to implement multi-way branches.

Modularize, use subroutines.

Use GOTOs only to implement a fundamental structure.

Avoid GOTOs completely if you can keep the program readable.

Don't patch bad code—rewrite it.

Write and test a big program in small pieces.

Use recursive procedures for recursively defined data structures.

Test input for plausibility and validity.

Make sure input doesn't violate the limits of the program.

Terminate input by end-of-file or marker, not by count.

Identify bad input; recover if possible.

Make input easy to prepare and output self-explanatory.

Use uniform input formats.

Make input easy to proofread.

Use free-form input when possible.

Use self-identifying input. Allow defaults. Echo both on output.

Make sure all variables are initialized before use.

Don't stop at one bug.

Use debugging compilers.

Initialize constants with DATA statements or INITIAL attributes; initialize variables with executable code.

Watch out for off-by-one errors.

TABLE C15 (continued)

Take care to branch the right way on equality.

Be careful when a loop exits to the same place from side and bottom.

Make sure your code "does nothing" gracefully.

Test programs at their boundary values.

Check some answers by hand.

10.0 times 0.1 is hardly ever 1.0.

Don't compare floating point numbers solely for equality.

Make it right before you make it faster.

Make it clear before you make it faster.

Don't sacrifice clarity for small gains in "efficiency."

Let your compiler do the simple optimizations.

Don't strain to re-use code; reorganize instead.

Make sure special cases are truly special.

Keep it simple to make it faster.

Don't diddle code to make it faster—find a better algorithm.

Instrument your programs. Measure before making "efficiency" changes.

Make sure comments and code agree.

Don't just echo the code with comments—make every comment count.

Don't comment bad code—rewrite it.

Use variable names that mean something.

Use statement labels that mean something.

Format a program to help the reader understand it.

Document your data layouts.

Don't over-comment.

B. W. Kernighan and P. J. Plauger, *The Elements of Style.* © 1978, McGraw-Hill, reprinted by permission.

5. The details of the inspection process should be covered, including the pertinent checklists, forms, standards, and reports.

6. Some class practice sessions should be held, and then the moderator trainees should participate in one or more inspections as reviewers or recorders. They are then ready to moderate their first inspection.

7. After they have moderated one or two inspections, the moderator trainees should attend a brief seminar to discuss their experiences, obtain guidance on their problems, and correct any bad habits or misconceptions. Videotaping or observation and comment by an experienced moderator can be very helpful at these sessions.

Training is also highly desirable for participants. If a competent moderator is available, however, the software professionals can often learn to become competent by participation in inspections. When practical, courses should teach inspection principles and provide practice sessions with the checklists and the methods in-

TABLE C16
CHECKLIST FOR DOCUMENTATION INSPECTIONS [6]

1. Have all phases of the document's life cycle been considered?
    a. Is there provision for user feedback?
    b. Is there provision for making changes?
    c. Will changes in the system cause difficult or expensive changes in the documentation?
    d. Is there adequate provision for distribution of the documents?
    e. Is there adequate provision for the distribution of changes to the documents?
    f. Can documents be reproduced easily?
    g. Can copying be prevented or controlled?
    h. Are there available people to supplement documents?
    i. Do the users and creators agree on the purpose of the documents?
    j. Is there adequate provison for keeping support people current and informed?
    k. Are tools available (e.g., fiche readers, terminals) for reading/accessing/storing these materials?
    l. Have the documents been properly approved?
    m. Do these documents show where they fall in the total plan?
    n. Do the documents indicate other documents that may be used as follow-up?

2. Are the contents of the documents adequate?
    a. Coverage of topics
        i. All essential topics complete?
        ii. Have irrelevant topics been kept out?
        iii. Topics complete, but is there completeness in detail, assumptions, facts, unknowns?
        iv. Is technical level appropriate to level of document?
        v. Who is the intended reader (readers)?
    b. Correctness
        i. No errors of fact?
        ii. Are there no contradictions?
    c. Evidence
        i. Is the evidence adequate to support the presentation?
        ii. Is the evidence realistic?
        iii. Is there a clear statement of goals of the documents? Are the goals consistent?
        iv. Does the presentation sound authoritative?

3. Are the materials in the documents clear?
    a. Are examples clear?
        i. Used where necessary?
        ii. Relevant where used?
        iii. Contribute to understanding?
        iv. Misleading?
        v. Wrong?
        vi. Less effective than their potential?

TABLE C16 (continued)

b. Are diagrams, pictures, or other visual materials clear?
   i.   Used where necessary?
   ii.   Relevant where used?
   iii. Contribute to understanding?
   iv.   Clearly rendered?
   v.   Misleading?
   vi.   Wrong?
   vii. Less effective than their potential?
   viii. Appropriate amount of information?
c. Is terminology clear?
   i.   Consistent throughout all documents?
   ii.   Conforms to standards?
   iii. Is there a glossary, if appropriate?
   iv.   Are definitions correct?
   v.   Are definitions clear?
   vi.   Is the glossary complete?
   vii. Is there too much technical terminology?
d. Is writing style clear?
   i.   Do paragraphs express only connected ideas and no more?
   ii.   Are larger logical units broken by subheadings?
   iii. Is the fog index too high for the audience?
   iv.   Does it talk down to the typical reader?
   v.   Does it put you to sleep?
   vi.   Is there an abstract?

4. Are the documents adequately supplied with referencing aids?
   a. Is there a table of contents, if appropriate?
   b. Is the table of contents well placed?
   c. Is the table of contents correct?
   d. Is there an index, if appropriate?
   e. Is the index well placed?
   f. Is the index correct?
      i.   Are page references accurate?
      ii.   Are there entries for the kinds of things the various classes of users will be seeking?
      iii. Are the entries under the right titles?
      iv.   Are there alternate titles for entries that might be accessed using different terminology?
      v.   Are major and minor entries for the same terms distinguished?
      vi.   Are terms broken down adequately, or are there too many page references under single terms, indicating that more subcategories are needed?
      vii. Are there superfluous entries?
   g. Is there a bibliography of prerequisite publications?
      i.   If there are no prerequisites, is this stated?
      ii.   Is the bibliography where it will be found before attempting to read the document?

TABLE C16 (continued)

---

    iii. Are the references complete enough to locate the publication?
    iv. Are there annotations to help the reader choose the approparite document?
  h. Is there a bibliography of related publications that may contain further information?
    i. If this is a unique source of information, is this stated?
    ii. Are the references complete enough to locate the publications?
    iii. Are there annotations to help the reader choose the appropriate document?
  i. Does the organization of the documents themselves contribute to the ease of finding information?
    i. Is page numbering sensible?
    ii. Is page numbering complete?

Daniel P. Freedman and Gerald M. Weinberg, *Handbook of Walkthroughs, Inspections and Technical Reviews.* © 1982, 1979, Scott Foreman and Company. Reprinted by permission.

volved. It is not a good idea, however, to delay the introduction of inspections until a full set of such courses is available. A brief overview by the moderator at the opening of the inspection is often sufficient to cover the purposes and principles of inspections. After the initial moderator training needs have been met, it is then desirable to broaden the training program to include all potential inspection participants.

References

1. Ackerman, A. F., and P. J. Fowler. "Software inspections and the industrial production of software," in Hans-Ludwig Hausen, ed., *Software Validation.* Amsterdam: North-Holland, 1984.
2. Collofello, J. S. "The Software Technical Review Process," SEI Curriculum Module SEI-CM-3-1.1 (Preliminary), Pittsburgh, PA: The Software Engineering Institute, Carnegie-Mellon University, April 1987.
3. Druffel, L. E. Private communication.
4. Fagan, M. E. "Design and code inspections to reduce errors in program development," *IBM Systems Journal,* vol. 15, no. 3, 1976.
5. Fisher, R., and W. Urey. *Getting to Yes.* Boston: Houghton Mifflin, 1981.
6. Freedman, D. P., and G. M. Weinberg. *Handbook of Walkthroughs, Inspections, and Technical Reviews, Evaluating Programs, Projects, and Products,* 3rd edition. Boston: Little, Brown and Company, 1982.
7. Fowler, P. J. "In-process inspections of work products at AT&T," *AT&T Technical Journal,* March–April, 1986.
8. Kernighan, B. W., and P. J. Plauger. *The Elements of Style.* New York: McGraw-Hill, 1978.
9. Weinberg, Gerald M. *The Psychology of Computer Programming.* New York: Van Nostrand Reinhold, 1971.
10. Yourdon, E. *Structured Walkthroughs,* 2nd edition. Englewood Cliffs, NJ: Prentice-Hall, 1979.

INDEX